The christianization of western Europe in late antiquity and the early middle ages required, in addition to simple conversion, the widespread adoption of Christian values, practices, and beliefs. As bishop of Arles from 502 to 542, Caesarius promoted tirelessly the christianization of townspeople and peasants alike through a program of patronage, teaching, and church reform. Yet his writings also reveal the community resistance his efforts evoked, the persistence of traditional "pagan" cultural and religious practices, and the community's own efforts at self-christianization. Indeed, the transformation of Arles into a Christian community entailed the adaptation of Christianity into a community religion that respected local expectations and traditions.

Utilizing insights provided by social history, archaeology, and anthropology, this book studies the problem of christianization in late Roman and early medieval Gaul from the perspective of Caesarius's career as monk, bishop, and church reformer. Subjects of inquiry include Caesarius's own training and preoccupations; the social and cultural history of Arles; the bishop's dealings with the Visigothic, Ostrogothic, and Frankish rulers of the city; his relations with fellow bishops, including the bishops of Rome; the effects of his strategies of christianization in city and countryside; and the fate of his program of church reform and christianization under the later Merovingians and Carolingians.

Cambridge Studies in Medieval Life and Thought

CAESARIUS OF ARLES

Cambridge Studies in Medieval Life and Thought
Fourth series

General Editor:

D. E. LUSCOMBE
Professor of Medieval History, University of Sheffield

Advisory Editors:

R. B. DOBSON
Professor of Medieval History, University of Cambridge, and Fellow of Christ's College

ROSAMOND MCKITTERICK
*Reader in Early Medieval European History, University of Cambridge, and Fellow of
Newnham College*

The series Cambridge Studies in Medieval Life and Thought was inaugurated by G. G. Coulton in 1921. Professor D. E. Luscombe now acts as General Editor of the Fourth Series, with Professor R. B. Dobson and Dr Rosamond McKitterick as Advisory Editors. The series brings together outstanding work by medieval scholars over a wide range of human endeavor extending from political economy to the history of ideas.

For a list of titles in the series, see end of book.

CAESARIUS OF ARLES

The Making of a Christian Community in Late Antique Gaul

WILLIAM E. KLINGSHIRN

The Catholic University of America, Washington D.C.

Published by the Press Syndicate of the University of Cambridge
The Pitt Building, Trumpington Street, Cambridge CB2 1RP
40 West 20th Street, New York, NY 10011–4211, USA
10 Stamford Road, Oakleigh, Melbourne 3166, Australia

© Cambridge University Press 1994

First published 1994

Printed in Great Britain at the University Press, Cambridge

A catalogue record for this book is available from the British Library

Library of Congress cataloguing in publication data

Klingshirn, William E.
Caesarius of Arles: the making of a Christian community in late
antique Gaul / William E. Klingshirn.
p.   cm. – (Cambridge studies in medieval life and thought;
4th ser., 22)
Includes bibliographical references and index.
ISBN 0 521 43095 X
1. Caesarius of Arles, Saint, 470–542.   2. Christian saints –
France – Arles – Biography.   3. Arles (France) – Biography.   4. Arles
region (France) – Church history.   1. Title.   11. Series.
BR1720.C2K57 1993
274.4′9102–dc   93-9578   CIP

ISBN 0 521 43095 X hardback

Dedicated to my father
Eugene Albert Klingshirn
and to the memory of my mother
Frances Mary Klingshirn

CONTENTS

MAPS

ACKNOWLEDGMENTS

This book could not have been written without the advice, encouragement, and assistance of many friends, teachers, colleagues, and institutions. I would first like to extend my deep gratitude to Sabine MacCormack, who directed the Stanford Ph.D. thesis on which the book is based and has continued to offer invaluable advice and encouragement in subsequent phases of the project. It was under her guidance that I came to realize how warily the historian must approach the delicate problems of religious conversion, christianization, and cultural identity. Thanks also go to my dissertation committee: Susan Treggiari offered numerous valuable suggestions, as did the late Jack Winkler, whose critical insight and warm good humor will be sadly missed by all who knew him. At Stanford I also benefited from discussions with Michael Jameson, Maud Gleason, Kenneth Wolf, and Roy Rike.

Many others deserve thanks as well. Peter Brown took an interest in the project from the very beginning and supplied a wealth of fresh perspectives, apt references, and stimulating criticism. Robert Markus has been a continuing source of support, advice, and fruitful ideas; I am especially indebted to his important analysis of asceticism and Christian self-definition in *The End of Ancient Christianity*. Raymond Van Dam has been unfailingly generous, reading numerous drafts of the book and offering wise counsel and helpful suggestions at every turn. Ralph Mathisen and Mark Vessey also read versions of each chapter and gave me the benefit of their specialist knowledge of late Roman history and literature. For reading and commenting on various chapters, I am also grateful to Uta-Renate Blumenthal, Frank Mantello, and James Rives. Caroline Nicholson not only read (and improved) the archaeological sections of the book, but also generously shared the results of an archaeological survey of the *territorium* of Arles that will constitute part of her forthcoming Bryn Mawr Ph.D.

thesis on late Roman Arles. Claude Sintès, Conservateur aux Musées d'Arles, responded most helpfully and promptly to repeated requests for information about recent excavations in Arles. For suggestive questions, stimulating ideas, and various other forms of assistance, I am also pleased to thank Henry Chadwick, Elizabeth Clark, Marie-José Delage, Jacques Fontaine, Walter Goffart, Thomas Halton, Cynthia Kahn, Mary Kiely, Conrad Leyser, William McCarthy, John Petruccione, Linda Safran, and Rebecca Weaver. For indexing, proofreading, and research assistance, I am indebted to Edward Strickland, and for cartography to Georgetta Cooper. Thanks are also due to William Davies of the Cambridge University Press and to the editors of *Cambridge Studies in Medieval Life and Thought*, particularly D. E. Luscombe and Rosamond McKitterick, who offered an abundance of helpful comments.

Generous financial support for the project was provided by a Whiting Fellowship in the Humanities from the Mrs. Giles Whiting Foundation, a Charlotte Newcombe Dissertation Fellowship from the Woodrow Wilson National Fellowship Foundation, and a Fellowship for University Teachers from the National Endowment for the Humanities. Additional funding for travel was provided by the Stanford Classics Department and the Catholic University of America. I am also grateful to the faculty research fund at Catholic University for a grant to cover the costs of cartography, proofreading, indexing, and research assistance.

To the many librarians and their staffs who have helped me over the years, I offer deepest thanks, especially to those at the Catholic University of America, Stanford University, Dumbarton Oaks, the Library of Congress, the New York Public Library, and the Bibliothèque Municipale in Arles. I am also grateful to the Musées d'Arles for help in obtaining research materials.

Finally, I would like to acknowledge the help, understanding, and encouragement that I have received over the years from my father and mother, my wife Patricia Ortega, and in his own way our infant son Michael. To them I offer this book as a small token of gratitude and love.

ABBREVIATIONS

ANRW	*Aufstieg und Niedergang der Römischen Welt*, ed. H. Temporini and W. Haase (Berlin, 1972–)
Arnold	C. F. Arnold, *Caesarius von Arelate und die gallische Kirche seiner Zeit* (Leipzig, 1894)
Beck	H. G. J. Beck, *The Pastoral Care of Souls in South-East France During the Sixth Century* (Rome, 1950)
CCSL	*Corpus Christianorum, Series Latina* (Turnhout, 1953–).
CE	*Carmina Latina Epigraphica*, ed. F. Buecheler and E. Lommatzsch, 3 vols. (Leipzig, 1895–1926)
CIL	*Corpus Inscriptionum Latinarum* (Berlin, 1893–)
CJ	*codex Justinianus*
CRAI	*Comptes rendus de l' Académie des Inscriptions et Belles-lettres*
CTh	*codex Theodosianus*
DACL	*Dictionnaire d' archéologie chrétienne et de liturgie*, ed. F. Cabrol, H. Leclercq, and H. Marrou (Paris, 1924–53)
Delage	M.-J. Delage, ed., *Césaire d' Arles. Sermons au peuple*, 3 vols., *SC* 175, 243, 330 (Paris, 1971–86)
DHGE	*Dictionnaire d' histoire et de géographie ecclésiastiques*, ed. A. Baudrillart *et al.* (Paris, 1912–)
DS	*Dictionnaire de spiritualité*, ed. M. Viller *et al.* (Paris, 1937–)

List of abbreviations

DTC	*Dictionnaire de théologie catholique*, ed. A. Vacant *et al.* (Paris, 1930–50)
Duchesne	L. Duchesne, *Fastes épiscopaux de l'ancienne Gaule*, 2nd edn., 3 vols. (Paris, 1907–15)
FIRA	*Fontes Iuris Romani Antejustiniani*, ed. S. Riccobono *et al.*, 3 vols. (Florence, 1940–43)
FOR V	*Forma Orbis Romani: Carte archéologique de la Gaule romaine*, V, ed. F. Benoit (Paris, 1936)
ILCV	*Inscriptiones Latinae Christianae Veteres*, ed. E. Diehl, 2nd edn. (Berlin, 1961)
Jones, *LRE*	A. H. M. Jones, *The Later Roman Empire, 284–602*, 3 vols. (Oxford, 1964)
JRS	*The Journal of Roman Studies*
JTS	*The Journal of Theological Studies*
Krusch	B. Krusch, ed., *Vitae Caesarii Episcopi Arelatensis Libri Duo*, MGH SRM, III, 433–501
LP	*liber pontificalis*, ed. L. Duchesne, *Le liber pontificalis*, 2nd edn., 3 vols. (Paris, 1955–57)
Malnory	A. Malnory, *Saint Césaire, évêque d'Arles*, Bibliothèque de l'école des hautes études 103 (Paris, 1894)
MGH	*Monumenta Germaniae Historica*
AA	*Auctores Antiquissimi*
Capit.	*Capitularia*
Capit. Episc.	*Capitula Episcoporum*
Conc.	*Concilia*
Ep.	*Epistolae*
SRM	*Scriptores Rerum Merovingicarum*
SS	*Scriptores*
Morin	G. Morin, ed., *Sancti Caesarii episcopi Arelatensis Opera omnia nunc primum in unum collecta*, 2 vols. (Maredsous, 1937–42)

PL	*Patrologia Latina*, ed. J.-P. Migne (Paris, 1844–64)
PLRE	*Prosopography of the Later Roman Empire*, ed. A. H. M. Jones *et al.*, 3 vols. (Cambridge, 1971–92)
PLS	*Patrologia Latina, Suppl.*, ed. A. Hamman (Paris, 1958–)
RAC	*Reallexikon für Antike und Christentum*, ed. T. Klauser *et al.* (Stuttgart, 1950–)
RBen	*Revue Bénédictine*
REA	*Revue des études anciennes*
REAug	*Revue des études Augustiniennes*
SC	*Sources chrétiennes*, ed. H. de Lubac *et al.* (Paris, 1942–)
Thiel	A. Thiel, ed., *Epistolae romanorum pontificum genuinae et quae ad eos scriptae sunt a s. Hilaro usque ad Pelagium II* (Braunsberg, 1867)
de Vogüé and Courreau	A. de Vogüé and J. Courreau, eds., *Césaire d'Arles Œuvres monastiques*, I, *Œuvres pour les moniales, SC* 345 (Paris, 1988)
ZRG KA	*Zeitschrift der Savigny-Stiftung für Rechtsgeschichte, Kan. Abt*

CONCORDANCE OF CAESARIUS'S
LETTERS

This list includes letters written by and to Caesarius. It correlates the numbering system used in this book and in my *The Life, Testament, and Letters of Caesarius of Arles* with the somewhat haphazard system Morin used in *Opera omnia*, II. Letters written to Caesarius are also identified by author and edition.

Klingshirn	Morin	Letters to Caesarius
ep. I	*ep.* I, Morin II, 3–4	Ennodius, *ep.* IX. 33 (Hartel)
ep. 2	*ep.* 2, Morin II, 4–5	Avitus, *ep.* II (Peiper)
ep. 3	*ep.* 3, Morin II, 5–7	
ep. 4	*ep.* 4, Morin II, 7–8	Ruricius, *ep.* II. 33 (Engelbrecht)
ep. 5	*ep.* 5, Morin II, 8	Ruricius, *ep.* II. 36 (Engelbrecht)
ep. 6	*ep.* 6, Morin II, 9–10	Pope Symmachus, *ep. Arel.* 25
ep. 7a	*ep.* 7, *exemplum libelli petitorii*, Morin II, 12	
ep. 7b	*ep.* 7, Morin II, 10–11	Pope Symmachus, *ep. Arel.* 27
ep. 8a	*ep.* 8, *exemplum libelli petitorii*, Morin II, 13–14	
ep. 8b	*ep.* 8, Morin II, 13	Pope Symmachus, *ep. Arel.* 29
ep. 9	*ep.* 9, Morin II, 14	Pope Hormisdas, *MGH Ep.*, III, 42
ep. 10	*ep.* 10, Morin II, 14–17	Pope Hormisdas, *ep. Arel.* 30
ep. 11	*ep.* 11, Morin II, 17–18	Pope Felix IV, *ep. Arel.* 31
ep. 12	*ep.* 12, Morin II, 18–19	Pope John II, *ep. Arel.* 32
ep. 13	*ep.* 13, Morin II, 19–20	Pope John II, *ep. Arel.* 33

ep. 14a	*ep.* 14, Morin II, 20–22	Pope John II, *ep. Arel.* 34
ep. 14b	*ep.* 14, Morin II, 22–28	
ep. 15	*ep.* 15, Morin II, 28–29	Pope Agapitus, *ep. Arel.* 36
ep. 16	*ep.* 16, Morin II, 29–31	Pope Agapitus, *ep. Arel.* 37
ep. 17	*ep.* 17, Morin II, 31–32	Pope Vigilius, *ep. Arel.* 38
ep. 18	Morin II, 125–27	Pope Hormisdas, Thiel I, 988–90
ep. 19	Morin II, 65–66	
ep. 20	Morin II, 67–70	Pope Boniface II, *CCSL* 148A, 66–69
ep. 21	Morin II, 134–144	

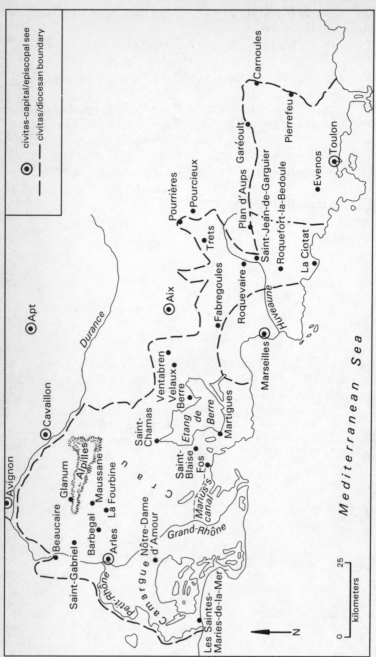

Map 1 The diocese of Arles and environs (c. 500). Source: based on A. L. F. Rivet, *Gallia Narbonensis: Southern France in Roman Times* (London: B. T. Batsford, Ltd., 1988), 204, and M. Chalon and M. Gayraud, "Notes de géographie antique, II," *Revue archéologique de Narbonnaise* 15 (1982), 399–406: 403.

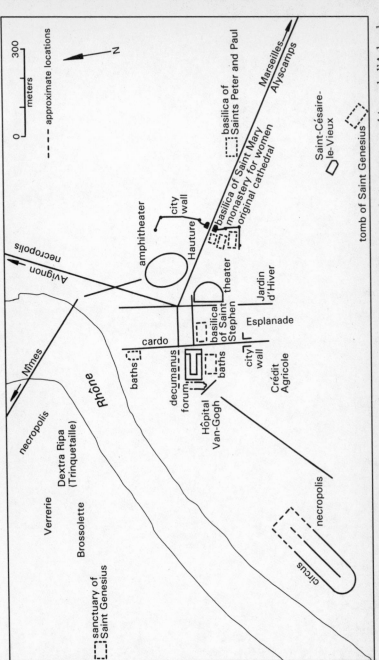

Map 2 The city and suburbs of Arles (c. 530). Source: based on C. Sintès, "L'évolution topographique de l'Arles du Haut-Empire à la lumière des fouilles récentes," *Journal of Roman Archaeology* 5 (1992), 130–47: 134, and *Topographie chrétienne des cités de la Gaule*, ed. N. Gauthier and J.-Ch. Picard, III, *Provinces ecclésiastiques de Vienne et d'Arles* (Paris: de Boccard, 1986), 75.

INTRODUCTION

Christianization in the late Roman and early medieval west was a process of slow, incomplete, inconsistent, and sometimes reversible social and religious change. It required not just the conversion of elites, the building of churches, or the founding of bishoprics and monasteries, but the widespread adoption of a Christian self-identity and a Christian system of values, practices, and beliefs. Unlike baptism or "conversion," which could be imposed from above, the social and religious changes required by christianization could not be put into effect without the consent and participation of local populations. The process of christian-ization was therefore reciprocal. Although its goals and strategies were established by theologians and its promotion entrusted to lay and clerical elites, its primary actors were the peasants and townspeople who made up local communities and who chose by their very way of life which of the church's teachings to accept, which to reject, and which to adapt for their own ends.

The power of local communities to define their own religious and cultural practices meant that the forms of christianization they chose to enact often differed from the program of christianization proposed by the official church. This occurred primarily because, unlike the traditional religion it sought to replace, Christianity had not arisen from within local culture, but had been imported from the outside and imposed on local populations, especially in the countryside. It was not in its origins a "community" religion, whose boundaries coincided with the boundaries of the local community and whose practices conformed to local traditions, attitudes, and expectations. It was rather an "organ-ized" religion, whose well-defined hierarchy, strict criteria of inclusion and exclusion, and highly regulated code of conduct and belief had all been devised by outside religious specialists and were in many ways ill-suited to the demands of local communities.[1] The result was that the Christianity practiced in local communities, while remaining an organized religion in many respects, also took on many of the characteristics of a community religion. Variously opposed and abetted by the clergy, this process was driven largely by the efforts of lay men and women to refashion Christianity according to their own expectations and traditions. The making of local communities into Christian communities thus entailed the making of Christianity into a community religion.

It would be difficult to find a better focus for studying these reciprocal processes of christianization than the life and writings of Caesarius, bishop of Arles from 502 to 542. As a monk, church reformer, bishop, and preacher, Caesarius devoted himself to the work of christianization with an ability and a vigor that few of his contemporaries displayed. He preached constantly to urban and rural congregations, not only in favor of Christian forms of worship, almsgiving, and spirituality, but also, according to his biographers, "against the evil of drunkenness and lust, against discord and hatred, against anger and pride, against the sacrilegious and fortune-tellers, ... worshippers of trees and springs, and vices of different kinds" (*vita* I. 55).[2] The originality of his message lay not in its content, which was based largely on the teachings of earlier churchmen, above all Augustine, but in the skill with which it was codified, simplified, and relentlessly propagated to a wide variety of audiences. But Caesarius's importance in the history of christianization goes well beyond the subject of his own efforts to christianize the population, although attention in the past has usually been confined to this subject. Through his writings, especially his sermons, we can also detect the community resistance

---

[1] For the difference between "organized" and "community" religions, see J. Davis, "Introduction," in *Religious Organization and Religious Experience*, ed. J. Davis, Association of Social Anthropologists, Monograph 21 (London, 1982), 1–8. The same distinction is often made between ethnic, local, or traditional religions on the one hand, and universal or world religions on the other, H.-D. Kahl, "Die ersten Jahrhunderte des missionsgeschichtlichen Mittelalters. Bausteine für eine Phänomenologie bis ca. 1050," in *Kirchengeschichte als Missionsgeschichte*, II, part 1, *Die Kirche des Früheren Mittelalters*, ed. K. Schäferdiek (Munich, 1978), 26–35; R. Horton, "African Conversion," *Africa* 41 (1971), 85–108: 85; J. D. Y. Peel, "Conversion and Tradition in Two African Societies: Ijebu and Buganda," *Past and Present* 77 (1977), 108–41: 108; W. A. Christian, *Local Religion in Sixteenth-Century Spain* (Princeton, 1981), 3–22.

[2] Translations are my own unless otherwise indicated. Some translations of Caesarius's sermons have been adapted from M. M. Mueller, *Caesarius of Arles. Sermons* (Washington, D.C., 1956–73).

his efforts evoked, the persistence of traditional practices, and the community's own efforts at self-christianization. Thus, by studying Caesarius, we can also study the community he sought to transform, and so fill in a portrait of Christian bishops and their communities in post-Roman Gaul that has up to now depended heavily on the writings of Gregory of Tours.[3] By focusing on Provence rather than on the Frankish heartland of central and northern Gaul, we may shed light on a more thoroughly romanized world with its own traditions and modes of life, which remained in regular communication with Rome, Ravenna, and the eastern Mediterranean, and resisted incorporation into the Merovingian realm longer than most other parts of Gaul. By concentrating on the writings of a preacher steeped in the traditions of Lérins rather than a hagiographer devoted to St. Martin, we may call attention to a strategy of christianization in which the power of rhetoric was more highly esteemed than the potency of relics, and to a measurement of christianization that does not equate its progress with the success of a local saint's cult. At the same time, because Christianity as a "cultural system" claimed for itself an exceedingly broad domain,[4] and because Caesarius's own career cannot be separated from the contemporary political situation, we shall also touch on a wide variety of problems in the social, political, and cultural history of late fifth- and early sixth-century Gaul.

Although it had long been the subject of commentary by his editors, Caesarius's career as a monk and pastor did not receive its first sustained critical attention until 1884, when Urbain Ville-vieille published his *Histoire de Saint Césaire, évêque d'Arles.*[5] This was followed in 1892/93 by Bruno Fürchtegott Gellert's accurate and succinct "Caesarius von Arelate."[6] These early efforts were soon superseded, however, by Arthur Malnory, *Saint Césaire, évêque d'Arles* (Paris, 1894), and Carl Franklin Arnold, *Caesarius*

---

[3] See for example the excellent studies by L. Pietri, *La Ville de Tours du IVe siècle au VIe siècle: naissance d'une cité chrétienne* (Rome, 1983); R. Van Dam, *Leadership and Community in Late Antique Gaul* (Berkeley and Los Angeles, 1985); and I. N. Wood, "Early Merovingian Devotion in Town and Country," in *The Church in Town and Countryside*, ed. D. Baker (Oxford, 1979), 61–76.

[4] C. Geertz, "Religion as a Cultural System," in his *The Interpretation of Cultures* (London, 1975), 87–125.   [5] Aix-en-Provence, 1884.

[6] Part 1, "Das Leben des Caesarius," *Programm des städtischen Realgymnasiums zu Leipzig*, Progr. Nr. 553 (Leipzig, 1892), 3–48, and part 2, "Seine Schriften," *Jahresbericht des städtischen Realgymnasiums in Leipzig*, Progr. Nr. 554 (Leipzig, 1893), 3–30.

von Arelate und die gallische Kirche seiner Zeit (Leipzig, 1894). Although both studies remain in demand, as recent reprints demonstrate, Arnold's more critical positivist approach has better endured the test of time, and still offers much of value, especially on chronology, prosopography, and ecclesiastical politics. An important shortcoming affecting both books was the inferiority of available editions for the study of Caesarius's life and work. This was partially remedied by Bruno Krusch in 1896 with the publication of an improved edition of the bishop's *vita*, accompanied by a learned introduction to his career.[7] A further step was taken in 1937 with the publication of a new edition of Caesarius's sermons by Germain Morin,[8] which more than doubled the size of the corpus.[9] Five years later, having already edited a number of other works by Caesarius, and taking particular account of Samuel Cavallin's studies of his *vita* (Lund, 1934, 1936),[10] Morin published a second volume containing Caesarius's *vita*, testament, monastic rules, letters, councils, and theological treatises.[11] The publication of these volumes spawned a flurry of articles and books in the post-war period on Caesarius's preaching, pastoral care, and theology.[12] Notable among these was Henry G. J. Beck, *The Pastoral Care of Souls in South-East France During the Sixth Century* (Rome, 1950), which relied heavily on Caesarius's sermons for its details about church order and pastoral practice in sixth-century Provence. More recently, new editions and translations of Caesarius with important introductions and notes have been made available in *Sources chrétiennes* by Marie-José Delage,

---

[7] *Vitae Caesarii Episcopi Arelatensis Libri Duo*, MGH SRM, III, 433–501.

[8] For his remarkable career, see G. Ghysens and P.-P. Verbraken, *La Carrière scientifique de Dom Germain Morin (1861–1946)* (Steenbrugge, 1986). On his aims and methods, see G. Morin, "Mes principes et ma méthode pour la future édition de saint Césaire," *RBen* 10 (1893), 62–78, and idem, "Comment j'ai fait mon édition des œuvres de saint Césaire d'Arles," *Nouvelle Revue de Hongrie* 58 (1938), 225–32.

[9] *Sancti Caesarii Episcopi Arelatensis Opera Omnia*, I, *Sermones* (Maredsous, 1937), repr. *CCSL* 103–4 (Turnhout, 1953). A concordance to the reprint is now available on CD-ROM in the *Cetedoc Library of Christian Latin Texts*, published by Brepols (Turnhout, 1991).

[10] Especially, *Literarhistorische und textkritische Studien zur Vita S. Caesarii Arelatensis* (Lund, 1934), and "Eine neue Handschrift der Vita S. Caesarii Arelatensis," *Kungl. Humanistiska Vetenskapssamfundet i Lund, Årsberättelse = Bulletin de la Société Royale des Lettres de Lund* (1935–36), 9–19. Cavallin also published a concordance to Krusch's edition of the *vita Caesarii* in *Vitae Sanctorum Honorati et Hilarii* (Lund, 1952).

[11] *Sancti Caesarii Episcopi Arelatensis Opera Omnia*, II, *Opera Varia* (Maredsous, 1942).

[12] An annotated bibliography can be found in G. Terraneo, "Saggio bibliografico su Cesario vescovo di Arles," *La scuola cattolica* 91 (1963), Suppl. bibliogr. 272*–94*.

Césaire d'Arles. Sermons au peuple (Paris, 1975–86), and Adalbert de Vogüé and Joël Courreau, *Césaire d'Arles. Œuvres monastiques*, I, *Œuvres pour les moniales* (Paris, 1988). Yet despite sustained interest in Caesarius over the years, no full-length study of his life and work has appeared since 1894.

This book seeks to fill that gap. At the same time, while necessarily building on the work of its predecessors, it attempts to avoid the triumphalism that has characterized much of the study of Caesarius in the past. Ever since Caesarius was first depicted by Cesare Baronio in the late sixteenth century as a great helmsman piloting the church amidst the waves of barbarian invasion and heretical attack,[13] he has consistently been portrayed as an agent of stability and orthodoxy in troubled times, "the fearless shepherd of a truly threatened flock troubled by catastrophes" in a recent description by Friedrich Prinz.[14] This book offers an alternative view of the bishop. Rather than treating him as the unquestioned representative of an already thoroughly christianized community, it focuses on his efforts to create precisely such a community. Rather than assuming that his main achievement was to sustain the religious *status quo*, it points to his controversial role as a proponent of reform. It devotes as much attention to his failures as to his successes, and as much analysis to the audience he sought to persuade as to the ideas and practices he sought to instill. It is neither a biography of Caesarius, strictly speaking, nor a study of his theology, but an examination of the history of christianization in the place and time so well illuminated by his writings.

The book begins with an account of Caesarius's birth in 469/70, his career as a junior cleric in Chalon-sur-Saône and his sojourn as a monk at Lérins. Chapter 2 surveys the history of Roman and late Roman Arles to provide the background for Caesarius's efforts to christianize and therefore disrupt and transform the city's existing culture. Chapter 3 discusses Caesarius's relocation to Arles in *c.* 495, his rapid promotion to deacon, priest, and abbot, and his education as a reformer under Julianus Pomerius. Chapter 4 is devoted to Caesarius's consecration as bishop of Arles in 502 and his stormy career under its Visigothic masters until 508, when an Ostrogothic administration replaced them. In Chapter 5 we

---

[13] C. Baronius, *Annales Ecclesiastici*, VI (Rome, 1595), 192, sub anno 453.
[14] F. Prinz, "Die bischöfliche Stadtherrschaft im Frankenreich vom 5. bis zum 7. Jahrhundert," in *Bischofs- und Kathedralstädte des Mittelalters und der frühen Neuzeit*, ed. F. Petri (Cologne and Vienna, 1976), 1–26: 13.

examine the long peaceful period of Ostrogothic administration (508–36), which saw Caesarius's greatest achievements as a politician, pastor, monastic founder, and reformer. The following three chapters explore his efforts at christianization and their limitations. Chapter 6 studies the diverse means of persuasion Caesarius employed to promote the values, practices, and beliefs of an "organized" Christianity. Chapter 7 examines the resistance his efforts called forth at the center of local society, primarily the urban population, while Chapter 8 examines resistance at the periphery, primarily among the peasantry, which took the form of a community religion that the bishop defined as "paganism." In Chapter 9 we discuss the transition from Ostrogothic to Frankish rule in Provence, the deterioration of Caesarius's political position after 536, his death in 542, and the fate of his reforms, his monastery, and his city under the Merovingians. The final chapter is devoted to Caesarius's considerable impact on the Carolingian reforms, which helped to create the kinds of Christian communities he had aimed to create, but at the cost of transforming Christianity itself into the community religion he had sought to repress.

Before we begin, it is necessary to discuss the most important sources for this study, the *vita* and *sermones* of Caesarius. At first glance, the genres of hagiography and homiletics might seem to offer the least promising materials for the writing of history. Yet, as we shall see, these are precisely the forms of available evidence best equipped to illuminate the complex relationship between the citizens of Arles and their bishop. Composed by churchmen well informed about their audiences, and designed as instruments of persuasion themselves, the *vita* and *sermones* of Caesarius can be interpreted to reveal the ideas and actions of those they were meant to convince, seldom accessible by other means.[15] As Emilio Gabba has written: "The fact that they addressed themselves to an audience which was all-embracing and not necessarily educated meant that Christian authors had to have not only direct experience of the life of a Christian community, but also a real feeling for its problems; otherwise they stood no chance of being understood in practical terms, concerned as they were with moral and religious themes. Their writings thus allow one to recognise

---

[15] On the possibility of using such forms of literature to investigate a largely non-literate "popular" culture, see A. Gurevich, *Medieval Popular Culture: Problems of Belief and Perception*, trans. J. M. Bak and P. A. Hollingsworth (Cambridge, 1988), 1–38.

and reconstruct the realities of contemporary situations, even where problems are formulated in moral terms and the aim is to portray an ideal society – as it should be and not as it was."[16]

The *vita* of Caesarius was composed within seven years of the bishop's death by five clerics of his acquaintance.[17] It consisted of two books. The architect of the work as a whole and the principal author of Book I was Cyprianus, bishop of Toulon (*c*. 517–*c*. 545) and a close associate of Caesarius. He was assisted in the composition of Book I by Firminus, bishop of Uzès (*c*. 534–*c*. 552), and Viventius, bishop of an unknown see (*c*. 541–*c*. 548). Book II in turn was composed by two diocesan clerics who had attended Caesarius since their adolescence, Messianus, a priest, and Stephanus, a deacon. The division of the *vita* into two books was intended to take advantage of the interests and capacities of its authors, who had acquired different kinds of knowledge about Caesarius on the basis of their different ecclesiastical ranks and duties. Thus, the authors of Book I, who knew Caesarius as a bishop and metropolitan, concentrated on official aspects of his monastic and clerical career, such as his training as a monk at Lérins, his political leadership of Arles, his travels outside the diocese, and his achievements as a preacher, a wonder-worker, and a monastic founder. The authors of Book II, on the other hand, portrayed Caesarius as he would have appeared to the local clergy. They recounted local, public activities such as his healings and exorcisms, his journeys to rural parishes, and the events surrounding his death and burial, as well as more private events, such as his dreams, his visions of Jesus, and his dinnertime conversations with the local clergy.

Cyprianus and his fellow clerics first undertook to write the life of Caesarius at the request of Caesaria the Younger, a close relation of Caesarius, who was serving at the time of his death as abbess of the convent he had founded in Arles. Like many other hagiographers, therefore, they designed the work, at least in part, to promote the interests of a monastery.[18] But as admirers and supporters of Caesarius, they also composed the *vita* to edify

---

[16] E. Gabba, "Literature," in *Sources for Ancient History*, ed. M. Crawford (Cambridge, 1983), 1–79: 74.

[17] For a useful introduction, see G. Sticca, "La biografia di Cesario vescovo di Arles, 470–549," (Tesi di Laurea, University of Turin, 1954).

[18] W. Klingshirn, "Caesarius's Monastery for Women in Arles and the Composition and Function of the 'Vita Caesarii'," *RBen* 100 (1990), 441–81.

anyone who read or listened to the work, to celebrate their own association with the bishop, and to defend the bishop's reputation from attack by rivals. In addition, they tried to promote after Caesarius's death the controversial reform ideas he had promoted all his life. The intended audience for the work must have included, besides the nunnery, succeeding bishops of Arles and their clergy, members of the Frankish royal family, and the population of Arles, but how wide a group the *vita* actually reached in late antiquity can no longer be determined. Clearly it was preserved and read in the women's monastery in Arles and in other closely related monasteries during the late sixth and early seventh centuries, but beyond these uses, the work's readership and influence remain unknown.[19]

Like other saints' lives, the *vita* of Caesarius is a valuable source for the mental world of its authors and their immediate audience.[20] Unlike many other saints' lives, however, the *vita* also serves as a valuable source for the career of its subject. It was written soon after his death by men deeply familiar with his life, who claimed to draw their information from reliable sources: Caesarius himself, their own eyewitness observations, and the eyewitness observations of others (*vita* I. 1; II. 1). While such claims are a commonplace of hagiography, the *vita* itself largely substantiates them. Quotations from Caesarius's sermons (*vita* I. 18, 54, 61; II. 5) and stories plausibly based on his own narration (*vita* I. 6, 29) can be identified throughout the work. Details supplied by one or another author are on many occasions of just the sort he was in a position to observe (*vita* I. 51; II. 6, 13–15, 19, 22). Reliance on the eyewitness testimony of others is confirmed in several instances by the naming of informants (*vita* II. 10–12, 41). In addition to these sources, the authors of the *vita* made use of the oral traditions they heard at various places. The edifying and amusing story of Benenatus and his daughter, for instance, was told at the Basilica of the Apostles in Arles (*vita* II. 24). These traditions were supplemented and elaborated by stories modeled directly on the Bible (*vita* II. 13) and on earlier saints' lives, especially the *vita* of Caesarius's predecessor Hilarius (*vita* I. 27; II. 49–50: cf. *vita Hilarii* 18, 28–29). Although the authors were no doubt responsible for some of these borrowings, in other cases the actors themselves may

---

[19] Ibid., 452–53, 474–80.
[20] F. Lotter, "Methodisches zur Gewinnung historischer Erkenntnisse aus hagiographischen Quellen," *Historische Zeitschrift* 229 (1979), 298–356: 298–305.

have modeled their behavior on biblical or patristic *exempla*.[21] It is for such reasons that the *vita Caesarii* can be considered trustworthy not only for the values and beliefs of its authors and audience, but also for the reconstruction of the life and work of Caesarius.

The sermons of Caesarius pose a different set of problems. That they survive at all is the result of his conviction that bishops, and under certain circumstances priests and deacons, should preach, and that many would not or could not do so unless they were given prepared sermons to recite to their congregations (*serm.* 1. 15; *vita* 1. 54), a practice Augustine had recommended for clergymen unable to compose sermons themselves.[22] Caesarius therefore assembled written copies of his sermons into collections, which he presented to bishops and other clerics, with orders to disseminate these further (*vita* 1. 55; *serm.* 2). Distributed throughout "the Frankish lands, Gaul, Italy, Spain, and other provinces" (*vita* 1. 55), these sermon collections formed the basis of collections surviving to the present.

But how had Caesarius's sermons come to be written down in the first place? And what was the connection between the sermons he delivered to his congregation and the versions he gathered into collections and distributed to other bishops? A comparison with Augustine's *sermones ad populum* is instructive. Written copies of these were made by stenographers (*notarii*) who recorded his sermons as they were delivered.[23] Although Augustine may have revised some of them subsequently, his alterations were probably slight, and his sermons thus appear in their present form as virtual transcripts of what he said to his congregation, or at least of what the *notarii* were able to record.[24] As such, they are filled with references to specific persons, places, and events, indications of date and place of delivery,[25] and descriptions of conditions of delivery, such as the eruption of applause.[26]

The recording of Caesarius's sermons, by contrast, depended on

[21] G. Scheibelreiter, "Der frühfränkische Episkopat: Bild und Wirklichkeit," *Frühmittelalterliche Studien* 17 (1983), 131–47: 136–37. [22] *doctr. christ.* IV. xxix. 62.

[23] Possidius, *vita Augustini* 7. See in general, R. J. Deferrari, "St. Augustine's Method of Composing and Delivering Sermons," *American Journal of Philology* 43 (1922), 97–123, 193–219, and C. Mohrmann, *Die altchristliche Sondersprache in den Sermones des hl. Augustin* (Nijmegen, 1932), 21–26.

[24] M. Pellegrino, "General Introduction," in *The Works of Saint Augustine*, ed. J. E. Rotelle, part 3, *Sermons*, I (Brooklyn, N.Y., 1990), 18.

[25] For details, see P.-P. Verbraken, *Etudes critiques sur les sermons authentiques de Saint Augustin* (Steenbrugge, 1976).

[26] Deferrari, "St. Augustine's Method," 193–211.

his own desire to furnish other clergymen with ready-made sermons for preaching. Caesarius probably had stenographers take down the sermons he delivered in Arles,[27] but then, in order to create more widely useful "generic" sermons, he revised these much more thoroughly than Augustine had done. He eliminated references to local persons, places, and events, and left out information about date and place of delivery, since these details were irrelevant to his purpose. His revision was not so complete, however, as to eliminate any connection between the sermons that left his scriptorium and those he delivered in Arles. In the first place, some references to specific conditions of delivery remain in his surviving sermons. In one sermon, for instance, Caesarius refers to a man possessed by the devil who had interrupted church services the Sunday before and caused great fear among the congregation (*serm.* 79. 1). In another sermon, he complained that there were women "even in this city" who honored Jupiter by refusing to spin wool on Thursdays (*serm.* 52. 2). In yet another, rather lengthy sermon, he indicated that he would stop speaking and resume his theme the following day, "on account of the poor, who are hurrying off to work" (*serm.* 91. 8); the next day he continued where he had left off (*serm.* 92. 1).[28] Moreover, although Caesarius's sermons contain no external indications of date, *Sermon* 6 can be shown from internal evidence to have been delivered shortly after the siege of Arles in 507/8. Likewise, although few sermons offer any evidence of the place of delivery, *Sermon* 233 can be shown to have been originally delivered to the monks "in Blandiacensi monasterio," the location of which is unknown.

But it is not just surviving references to conditions of delivery that testify to the connection between Caesarius's written sermons and the versions he originally delivered. The whole logic behind his distribution of sermons to clergymen outside Arles rested on the assumption that similar conditions prevailed elsewhere. Unlike classical orators, whose written speeches for various reasons often differed remarkably from the versions they actually delivered,[29] Caesarius had his sermons written down precisely so that they

---

[27] For the existence of ecclesiastical *notarii* in Arles, see *vita* I. 21.

[28] See also *serm.* 146. 4.

[29] The classic example is Cicero's *pro Milone*. After receiving a copy of the speech as later revised by Cicero, Milo commented from his exile in Marseille that he was fortunate it had not been delivered in the same form at the trial; otherwise he would not be enjoying the seafood delicacies of Provence, Cassius Dio XL. 54. 3.

could be delivered again in similar circumstances. They were designed to address the same kinds of problems Caesarius faced and to offer the same kinds of solutions. There was no reason for any large-scale revision in either content or style. Caesarius had composed the themes and arguments of his sermons for the diocese he knew best; he could not have composed more effective sermons on any other basis. Moreover, his sermons were already suitable for delivery in other dioceses. Their length suited conditions at Arles and presumably elsewhere, and their syntax and diction made them accessible to educated and uneducated listeners alike (*serm.* 86. 1), especially when they were delivered with a pronunciation that conformed not to their classically correct orthography, but to the vernacular Latin spoken by both preachers and congregations.[30] All this would suggest that the sermons Caesarius distributed to outsiders were very close to those he delivered in Arles.

Yet Caesarius's sermons are afflicted with an additional problem for the historian. Many contain extensive verbatim borrowings from other patristic homilies, ranging in extent from a few sentences to virtually the entire sermon. At issue here is not only the value of such borrowings as evidence, but more fundamentally the possibility that the sermons in which they appear were products of the study rather than the pulpit, and do not reflect a close connection between the preacher and his audience. In exploring this problem, it is first important to note that Caesarius's use of borrowed material varies widely from sermon to sermon. Morin's edition is divided into three categories on this basis. The 149 sermons of Class I, which make up 62·6% of the total, are those Morin considered original compositions by Caesarius; in these, direct borrowing was kept to a minimum. Class II, with 52 sermons (21·8%), consists of sermons Morin believed to have been modeled on the sermons of others, but within which he found a substantial number of passages attributable to Caesarius's style of speech or thought. Class III (37 sermons, 15·5%) contains sermons that are essentially copies of earlier models, but display evidence of minimal reworking by Caesarius, for instance in an introduction or conclusion. Although we have most often relied for evidence on sermons in the first class, which clearly maintain the closest

---

[30] R. Wright, *Late Latin and Early Romance* (Liverpool, 1982); on his thesis, see the papers in *Latin and the Romance Languages in the Early Middle Ages*, ed. R. Wright (London and New York, 1991).

connection to Caesarius's world, we have also used sermons in the second and third classes, since these too supply valuable information, especially when they can be compared with their models. It is, for instance, on the basis of Caesarius's addition of just three words – "Natalis Domini imminet" ("Christmas is approaching") – to a sermon originally delivered by Augustine on the occasion of his ordination as bishop (Augustine, *serm.* 339; Caesarius, *serm.* 231. 3) that we can surmise that Caesarius was ordained a bishop just before Christmas in 502. Indeed, we may generally assume that whenever Caesarius borrowed from other preachers, he did so because he believed that this material was relevant to the audience he addressed, not because he was incapable of producing material of his own.[31]

But if we are to maintain a close connection between Caesarius and his audience, even in the case of derivative sermons, we must ask how his sermons were composed and delivered. Did Caesarius compose them mentally in advance and deliver them extempore or did he dictate them beforehand and deliver them from verbatim memory? That this question mattered in Christian preaching is clear from the case of Atticus, bishop of Constantinople from 406 to 425. According to the church history of Socrates, "formerly while a presbyter he had been accustomed, after composing his sermons, to commit them to memory, and then recite them in the church; but by diligent application he acquired confidence and made his instruction extemporaneous and eloquent."[32] As Augustine explained in the *de doctrina christiana*, extemporaneous preaching was superior because it allowed the preacher to adjust his message to the reactions of his audience, "which is not possible for those who preach what they have prepared in advance and memorized verbatim."[33]

Caesarius's biographers tell us that he delivered his sermons *memoriter*, "from memory" (*vita* I. 54; II. 20). This does not necessarily refer to verbatim memory, however, since *memoriter* in patristic Latin and particularly in the sermons of Caesarius can refer to either of the two divisions of memory treated in ancient rhetorical handbooks: "memory for things" (*memoria rerum*) or

[31] See in general, L. Cracco Ruggini, *Economia e Società nell' "Italia Annonaria"* (Milan, 1961), 13–16.
[32] Socrates, *historia ecclesiastica* VII. 2, *PG* 67: 741, trans. A. C. Zenos, Nicene and Post Nicene Fathers, 2nd series, II (Grand Rapids, Mich., 1979).
[33] *doctr. christ.* IV. X. 25.

"memory for words" (*memoria verborum*).[34] While professional orators employed both forms of memory in the composition of a speech, it was memory for things that they used for its actual delivery; memory for words was used only in quoting others or in delivering a particularly intricate passage.[35] Given the rules of classical and Christian rhetoric and Caesarius's pastoral concern for instructing his audience, it makes sense to argue that he delivered his sermons extemporaneously, even those containing derivative material. It is not difficult to imagine how he did this. For Caesarius, patristic texts were nearly as worthy of study and emulation as the Bible, and he was prepared to use them as creatively as he used the scriptures.[36] Having memorized a wide variety of patristic sermons, he could draw upon these in his own preaching, just as he did the Bible, selecting appropriate passages, abbreviating and paraphrasing where necessary, and improvising *ad libitum*. Such extensive memorization was certainly not beyond Caesarius's capacities. His biographers noted his "wonderfully retentive memory" (*vita* I. 9) and the facility with which "he recited in succession countless *exempla* from the divine books. He did this as if he were reading what he knew out of a book, not as if he were drawing forth what he had once read from the storehouse of his memory" (*vita* I. 16).

The scope and accuracy of his verbatim memory allowed Caesarius to freely manipulate both biblical and patristic texts, and thus to create sermons that exactly suited the conditions of delivery he faced. Sermons composed in this way could remain faithful to their original sources while still taking into account (and reflecting) reactions of perplexity, indifference, skepticism, or hostility from the audience. The advantage of this explanation is that it allows for the kind of interaction with his audience that was essential for propagating a Christian system of values and beliefs. In addition, it takes account of classical and patristic habits of composition, and in particular the use of "active memory," not

---

[34] For the two kinds of memory, see *ad Herennium* III. xxiv. 39, and Caesarius, *serm.* 22. 1. For *memoriter* in the sense of *memoria verborum*, see Augustine, *de catechizandis rudibus* iii. 5; Fulgentius of Ruspe, *ep.* 11. 2, ed. J. Fraipont, *CCSL* 91; and Caesarius, *serm*, 9. 1, 16. 2, 130. 5, 136. 1, and 238. 1. For *memoriter* in the sense of *memoria rerum*, see Gregory the Great, *ep.* VI. 19, and Caesarius, *serm.* 19. 6, 22. 1, 23. 2, 36. 1, 74. 4, 104. 6.

[35] M. J. Carruthers, *The Book of Memory: A Study of Memory in Medieval Culture* (Cambridge, 1990), 196–208. This excellent study has influenced much of my discussion of memory in Caesarius's sermons.

[36] On Caesarius's attitude to his biblical and patristic sources, see Delage I, 94–117.

only to recall what was stored in the mind but equally important to create something new out of memorized material.[37] Finally, for the historian, such an explanation allows the full range of Caesarius's sermons to be used as evidence for what he believed his audience needed to hear.

Yet the most serious problem with using Caesarius's sermons as historical sources might seem to lie precisely in the normative character of the genre itself. The bishop delivered sermons to instruct and convince his audiences of what ought to be, not to describe what actually was.[38] And while his use of the analogy is understandable, it is impossible to take at face value Caesarius's claim that his preaching was "like a mirror," which revealed to his people the details of their sinful behavior (*serm.* 42. 6). For if so, it was a mirror of a peculiarly distorted and selective kind, which represented only those aspects of attitude or behavior the bishop could observe for himself or learn from others, reflected only those matters he chose to discuss, and presented only those interpretations he chose to present. But sermons could only persuade if they related what ought to be to what actually was. Caesarius was a master of this skill, and used a wide variety of analogies from daily life to make his point. It is therefore precisely as instruments of rhetoric and polemic that his sermons constitute irreplaceable sources of evidence. In expressing what he thought his audience agreed with or took for granted, Caesarius's sermons point to the issues on which a consensus existed. In expressing what he thought they disagreed with, they provide evidence of points of dissent. In describing behaviors he disapproved of, they provide evidence of what people were actually doing. Of particular value is his frequent practice of anticipating objections to the doctrines and practices he preached in order to refute them, a rhetorical technique that often suggests, in the bishop's view, the reasons members of his congregation advanced for their disagreement with him. These constitute the only available fragments of his congregation's views, and they would not have had any rhetorical effect at all if they did not represent the authentic views of at least some in the community. For these reasons, despite their flaws as sources, the sermons of Caesarius provide us with the best available evidence for the values, practices, and beliefs of his congregation. The fact that they were composed with particular audiences in

---

[37] Carruthers, *The Book of Memory*, 189–220.
[38] Cracco Ruggini, *Economia e società*, 9–10.

mind, and delivered under particular conditions and at particular times, guarantees their value as sources for these audiences, conditions, and times, even when they are the only sources available. Combined with other literary, documentary, and archaeological evidence, they constitute a precious resource for the study of Caesarius and the people of Arles.

Chapter 1

IN SEARCH OF THE *VITA PERFECTA*

At the time of Caesarius's birth in 469/70, the western Roman empire was on the verge of permanent dissolution. In many regions barbarian rulers had already exercised a virtual sovereignty for some time, with or without the cooperation of local Roman officials. Vandals controlled north Africa, and Saxons Roman Britain; Visigoths and Suevi ruled much of Spain, and Rugians dominated Noricum.[1] Control over Gaul was divided among Bretons and Saxons in the west, Franks in the north, Burgundians and Alamanni in the east, and Visigoths in the southwest.[2] Only Italy and Provence remained under the direct control of the west Roman government in Ravenna. In other areas, such as the province of Tarraconensis in Spain and the territory of Clermont in Gaul, Roman officials and local nobles maintained a tenuous independence without the help of imperial armies. This soon came to an end, however. By the mid-470s Visigothic armies were in control of Tarraconensis.[3] In 475, Clermont was ceded to the Visigoths in exchange for Provence, an agreement that acknowledged Gothic conquests without acknowledging Gothic sovereignty.[4] When Odovacar deposed the usurper Romulus Augustulus in 476 and refrained from replacing him, imperial rule in the west came to an end. Odovacar took charge of Italy and the Visigoths annexed Provence.[5] The apparently independent Roman officials who surface in Gaul after this date, such as Arbogast, count of Trier, and Syagrius, "king" of the Romans at

---

[1] E. Stein, *Histoire du Bas-Empire*, ed. J.-R. Palanque, I (Paris, 1959), 319–22, 329–32.

[2] E. James, *The Origins of France: From Clovis to the Capetians, 500–1000* (London, 1982), 15–36.

[3] R. Collins, *Early Medieval Spain: Unity in Diversity, 400–1000* (New York, 1983), 24.

[4] H. Wolfram, *History of the Goths*, trans. T. J. Dunlap (Berkeley and Los Angeles, 1988), 186–87.   [5] Stein, *Histoire*, I, 397.

Soissons, may well have exercised a restricted authority in cooperation with the Franks.[6]

Caesarius was born and brought up in the territory of Chalon (Cabillonum), a busy port on the Saône, located at the strategic crossroads between Langres, Besançon, Lyon, and Autun. Of Celtic origin, it was for most of the Roman period one of several important towns in the vast district (*civitas*) of the Aedui, whose capital was established by Augustus at Autun. By the fifth century, it had become the capital of its own district, located in the province of Lugdunensis I. As such, Chalon possessed its own municipal council, its own magistrates, and its own bishop.[7] Ammianus Marcellinus reckoned it one of the most prosperous cities in the province, no doubt because of its location on the major waterway connecting the Rhine frontier and the Mediterranean.[8]

It was probably in the late 460s or early 470s that Chalon and its territory had come under the control of the Burgundians, who had been settled in Sapaudia as Roman federates in *c.* 442.[9] Under the leadership of King Gundioc (d. *c.* 470), they had demonstrated their willingness to enlarge the area of their influence.[10] Under Gundioc's successors – especially his brother Chilperic I (*c.* 470–*c.* 480), his son Gundobad (*c.* 480–516), and Gundobad's son Sigismund (516–23) – the Burgundian realm grew larger, including at its maximum extent the whole of Lugdunensis I, most of Maxima Sequanorum, and portions of Viennensis, Narbonensis II, Alpes Graiae, and Alpes Maritimae.[11]

By the terms of their agreement with the imperial government, the Burgundians were considered Roman federates and their kings were designated as Roman officers.[12] Gradually, however, they replaced the imperial government in the territories under their control. Although the kings left matters of local jurisdiction to the

[6] E. James, *The Franks* (Oxford, 1988), 70–74.
[7] B. Beaujard, "Chalon-sur-Saône," in *Topographie chrétienne des cités de la Gaule*, ed. N. Gauthier and J.-Ch. Picard, IV, *Province ecclésiastique de Lyon* (Paris, 1986), 68–70.
[8] Ammianus Marcellinus XV. 11. 11; see also XIV. 10. 3.
[9] L. Schmidt, *Die Ostgermanen*, 2nd edn. (Munich, 1941), 143–44.
[10] The territorial extent of Burgundian control is complicated by questions about their sovereignty before 476. Did they occupy territory as Roman federates or as Burgundian warriors? See further, I. N. Wood, "Avitus of Vienne: Religion and Culture in the Auvergne and the Rhône Valley, 470–530" (D. Phil. thesis, Oxford University, 1980), 1–9. I am grateful to Dr. Wood for permission to cite this study.
[11] Schmidt, *Ostgermanen*, 169–70. A map of the *civitates* and provinces of late antique Gaul may be found in James, *The Origins of France*, xix–xx.
[12] Schmidt, *Ostgermanen*, 170, 176.

existing municipal councils and their magistrates,[13] just as the imperial government had done, they exercised a general supervision over the Roman *civitates* through their own officers, in particular, the counts.[14] In time the kings took over imperial lands, tax revenues, and mints.[15] Individual Burgundians were probably allocated a fixed proportion of tax revenues and given residences and the right to cultivate uncultivated property.[16] This arrangement minimized losses to the Roman population, and allowed the local aristocracy to remain wealthy. Indeed, in areas where the Burgundians did not settle in large numbers, which included Chalon, the social structure remained largely unchanged.

FAMILY AND EARLY LIFE

Caesarius's parents probably belonged to the local Gallo-Roman aristocracy of Chalon, although they lived, as did many aristocrats of the period, not in the city itself, but in its countryside (*territorium*, *vita* I. 3). The *vita* identifies them only as aristocrats and Christians, without revealing their names.[17] Caesarius had at least one sister, named Caesaria (the Elder),[18] as well as a nephew, perhaps another sister's son, named Teridius,[19] and another close relation, perhaps a brother's daughter, named Caesaria (the Younger).[20] In southern Gaul, Caesarius's best-known relative was Aeonius, who served as bishop of Arles from *c.* 485 to 501/2 (*vita* I. 10). Another relative from Chalon, an unnamed cleric, lived in Arles at the same time as Caesarius (*vita* I. 29). Several other possible relations can also be identified in the neighborhood of Chalon and further south.[21]

Caesarius received a good education in Latin grammar at Chalon, which provided a solid foundation for his later studies at

---

[13] For instance, in Vienne (Avitus, *hom.* 6, *MGH AA*, VI. 2, 110) and Lyon (Sidonius Apollinaris, *ep.* I. 6. 4; v. 20. 1).   [14] Schmidt, *Ostgermanen*, 181–83.

[15] Ibid., 186–87.

[16] W. Goffart, *Barbarians and Romans: The Techniques of Accommodation* (Princeton, 1980), 127–61, esp. 149–51.

[17] "whose parents as well as his family – an exceptionally great example of honor and nobility – were distinguished above all their fellow citizens because of their faith and even more their conduct," *vita* I. 3. See also "stirpibus nobilibus," *vita* I. 4.

[18] *vita* I. 35, 58.

[19] Caesarius, *reg. mon.*, Morin II, 149; G. Morin, "Le Prêtre Arlésien Teridius," *Recherches de science religieuse* 28 (1938), 257–63.

[20] *vita* I. 1, 58. On the relationship, see Arnold, 14.

[21] R. W. Mathisen, "The Ecclesiastical Aristocracy of Fifth-Century Gaul: A Regional Analysis of Family Structure" (Ph. D. diss., University of Wisconsin-Madison, 1979), 435–38.

Lérins and Arles. We can infer this from the report that he later instructed Florianus in Latin grammar,[22] and from his later career as a preacher and an author. Although composed in a simple Latin style, his sermons display a wide range of rhetorical devices, a good knowledge of Latin orthography and syntax, and a deep familiarity with the Bible and Latin patristic literature. Writings meant for more sophisticated audiences, such as his letters, monastic rules, and theological treatises, demonstrate a correspondingly more sophisticated style. His almost total avoidance of references to classical literature,[23] his dream about the dangers of "secular wisdom" (*vita* 1. 9), and his public condemnations of classical literature and philosophy (*serm.* 99. 2, 3; 100. 3; 163. 1) should not be attributed so much to a hostility toward classical culture, which no longer posed a serious threat, as to a well-conceived strategy of christianization, as we shall demonstrate in subsequent chapters.

In 486/87, at the age of seventeen ("in his eighteenth year," *vita* 1. 4), Caesarius decided to enter the local clergy of Chalon, under Bishop Silvester (*c.* 485–*c.* 527).[24] His biographers suggest that he did so without the knowledge or permission of his parents, and furthermore that he asked the bishop to prevent his family from recalling him to the family estate and his family relations (*vita* 1. 4). This is certainly a plausible scenario. So abrupt a departure from family responsibility might well have been opposed by Caesarius's parents, and particularly his father, whose authority the young man was morally and legally obliged to respect.[25] Still, in view of the tendency of hagiographers to exaggerate their heroes' rejection of family ties, such an assertion needs to be viewed skeptically.[26] It is equally likely that, in entering the local clergy of Chalon, Caesarius was embarking upon a traditional family career. In either case, by entering the local clergy, perhaps as a lector,[27] Caesarius removed himself from his father's authority and placed

---

[22] "ipse igitur mihi Latinis elementis inposuit alfabetum," Florianus, *epistolae Austrasicae* 5, ed. W. Gundlach, *MGH Ep.*, III, 116–17.

[23] P. Riché, *Education and Culture in the Barbarian West, Sixth Through Eighth Centuries*, trans. J. J. Contreni (Columbia, S.C., 1976), 114, nn. 88, 89.

[24] Duchesne II, 193. He took part in the synods of Epaone (517) and Lyon (518/23), *Concilia Galliae, A. 511–A. 695*, ed. C. de Clercq, *CCSL* 148A, 35, lines 256–57; 41, line 60. The healing powers of his bed are related in Gregory of Tours, *glor. conf.* 84.

[25] Cf. Gregory of Tours, *vita patrum* 6. 1.

[26] See in general, L. Theis, "Saints sans famille? Quelques remarques sur la famille dans le monde franc à travers les sources hagiographiques," *Revue historique* 255 (1976), 3–20.

[27] Riché, *Education and Culture*, 122–23.

himself under the bishop's authority, a transition symbolized by a change of clothes and tonsure (*vita* I. 4). After a little more than two years in the local clergy (*vita* I. 4), he decided to enter the monastery of Lérins in southern Gaul, intent on becoming, in the words of a well-known topos, "a stranger not only to his parents, but also to his homeland" (*vita* I. 4).

Caesarius's decision to relinquish his homeland for Lérins was far from unique among the Christian aristocrats of northern and central Gaul during the fifth century.[28] Honoratus, the founder of Lérins and later bishop of Arles, had been the first to do so when, in the early fifth century, he and his brother Venantius sold their shares of the family estates located in north-central Gaul, possibly at Langres.[29] They then left for a tour of monasteries in the Mediterranean world that culminated in the founding of Lérins. Honoratus was followed to Lérins by other northern aristocrats: his young relative Hilarius, later bishop of Arles; Hilarius's brother-in-law Lupus, later bishop of Troyes, originally from Toul;[30] Lupus's brother Vincentius, author of the *commonitorium*;[31] Salvian, author of the *de gubernatione dei*, originally from Cologne or Trier;[32] and, finally, Faustus, abbot of Lérins and later bishop of Riez, originally from Britain.[33] The influx of these and other aristocrats into the monastery and their later fame as monks, abbots, bishops, and theologians helped to promote the island as a center of spirituality and learning and, equally important, as a source of leaders for the church.[34]

Entrance into the monastery of Lérins not only provided recruits with a congenial environment for the pursuit of Christian asceticism, but also with opportunities for advancement in the church hierarchy. Such opportunities were increasingly sought after in Gaul during the fifth century, as Roman control gradually diminished.[35] This reduced the chances for aristocrats to hold the

---

[28] S. Pricoco, *L'isola dei santi. Il cenobio di Lerino e le origini del monachesimo gallico* (Rome, 1978), 59–60, and F. Prinz, *Frühes Mönchtum im Frankenreich* (Munich and Vienna, 1965), 47–58. As Pricoco shows, however (70–72), Prinz goes too far in characterizing Lérins in the fifth century as primarily a place of refuge for aristocrats fleeing barbarian invasions in the north.

[29] Hilarius, *vita Honorati* 11. 4. On the location of the estates, see Mathisen, "Ecclesiastical Aristocracy," 428. [30] *vita Lupi* 1. [31] Pricoco, *L'isola dei santi*, 52–53.

[32] Ibid., 53–54. [33] Sidonius Apollinaris, *ep.* IX. 9. 6.

[34] Eucherius, *de laude eremi* 42; Prinz, *Frühes Mönchtum*, 59–62.

[35] K. F. Stroheker, *Der senatorische Adel im spätantiken Gallien* (Tübingen, 1948), 92; R. W. Mathisen, *Ecclesiastical Factionalism and Religious Controversy in Fifth-Century Gaul* (Washington, D.C., 1989), 7–9; R. Van Dam, *Leadership*, 141–56.

imperial offices that had been seen in Gaul, particularly in the fourth and early fifth centuries, as stages in a successful aristocratic career.[36] In such circumstances, some aristocrats forsook political careers entirely, preferring to withdraw to self-sufficient country estates; others served in barbarian administrations. Still others, however, began to perceive the episcopate as an office for which it was worth competing. Bishops exercised wide-ranging, lifetime powers within their dioceses, which included the control of church wealth, the appointment and supervision of the lower clergy, and a moral authority over the entire diocese. Moreover, at a time when many aristocrats were disengaging themselves from their towns and retreating to secure country properties, bishops often became the most powerful aristocrats in their cities, monopolizing the role of civic patron and protector that had formerly been the object of keen aristocratic competition.[37] As a result of increased interest in episcopal office and lifetime tenure, which kept the number of vacancies low, the competition for available positions increased dramatically over the fifth century. Openings for episcopal office could sometimes be contested by dozens of candidates.[38] A variety of qualifications might win a candidate success: an illustrious family background, high standing in the local clergy, a reputation for asceticism, the holding of public office, civic generosity, and links of kinship and patronage with powerful local bishops and aristocrats.

Monasteries could not confer additional wealth on their monks or increase the prestige of their families, but they could and did furnish them with other qualifications much prized by Gallic communities in search of a bishop. First and foremost, monks automatically acquired a reputation for probity, spiritual learning, and asceticism. Aristocrats sought recognition for these qualities to attain credibility as religious leaders. That congregations also considered them important is clear from episcopal epitaphs, which regularly praised deceased prelates for their spiritual teaching,

---

[36] J. Matthews, *Western Aristocracies and Imperial Court, A.D. 364–425* (Oxford, 1975), 348–51. Where opportunities for imperial office were still available, as they were in Ostrogothic Italy, many fewer aristocrats held church office, T. Brown, *Gentlemen and Officers: Imperial Administration and Aristocratic Power in Byzantine Italy A.D. 554–800* (Rome, 1984), 34, 181. See also S. J. B. Barnish, "Transformation and Survival in the Western Senatorial Aristocracy, c. A.D. 400–700," *Papers of the British School at Rome* 56 (1983), 120–55: 138–40.

[37] For example, Bishop Patiens of Lyon, Sidonius Apollinaris, *ep.* VI. 12.

[38] Sidonius Apollinaris, *ep.* VII. 9. 2.

generosity, love of justice, and ascetic style of life.[39] Not only could aristocrats strive to achieve a reputation for such qualities in a monastery; they could also form valuable connections there with other aristocrats. Moreover, because entrants were normally required to give away all their property upon entrance into the monastery, they were presented with unavoidable opportunities for creating links of patronage.[40] Finally, monks could aspire to the office of abbot. This was recognized as the ecclesiastical office most like a bishop's, since it involved the exercise of authority, control of property, and participation in local networks of politics and influence. The most significant difference between the two positions was that, unlike bishops, abbots could relinquish their office if they were chosen as bishops. It is therefore not surprising that many of the monks who became bishops in late antique Gaul had previously held the office of abbot.[41] For a monk without illustrious family connections or substantial wealth, the only other avenue to the episcopate was service in the local clergy, from whose ranks bishops were also chosen.[42]

Like other pious and ambitious young aristocrats drawn to Lérins in previous generations, Caesarius may well have felt that his prospects for advancement in the local clergy were poor. His family, while wealthy, was not closely linked by kinship to the family that controlled the episcopal see of Chalon, to which both Silvester and his predecessor Johannes appear to have belonged.[43] On the other hand, Caesarius did have links of kinship with Aeonius, who became bishop of Arles around the time Caesarius left for Lérins. In view of his kinsman's success in the south and the

---

[39] For the Gallic evidence, see M. Heinzelmann, *Bischofsherrschaft in Gallien* (Zurich and Munich), esp. 84–98, 168–74. For Italy, see *ILCV* 1011, 1024, 1044, 1046, 1049, 1053, and 1054.

[40] Such opportunities continued as long as there was wealth to distribute. For instance, Lupus was made bishop of Troyes while bestowing his wealth on the people of Mâcon, *vita Lupi* 3.

[41] E.g., Honoratus of Arles, Maximus of Riez, and Faustus of Riez, all abbots of Lérins; Germanus of Paris and Virgilius of Arles, abbots of St. Symphorian in Autun (Venantius Fortunatus, *vita Germani* 9; Gregory of Tours, *hist.* IX. 23); Guntharius of Tours, abbot of St. Venantius in Tours (Gregory of Tours, *hist.* X. 31. 17); Salvius of Albi, abbot of an unnamed monastery in Albi (Gregory of Tours, *hist.* VII. 1); and Mummolinus of Langres, abbot of Reomaus (Jonas, *vita Johannis* 19).

[42] For example, Rusticus of Narbonne (H.-I. Marrou, "Le dossier épigraphique de l'évêque Rusticus de Narbonne," *Rivista di archeologia cristiana* 46 [1970], 331–49: 332–34); Venerius of Marseille (Marrou, "Le dossier," 332–34); and Gallus of Clermont (Gregory of Tours, *vita patrum* 6. 2–3).

[43] Mathisen, "Ecclesiastical Aristocracy," 423.

Lerinian tradition of supplying the Gallic church with distinguished leaders, Caesarius might well have believed that better opportunities for fulfilling his religious aspirations and political ambitions lay further south. Around 488/89 therefore, at the age of nineteen or twenty, Caesarius embarked on the most important journey of his life. Accompanied by a single slave and probably carrying a letter of introduction from some powerful person (such as the letter Salvian once sent on behalf of a relative, probably to Lérins[44]), he left behind his *patria*, his parents and family, their estates, and the local clergy, and set out for the island monastery of Lérins, 250 Roman miles to the south, in Provence (*vita* I. 5).

LÉRINS

Honoratus had founded his monastery between 400 and 410 on the island of Lerina (Saint-Honorat), located about 4 km from Cannes.[45] Though small – only 3 km in circumference and 105 ha in area[46] – Lerina was fertile,[47] well watered,[48] and suitably remote.[49] Although the remains of a villa and fragments of pottery, stonework, and inscriptions dating to the Roman period have been found on the island, it seems to have been deserted by the early fifth century.[50] After an initial period of organization, Honoratus set up a church and shelter for monks.[51] The population of the monastery grew under his supervision, and at the time of his departure for Arles in 427, Cassian could speak of Lérins as an "enormous community of monks."[52] Under Honoratus's immediate successors, Maximus (427–33) and Faustus (433–*c*. 451), the population of Lérins continued to grow, along with its prestige, as scores of Gallic aristocrats, some with their wives and children, took up residence in the monastery and on the adjacent

[44] Salvian, *ep.* I; Pricoco, *L'isola dei santi*, 54.   [45] Pricoco, *L'isola dei santi*, 25–40.
[46] M.-D. Valentin, ed., *Hilaire d'Arles. Vie de Honorat*, SC 235 (Paris, 1977), 108, n. I.
[47] Eucherius, *de laude eremi* 42.   [48] Hilarius, *vita Honorati* 17. I.
[49] An excellent map may be found in I. M. Smith, "The Lérins Survey," Durham University Excavation Committee and Committee for Excavation and Fieldwork, University of Newcastle upon Tyne, *Archaeological Reports for 1983* (1984), 61–66: 62.
[50] Ibid., 61–63.
[51] Hilarius, *vita Honorati* 17. I. The chapel of La Trinité, located at the eastern end of the island and probably dating to its earliest Christian occupation, may mark the site of this early foundation, Smith, "The Lérins Survey," 63. See also F. Benoit, "Les chapelles triconques paléochrétiennes de la Trinité de Lérins et de la Gayole," *Rivista di archeologia cristiana* 25 (1949), 129–54.   [52] Cassian, *conl.* XI, pref. I.

island of Lero (Sainte-Marguerite).[53] With the arrival of such learned men as Hilarius, Eucherius, Vincentius, Salvian, and Faustus,[54] the monastery acquired a reputation as the center of Christian culture in Gaul.[55]

Unfortunately, we know little about the monastery after the departure of Faustus in the early 450s. The *vita* informs us that Porcarius was serving as abbot when Caesarius arrived in 488/89 (*vita* I. 5), but the names of his predecessors back to Faustus as well as most of his successors are unknown. Still, the monastery seems to have retained its reputation as a center of monastic spirituality and Christian culture and a source of bishops through the sixth century.[56] Certainly the fact that a well-educated and ambitious young man like Caesarius chose to enter the monastery suggests that it still offered outstanding intellectual and spiritual opportunities in the late fifth century.

The most lamentable gap in our knowledge about Lérins concerns its rule. Although we know that the monastery was governed by a written rule from an early date,[57] and continued to be governed by a rule at the time of Caesarius's arrival (*vita* I. 5), no extant document can be identified with absolute certainty as a Lerinian rule. Recently, however, Adalbert de Vogüé has revived the idea that three rules of unknown date and provenance – part of a collection of five rules known as the "Rules of the Fathers" – can be identified as Lerinian rules.[58] The possibility of using these rules as evidence for the monastic routine at Lérins during Caesarius's sojourn there justifies a brief discussion of this suggestion. Dom de Vogüé divided his argument into two parts. He first arranged the

---

[53] Prinz, *Frühes Mönchtum*, 53.

[54] Prinz, *Frühes Mönchtum*, 457–61, 470–73; L. Alliez, *Histoire du monastère de Lérins*, I (Paris, 1862), 417–91.

[55] P. Courcelle, "Nouveaux aspects de la culture lérinienne," *Revue des études latines* 46 (1968), 379–409: 406–9; Fr. Glorie, "La culture lérinienne," *Sacris Erudiri* 19 (1969–70), 71–76.

[56] Sidonius Apollinaris, *ep.* VIII. 14. 2; Ennodius, *vita Epiphani* 93; *vita Antonii* 37, 38, 40. For aborted journeys to Lérins in the sixth century, see *vita Leobini* xiii. 41 (Leobinus of Chartres) and Ado of Vienne, *vita Theudarii* 2, ed. B. Krusch, *MGH SRM*, III, 526 (Theudarius of Vienne); for the seventh century, see *vita Arnulfi* 6, ed. B. Krusch, *MGH SRM*, II, 433 (Arnulf of Metz). See also I. N. Wood, "A Prelude to Columbanus: The Monastic Achievement in the Burgundian Territories," in *Columbanus and Merovingian Monasticism*, ed. H. B. Clarke and M. Brennan (Oxford, 1981), 3–32: 5.

[57] Prinz, *Frühes Mönchtum*, 50; *CCSL* 148, 134, lines 34–36; Caesarius, *regula virginum* 66; Sidonius Apollinaris, *ep.* VII. 17. 3; but see Pricoco, *L'isola dei santi*, 83–84.

[58] A. de Vogüé, ed., *Règles des saints pères*, 2 vols., *SC* 297–98 (Paris, 1982).

Rules of the Fathers in order from earliest to latest: the *regula sanctorum patrum* (*RIVP*), *statuta patrum* (*2RP*), *regula Macarii* (*RMac*), *regula orientalis* (*ROr*), and *regula "tertia" patrum* (*3RP*).[59] Second, he argued that two of the rules, the *regula Macarii* and the *regula orientalis*, could be linked by external evidence to Lérins.[60] It was essentially on the strength of these connections with Lérins that de Vogüé asserted that the *regula sanctorum patrum*, the *statuta patrum*, and the *regula Macarii* could be identified as Lerinian rules. In his view, the *regula sanctorum patrum* was Honoratus's original rule for the monks, which was replaced by the *statuta patrum* around the time of his departure for Arles; this rule in turn was replaced around the end of the fifth century by the *regula Macarii*, which may have been composed by the abbot Porcarius.[61]

Although de Vogüé's hypotheses are attractive, they cannot be considered proven beyond doubt. Indeed, de Vogüé himself admits that they are to some extent conjectural.[62] But doubts about the *regula sanctorum patrum* and the *statuta patrum*, on which skeptical reviewers have concentrated,[63] do not necessarily affect what is for us the most important of de Vogüé's propositions: that the *regula Macarii* was in fact the rule in use at Lérins in the late fifth century. To demonstrate this point, it is first necessary to establish a connection between the *regula Macarii* and Lérins. In about 506/10, according to Jonas of Bobbio, abbot John of the monastery of Reomaus near Langres returned to his monastery after an eighteen-month stay in Lérins. At that time he began to instruct his monks according to a certain "rule of Macarius."[64] The same *regula Macarii* was mentioned in the seventh century in connection with two other monasteries, at Grausel and Rebais.[65] Although nothing is known of the contents of this rule, it is reasonable to argue, as de Vogüé does, that it is identical with the extant *regula Macarii*, and further to suggest that it was originally brought to Reomaus in the early sixth century from Lérins, where John first learned of it.[66]

Even if we do not follow de Vogüé in ascribing the authorship of the *regula Macarii* to Abbot Porcarius, the rule could still have

[59] Ibid., I, 41–54.   [60] Ibid., I, 339–56; II, 435–54.   [61] Ibid., I, 21–34.
[62] Ibid., I, 39.
[63] M. Carrias, "Vie monastique et règle à Lérins au temps d'Honorat," *Revue d'histoire de l'église de la France* 74 (1988), 191–211; J. Gribomont, review of *Règles des saints pères* by A. de Vogüé, *Revue d'histoire ecclésiastique* 78 (1983), 849–51.
[64] "sub regulare tenore quam beatus Macharius indedit," Jonas, *vita Johanni* 4–5.
[65] de Vogüé, *Règles*, I, 351.   [66] Ibid., I, 352–56.

been in effect at Lérins when Caesarius arrived there. This possibility is suggested by resemblances between Caesarius's reception at Lérins and procedures described in the *regula Macarii*. According to the *vita* Caesarius was welcomed not by the abbot alone, as he would have been in monasteries following Cassian's *Institutes*[67] or in the monastery for which the *regula sanctorum patrum* was written,[68] but rather by the abbot and all the senior monks (*vita* I. 5). This accords well with the procedure described in the *regula Macarii*: "Thus if someone from the world should wish to be converted in the monastery, let the rule be read to him when he enters, and let every practice of the monastery be made clear to him. And if he should accept all things suitably, let him thus be fittingly received by the brothers in the cell."[69] It is also worth pointing out that in entering the monastery, Caesarius does not seem to have undergone a probationary period of any length, which Cassian recommended and the *regula sanctorum patrum* required.[70] This too accords well with the *regula Macarii*, which allowed for the immediate entrance of the novice into the monastery once the rule had been explained to him.[71] These pieces of evidence suggest that the *regula Macarii* can be used, along with the *vita Caesarii*, a brief treatise by Porcarius entitled the *monita*, and the writings of other Lerinian monks, to reconstruct the prescribed mode of life at Lérins at the end of the fifth century.

The most important consequence of using the Rules of the Fathers, especially the *statuta patrum*, is that they add an "Augustinian" element to the "Cassianic" core of Lerinian spirituality.[72] To Cassian's emphasis on obedience, the Rules of the Fathers add Augustine's emphasis on charity; to Cassian's emphasis on the individual monk's pursuit of perfection, the Rules of the Fathers add Augustine's emphasis on the perfection of the whole community; and to Cassian's emphasis on the monastery as a retreat from the world, the Rules of the Fathers add Augustine's emphasis on the monastery as a model for the world.[73] Indeed, by the end of the fifth century, as the result of a complex development of monastic ideas, Lérins had come to represent above all a

---

[67] Cassian, *inst.* IV. 3–7.   [68] *RIVP* 7.
[69] *RMac* 23, trans. C. V. Franklin, I. Havener, and J. A. Francis, *Early Monastic Rules* (Collegeville, Minn., 1982).   [70] *RIVP* 7.   [71] *RMac* 23.
[72] de Vogüé, *Règles*, I, 25–27.
[73] These differences are expounded in R. A. Markus, *The End of Ancient Christianity* (Cambridge, 1990), 157–77.

monastic *community*.[74] Men entered the monastery to lead the *vita perfecta* there,[75] and while they lived in separation from the world, they did so in common with other men. From the day a man entered the monastery, he was continually reminded of the importance of the monastic community and its communal pursuit of perfection. The requirement that entrants give up their wealth was designed to signal not only their total separation from the world, but also their equality with their fellow monks, who came from a variety of places and statuses.[76] If not given away to relatives or the needy, this wealth was conveyed to the monastic community itself to ensure its continued survival.[77] Monks were housed either in individual cells under a common roof,[78] or if they were prepared to live a semi-eremitical lifestyle, in cells dispersed over the island.[79] All monks took their meals in common.[80] Their life together was structured by a daily routine that allowed for periods of private reading and prayer, but emphasized above all common worship and service to the community. After communal prayers conducted at daybreak, monks were given two hours for solitary prayer and spiritual reading.[81] From the third to the ninth hour, with interruptions for further periods of communal worship, they performed the tasks assigned to them, which no doubt included cooking, cleaning, gardening, mending, and other housekeeping tasks.[82] This regime was required not only to satisfy the community's needs,[83] but also to reinforce the monks' sense of humility,[84] to test their capacity for obedience,[85] and to restrain them from idleness.[86] Their main meal of the day was probably taken after the ninth hour,[87] with further periods of communal worship and solitary prayer to follow until nightfall, when the monks were advised, in Jerome's words, to "go to your bed weary and believe that you rest with Christ."[88]

But the physical arrangement of the monastery and the enforcement of a strict routine could not in themselves maintain community harmony and overcome the inevitable strains in social

---

[74] Ibid., 181–97.   [75] The phrase comes from Cassian, *inst.*, pref. 7.
[76] Hilarius, *vita Honorati* 19. 1; Ennodius, *vita Antonii* 40.   [77] *RMac* 24, 25.
[78] *RMac* 13, where *oratorium* is the equivalent of the *monasterium* of *2RP* 5.
[79] Eucherius, *de laude eremi* 42; *RMac* 13; Pricoco, *L'isola dei santi*, 116–17.
[80] *RMac* 18; Eusebius Gallicanus, *hom.* 72. 4.   [81] *RMac* 10.
[82] *RMac* 11; Pricoco. *L'isola dei santi*, 121–22, n. 157. It is uncertain whether the monks actually supported themselves by working, as A. Quacquarelli argues, *Lavoro e ascesi nel monachesimo prebenedettino del IV e V secolo* (Bari, 1982), esp. 61–66.
[83] *RMac* 30. 4.   [84] *RMac* 5. 1.   [85] *RMac* 11. 2.   [86] *RMac* 8. 1–2.
[87] *RIVP* 9.   [88] *RMac* 8. 4.

27

relations brought on by ascetic competition, envy, pride, and sheer physical proximity. In addition, the monks needed to be reminded – by the rule, the exhortations of their superiors, and the examples of other monks – to practice the virtues that assured their spiritual progress and made their living together possible. Pre-eminent among these were the virtues of obedience and charity, on which all other virtues depended.

To monastic legislators, emphasizing the importance of obedience was an abiding preoccupation. Obedience confirmed the authority of superiors and ensured good order in a coenobitic monastery; it promoted the humility of inferiors and assisted in their spiritual progress; it restrained ascetic competition and reinforced a sense of communal endeavor.[89] Not surprisingly, it received a heavy emphasis at Lérins from the very beginning,[90] and continued to be encouraged throughout the fifth century. The *regula Macarii* exhorted monks to obedience at many points,[91] as did Caesarius in a sermon delivered to the monks of Lérins after he had become bishop of Arles (*serm.* 234. 2). Yet by the late fifth century, obedience was no longer the only virtue to receive so heavy an emphasis at Lérins. With the composition of the *regula Macarii*, charity was placed on an equal level with obedience, thanks in part to the influence of Augustine's monastic rule, in which charity, and not obedience, had been made the cornerstone of monastic harmony and the common life.[92] In its prologue the *regula Macarii* urged monks not only to pursue *perfectissima oboedientia* among themselves,[93] but also to maintain *perfectissima caritas*.[94] Further on, quoting Jerome, the rule urges monks to "fear the superior of the monastery as God and love him as a parent,"[95] and to "love all of your brothers"[96] and not to "consider any to be closer relations to you than those who are brothers with you in the monastery."[97]

Other virtues, such as humility, kindness, purity of heart, patience, gentleness, mercy, and magnanimity,[98] were thought to follow naturally from the practice of obedience and charity. Like

[89] See Cassian, *inst.* IV. 8–10, 24–29; see also Rousseau, *Ascetics, Authority and the Church in the Age of Jerome and Cassian* (Oxford, 1978), esp. 194–98.

[90] Hilarius, *vita Honorati* 23. 8; Eucherius, *de laude eremi* 43; Pricoco, *L'isola dei santi*, 95–96. [91] *RMac* 2. 1, 7; 4. 1, 3; 7. 1; 11. 1–2; 12. 1–6; 19. 1–2.

[92] Especially *praeceptum* 1. 2. See A. Zumkeller, *Augustine's Ideal of the Religious Life*, trans. E. Colledge (New York, 1986), 260–62. [93] *RMac* 2. 1. [94] *RMac* 1. 2.

[95] *RMac* 7. 1. [96] *RMac* 7. 2. [97] *RMac* 21. 5–6.

[98] Porcarius, *monita* 61–66.

obedience and charity, they were encouraged not only because they were considered conducive to a monk's spiritual progress, but also because without them the monastery could not have functioned as a community. It is therefore not surprising that the *vita* reports, in language reminiscent of the *regula Macarii*, that upon his entrance into the monastery, Caesarius perfectly practiced the virtues suited to community living.

Therefore, having been admitted by the holy abbot Porcarius and by all the senior monks, he began to be well disposed at vigils, attentive in observation, quick in obedience, dedicated to work, distinguished in humility, and remarkable in gentleness. As a result, the monks rejoiced to discover that he whom they had received for instruction in the rudiments of the discipline of the rule had already been made perfect in the advanced principles of the whole teaching. (*vita* I. 5)[99]

Yet despite the efforts of his biographers to put the best possible face on Caesarius's behavior at Lérins, their account of his sojourn there casts doubt on his suitability for the common life. Sometime after he arrived at Lérins – it may have been months or years; the *vita* does not say – Caesarius was chosen cellarer of the community (*vita* I. 6). As we learn from a number of Rules, the cellarer was responsible for supervising the storage and distribution of the monastery's food, clothing, tools, and other items for daily use.[100] He was to be, in the words of the Benedictine Rule, "like a father to the whole community."[101] Because the cellarer was responsible for the monastery's property, he had to be, in the first place, honest, diligent, sober, and abstemious.[102] Because he was responsible for the monks' access to that property, he had to be, in addition, extremely judicious in his disbursements, maintaining a delicate balance between avarice and prodigality,[103] and acting at all times with humility and kindness.[104] Finally, because the property that he guarded was not his own but the community's, and more precisely God's,[105] he had to be, above all, responsive to the needs of the community, and willing to follow the community's standards for distributing property. In practical terms, this meant following the directions of the abbot and other senior monks, rather than his own judgment.[106]

---

[99] See *RMac* 2. 6–7 for a similar passage.
[100] *ROr* 25. 3–4, *regula magistri* (= *RM*) 16. 57; *regula Benedicti* (= *RB*) 31. 10.
[101] *RB* 31. 2.   [102] *RIVP* 3. 24; *ROr* 25. 1; *RM* 16. 62–3; *RB* 31. 1.
[103] *ROr* 25. 6; *RB* 31. 1, 12.   [104] *RB* 31. 6–8, 13.   [105] *RM* 16. 11–17, 58–61.
[106] *ROr* 25. 10; *RM* 16. 32; *RB* 31. 4–5, 12, 15.

We do not know by whose influence the young Caesarius was chosen for this important position or what opposition there might have been to his promotion. What is clear is that he soon encountered widespread resistance among his brother monks, who accused him of withholding supplies from them. They petitioned the abbot to remove him from the post, and he did so (*vita* I. 6). This story has frequently been cited as evidence of the "degeneration" of ascetic standards at Lérins and the weakness of its abbot for allowing this to occur.[107] Porcarius, it is said, too easily gave in to the demands of the weaker brothers, who could not live up to Caesarius's high standards. But this view ignores the fact that the cellarer was not supposed to set standards on his own, but rather to enforce the standards established by the abbot and senior monks. In fact, the *vita* provides too little information for us to deduce exactly why opposition arose against Caesarius. It may have resulted from continued opposition to his selection as cellarer or from his misjudgment of community standards. If that misjudgment resulted from his failure to consult the wishes of his superiors before acting, it would have been Porcarius's duty to remove him, for disobedience if for no other offence.

Having failed as cellarer, Caesarius initiated a program of ascetic activity more characteristic of eremitic than coenobitic monasticism. He began to weaken his body with continual prayer, reading, singing, and vigils. He ate only on Sundays and restricted his diet to "a meager concoction of vegetables and gruel" (*vita* I. 6). No further mention is made of his devotion to the community labor required at Lérins. Instead, he "wore down the robustness of his flesh so that he might firm up the power of his spirit by the solidity of hope and faith" (*vita* I. 7). Through these actions, Caesarius sought to recover his prestige by imitating the desert fathers of Egypt, the ultimate exemplars of monastic holiness. But in so doing, he deliberately rejected well-established standards of coenobitic monasticism in Gaul, especially as laid down by the authority of John Cassian. In particular, by eliminating bread from his diet and eating only once a week, he specifically broke two of Cassian's cardinal rules for fasting.[108] In addition, by devoting himself exclusively to the challenges of self-

---

[107] Alliez, *Histoire*, I, 270; Villevieille, *Histoire de saint Césaire*, 52; Malnory, 12; S. Dill, *Roman Society in Gaul in the Merovingian Age* (London, 1926), 97–98; de Vogüé, *Règles*, I, 346.

[108] Cassian, *inst.* V. 23; *conl.* II. 17–24. I owe this observation to Sr. Mary Kiely.

conquest, he violated Cassian's dictum that fasting like other ascetic practices should not be carried out for their own sake, but rather in pursuit of "perfect charity."[109]

Even Caesarius's biographers thought he had gone too far: "Caesarius so afflicted himself by his constant desire for reading, singing psalms, praying, and keeping vigils that finally, by an excess of asceticism, he brought it about that his feeble young body, which should properly have been coddled rather than weakened, was bent and broken" (*vita* I. 6). His behavior eventually led to a serious illness, described as a quartan fever. Cassian had warned that exactly such an outcome could result from excessive fasting.[110] Because he refused to alter his ascetic practices, and because no physician was available at Lérins, Caesarius was ordered by the abbot to leave for the city of Arles to recover his health (*vita* I. 7). Arles was chosen for a number of reasons. Not only did the city have a reputation for excellent physicians,[111] but from the time of Honoratus's episcopate, close ties had existed between Arles and Lérins. Most importantly, Caesarius had an important relative in the city, Bishop Aeonius himself. The fact that sick monks were later prohibited from leaving their monasteries to be cared for by their families shows that this practice was widespread.[112]

And so, at some point before 499, perhaps as early as 495, Caesarius left Lérins for Arles. In a sense, his life as a monk had been a failure, since he had been unable to conform to either of the styles of life Lérins offered, the coenobitic or the semi-eremitic. But the success of Caesarius's life at Lérins should not be measured by what happened there but by what he took away from there: a set of habits, ideas, and values that would have a profound impact on his career as a bishop, preacher, pastor, and reformer. He first of all took away from Lérins a way of life, a routine of work, prayer, and renunciation, that he would continue to observe after his departure from Lérins (*vita* I. 11). It was this ascetic style of life, as perceived by his congregation and praised by his supporters, that would provide the most secure foundation for the style of authority that he was to cultivate as bishop, based not so much on personal wealth, high birth, or clerical office – although these were also involved – as on a knowledge of scripture, a record of ascetic achievements, and a talent for spiritual direction.[113] He also

---

[109] Cassian, *conl.* I. 7.   [110] Cassian, *inst.* V. 9.   [111] Arnold, 66–67.
[112] *3RP* 12.   [113] Rousseau, *Ascetics*, 189–98.

brought with him to Arles the intellectual fruits he had gathered at Lérins: a deeper acquaintance with the literature produced in Lerinian circles and the Latin patristic tradition in general, and sympathy for a moderate Augustinianism (sometimes termed "semi-Pelagianism"), which gave individuals credit for their spiritual exertions at the same time as it admitted the essential role of divine grace in their salvation. Finally and most significantly, he brought away from the island Augustine's vision of the ideal Christian community, a city of God on earth, imperfect, to be sure, and never to be confused with the true *civitas dei*, but imaginable nonetheless.[114] This was a vision of community based not only on Caesarius's reading of Augustine's monastic ideals, but also on his living of those ideals at Lérins. It was on the memory of this experience that he would most rely in designing the strategies of christianization and pastoral care by which he hoped to recreate such a community in the world outside the monastery.

[114] Markus, *Ancient Christianity*, 78–82.

Chapter 2

LATE ROMAN ARLES

By emigrating from Chalon to Lérins, and from there to Arles, Caesarius had transported himself from the periphery of the Roman world to its Mediterranean heartland. A Roman possession for nearly 600 years, until the Visigoths took control of it in 476/77, Provence was the most romanized region in Gaul, in the words of Pliny the Elder, writing in the first century AD, "Italy rather than a province."[1] It was the familiar, Mediterranean character of the place that struck ancient observers most forcefully. Strabo noted that the rivers of Provence, especially the Rhône, drained into the Mediterranean Sea "which is better than the outer sea."[2] He also observed that the region yielded the same produce as Italy, and that olives, grapes, and figs ceased to grow well at its outer limits.[3] Indeed, in climate, geography, and culture, Roman Provence more closely resembled northern Italy than the rest of Gaul, where people wore trousers instead of tunics,[4] drank beer instead of wine,[5] and in the later empire still measured distances in Celtic leagues rather than Roman miles.[6]

It was in this most Mediterranean and Roman of settings, and specifically in the city and countryside of Arles, that Caesarius would attempt to enact the Christian principles that he had acquired as a monk at Lérins. But Arles had little in common with the tranquil island monastery. It was a bustling, noisy, crowded,

---

[1] Pliny, *hist. nat.* III. 4. 31. The modern bibliography is extensive. For surveys of recent work, see R. Chevallier, "Gallia Narbonensis. Bilan de 25 ans de recherches historiques et archéologiques," *ANRW* II. 3 (1975), 686–828, and *Provincia* (Paris, 1982); A. L. F. Rivet, *Gallia Narbonensis: Southern Gaul in Roman Times* (London, 1988); and the annual "Chronique gallo-romaine" in *Revue des études anciennes*. Excellent maps may be found in E. Baratier *et al.*, *Atlas historique. Provence, Comtat, Orange, Nice, Monaco* (Paris, 1969), and in the "Blue" series of topographical maps (1:25,000) published by the Institut Géographique National (IGN) in Paris.   [2] Strabo IV. 1. 2.

[3] Ibid., IV. 1. 2; see also Diodorus Siculus V. 26. 2.

[4] Strabo IV. 4. 3; Diodorus Siculus V. 30. 2.

[5] E. Salin, *La Civilisation mérovingienne*, I (Paris, 1949), 444; Diodorus Siculus V. 26. 2.

[6] Ammianus Marcellinus XV. 11. 17; C. Jullian, *Histoire de la Gaule*, IV (Paris, 1924), 283.

shabby river port; its territory stretched from the river delta in the south (the Camargue) to the mountains of the north (the Alpilles) and the stony plains of the east (the Crau). Its inhabitants had their own ways of life and religious traditions, which were in many ways contrary to the ideals Caesarius proposed. Deeply rooted in past and present realities, their native culture had changed only very slowly under the impact of hellenization and romanization, and was just beginning to change further under the more thorough and direct pressure of christianization. To understand the full context in which Caesarius attempted to implement his Christian ideals, we need to go well beyond the study of those ideals in themselves. We also need to pay attention to the social, cultural, and political setting in which they were introduced. A survey of the history of Arles and its countryside to the end of the fifth century will help to explain the political and administrative framework in which Caesarius was to operate as bishop, the social structure of his diocese, the progress that Christianity had already made in its constituent communities, and the patterns of religion and culture that resisted his efforts of disruption and trans-formation. The evolution of late Roman Arles cannot, however, be understood apart from its Roman past, partly because there was a high degree of continuity from one period to the next, and partly because many of the changes that did occur were rooted in larger processes of transformation affecting both periods. We therefore begin this survey with a brief sketch of the history of Roman Arles.

ROMAN ARLES

Located on a limestone hill (the Hauture) that rose twenty-five meters above the Rhône and the surrounding swamps, Arles was inhabited from the sixth century BC,[7] probably by the Nearchi, a Celto-Ligurian tribe of the federation of the Salluvii.[8] Its original name, Arelate, may be either Ligurian or Celtic.[9] The site was well placed for strategic and commercial advantage. It was located at

---

[7] For recent research on pre-Roman Arles, see P. Arcelin, "Arles protohistorique" and "Les fouilles du jardin d'Hiver," in *Du nouveau sur l'Arles antique*, ed. C. Sintès, *Revue d'Arles* 1 (1987), 17–31; G. Congès, "L'histoire d'Arles romaine precisée par les fouilles archéologiques," *Archéologia*, no. 142 (May 1980), 10–23; and C. Sintès, "L'évolution topographique de l'Arles du Haut-Empire à la lumière des fouilles récentes," *Journal of Roman Archaeology* 5 (1992), 130–33.

[8] G. Barruol, *Les Peuples préromains du Sud-Est de la Gaule* (Paris, 1969), 193–94.

[9] Ch. Rostaing, *Essai sur la toponymie de la Provence* (Paris, 1950), 58–61.

the first landing place for ships sailing up the Rhône, at the closest point to the sea that the Rhône can be crossed, and in the midst of marshes and lakes navigable by barges and flat boats.[10] In addition, the right bank of the Rhône and the plain of the Camargue were covered with vast forests, which supplied materials for ship-building.[11] The local inhabitants made a living from growing typical Mediterranean crops, raising livestock, and collecting and processing fish, shellfish, and salt throughout the delta.[12]

The resources of Arles did not escape the notice of the Greeks of Marseille, who soon took an interest in the place. After the last quarter of the sixth century, signs of Greek influence began to appear in Arles, in the form of fine pottery and a regular town plan, likely indications of its transformation into a Greek outpost for trade with the interior of Gaul.[13] Its Greek name, Theline, probably dates to this period.[14] After the middle of the fourth century BC, native Celto-Ligurian elites appear to have returned to power and to have readopted the original name.[15] A sizeable Greek population remained in the vicinity, however, especially in the Camargue, where trade in salt, fish, and the fish sauce known as *garum* continued.[16]

Romans first appeared in southern Gaul as trading partners and allies of the Marseillais. There is abundant archaeological evidence from the end of the third century BC for the movement of goods between Campania and southern Gaul,[17] although how much of this movement involved trade for profit and how much the exchange of gifts for prestige remains unclear.[18] More important

[10] Polybius III. 42. 2; L.-A. Constans, *Arles antique* (Paris, 1921), 185.

[11] Polybius III. 42. 3; Constans, *Arles antique*, 52. The presence of ancient forests in the Camargue is suggested by place names such as Bois des Rièges (*FOR* V, 403), as Caroline Nicholson has suggested to me.

[12] F. Benoit, *Recherches sur l'hellénisation du Midi de la Gaule* (Paris, 1965), 199–202, 207–11; Barruol, *Les Peuples préromains*, 90–91; F. Benoit, "L'économie du littoral de la Narbonnaise à l'époque antique: le commerce du sel et les pêcheries," *Rivista di studi liguri* 25 (1959), 87–110.   [13] Arcelin, "Arles protohistorique," 22.

[14] Avienus, *ora maritima* 689–91, ed. A. Schulten, *Fontes Hispaniae Antiquae 1* (Barcelona and Berlin, 1922), 74.   [15] Arcelin, "Arles protohistorique," 23.

[16] Evidence for fish basins possibly used for the production of *garum* can be found in several villas in the Camargue with Greek foundations: le Fournelet (*FOR* V, 401), Carrelet (*FOR* V, 410), and Nôtre-Dame d'Amour (*FOR* V, 414). For the presence of fish basins on these sites, see F. Benoit, "L'archéologie sous-marine en Provence," *Rivista di studi liguri* 18 (1952), 237–307: 294–97.

[17] F. Benoit, "La romanisation de la Narbonnaise à la fin de l'époque républicaine," *Rivista di studi liguri* 32 (1966), 287–303: 288.

[18] A. Tchernia, "Italian wine in Gaul at the end of the republic," in *Trade in the Ancient Economy*, ed. P. Garnsey, K. Hopkins, and C. R. Whittaker (London, 1983), 87–104.

was the military alliance between Marseille and Rome. This was first invoked against the Carthaginians in the Second Punic War, then during the second century against neighboring Ligurian and Celtic tribes, and finally at the end of the second century against the German Cimbri and Teutones.[19] It was after the last of these wars, around 100 BC, that southern Gaul appears as a fully functioning province,[20] although parts of it may have been formally annexed as early as 120.[21] The new province was known initially as Gallia Transalpina or simply *Provincia*, The Province (hence Provence). Marseille remained an ally, free from the interference of the Roman governor.[22] By annexing southern Gaul, the Romans acted to protect Italy, to acquire a land route to their possessions in Spain, and to open up territory for Roman settlement. As in other urbanized and hellenized regions of the Mediterranean newly annexed by Rome, members of the local upper classes, both Greek and Celto-Ligurian, were quick to see the advantages of cooperating with the Romans. They began to enter into networks of commerce and patronage with their new masters, often growing rich in the process, like the family of the Domitii, whose vast estates northwest of Aix have recently been studied.[23] In such families, the knowledge of Latin became indispensable, as it had long been in Marseille.[24] The acquisition of Roman culture followed,[25] and although deep anti-Roman sentiment persisted,[26] especially among non-elites, it did not prevent Caesar from relying on the province as a base from which to conquer the rest of Gaul.[27]

During the civil war that followed Caesar's conquest of Gaul, Marseille remained loyal to Pompey, and was besieged by Caesar in 49 BC with the help of twelve ships built in Arles.[28] When it fell,

---

[19] Rivet, *Gallia Narbonensis*, 27–48.   [20] Ibid., 47.

[21] W. V. Harris, *War and Imperialism in Republican Rome* (Oxford, 1979), 150–51.

[22] Strabo IV. 1. 5.

[23] Y. Burnand, *Domitii Aquenses. Une famille de chevaliers romains de la région d'Aix-en-Provence. Mausolée et domaine* (Paris, 1975).

[24] Varro says that the Marseillais were tri-lingual in Latin, Greek, and Celtic, ap. Jerome, *commentarii in epistulam ad Galatas* II, pref., *PL* 26: 354.

[25] Benoit, "La romanisation," 287–303.

[26] G. Barruol, "La résistance des substrats préromains en Gaule méridionale," in *Assimilation et résistance à la culture gréco-romaine dans le monde ancien*, ed. D. M. Pippidi (Bucharest and Paris, 1976), 389–405.

[27] Jullian, *Histoire*, III, 189–93. Natives of Arles even provided Caesar with direct assistance, *bell. Gall.* I. 19. 3, 23. 2, 47. 4; v. 36. 1; VII. 65. 2.

[28] Caesar, *bell. civ.* I. 36. 4.

Marseille was deprived of its extensive coastal territory, much of which was given to Arles as a reward.[29] The prestige of Arles was further increased in 46 BC when Ti. Claudius Nero designated it as a colony for veterans of Caesar's sixth legion.[30] After an interval of uncertainty following Caesar's assassination, the colonial status of Arles was reconfirmed by Octavian in 39 BC.[31] At some point the city received a new name to commemorate the foundation: Colonia Julia Paterna Arelate Sextanorum.[32]

By the end of Augustus's reign, reorganized and renamed Gallia Narbonensis,[33] The Province consisted of twenty-three *civitates*.[34] Although somewhat artificial, these *civitates* corresponded in general to the areas controlled either by federations of native tribes[35] or by city-states like Marseille. They were enduring administrative creations, which largely persisted in the form of Christian dioceses to the French Revolution. Each *civitas* was placed under the administration of a single self-governing urban center, the *civitas*-capital, usually the most populous and important town in the *civitas*. With a territory of some 3,000 km², Arles was designated as capital of the sixth largest *civitas* in Narbonensis[36] and the largest in Provence.[37] The rural territory of the *civitas* was divided in turn into geographically and culturally well-defined districts known as *pagi*, at least some of which closely matched the territory of particular native peoples.[38] Each *pagus* was then placed under the supervision of a village center. It is not certain how many *pagi* made up the *civitas* of Arles, but Jullian's estimate of five

[29] Rivet, *Gallia Narbonensis*, 66–68.
[30] Suetonius, *Tiberius* 4.
[31] F. Benoit, "Le développement de la colonie d'Arles et la centuriation de la Crau," *CRAI* (1964), 159–69: 163, and "Le sanctuaire d'Auguste et les cryptoportiques d'Arles," *Revue archéologique* 39, part 1 (1952), 31–67: 44–46.
[32] Arles: *CIL* XII. 689, 694, 700, 702, 704, 705, 712, 719, 731, 738; St. Remy: 1005; Saint-Jean-de-Garguier: 594, 595.
[33] Cassius Dio LIII. 12. 5.
[34] Rivet, *Gallia Narbonensis*, 79–80.
[35] J. F. Drinkwater, *Roman Gaul* (Ithaca, N.Y., 1983), 30, n. 2.
[36] The only larger *civitates* in Narbonensis – Vienne, Vaison, Toulouse, Narbonne, and Nîmes – were located in mountainous or under-urbanized areas to the north and west of Provence.
[37] For the area of the *civitas*, see Delage I, 118. For its boundaries, see in general Constans, *Arles antique*, 61–76, and Rivet, *Gallia Narbonensis*, 196–206, with Map 26. For the northwestern boundary, however, which included Beaucaire and surrounding places, see M. Chalon and M. Gayraud, "Notes de géographie antique, II," *Revue archéologique de Narbonnaise* 15 (1982), 399–406: 402–6.
[38] A. Grenier, *Manuel d'archéologie gallo-romaine*, I (Paris, 1931), 145–50; Barruol, *Les Peuples préromains*, 128–29.

or six may be correct.[39] Among them would have been the *pagus Lucretius*, whose capital was located at Gargarius (Saint-Jean-de-Garguier),[40] the *pagus* headed by Citharista (La Ciotat), which like Gargarius briefly became an episcopal see in the early fifth century,[41] and the *pagus* of Telo Martius (Toulon), which permanently became an episcopal see in the later fifth century.[42] Other important towns in the *civitas*, including Glanum and Ernaginum (Saint-Gabriel), may have been the centers of their own *pagi*.

Like most other cities and towns in Provence, Arles began to take on a distinctly Roman appearance only in the Augustan Age.[43] Because the urban fabric created at this time largely persisted into late antiquity, a brief discussion is warranted here.[44] Late in the first century BC, a rectilinear street plan was laid out in the low-lying zone between the banks of the Rhône and the Hauture.[45] Its main feature was a four-meter wide boulevard, identified as the *cardo maximus*, which ran south from the Rhône to the city wall. On the west side of this boulevard, at its intersection with the city's major east–west street (the *decumanus*), lay the forum,[46] and adjacent to it a smaller monumental open space built in the reign of Tiberius.[47] To the east of the *cardo maximus* were constructed two of the city's major monuments, which still stand today: a theater built in the first half of the first century AD[48] and a 21,000-seat amphitheater built during the second half of the century.[49] Baths were built to the south of the forum,[50] and water was brought in by an aqueduct that led from the Alpilles.[51] A

---

[39] C. Jullian, "Inscriptions de la vallée de l'Huveaune," part 4, *Bulletin épigraphique* 5 (1885), 165–84: 182.

[40] *CIL* XII. 594, with commentary in Jullian, "Inscriptions" (1885), 175–84.

[41] *ep. Arel.* 1.

[42] P.-A. Février, "Toulon," in *Topographie chrétienne des cités de la Gaule*, ed. N. Gauthier and J.-Ch. Picard, II, *Provinces écclesiastiques d'Aix et d'Embrun* (Paris, 1986), 61–63: 61–62.

[43] P. Gros, "Un programme Augustéen: le centre monumental de la colonie d'Arles," *Jahrbuch des deutschen archäologischen Instituts* 102 (1987), 339–63.

[44] A survey of recent research can be found in Sintès, "L'évolution topographique," 133–41.

[45] F. Benoit, "Essai de quadrillage d'un plan d'Arles," *CRAI* (1941), 92–100.

[46] Attested epigraphically in *CIL* XII. 5805.

[47] Gros, "Un programme Augustéen," 357–61; R. Amy, "Les cryptoportiques d'Arles," in *Les cryptoportiques dans l'architecture romaine* (Rome, 1973), 285.

[48] Grenier, *Manuel d'archéologie*, III, 742–53.   [49] Ibid., 613–39.

[50] Constans, *Arles antique*, 270–73; F. Benoit, "Informations archéologiques: Circonscription d'Aix-en-Provence (région sud)," *Gallia* 18 (1960), 287–327: 303; Grenier, *Manuel d'archéologie*, IV, 255–56.   [51] Grenier, *Manuel d'archéologie*, IV, 75–88.

circuit wall was erected in the late first century BC to surround this compact urban ensemble.[52] Remnants of the wall, its towers, and one of its gates are still visible to the east and southeast of the city.

Populated suburban areas were located just outside the city walls. To the southwest, along the left bank of the Rhône, a circus was built at the end of the first century AD,[53] and connected to the city by a major new road.[54] To the south, in the modern Crédit Agricole, Esplanade, and Jardin d'Hiver, archaeologists have discovered baths, shops, and houses decorated with splendid mosaics which date to the first and second centuries AD.[55] Across the river was the district probably known in antiquity as the Right Bank (Dextra Ripa), now called Trinquetaille.[56] It was connected to the city by a bridge built on boats, and hence movable if necessary.[57] In this district were located the city's marine docks, warehouses, and shipyards,[58] as well as workshops, private baths,[59] and several large luxurious houses of early imperial date.[60]

The formal designation of Arelate as a Roman colony meant that burials could not be performed within the city walls. This is clear from the surviving charters of other Caesarian colonies in the west, such as Urso (Osuna) in Spain, founded at almost the same time as the colony of Arles.[61] As a result, indigenous cemeteries

---

[52] This complicated subject is discussed, with bibliography, in Rivet, *Gallia Narbonensis*, 191–93, and in Sintès, "L'évolution topographique," 134–35.

[53] G. Hallier, "Le cirque romain: Etude historique et monumentale," in *Du nouveau sur l'Arles antique*, ed. C. Sintès, 56–62.

[54] J.-P. Jacob *et al.*, "Provence-Alpes-Côte d'Azur," *Gallia Informations* (1987–88), part 2, 185–343: 231–33.

[55] Congès, "L'histoire d'Arles romaine," 20–23; C. Sintès, "L'habitat du haut-empire au Jardin d'Hiver," in *Du nouveau sur l'Arles antique*, ed. C. Sintès, 41; J.-M. Rouquette, "Les découvertes du Crédit Agricole," in *Du nouveau sur l'Arles antique*, ed. C. Sintès, 70–77.

[56] On the ancient name, see Ausonius, *Mosella* 481, and R. P. H. Green, *The Works of Ausonius* (Oxford, 1991), 514.

[57] Such a bridge is depicted on a mosaic in the pavement of *statio* 27 in the Piazzale delle Corporazioni in Ostia, *Scavi di Ostia*, IV, part 2 (Tavole), ed. G. Becatti (Rome, 1961), pl. clxxxiv. The mosaic may in fact represent the bridge at Arles, as many have thought; Becatti, however, argues that it was intended to depict a bridge over the Nile, *Scavi di Ostia*, IV, part 1, 74–76.

[58] Sintès, "L'évolution topographique," 137.

[59] F. Benoit, "Informations archéologiques: Circonscription d'Aix-en-Provence (région sud)," *Gallia* 22 (1964), 573–610: 575–76.

[60] There are two main sites. For the Verrerie, see C. Sintès, "Les fouilles de la Verrerie de Trinquetaille," in *Du nouveau sur l'Arles antique*, ed. C. Sintès, 80–88, and J.-M. Rouquette, "Mosaïque du génie de l'année," in *Du nouveau sur l'Arles antique*, ed. C. Sintès, 89–93. For Brossolette, see J.-P. Jacob *et al.*, "Provence-Alpes-Côte d'Azur," *Gallia Informations* (1987–88), part 2, 236–37.

[61] *lex coloniae Genetivae Iuliae Ursonensis* 73.

located in areas enclosed by the walls were abandoned.[62] The burial places of Roman Arles were situated outside the walls, along the roads leading into the city: to the north along the road to Avignon, to the southeast along the road to Marseille (site of the medieval Alyscamps, made famous by Dante[63]), to the southwest along the road leading to the circus, and to the northwest, on the opposite bank of the Rhône, along the road to Nîmes.[64]

The transformation of Arles into a Roman city was for the most part the work of local aristocrats who competed for honor with one another by serving on the town council, holding public office, serving in prestigious priesthoods, and giving the city lavish gifts. It was owing to such men that the town acquired its monuments, and could afford to hold festivals, performances, and games. There were many men like Aulius Annius Camars, who bequeathed 200,000 sesterces to the city for the celebration of circus games on the anniversary of his death.[65] The wealth of these local dignitaries and their willingness to spend it on their cities therefore constituted crucial elements in the process of romanization. Since most aristocrats in this pre-industrial economy drew most of their income from agriculture, it is clear that the amenities of city life depended to a great extent on the output of the surrounding countryside, where most of the wealth in the *civitas* was produced, and where most of its inhabitants lived and worked.

One of the first changes to take place in the countryside of Arles after the city's acquisition of colonial rank was the surveying of land and its allotment to veterans of Caesar's sixth legion.[66] A second, even more profound change was the registration of land for purposes of taxation, which probably initiated a long series of displacements and seizures of land, as Roman and native aristocrats attempted to register as much land as possible under their own names.[67] The disturbance these procedures would have created in existing patterns of population distribution and land tenure is completely unknown, in Arles as elsewhere in Provence, since we lack even the most elementary idea of what these patterns might

[62] For example, the small cemetery found in recent excavations of the Hôpital Van-Gogh, C. Sintès, "La nécropole protohistorique de l'Hôpital Van-Gogh," in *Du nouveau sur l'Arles antique*, ed C. Sintès, 100–04.

[63] *Inferno* IX, 112–15.

[64] C. Sintès, "Les nécropoles," in *Du nouveau sur l'Arles antique*, ed C. Sintès, 95–99.

[65] *CIL* XII. 670.   [66] Benoit, "Le développement," 162–69.

[67] E. M. Wightman, "Rural Settlement in Roman Gaul," *ANRW* II. 4 (1975), 584–657: 619–21.

have been.[68] Nonetheless, it is clear that Roman settlement and registration of land in the *civitas* brought about significant changes in the countryside.

Perhaps the most obvious indication of these changes was a rapid increase in the number of villas located throughout the countryside; these can be defined as substantial, well-furnished rural dwellings built on stone foundations.[69] Although Greek settlement and investment had brought with it the erection of similar structures in the vicinity of Arles, especially in the Camargue,[70] the first century AD saw the construction of many more such buildings throughout the *civitas*, particularly around the Etang de Berre and in the lower valley of the Huveaune between Marseille and Toulon.[71] Villas served both as country houses for Gallo-Roman landowners and as centers of exploitation for the surrounding estates. They represented a system of production in which goods were produced on an intensive scale not only for the villa's subsistence, but also for local and regional markets,[72] and even beyond. The massive water mill that operated at Barbegal from at least the third century AD to Caesarius's day[73] must have processed much of the grain supplied to it by local villas for shipment to Roman armies in the north.[74] Despite the importance of the villa system, however, it is unclear how much the existing peasant economy was altered. Not only did isolated

---

[68] For suggestions based on the Three Gauls, see E. M. Wightman, "Peasants and Potentates," *American Journal of Ancient History* 3 (1978), 97–128: 99–101, and Wightman, "Rural Settlement," 592–602. For the limitations of this methodology, see Drinkwater, *Roman Gaul*, 171–78.

[69] For the definition, see E. M. Wightman, *Gallia Belgica* (Berkeley and Los Angeles, 1985), 105–6.

[70] Grau de la Fourcade (*FOR* V, 398), le Fournelet (*FOR* V, 401), Ile de Mornès (*FOR* V, 404), Carrelet (*FOR* V, 410), Mas de Cabassole (*FOR* V, 413), Nôtre-Dame d'Amour (*FOR* V, 414), and Sainte-Cécile (*FOR* V, 437).

[71] For a (very incomplete) map of villa sites, see Rivet, *Gallia Narbonensis*, Map 26. Many new villa sites have recently been discovered by Caroline Nicholson, to be published in her Bryn Mawr Ph.D. thesis on late Roman Arles.

[72] J.-L. Fiches, "L'éspace rural antique dans le sud-est de la France: ambitions et réalités archéologiques," *Annales ESC* 42 (1987), 219–38: 229. For regional markets in olive oil, see J.-P. Brun, "L'oléiculture antique en Provence d'après les recherches archéologiques récentes," *Echos du monde classique/Classical News* 28 (1984), 249–62: 258.

[73] Although its original excavator dated the mill to the early fourth century, recent opinion has dated the mill earlier, H.-P. Eydoux, "La meunerie hydraulique de Barbegal," *Congrès archéologique de France* 134 (1979), 165–71. For its survival into the sixth century, see J.-P. Jacob *et al.*, "Provence-Alpes-Côte d'Azur," *Gallia Informations* (1990), 81–315: 163; see also Caesarius, *serm.* 8. 4.

[74] F. Benoit, "L'usine de meunerie hydraulique de Barbegal (Arles)," *Revue archéologique* 15, part 1 (1940), 19–80: 68–71.

and marginally fertile properties remain outside of this system, but even on the estates of larger villas, much land continued to be divided into smaller tenant properties worked by individual peasant families rather than gangs of slaves.[75]

Another change brought about in the countryside by romanization affected the siting of nucleated settlements (*vici*). Increasingly during the Roman period these tended to be located in the plains rather than in the hills, as previously.[76] In fact, it was during the first century BC that many, though by no means all, of the fortified hilltop villages (*oppida*) in the *civitas* were abandoned.[77] The reasons for this shift of population are still much disputed, but they are certainly connected with the creation of new patterns of land ownership, greater political security, and changes in the rural economy brought by Rome. As a result of these changes, villages served not only as places of habitation for peasants, tradesmen, and artisans, but also as markets and nodes in the transportation system.[78]

The marketing of surpluses from the countryside, which was crucial to the profitability of the villa system, was made easier in Roman times by the improvement of the system of primary, and perhaps more important, secondary and tertiary roads, as well as river fords and bridges,[79] such as the bridge near Saint-Chamas.[80] Unfortunately, not much is known at present about secondary and tertiary roads in the *civitas*, since it was the primary roads that tended to be well built enough to survive, marked with milestones, and cited on maps and itineraries.[81] For Arles itself, the most important avenues of trade were the Rhône and the canal that C. Marius had dug to connect it to the seaport of Fossae Marianae (Fos-sur-Mer) in 102 BC.[82] Strabo called Arles "no small emporium," and, together with Narbonne and Marseille, it was one

---

[75] Wightman, *Gallia Belgica*, 127.

[76] The *vici* of the *civitas* of Arles are surveyed in Rivet, *Gallia Narbonensis*, 196–206.

[77] P.-A. Février, "The Origin and Growth of the Cities of Southern Gaul to the Third Century, A.D.: An Assessment of the Most Recent Archaeological Discoveries," *JRS* 63 (1973), 1–28: 17–18. See for example the *oppidum* of Saint-Blaise, H. Rolland, *Fouilles de Saint-Blaise (Bouches du Rhône)* (Paris, 1951), and idem, *Fouilles de Saint-Blaise (1951–1956)* (Paris, 1956).

[78] P.-A. Février, "A propos du *vicus* en Gaule méridionale," in *Le vicus gallo-romain, Caesarodunum* 11 (1976), 309–21.   [79] Drinkwater, *Roman Gaul*, 170.

[80] *FOR* V, 97.

[81] For a survey of roads in the *civitas*, see I. König, *Die Meilensteine der Gallia Narbonensis* (Bern, 1970) and *Miliaria Imperii Romani*, ed. G. Walser, *CIL* XVII. 2 (1986).

[82] Rivet, *Gallia Narbonensis*, 46, 203.

of the great ports of southern Gaul.[83] Its main function was to serve as a transfer point between the Rhône and the Mediterranean Sea. Goods coming in from the Mediterranean were brought up Marius's canal by one of the city's corporations of *navicularii marini*, the merchants and sailors responsible for seaborne shipping.[84] At the docks in Arles, cargoes were transferred to river boats owned and operated by the *nautae Druentici*, if the shipment was going up the Durance, or the *nautae Rhodanici*, if the shipment was going up the Rhône.[85] From there, shipments made their way into Upper Provence or into central and northern Gaul, often to the armies on the Rhine frontier. Traffic downriver worked in the same way. In addition, Arles also served as a market for agricultural products from its own countryside, and as an exporter back to the countryside of imported and locally manufactured articles. These goods were shipped to and from the city by way of the lakes and marshes that surrounded it; they were carried on shallow boats and rafts operated by raftsmen, *ratiarii* or *utricularii*, the latter named from the *utres*, inflated goat-skins, that kept their crafts afloat.[86]

We can conclude from such evidence that annexation and colonization by Rome brought important changes to Arles and its territory in the first and second centuries AD: a long era of peace, the building of roads, bridges, and aqueducts, and the opening of new markets for trade. As a result, it is likely that a wide segment of the population of the *civitas* enjoyed greater prosperity than previously.[87] But at the same time we must not overemphasize the impact of romanization, especially on local culture, since the population widely continued to maintain their traditional system of values, beliefs, and practices. It is to the continuity and discontinuity of these cultural – and particularly religious – traditions that we now turn, in an effort to establish the background against which christianization was later to take place.

---

[83] Strabo IV. I. 6. For a comparison of Arles and Marseille as ports, see now S. T. Loseby, "Marseille: A Late Antique Success Story?" *JRS* 82 (1992), 165–85.

[84] Grenier, *Manuel d'archéologie*, II, 530–35.   [85] Ibid., 546–55.

[86] Ibid., 536–46.

[87] Drinkwater demonstrates this point for the Three Gauls in general, *Roman Gaul*, 173–76, 186–206.

COMMUNITY AND RELIGION IN ROMAN ARLES

In a famous passage, Cicero defined the *res publica* as "an assemblage of people in large numbers associated in an agreement (*consensus*) with respect to law and common self-interest."[88] Limited in size and given a local, territorial focus, Cicero's definition of the *res publica* can be treated as a Roman version of the concept of "community," a concept notoriously difficult to define, but arguably rooted in objective social reality.[89] It is admittedly a Roman aristocrat's definition – the *consensus* it speaks of takes for granted a thoroughly hierarchical social system – but this was after all the social system in which local communities found themselves in the Roman empire. The value of adapting Cicero's definition to our purposes is that it allows us to define ancient communities in terms of the values they held as a group while at the same time emphasizing the hierarchical system of consensus by which those values were maintained, legitimated, and transmitted. It is important to establish in principle the existence of such local systems of values, beliefs, and practices, even if we lack the evidence to spell out the details, for the ways in which Christianity was adopted in local communities ultimately depended on the moral and religious system it was intended to disrupt and replace. Cicero's definition of the *res publica* is all the more suitable for this purpose in view of its later adoption by Augustine as a standard against which to measure the rival claims of Rome and the "city of God" to true civic status.[90]

There were many communities in the *civitas* of Arles. They ranged in size from the city of Arles, itself diverse and composed of smaller communities, to more homogeneous villas or villages of perhaps a hundred of fewer inhabitants. In each of these communities we can assume the existence of a central system of values, beliefs, and practices, which defined the community's view of the "good life" and prescribed how its members should act to attain the goods it collectively valued: honor, wealth, privilege, power, autonomy, good health, and divine favor. Those who belonged to the community stood in varying degrees of proximity to this system, depending on gender, age, social, economic, and

---

[88] "coetus multitudinis iuris consensu et utilitatis communione sociatus," Cicero, *de re publica* I. 25. 39, trans. adapted from C. W. Keyes, Loeb Classical Library, 1928.
[89] C. Bell and H. Newby, *Community Studies: An Introduction to the Sociology of the Local Community* (New York, 1972), 27–32.   [90] Augustine, *civ. dei* II. 21; XIX. 21.

legal status, and other variables. Depending on the type of community, the distance between center and periphery would likely have varied as well, with a greater distance in larger, more heterogeneous communities sharply divided by wealth and privilege, and a lesser distance in smaller, more homogeneous communities. Diversity within communities was reflected on a larger scale in the diversity of the *civitas* as a whole, where entire communities could be said, on the basis of the makeup of their populations, to stand in varying degrees of proximity to the central value and belief system upheld by the aristocracy of Arles, and ultimately, by the emperor and the imperial aristocracy.[91]

This model of the *civitas* of Arles can be illustrated by an inscription of the second century AD discovered in the village of Gargarius (Saint-Jean-de-Garguier).

The inhabitants (*pagani*) of the district (*pagus*) of Lucretius located in the territory of Arles in the place known as Gargarius in honor of Quintus Cornelius Zosimus, freedman of Marcellus and priest of Augustus in the colony of Julia Paterna Arelate: for he made known our grievance to the Emperor Titus Aelius Antoninus, most sacred of all ages. He sent letters to Rome on three occasions and pursued the matter with provincial governors for many years at his own expense. He donated to us the expenses he had incurred in this matter, so that the favors of the Emperor Caesar Antoninus Augustus Pius, most sacred of all the ages, might last and endure, by which favors we enjoy water and a bath house free of charge, which had been taken away from the inhabitants of the district of Lucretius, which they had used for more than forty years.[92]

Although some of its details remain obscure, the sense of the inscription is clear. The inhabitants of Gargarius had lost the privileges of free bathing which they had enjoyed for many years, perhaps because the heirs of their original benefactor took back the endowment that had made this possible.[93] They then persuaded a wealthy and influential freedman from Arles to petition several governors of Narbonensis and finally the emperor Antoninus Pius (138–61) on their behalf. In gratitude to their patron for his success and for the donation of his services, the *pagani* set up and paid for an inscription in his honor.

---

[91] For the model of center and periphery on which this analysis is based, see E. Shils, "Center and Periphery," in his *Center and Periphery: Essays in Macrosociology* (Chicago and London, 1975), 3–16.

[92] Text, with supplements and commentary, in Jullian, "Inscriptions" (1885), 175–84, with the emendation to [aquis] noted in the *additamentum* to *CIL* XII. 594.

[93] Jullian, "Inscriptions" (1885), 184.

This inscription contributes to our understanding of local communities by revealing the extent to which the inhabitants of Gargarius shared a sense of "law and common self-interest" with one another, and by demonstrating how actively they were prepared as a community to defend their interests. The inscription also shows the degree to which the individual *pagani* of Gargarius shared a common culture and a common social system with the townspeople of Arles. To both communities, the social act of bathing represented the essence of civilized Mediterranean living. "To hunt, to bathe, to gamble, to laugh – that's what it is to live," according to the famous inscription from the forum in Timgad in north Africa.[94] When their access to this cultural privilege was curtailed, it was to a patron in Arles that the inhabitants of Gargarius turned for help. In doing so, they demonstrated both their autonomy as a community and the limits of that autonomy. But it is difficult to say just how typical a rural community Gargarius was. For it was the administrative center of the *pagus Lucretius*, and clearly a prosperous village, with extant remains not only of a bath, reservoir, and aqueduct (which confirm the details of the inscription), but also of large numbers of inscriptions, mosaics, fragments of sculpture and pottery, and coins.[95] Its inhabitants probably stood closer to the social and cultural center than those who lived in many other rural communities. In those more remote environments, hidden from our scrutiny by their very marginality, a somewhat different system of values, beliefs, and practices would likely have prevailed, important to the local population, but peripheral to the central system of values in the *civitas* as a whole.

Nowhere is the distinction between central and peripheral values, practices, and beliefs more evident than in the realm of religion. The traditional religions of antiquity were local and "community" religions, practiced both publicly and privately by members of the community. Deeply rooted in the local and communal realities of life, these religions reflected the diversity of local communities. Unlike universal, "organized" cults, such as Mithraism, Judaism, or Christianity, community religions were attached to specific places and specific groups. They did not proselytize or accept converts. People belonged to them by virtue

[94] *CIL* VIII. 17938.
[95] *FOR* V, 5–6; Benoit, "Informations archéologiques," *Gallia* 20 (1962), 695.

of belonging to a local kinship group and a local community, not
by virtue of individual choice.[96] Their structure reflected the local
social order: their gods were local gods, their sanctuaries were
local sanctuaries, and their priests were local priests. Thus was
"paganism" truly a religion of place.[97] This did not make it
immutable. On the contrary, it was affected, like other cultural
systems, by changes and continuities in local conditions.

The romanization of the *civitas* of Arles over the first and second
centuries AD affected existing religious practices differently in
different communities, as it did other cultural practices, like
language. On the whole, it further widened cultural distinctions
that had already opened up between hellenized towns and the
Celto-Ligurian countryside, and within towns, between more and
less hellenized (and now romanized) elements of the population.[98]
The religious landscape these differences created is important to
our inquiry because it helps to explain the uneven success of
christianization in subsequent centuries. To establish a background
for our discussion of christianization, we shall therefore survey
expressions of community religion in Arles and its countryside
during the first and second centuries AD.

During the empire, the community religion of the *colonia* of
Arles was, at least officially, identical with the Roman state
religion, which consisted chiefly of subsidized public sacrifices,
processions, festivals, and games in honor of the Capitoline triad
and the deified and living emperors, particulary Augustus. In
Caesar's colony at Urso, duovirs and aediles were required to
celebrate gladiatorial games or dramatic shows in honor of the
Capitoline triad of Jupiter, Juno, and Minerva at least once in their
magistracies.[99] Evidence for the existence of a Capitolium in Arles
is not strong, but it is a reasonable conjecture that such a structure
existed to support the cult.[100] Moreover, as elsewhere in Narbonensis, the official priesthoods of the Roman civic religion and
emperor cult flourished in Arles.[101] Its inhabitants celebrated these

---

[96] A. D. Nock, *Conversion: The Old and the New in Religion from Alexander the Great to Augustine of Hippo* (Oxford, 1933), 1–16.

[97] P. Chuvin, *A Chronicle of the Last Pagans*, trans. B. A. Archer (Cambridge, Mass., 1990), 8–9.

[98] A. Grenier, "Aspects de la religion romaine en Provence," *CRAI* (1954), 328–35.

[99] *lex coloniae Genetivae Iuliae Ursonensis* 70–71.

[100] Constans, *Arles antique*, 254–55; Grenier, *Manuel d'archéologie*, III, 270–71.

[101] *Flamines*: *CIL* XII. 692, 697, 701; *pontifices*: *CIL* XII. 692, 696, 701; *seviri Augustales*, *CRAI* (1898), 683–85, *CIL* XII. 594, 642, 689, 694, 699, 700, 702, 704, 705, 709,

official rituals together as a communal expression of consensus.[102] In addition, they honored an extensive pantheon of Roman and Italian deities. These included, not surprisingly for Narbonensis, Apollo,[103] Neptune,[104] Hercules,[105] Bona Dea,[106] and the thoroughly local "Genius of the colony"[107] and "Fortuna of Arles."[108] Equally typical for the lower Rhône valley was the employment of "Egyptian" magical amulets[109] and participation in the "oriental" cults of Isis,[110] Mithras,[111] and Cybele,[112] whose cult appears to have been merged with that of Bona Dea.[113] At the same time, however, the cults of traditional local and Celtic gods were never abandoned in Arles.[114] In some instances, this meant revering superficially romanized indigenous deities, for example, the Celtic god Succellus, who was honored under the name of the Italian Silvanus.[115] In other instances, the cults of traditional gods continued without any apparent romanization, as demonstrated in the inscription dedicated by T. Attius Quartus to the local god Caiiarus, elsewhere unattested,[116] and in the altar to the Proxsumes, Celtic *genii*, discovered near Arles.[117]

As we move away from the Roman center of the *civitas* to consider its other important towns, the religious landscape remains similarly diverse, but less thoroughly romanized. At Glanum, for instance, where extensive excavations have been conducted, better evidence of the worship of the Capitoline triad has been found than has yet been discovered at Arles, the presumed center of such

---

1005. On the foundation of the emperor cult in Arles, see Benoit, "Le sanctuaire," 31–67. For the cult in Narbonensis generally, see E. Demougeot, "Remarques sur les débuts du culte impérial en Narbonnaise," *Provence historique* 18 (1968), 39–65.

[102] For the communal aspect of such celebrations, see S. R. F. Price, *Rituals and Power: The Roman Imperial Cult in Asia Minor* (Cambridge, 1984), 107–14.

[103] Constans, *Arles antique*, 283–85; E. Espérandieu, *Recueil général des bas-reliefs de la Gaule romaine*, I (Paris, 1907), nos. 138, 140.   [104] *CIL* XII. 660, 697.

[105] Constans, *Arles antique*, 263.   [106] *CIL* XII. 654.

[107] Constans, *Arles antique*, 266–67; Jullian, *Histoire*, VI, 66–67; Grenier, *Manuel d'archéologie*, III, 292–94.   [108] *CIL* XII. 656.

[109] H. Guiraud, "Une intaille magique au Musée d'Arles (Bouches-du-Rhône)," *Revue archéologique de Narbonnaise* 7 (1974), 207–11.

[110] *CIL* XII. 734; Constans, *Arles antique*, 122.

[111] Espérandieu, *Recueil*, I, no. 14; Constans, *Arles antique*, 123–24; *FOR* V, 137, no. 7b.

[112] Espérandieu, *Recueil*, I, nos. 181, 199; *CIL* XII. 703, 708, 5697. 3; Constans, *Arles antique*, 124–27.

[113] R. Turcan, *Les Religions de l'Asie dans la vallée du Rhône* (Leiden, 1972), 58.

[114] On their identities and characteristics, see P.-M. Duval, *Les Dieux de la Gaule*, 2nd edn. (Paris, 1976).

[115] Constans, *Arles antique*, 115–16; *CIL* XII. 662, 4103 (Fourques).

[116] *CIL* XII. 655.   [117] *CIL* XII. 661.

a cult.[118] Similarly, there are indications of cults of Hercules,[119] Bona Dea,[120] and Mithras,[121] as at Arles, along with those of Bona Fortuna[122] and the Parcae.[123] At the same time, however, Glanum appears to have supported the worship of a higher proportion of indigenous deities than Arles, in part because its Celtic population was never as thoroughly romanized,[124] and in part because its location at the foot of the Alpilles provided many more caves, springs, and forests where local deities could be thought to live.[125] The cult of the Celtic Silvanus-Succellus, for instance, is far better attested in Glanum than in Arles, with at least eleven extant dedications.[126] The cult of the Celtic Matres – the triple mothers and fertility goddesses of earth and water – so far unattested at Arles, is represented in two inscriptions from Glanum, one in Latin[127] and the other in Celtic.[128] Both inscriptions are associated with a native healing spring at Glanum,[129] and represent the goddesses in their local form as *Matres Glanicae*.[130] Also associated with the spring were dedications to Apollo[131] and Valetudo.[132]

When we move from cities and towns into villages, the rural strength of Celto-Ligurian religion becomes clear. To be sure, there are occasional signs of Roman and oriental religion. For example, a small votive altar to Jupiter Optimus Maximus has surfaced at Fabregoules, near Marseille, dedicated by Firmus and Bituna, the latter certainly Celtic by name.[133] But on the whole, the religion of the countryside was a native religion, romanized either superficially or not at all. Many communities worshiped purely local or regional gods, unattested elsewhere. A divinity named Lauscus was honored at Roquevaire[134] and Garéoult;[135]

---

[118] H. Rolland, "Inscriptions antiques de Glanum," *Gallia* 3 (1944), 167–223: no. 13 = *CIL* XII. 996.

[119] H. Rolland, *Fouilles de Glanum, 1947–1956* (Paris, 1958), 106–15.

[120] Rolland, "Inscriptions," nos. 18–20; Rolland, *Fouilles de Glanum, 1947–1956*, 96–98.

[121] Rolland, "Inscriptions," no. 25 = *CIL* XII. 1003.

[122] Rolland, "Inscriptions," no. 22.   [123] Rolland, "Inscriptions," no. 24.

[124] Constans, *Arles antique*, 116.   [125] I owe this point to Caroline Nicholson.

[126] Rolland, "Inscriptions," nos. 29–33, 33A, 34–38.

[127] Rolland, *Fouilles de Glanum, 1947–1956*, 88.   [128] Ibid., 115.

[129] Grenier, *Manuel d'archéologie*, IV, 485.

[130] An inscription to "Tellura of the earth, Mana of the earth, and the fertility of the earth" may also be associated with the Matres, Grenier, "Aspects," 330.

[131] *CIL* XII. 991; Rolland, *Fouilles de Glanum, 1947–1956*, 98.

[132] Rolland, *Fouilles de Glanum, 1947–1956*, 98–106.

[133] M. Chaillan and C. Jullian, "Inscriptions de Fabregoules," *REA* 13 (1911), 466.

[134] *CIL* XII. 616.

[135] M. Clerc, "Inscriptions romaines de Garéoult (Var)," *REA* 16 (1914), 79–80.

Trittia was worshiped at Carnoules[136] and Pierrefeu;[137] an inscription to Celleus was discovered between Pourrières and Pourcieux;[138] and a fragmentary dedication to Acilus or Aciludeus was discovered at Trets.[139] The Matres were worshiped at Ventabren[140] and Les Saintes-Maries-de-la-Mer;[141] they took on local names and associations with bodies of water in the Huveaune valley (*Matres Ubelnae*)[142] and in Plan d'Aups (*Matres Almahae*).[143] In addition to these divinities, honored by those who could afford to put up inscriptions, a wide variety of other divinities were worshiped by the Celto-Ligurian peasantry, seldom or never commemorated in inscriptions, but known from literary or archaeological evidence. These included springs, lakes, rivers, groves, mountains, and other divinities of the landscape itself;[144] divine stags, boars, and other animals;[145] and gods and goddesses of healing[146] and fertility.[147] As elsewhere, the cult of these divinities took the form of sacrifices, libations, prayers, and votive offerings, and, where public, processions and festivals as well.[148] Rituals were normally conducted out of doors at sacred places in each locale: on mountains and hills, by springs, rivers, and lakes, in groves of trees, or simply in open spaces.[149]

It is clear from such evidence that the religion of the *civitas* of Arles, like the religion of Roman Provence in general, was "much more indigenous than Roman" especially in the countryside, but also in the towns.[150] Reasons for this state of affairs are not difficult to find. The majority of the population of the *civitas*, and the province in general, were affected only very gradually and imperfectly by the process of romanization. Peasants continued to speak the Gaulish language well into the second century and

---

[136] *CIL* XII. 255.   [137] *CIL* XII. 316.
[138] C. Jullian, "Notes gallo-romaines," *REA* 2 (1900), 233–36.   [139] Ibid., 233–36.
[140] *CIL* XII. 634.   [141] *CIL* XII. 4101.   [142] Jullian, "Inscriptions," 74–76.
[143] Ibid., 8–10.
[144] J. Toutain, *Les Cultes païens dans l'empire romain*, III (Paris, 1920), 292–311. For instance, the cave at Gignac where archaeologists have discovered offerings of coins dating from the second to the fourth century AD, probably made to a divinity of the spring at its base, M. Dalloni, "Grotte votive de l'époque gallo-romaine à Gignac (Bouches-du-Rhône)," in *Cinquième Congrès international d'archéologie* (Alger, 1933), 153–57. Coins dating between 150 and the beginning of the fifth century were also discovered in a cave at Les-Pennes-Mirabeau, F. Benoit, "Informations archéologiques: XIIᵉ circonscription," *Gallia* 8 (1950), 116–32: 123–24.
[145] M. Green, *The Gods of the Celts* (Gloucester, 1986), 179–99.   [146] Ibid., 148–66.
[147] Ibid., 72–102.   [148] Toutain, *Les Cultes païens*, III, 364–407.
[149] Ibid., 331–64.   [150] Grenier, "Aspects," 335.

beyond,[151] and along with many urban dwellers continued to retain the native forms of their names.[152] Changes in religion were even less likely, since this was the most traditional feature of ancient culture, and there was little pressure for conformity.[153] Especially for those at the social periphery, largely unaffected by Roman culture, there would have been no reason at all to make changes in traditional forms of religion. For those nearer the center, who had at least partially romanized their Celtic names and learned Latin, it was apparently enough to worship the old divinities under Roman names. Of the fifty dedications offered in Narbonensis to the Celtic Teutates under the name of Mars, only three were discovered in important towns.[154] Of the thirty-eight votaries in this group whose names bear some indication of ethnic identity, 58 % were Celtic.[155] That cultural autonomy mattered to the indigenous peoples of Provence is clear from the way in which they retained their traditional cultural practices, including religion.[156] Above all, for the peasantry in particular, but also for urban dwellers, adherence to traditional practices was grounded in their daily dependence on nature. The survival of individuals, families, and whole communities depended on their ability to explain, predict, and control the forces by which the rains came, the crops grew, and prosperity abounded.[157] It was their dependence on this hard-won knowledge that made peasants so loyal to the traditions of their ancestors and so reluctant to abandon what had worked in their native places for centuries.

THE LATE ROMAN CITY

In the middle of the third century, the people of central and southern Gaul saw 300 years of peace and political stability come to an end as marauding groups of Germans invaded the country, and a series of imperial usurpers arose to manage provincial defenses. In Arles between 250 and 280, all the houses, shops, and baths so far excavated outside the walls were destroyed, largely by fire, and subsequently abandoned (though later reoccupied).[158]

[151] J. Whatmough, "Κελτικά, Being Prolegomena to a Study of the Dialects of Ancient Gaul," *Harvard Studies in Classical Philology* 55 (1944), 68–76.

[152] G. Barruol, "La résistance," 403–4.   [153] I owe this observation to James Rives.

[154] H. Lavagne, "Les dieux de la Gaule Narbonnaise: 'romanité' et romanisation," *Journal des savants* (1979), 155–97: 165.   [155] Ibid., 162.

[156] Barruol, "La résistance," 404–5.

[157] For this description of community religion, see Horton, "African Conversion," 101.

[158] Sintès, "L'évolution topographique," 141–46.

Similar events occurred elsewhere in the region. The Maison du Dauphin in Vaison was probably destroyed at this time,[159] as was the town of Glanum.[160] In addition, many villas in the *civitas* were abandoned, some permanently,[161] and caves and hill forts temporarily reoccupied.[162] It is unclear whether this pattern of destruction, abandonment, and displacement was the direct result of barbarian attack, or whether it was a byproduct of the political and economic instability such attacks engendered.[163] Whatever the cause, it is clear that while Provence may have been spared the most serious consequences of barbarian invasion, it suffered the same general political and economic disruption as the rest of the empire at this time.

By the early fourth century, however, Arles appears not only to have recovered from the damage it had suffered in the late third century, but also to have embarked on a period of renewed prosperity and heightened administrative importance, which depended, as always, on the city's strategic location.[164] Milan and Trier had earlier undergone the same transformation as a result of political unrest along the Rhine and Danube frontiers. Already in the third century, Milan had become a favorite imperial residence because of its location near, but not directly on, the Danube frontier. Trier was located in a similar position near the Rhine frontier, and by the fourth century had been established as capital of the newly created province of Belgica I and of the diocese of northern Gaul, as well as an imperial residence and headquarters of the praetorian prefect of Britain, the Gauls, and Spain.[165] Arles was strategically located between these two centers, accessible to Milan

---

[159] C. Goudineau, *Les Fouilles de la Maison au Dauphin. Recherches sur la romanisation de Vaison-la-Romaine* (Paris, 1979), 37.

[160] H. Rolland, *Fouilles de Glanum* (Paris, 1946), 20.

[161] For instance, the villa at Martigues, Benoit, "Informations archéologiques" (1962), 687–90; M. Euzennat, "Informations archéologiques: Circonscription de Provence-Côte d'Azur-Corse (région sud)," *Gallia* 27 (1969), 419–63: 432; F. Salviat, "Informations archéologiques: Circonscription de Provence," *Gallia* 35 (1977), 511–37: 525.

[162] S. Gagnière and J. Granier, "L'occupation des grottes du IIIᵉ au Vᵉ siècle et les invasions germaniques dans la basse vallée du Rhône," *Provence historique* 13 (1963), 225–39.

[163] P.-A. Février, "Problèmes de l'habitat du midi méditerranéen à la fin de l'antiquité et dans le haut moyen âge," *Jahrbuch des römisch-germanischen Zentralmuseums Mainz* (1978), 208–47: 227–28.

[164] For a useful survey, see P.-A. Février, "Arles au IVᵉ et Vᵉ siècles: ville impériale et capitale régionale," *XXV Corso di cultura sull'arte Ravennate e Bizantina* (Ravenna, 1978), 127–58, and "Vetera et nova: le poids du passé, les germes de l'avenir, IIIᵉ-VIᵉ siècle," in *Histoire de la France urbaine*, I, *La Ville antique*, ed. G. Duby (Paris, 1980), 393–493.

[165] E. M. Wightman, *Roman Trier and the Treveri* (London, 1970), 58–59.

by way of the upper Durance and the Col de Mont-Genèvre, and to Trier by way of the Rhône–Saône–Mosel corridor.[166] The city therefore rose in importance, even gaining recognition in a text of the mid-fourth century as the "port of Trier."[167] It was a measure of the new importance of Arles that Constantine the Great established an imperial residence there. In 313 he transferred the mint of Ostia to Arles,[168] where it would remain in operation to the end of Roman rule in the west.[169] After 328 its issues bore the mintmark CONST (Constantina) to indicate a change in the city's name that commemorated its special relationship with the imperial family.[170] This relationship was renewed on the visit of Constantine's son Constantius, who resided in the city from late 353 to early 354.[171]

The administrative importance of Arles was further increased around 395, when the capital of the praetorian prefecture of the Gauls was moved there from Trier.[172] In addition, by 408, Arles had displaced Bordeaux as capital of the civil diocese of Septem-provinciae (formerly Quinqueprovinciae),[173] and took the place of Vienne as metropolitan capital of the province of Viennensis.[174] Finally, in 402/8, Arles was designated as the venue for an annual council of the seven provinces that made up the civil diocese.[175] It was not coincidental that these changes occurred at the same time as the imperial residence was transferred from Milan to the port of Ravenna. Both actions signaled a policy of retreat from earlier frontiers and the creation of an "east–west axis" between Ravenna and Arles to replace the northern route from Milan to Trier.[176] Thus did Arles become in effect the Roman capital of Gaul, "Gallula Roma Arelas" in Ausonius's prescient phrase,[177] a status confirmed by the usurper Constantine III when he established his

---

[166] Rivet, *Gallia Narbonensis*, 4–9.   [167] *expositio totius mundi et gentium* 58.

[168] P. Bruun, *The Constantinian Coinage of Arelate* (Helsinki, 1953), 3.

[169] R. A. G. Carson, *Coins of the Roman Empire* (London and New York, 1990), 254.

[170] Bruun, *Constantinian Coinage*, 48, 101. The emperor's son Constantine II was born in Arles in 317.

[171] O. Seeck, *Regesten der Kaiser und Päpste für die Jahre 311 bis 476 n. Chr.* (Stuttgart, 1919), 200–1.

[172] For this date, see J.-R. Palanque, "La date du transfert de la Préfecture des Gaules de Trèves à Arles," *REA* 36 (1934), 359–65, and "Du nouveau sur la date du transfert de la préfecture des Gaules de Trèves à Arles," *Provence historique* 23 (1973), 29–38. For a later date (*c.* 407), see A. Chastagnol, "Le repli sur Arles des services administratifs gaulois en l'an 407 de notre ère," *Revue historique* 249 (1973), 23–40.

[173] Chastagnol, "Le repli sur Arles," 32.   [174] Ibid., 32.

[175] Mathisen, *Ecclesiastical Factionalism*, 42.

[176] Matthews, *Western Aristocracies*, 333.   [177] *ordo nobilium urbium* 74.

capital at Arles in 407.[178] Arles remained an imperial capital – and occasionally an imperial residence[179] – to the end of Roman rule in Provence.

Status as an administrative capital and imperial residence brought numerous economic and demographic changes to the city and countryside of Arles. The presence of an emperor led to the erection of suitable imperial structures. Extensive baths were built near the Rhône,[180] and a palace was built, possibly on the Hauture[181] or near the baths along the Rhône.[182] Headquarters were also found for the praetorian prefect, diocesan vicar, provincial governor, and other officials resident in the city. In addition to the mint, a treasury was located in the city, and state-owned factories were established for the production of woolens and armor embellished with gold and silver.[183] The population of the city rose accordingly, as factory workers, construction workers, artisans, and imperial officials took up residence.[184] The demands of these new residents for housing, food, entertainment, and luxury goods enlarged the local market for these products.

Archaeological evidence from areas outside the city walls reflects the changes that came about as a result. Quarters outside the walls that had been destroyed and abandoned at the end of the third century were reoccupied in the fourth, though not with the luxury housing that had previously existed there. The baths of the Esplanade were refurbished, and continued in use up to about 360, when a kiln was set up to convert the marble into lime.[185] Early in the fifth century, a house was erected over an earlier structure on the east side of the *cardo*, which stood for a short time until it was replaced by a road leading from the city to the Alyscamps.[186] In Trinquetaille, a room in one house was reoccupied in the fourth century after the ashes had been carefully cleared away and the mosaic floor had been somewhat crudely repaired.[187] The absence

---

[178] Stein, *Histoire*, I, 252.
[179] Avitus was named emperor there and resided there in 456 and Majorian resided there between 459 and 461, Stein, *Histoire*, I, 368, 372, 380.
[180] Grenier, *Manuel d'archéologie*, IV, 256–63; F. Salviat, "Informations archéologiques: Circonscription de Provence," *Gallia* 32 (1974), 501–28: 507–9.
[181] Février, "Arles au IVe et Ve siècles," 132.
[182] C. Brühl, *Palatium und Civitas*, I, *Gallien* (Cologne, 1975), 243.
[183] *notitia dignitatum in partibus occidentis* XI. 33, 43, 54, 75.
[184] For example, Geminus (*CIL* XII. 674) and Tolosanus (F. Benoit, *Sarcophages paléochrétiens d'Arles et de Marseille* [Paris, 1954], no. 98).
[185] Congès, "L'Esplanade," in *Du nouveau sur l'Arles antique*, ed. C. Sintès, 37.
[186] Ibid., 37.   [187] Sintès, "Les fouilles de la Verrerie," 84.

of evidence for luxury housing outside the walls during this period is probably best explained by assuming that the wealthy inhabitants of the *civitas* did not live in the lands just outside the city walls, which were now dangerously exposed, but rather within the walls, in areas that have not yet been excavated, or in well-protected country villas. The discovery in cemeteries around the city of high-quality fourth- and fifth-century Christian sarcophagi, many imported from Italy and the east, demonstrates not only the christianization of local aristocrats and imperial officials, as we shall see, but also the success with which their demand for luxury goods was met.[188] A high demand from all classes in the city for the surpluses of the countryside, together with the renewed confidence of landowners and repressive laws designed to tie tenants to the soil, ensured the continuation of the villa system. Not only did many villas in the region remain occupied during this period,[189] but a number of villas abandoned in the third century were reoccupied in the fourth or fifth centuries.[190] In addition, salt-works at a distance of thirty Roman miles from Arles continued to function on church-owned property in the middle of the fifth century.[191] Trade between the countryside and the city also continued, as did long-distance trade. Arles continued to serve

---

[188] P.-A. Février, "La sculpture funéraire à Arles au IVe et début du Ve siècle," *XXV Corso di cultura sull'arte Ravennate e Bizantina* (Ravenna, 1978), 159–81.

[189] For instance,the villa at L'Anjoly in Vitrolles (M. Gauthier, "Informations archéologiques: Circonscription de Provence-Alpes-Côte d'Azur," *Gallia* 44 [1986], 375–483: 456), the villa at Nôtre-Dame d'Amour in the Camargue (Benoit, "Informations archéologiques" [1964], 589–90; *FOR* V, 414), and the villa near the chapel of Saint-Julien in Martigues (Salviat, "Informations archéologiques" [1977], 525).

[190] For instance, the villa at Saint-Julien in the commune of Martigues shows some signs of abandonment in the late third century (stage IIIC), but seems to have been reoccupied, at least in part, at the beginning of the fourth century (stage IVA), Gauthier, "Informations archéologiques" (1986), 436. Another villa in Martigues, at Sénèmes, which seems to have been destroyed in the third century, was reoccupied in the fourth (Euzennat, "Informations archéologiques" [1969], 432; cf. Benoit, "Informations archéologiques" [1962], 687–90), as was a villa at Mas de la Plantade, surveyed by Caroline Nicholson. But this picture of prosperity is complicated by the permanent abandonment of some villas at the end of the third or beginning of the fourth century AD, such as the villa at le Griffon in Vitrolles (Salviat, "Informations archéologiques" [1977], 530; Gauthier, "Informations archéologiques" [1986], 456), the villa at Baumajour in Grans (Salviat, "Informations archéologiques" [1977], 518), and the villa at Touret in Martigues (Benoit, "Informations archéologiques" [1964], 585–86). Since it is found only in preliminary excavation reports, however, all of this information is subject to further revision and precision, and at this stage it would not be wise to draw any firm conclusions about the entire *civitas* on the basis of a few sites which are still not completely excavated or securely dated.

[191] *vita Hilarii* 15. See further, Benoit, "L'économie," 97.

as the exchange point for goods passing between the Mediterranean Sea and the interior of Gaul, as well as the origination point for the products of its shops and factories and the destination for luxury goods from Italy and the east. Despite its exaggerations, a decree of the emperor Honorius (418) confirms the commercial importance of late antique Arles:

> For so great are the advantages of the place, so great is the flow of merchandise, so great is the multitude of those coming and going there, that whatever is produced anywhere is very easily conveyed there…
> Whatever celebrated products are available in the rich Orient, fragrant Arabia, luxurious Assyria, fertile Africa, beautiful Spain, or brave Gaul, all those things held everywhere to be magnificent, abound there in such a quantity as if they were actually produced there.[192]

Ausonius likewise remarked on the city's role in facilitating trade between Gaul and the rest of the Mediterranean world, noting in particular that Arles remained a double city, *duplex Arelate*, with the bridge of boats connecting the right and left banks of the Rhône.[193] Although no surviving inscriptions attest to the continued existence of corporations of *navicularii* and *nautae* in Arles, the volume and diversity of seaborne trade passing through Arles make it certain that these bodies continued to function in some form.[194]

Despite the changes that Arles underwent during the fourth and fifth centuries, life in the city went on in much the same way it had for centuries. When Sidonius visited Arles in 461, he found it bustling with activity and gossip.[195] The forum remained a meeting place, adorned with statues and a portico, although part of this had been dismantled earlier in the fifth century.[196] In

---

[192] *ep. Arel.* 8.

[193] Ausonius, *ordo nobilium urbium* 73–80. For the survival of the bridge into the fifth century, see Paulinus of Périgueux, *vita Martini* VI. 140–44, ed. M. Petschenig, *CSEL* 16; for the sixth century, see Cassiodorus, *var.* VIII. 10. 6.

[194] Imperial constitutions of the fourth through sixth centuries make frequent mention of *navicularii marini*, who were closely regulated by the government, like members of other essential occupations in late antiquity (*CTh* XI. 28. 8; XII. 1. 149; XIII. 5–9; Valentinian, *nov.* 29; *CJ* 11. 1–5; Justinian, *edict.* XIII. 4–8). No mention is made of *nautae* in these laws, but the *notitia dignitatum* mentions the existence of fleets at Vienne, Arles, Chalon, and Lyon (*notitia dignitatum de partibus occidentis* XLII. 14), and Constantine's rapid journey by river from Chalon to Arles in 310 (*panegyrici Latini* 6. 18, ed. R. A. B. Mynors [Oxford, 1964]) suggests that there were still organized bodies of riverboat captains and sailors at his disposal, Grenier, *Manuel d'archéologie*, II, 534–35, 558–60. [195] *ep.* I. 11. 7.

[196] Jacob *et al.*, "Provence-Alpes-Côte d'Azur," *Gallia Informations* (1987–88), part 2, 233–34.

addition, circus games are attested under Constantius II in 353[197] and Majorian in 461.[198] But in the midst of such continuities, profound changes in the fabric of urban life were also taking place, as Christian festivals, churches, and forms of entertainment began to function as new ways of expressing social relationships, dispensing patronage, and promoting civic unity.

THE BEGINNINGS OF CHRISTIANIZATION

In the judgment of Sulpicius Severus, Christianity came late to Gaul.[199] His assessment is confirmed by literary evidence, which places the earliest Christian communities in Gaul at Lyon and Vienne in the middle of the second century.[200] Christians are first attested at Arles around 254, when Cyprian of Carthage criticized their bishop Marcianus for supporting Novatian.[201] Nothing more is heard of the Christians of Arles until the time of Constantine the Great, whose promotion of the Christian religion immediately after his own conversion had the effect of conferring both respectability and prominence on individual Christians and Christian institutions. In particular, his determination to invest his private conversion with public consequences had an immediate impact on Arles. In 314 he selected the city as the site of a council of bishops who were to settle the Donatist schism in the African church.[202] He thus honored the city in an unusual way. By convening under his own patronage a great council in the city, attended by over eighty bishops and other clerics from Spain, Britain, Africa, Italy, Illyricum, and Gaul, Constantine was treating the leaders of a private religious society as public officials, whose deliberations were to produce public benefits – not just the restoration of religious harmony among Christians, but a Christian version of the *pax deorum* that would benefit the empire as a whole. The attitudes of the people of Arles to this radical shift in imperial religious policy are unfortunately impossible to determine with any accuracy. In the case of the ruling class, however, two trends become apparent, both abundantly paralleled elsewhere: for pagans, a gradual shift in religious affiliation, and for Christians,

---

[197] Ammianus Marcellinus XIV. 5. 1.   [198] Sidonius, *ep*. I. 11.

[199] "serius trans Alpes Dei religione suscepta," Sulpicius Severus, *chron*. II. 32. 1.

[200] Eusebius, *historia ecclesiastica* V. 1–4, ed. G. Bardy, *SC* 41.

[201] *ep*. 68, ed. G. Hartel, *CSEL* 3.

[202] *epistula ad Silvestrum, Concilia Galliae, A. 314–A. 506*, ed. C. Munier, *CCSL* 148, 4.

the opening up of new opportunities for political and social prominence.

The extensive and still-growing series of Christian sarcophagi found in Arles – some with inscriptions – provides the largest and most reliable body of evidence for the presence of Christian aristocrats in Arles in the fourth century. Although they varied in quality, carved marble sarcophagi – many imported from Greece, Italy, and Asia Minor – were generally quite expensive, and could only be purchased by wealthier Christians. Poorer Christians were buried in wooden coffins, under tiles, or in the bare earth.[203] It is therefore most revealing that of the fifty Christian sarcophagi in Arles he dated in 1954, F. Benoit assigned twenty-three to a period before the end of the fourth century, twenty-five to the end of the fourth or beginning of the fifth century, and two to the middle or end of the fifth century.[204] These figures suggest that already in the fourth century, even before the relocation of the prefecture, there were numerous wealthy Christians in Arles.[205]

The survival on some sarcophagi of inscriptions datable to the fourth century supports this conclusion. The most prominent Christian aristocrat discovered so far in this material is Marcia Romania Celsa, whose death at the age of 38 was commemorated by her husband Flavius Ianuarinus, ordinary consul for 328.[206] Another inscription, found on a sarcophagus dated to *c.* 340, was composed by Terentius Museus to his wife Hydria Tertulla and his daughter Axia Aeliana.[207] Still another Christian inscription, now lost, was composed by Iulia Victoria for her husband, M. Aurelius Asclepiodotus.[208] But it was a long way to go from the conversions of individual citizens to the christianization of the city as a whole.[209] To take only the most obvious index of civic self-identity in the Roman world – the city's appearance – it is clear that the process by which Arles defined itself as a "Christian" city had only just begun in the early fourth century.

---

[203] Sintès, "Les nécropoles," 96.   [204] Benoit, *Sarcophages paléochrétiens.*

[205] Février, "La sculpture," 163.

[206] J.-M. Rouquette, "Trois nouveaux sarcophages," *CRAI* (1974), 257–63.

[207] *CIL* XII. 675.

[208] *CIL* XII. 834. Although the inscription cannot be dated precisely, retention of the *tria nomina* indicates a relatively early date, perhaps in the fourth century, J. Guyon, "Arles," *RAC* Suppl., fasc. 4 (1986), cols. 612–13, who cites *Sylloge inscriptionum christianarum veterum*, ed. H. Zilliacus, II (Helsinki, 1963), 43.

[209] P. Brown, "Dalla 'plebs romana' alla 'plebs dei': aspetti della cristianizzazione di Roma," in *Governanti e intellettuali: popolo di Roma e popolo di Dio (I–VI secolo)*, ed. P. Brown, L. Cracco Ruggini, and M. Mazza (Turin, 1982), 123–45: 123–24.

Although the date is uncertain, it was probably under Constantine that the Christians of Arles built the city's first cathedral and baptistery.[210] This date is suggested by the location of the two structures: inside the city walls, but far from the forum and other centers of activity. It was exactly the same setting that the emperor had chosen for the Lateran basilica he erected in Rome between 313 and 318: just far enough inside the walls to indicate its privileged status, but distant enough from the monumental core of the city to avoid offending the pagan majority, especially the aristocracy.[211] The location of the original cathedral and baptistery of Arles can probably be explained by the same logic. Despite its prominent location on a high point in the southeastern corner of the city, it was far removed from the normal routes of circulation, and therefore less likely to create friction between pagans and Christians.

Christian sanctuaries outside the walls were located further from centers of everyday activity, but for different reasons. Two were particularly important in Arles, both consecrated to the memory of the martyr Genesius, the first patron saint of Arles. The first sanctuary was located at the site of his martyrdom in Trinquetaille, where a mulberry tree and later an ancient column were venerated as *loci* for the saint's miraculous healings.[212] The second sanctuary was located at his burial place in the Alyscamps, where a basilica was erected before 449.[213] During the fourth century, Christian cemeteries developed around both sites,[214] particularly at his grave, where several of the bishops of Arles were to be buried,[215] along with other members of the Christian community.[216] This was a normal, Roman use of these marginal suburban lands, but Christians also made a habit of visiting both sites on August 25, the saint's feast, in a public procession of the

---

[210] P. A. Février, "Arles," in *Topographie chrétienne des cités de la Gaule*, ed. N. Gauthier and J.-Ch. Picard, III, *Provinces ecclésiastiques de Vienne et d'Arles* (Paris, 1986), 73–84: 80, no. 1.

[211] R. Krautheimer, *Three Christian Capitals: Topography and Politics* (Berkeley and Los Angeles, 1983), 12–15, 28–29.

[212] Gregory of Tours, *glor. mart.* 67; Février, "Arles," 84, no. 14.

[213] *vita Hilarii* 29; Février, "Arles," 83, no. 13.

[214] F. Benoit, *Les Cimetières suburbains d'Arles dans l'Antiquité chrétienne et au Moyen Age* (Rome, 1935), 18, 41.

[215] Hilarius was certainly interred there (*vita Hilarii* 29 and *CIL* XII. 949), and Concordius (d. 374) and Aeonius (d. 501/2) possibly were, Benoit, *Les Cimetières*, 43–44. According to a later tradition, Honoratus, Virgilius (d. *c.* 610), and Rothlandus (d. 869) were also buried there, Février, "Arles," 83.

[216] F. Benoit, "Fouilles aux Aliscamps," *Provence historique* 2 (1952), 115–32; *CIL* XII. 961.

living that streamed out of the city, beyond the walls, and came to rest in two places normally reserved for the dead and the families that remembered them.[217] As Peter Brown has rightly pointed out, it was precisely such regular, ritual separations from everyday urban space that helped Christians to revisualize their cities in Christian terms.[218] But these developments occurred very slowly, and it was not until the city's ruling class and a majority of its citizens began to participate in such festivals that they could be seen, despite their apparently marginal character, as essential elements in the self-definition of the Christian city.

This more widespread participation had in fact begun to be noticeable by the middle of the fifth century. A miracle story set in the episcopate of Honoratus and composed by one of his successors, possibly Hilarius, furnishes precious evidence for the social composition of the Christian community in Arles at the time of its redaction in the middle or later fifth century. One year, according to the preacher, Arles was crowded with Christians from the city and countryside intent upon celebrating the feast of St. Genesius. Just before dawn on the morning of August 25, after a vigil in the *ecclesia* (probably the cathedral church), the crowd of men, women, children, and slaves went out to the sanctuary of Genesius in Trinquetaille. On their way over the bridge of boats that led across the Rhône, they had an accident that terrified the whole city. Burdened with so much weight, the bridge collapsed, and spilled people into the swift-flowing river, together with the splendidly decorated horses that some were riding. Among those who fell were slaves loaded down with children and their mistresses' drinking cups, and beautifully dressed maidens wearing jewelry. Seeing their great danger, Bishop Honoratus said a prayer, and with the assistance of St. Genesius, everyone was rescued.[219] This story gives the impression that by the middle of the fifth century the festival of St. Genesius was considered to be an affair of the entire city, with the potential to attract a crowd large enough to cause the bridge to collapse. Notable among the participants were the city's wealthiest citizens, who feared the loss of their expensive possessions as much as their lives.

[217] P. Brown, *The Cult of the Saints: Its Rise and Function in Latin Christianity* (Chicago, 1981), 40–44.   [218] Brown, "Dalla 'plebs romana'," 130.
[219] *sermo seu narratio de miraculo s. Genesii*. The miracle is abridged by Gregory of Tours, *glor. mart.* 68.

It was these wealthy Christians along with their bishops who were responsible for changes in the city's Christian topography during the first half of the fifth century.[220] The most important change was the erection of a new cathedral church dedicated to St. Stephen, which was soon followed by the construction nearby of a new baptistery (*vita* II.17) and an episcopal residence (*domus ecclesiae*), with individual cells for the bishop and his clergy. This new episcopal complex was not built on the site of the old cathedral, but adjacent to the forum, along the road leading from the theatre, where the Romanesque church and cloister of Saint-Trophime now stand.[221] It was a far more central (and therefore privileged) location than the old cathedral had occupied, which in itself indicates how far the Christian reshaping of the urban landscape had proceeded. The construction date for the basilica is uncertain, but it must lie between 415, when Stephen's relics were discovered in Palestine, and 449, when Hilarius's body was put on view in the church.[222] Only four bishops could have been responsible for the edifice – Patroclus, Helladius, Honoratus, or Hilarius – and Hilarius is perhaps the most likely candidate, for, according to his biographer, he established *monasteria* and erected *templa* in the city.[223] This hypothesis is strengthened by the report in the *vita Hilarii* that the deacon Cyril, whom Hilarius had put in charge of constructing *basilicae*, was injured while removing building materials from the *proscenium* of the theatre.[224] The proximity of the theatre to the site of the new cathedral suggests that the *spolia* were intended for that structure.[225] The story further illustrates, of course, how Christian leaders attempted to rearrange the city's topography by demolishing a center of Roman, pagan entertainment in order to embellish a center of Christian worship.[226] It is important to note, however, that the far

---

[220] For the contribution of aristocrats to church-building, see Marrou, "Le dossier."

[221] There is some disagreement about the date at which the cathedral was moved to this site. I have followed F. Benoit, "Le premier baptistère d'Arles et l'abbaye Saint-Césaire," *Cahiers archéologiques* 5 (1951), 31–59: 53–59, and Février, "Arles," 80, rather than J. Hubert, "La topographie religieuse d'Arles au VIᵉ siècle," *Cahiers archéologiques* 2 (1947), 17–27: 23, and de Vogüé and Courreau, 98–101, who date the relocation of the cathedral to the late sixth century.

[222] *vita Hilarii* 28. On the use of Stephen as a patron for churches in Gaul, see E. Ewig, "Die Kathedralpatrozinien im römischen und im fränkischen Gallien," in his *Spätantikes und fränkisches Gallien*, II, 260–317: 297–302.   [223] *vita Hilarii* 11.

[224] *vita Hilarii* 20.   [225] Benoit, "Le premier baptistère," 56–57.

[226] That the attempt did not succeed is clear from the fact that the theater remained in use during the sixth century, *infra*, p. 174.

more radical step of replacing the forum with a basilica and baptistery, as happened at Aix around 500,[227] was not attempted in Arles; the forum remained in use.

Other church structures were erected in the city before the middle of the fifth century. The *basilica Constantia*, where Bishop Hilarius preached on one occasion, may have been erected by Fl. Constantius after his defeat of Constantine III in 411 and before his death in 421.[228] Unfortunately, the basilica cannot be identified with any known structure, and its location remains unknown. The *basilica Apostolorum*, mentioned in the *vita Caesarii* (II.24), may also have been in existence around this time, but its location too is unknown.[229] Finally, a monastery for men, located *in suburbana insula civitatis* (probably the Ile de la Cappe, about 3 km southwest of the walled city), was built before 498/99, when Caesarius became its abbot.[230] Its foundation has been plausibly attributed to Hilarius, on the strength of his biographer's report about the bishop's building activities and his close connection with Lérins, but it could as well be the work of one of his successors in the later fifth century.[231]

The reasons for this building up of the city's Christian landscape during the early and middle years of the fifth century are not difficult to discern, even if we cannot assign individual responsibility for specific projects. In general, the construction of basilicas, monasteries, and baptisteries brought renown to the churchmen or laymen responsible for them, in much the same way as the construction of amphitheaters, theaters, and circuses enhanced the prestige of aristocrats in an earlier age, by establishing them as generous patrons of their cities.[232] With the conversion of more aristocrats to Christianity and the entry of more aristocrats into the episcopate, there were bound to be more efforts to practice a Christian idiom of patronage. At a time when church

---

[227] R. Guild *et al.*, "Saint-Sauveur d'Aix-en-Provence," *Congrès archéologique de France* 143 (Paris, 1988), 17–64: 18.

[228] *vita Hilarii* 13; Benoit, "Le premier baptistère," 55–56.

[229] Février, "Arles," 82.

[230] *vita* I. 12; P.-A. Février, *Le Développement urbain en Provence de l'époque romaine à la fin du XIVe siècle* (Paris, 1964), 70–71.   [231] *vita Hilarii* 11.

[232] The crucial difference, of course, was that amphitheaters, theaters, and circuses were built for all the free inhabitants of the city in their capacity as citizens, while churches and other ecclesiastical buildings were constructed only for those inhabitants of the city who happened to be Christians. Moreover, in cities divided into Arian and orthodox factions, they were intended only for those who belonged to the proper faction. On the Arian church in Vienne, see Gregory of Tours, *hist.* II. 33–34.

membership was expanding rapidly, these efforts would most naturally have been devoted to the construction of suitably grand and spacious structures for baptism and worship. In those cases in which a bishop built himself a new cathedral church, as Hilarius or one of his predecessors did in Arles, the prestige involved was doubled in value, for in addition to enjoying the honor that came from serving his fellow Christians, the bishop directly enhanced his own prestige by establishing an impressive physical setting in which to show off his personal power and his ministrations to the community. In addition, perhaps most importantly, the appearance of Arles as a Christian city had to keep pace with the enhancement of the city's ecclesiastical status, which resulted directly from its rise in civil status, as we shall see in the following section.

Over the course of the fourth and fifth centuries, as Arles took on an increasingly Christian aspect, similar changes were beginning to occur in the countryside, although far more slowly. One indication of the progress that christianization made there is provided by the gradual construction of a network of rural churches and parishes, which parallels developments in other dioceses.[233] If we can take a reference to "urban deacons" in canon 18 of the council of Arles (314) to imply the existence of rural deacons, then we can date the beginnings of the rural clergy in Arles, if not rural parishes as such, to the late third or early fourth century.[234] The first indication of rural parishes in the *civitas* appears a century later, when a papal letter of 417 mentions two parishes "located in the territory of Arles": the *vici* of Cytharista and Gargarius.[235] It is not surprising that the first parishes known in the diocese were established at these *vici*, particularly Gargarius, for it was in just such places, closely linked to the city of Arles, as we have seen, by ties of patronage and similarities of culture, that the local population would be most likely to welcome the urban Christianity of the fourth century. It was also in this sort of place that a bishop might be motivated to display his pastoral concern or a local aristocrat his patronage by the construction of a village church.[236] With the assignment of clergy and financial support to

---

[233] I. de la Tour, *Les Paroisses rurales du 4ᵉ au 11ᵉ siècle* (Paris, 1900), 10–26; C. E. Stancliffe, "From Town to Country: The Christianisation of the Touraine," in *The Church in Town and Countryside*, ed. D. Baker (Oxford, 1979), 43–51: 47–48.

[234] de la Tour, *Les Paroisses*, 6.   [235] *ep. Arel.* 1.

[236] Cytharista had a parish church in Caesarius's time (*vita* II. 21).

the church, a parish was created. Parish churches and rural clergy were set up in other villages in the diocese as well, for instance, at Cataroscensis (Berre, *vita* II. 20), the vicus Arnaginensis (Saint-Gabriel, *vita* II. 11), and the *castellum* of Luco (*vita* II. 18). But rural parishes were not only set up in villages. The bishops of Arles also established them for the peasants who worked ecclesiastical estates, for example, Succentriones, located in the vicinity of an abandoned bath house (*vita* II. 22). At the same time, large landowners also began to construct churches on their properties for the use of their families, slaves, and tenants; many of these were eventually given full status as local parishes.[237] It is not certain exactly how many parishes there were in the diocese of Arles at the end of the fifth century, but comparison with other Gallic *civitates* suggests that there were perhaps twenty or twenty-five,[238] about half the number the (far smaller) diocese was to have under the *ancien régime*.[239]

Once established in villages and country estates, parishes served as centers for the administration of baptism, the celebration of the Mass, and the instructional activities of the parish clergy.[240] But it is difficult to say how effectively the parish system of Arles promoted the christianization of the peasantry in the fourth and fifth centuries, since the parish church was still seen as an extension of the cathedral church, and the deacons and priests who constituted its clergy were given a very limited range of authority, and consequently of effective action. For instance, although deacons and priests were permitted to read the scriptures at Mass, they were not permitted to explain them in sermons, a privilege reserved for bishops alone. Moreover, until the early sixth century, control over all the offerings made to parish churches remained in the hands of the bishop, who could distribute them as he deemed fit,[241] depriving priests and deacons of the opportunity to function

[237] de la Tour, *Les Paroisses*, 28–29, 57–58.
[238] The *civitas* of Tours, for instance, approximately the same size as Arles, but more sparsely populated, already had over twenty village parishes by the year 500, Gregory of Tours, *hist.* X. 31. A single district (*pagus*) in the diocese of Nîmes was said to have contained fifteen parishes, ibid., V. 5. The diocese of Auxerre had a total of twenty parishes, eight in *vici* and twelve in villas, M. Chaume, "Le mode de constitution et de délimitation des paroisses rurales aux temps mérovingiens et carolingiens," *Revue Mabillon* 27 (1937), 61–73: 65.
[239] L. Royer, "Arles," *DHGE* IV (1930), col. 231.
[240] A. Angenendt, "Die Liturgie und die Organisation des kirchlichen Lebens auf dem Lande," in *Cristianizzazione ed organizzazione*, 169–226: 199–226.
[241] de la Tour, *Les Paroisses*, 59–73.

as local patrons. Such restrictions on the parish clergy would not have mattered much if bishops, in Arles and elsewhere, had concentrated their attention on the christianization of the peasantry. But *rustici* were not generally of much interest to fourth- and fifth-century bishops, who felt more comfortable dealing with aristocrats and townspeople than peasants[242] – Martin of Tours was of course the great exception, along with other monks and soldiers like himself.[243] Indeed, bishops entrusted much of the responsibility for converting peasants to Christianity and dissuading them from paganism to aristocratic landowners, whose powers over their tenants and slaves were much greater than any bishop could muster on his own.[244] It was probably by a combination of their efforts with those of the urban and parish clergy that large numbers of peasants were converted to at least the appearance of Christianity by the end of the fifth century, although the details of this process remain uncertain.

TOWARDS ECCLESIASTICAL PRIMACY

Throughout the fourth century, the city of Arles was not particularly important in the structure of the Gallic church: it served only as the capital of a diocese coterminous with the *civitas*. The diocese, in turn, belonged to the ecclesiastical province of Viennensis, whose capital, like the capital of the civil province, was located at Vienne. As Arles became more important in the civil framework of the empire, however, its bishops began to argue for correspondingly greater ecclesiastical status. By 398, just after the relocation of the praetorian prefecture from Trier to Arles, the bishop of Arles could be found maintaining that his city and not Vienne should be considered the metropolitan capital of the ecclesiastical province of Viennensis, and that he and not the bishop of Vienne should exercise the rights due to bishops of metropolitan cities, principally the right to ordain suffragan

---

[242] For example, *vita Hilarii* 14. But note that Hilarius had also once gone out to baptize shepherds in the Crau, *vita Hilarii* 32. Although Cavallin marks the passage as an interpolation in his edition, it may simply be misplaced.

[243] Victricius of Rouen for example, Paulinus of Nola, *ep.* 18. 4, 7, ed. W. Hartel, *CSEL* 29.

[244] F. J. Dölger, "Christliche Grundbesitzer und heidnische Landarbeiter," *Antike und Christentum* 6 (1950), 297–320. On the evidence from Maximus of Turin, see R. Lizzi, "Ambrose's Contemporaries and the Christianization of Northern Italy," *JRS* 80 (1990), 156–73: 167–68.

bishops and to convene provincial councils.[245] In 398 a meeting of Gallic bishops was convened at Turin to settle this and other disputes. Recognizing the claims of both cities and unwilling to disappoint the supporters of either side, the bishops ruled that the ecclesiastical province of Viennensis should be divided between Arles and Vienne, with each city exercising metropolitan rights over the cities closest to it.[246] By not specifying these cities, however, they left the way clear for future disagreements.

The transfer to Arles of the civil capital of Viennensis sometime after 407, the establishment of an annual provincial council in Arles *c.* 402/8, and the choice of Arles as capital by the usurper Constantine III (407–11) only served to strengthen the city's claims to greater ecclesiastical prominence. In 412, a year after Constantius's defeat of Constantine III, Bishop Heros, a disciple of St. Martin and a partisan of the usurper, was replaced by Patroclus, a supporter of Constantius.[247] With the help of his patron, Patroclus immediately began a campaign to enhance the ecclesiastical status of his city. He not only invoked the city's civil status but also made skillful use of the legend of St. Trophimus, traditionally the first bishop of Arles, who had reportedly been sent by the bishop of Rome to convert Gaul.[248] In addition, it was Patroclus's good fortune to be in Rome on March 18, 417 when Zosimus was ordained bishop of the city. Four days later, perhaps in return for the support of Patroclus and Constantius in the election,[249] and certainly in expectation of some acknowledgment from Patroclus of papal primacy, Zosimus granted Patroclus unusually broad powers over Gaul in general and southern Gaul in particular.[250] In the first place, any cleric who wished to travel to Rome to see the bishop or to go to "other places" was required to obtain a letter of introduction (*litterae formatae*) from Patroclus. In addition, Patroclus was given the right to ordain bishops not only in the ecclesiastical province of Viennensis, but also in the provinces of Narbonensis I and Narbonensis II, which seems at the time to have included Alpes Maritimae as well.[251] This was an unprecedented step, which trampled on the rights of bishops in at least four other

---

[245] The controversy has been well studied. For recent bibliography, see Mathisen, *Ecclesiastical Factionalism.*   [246] Turin (398), can. 2.

[247] Prosper Tiro, *epitoma chronicon* 1247, ed. T. Mommsen, *MGH AA,* IX, 466.

[248] E. Duprat, "Histoire des légendes saintes de Provence," part 1, *Mémoires de l'Institut historique de Provence* 17 (1940), 118–98: 148–69.

[249] Mathisen, *Ecclesiastical Factionalism,* 48–51.   [250] *ep. Arel.* 1.

[251] Mathisen, *Ecclesiastical Factionalism,* 49, n. 29.

cities that claimed metropolitan status in these provinces: Vienne, the former capital of Viennensis, Narbonne, the capital of Narbonensis I, and Marseille and Aix, which disputed control over Narbonensis II.[252] Not surprisingly, Zosimus's decision raised fierce objections in Gaul,[253] and shortly after the death of Constantius in 421, Zosimus's successor Boniface appears to have withdrawn Patroclus's right to ordain bishops outside the province of Viennensis.[254] Two years after Patroclus's assassination in 426, during the episcopate of Honoratus of Arles, Pope Celestine reconfirmed this decision.[255]

Despite the loss of Roman support, it was still to Patroclus's papally-defined status as metropolitan bishop of Viennensis, Narbonensis I and II, and Alpes Maritimae that his successors continued to aspire. By 442, with the closing of the Council of Vaison, it is evident that Honoratus's successor Hilarius had made remarkable progress in advancing his claim to metropolitan control over these provinces. By controlling episcopal ordinations throughout the region and sponsoring a series of church councils for the bishops not only of Viennensis, but of other provinces as well, he had built up a network of support that made him the most powerful of a number of powerful bishops in southern Gaul.[256] But because this power, unlike Patroclus's, depended on local political support, and not on authorization from Rome, Hilarius soon came into conflict with Pope Leo (440–61), whose own aspirations to primacy could not tolerate such independence. In 445, in response to the complaints of Hilarius's fellow metropolitans and other Gallic opponents of Hilarius, Leo ordered Hilarius stripped of his metropolitan rights over all the provinces involved, including Viennensis.[257] The order was confirmed by an imperial rescript issued the same year.[258] Hilarius spent the last four years of his life fighting to regain his status, but died before he could succeed.

Ravennius, who succeeded Hilarius in 449, found himself an heir to his predecessor's considerable local support. In 450 nineteen bishops ordained by Hilarius wrote to Pope Leo to ask him to reverse his decision of 445.[259] In particular, they asked that

---

[252] Turin (398), can. 1.   [253] Mathisen, *Ecclesiastical Factionalism*, 51–60.
[254] Boniface, "Difficile quidem" 1, *PL* 20: 772–73.
[255] Celestine, "Cuperemus quidem" 6, *PL* 50: 434.
[256] Mathisen, *Ecclesiastical Factionalism*, 101–16.
[257] Leo, "Divinae cultum," *PL* 54: 628–36.   [258] Valentinian, *nov.* 17.
[259] *ep. Arel.* 12.

Ravennius be granted authority over the provinces from which they themselves came, that is, not only over Viennensis but also over the provinces of Narbonensis I and II and Alpes Maritimae. Among the reasons they cited were the traditional primacy of Arles, the city's secular prominence, and the missionary role of Trophimus in Gaul. On May 5, 450 Leo responded to their request by elaborating on the solution first proposed a half century earlier at the council of Turin.[260] He assigned the cities of Valence, Grenoble, Geneva, and Tarantaise to the bishop of Vienne, and "the rest of the cities of the same province" to the bishop of Arles. By not defining "the same province" more specifically, however, Leo left the exact composition of the metropolitan province of Arles open to differing interpretations. It is now impossible to say, as it may have been in 450 as well, whether Leo intended "the same province" to mean the province of Viennensis or the four provinces from which the authors of the letter came, which Leo referred to in his letter as *vestra provincia*.[261] But what matters more than Leo's own intentions is the fact that his letter did nothing to discourage Ravennius or his successors from claiming metropolitan control over nearly the same extensive province as Patroclus and Hilarius.

Leo's solution to the problem of the status of Arles won widespread support in Gaul, even among some of Ravennius's rival metropolitans, in part because it followed the outlines of the Gallic solution proposed to the problem at the Council of Turin.[262] A letter commending Leo's decision was signed by Ravennius of Arles, Rusticus of Narbonne, Venerius of Marseille, and forty-one other bishops.[263] Not surprisingly, however, the settlement provoked opposition from other bishops, including Mamertus of Vienne, whose metropolitan province was greatly reduced in size,[264] and the bishop of Aix, whose metropolitan rights to Narbonensis II still had not been explicitly recognized by Rome.[265] Such opposition continued despite various efforts by Leo's successor Hilarus (461–68) to promote the primacy of Arles in the person of its new bishop, Leontius (461–c. 480).

But the interference of the bishop of Rome in the Gallic church

---

[260] *ep. Arel.* 13; Mathisen, *Ecclesiastical Factionalism*, 182, n. 41 for references.
[261] *pace* Mathisen, *Ecclesiastical Factionalism*, 182–83.
[262] Mathisen, *Ecclesiastical Factionalism*, 182. [263] *CCSL* 148, 107–10.
[264] Ceretius *et al.*, "recensita epistola," *PL* 54: 887–90; Mathisen, *Ecclesiastical Factionalism*, 188–90. [265] Mathisen, *Ecclesiastical Factionalism*, 188.

was coming to matter less and less in the 460s, since Roman political control over the provinces of southeastern Gaul was rapidly slipping away to the Visigoths in the west and the Burgundians in the north. This meant in addition that the bishop of Arles had to exercise whatever metropolitan rights he claimed over a progressively shrinking territory. Most of the province of Narbonensis I, including Narbonne, was already in Visigothic hands by 462.[266] A large part of Viennensis and smaller parts of Alpes Maritimae and Narbonensis II, perhaps as far south as the Durance, were likewise in Burgundian hands by around the same time.[267] Although a Burgundian king could still insist in 463 on the right of the bishop of Arles to consecrate the bishop of Die, located in Burgundian territory,[268] the trend was about to turn in the other direction. Metropolitan control was coming to be based not on Roman provincial organization or pronouncements from the bishop of Rome, but on the political boundaries established by barbarian kings. In 476/77 Arles itself became part of the Visigothic kingdom. Within a generation its bishop would preside over the council of Agde, the first "national" council in any of the Germanic kingdoms, which was convened not by a metropolitan bishop but by the Gothic king, and was attended not by bishops from the same ecclesiastical province, but by bishops from the same kingdom.

VISIGOTHIC ARLES

In 412 a large body of Goths under the command of Alaric's brother-in-law Athaulf entered Gaul in search of what they could not obtain in Italy, a homeland of their own within the empire. By 418, after years of warfare and negotiation, they were permanently established as federates in Aquitaine under the terms of a treaty that would last to 466. Eager to improve the terms of their settlement by intimidation and force, as well as by their service as federate soldiers, the Goths regularly marched on Arles, the capital of Roman Gaul, in much the same way as Goths under Alaric had marched on Rome. These assaults, recorded for the years 425, 430, and 458, never succeeded in breaching the city walls, but they did spread death, destruction, and famine in the surrounding country-side, and helped to create deep feelings of insecurity on the part of rural dwellers. After Euric became king in 466, the treaty of

---

[266] Wolfram, *Goths*, 180–81.   [267] Schmidt, *Ostgermanen*, 143.
[268] *ep. Arel.* 19.

416/18 was abrogated, and Gothic policy changed.[269] No longer content with federate status within the empire on any terms, Euric wanted an independent kingdom that would replace the Roman empire in Gaul. He soon found himself in a position to act on these intentions, and between 471 and 475 Gothic armies managed to win control over most of Aquitaine from a series of emperors who faced their own problems in northern Italy. The Goths threatened Provence as well. In 473 Euric captured both Arles and Mar-seille,[270] but ceded them back to Rome in 475 in return for the remainder of the Auvergne.[271] Within a year, however, Euric had regained Arles, and the Visigoths occupied the city and all of Provence between the Durance and Rhône.[272]

It was thus in 476/77 that Arles permanently passed out of the control of the Roman empire. The praetorian prefecture also came to an end, although not permanently, since it would be reinstituted by Theoderic a generation later. Although it had been the fifth-century capital of Roman Gaul, Arles did not become the capital of the Visigothic kingdom, which remained at Toulouse, but it did serve occasionally as a royal residence.[273] As in all *civitates* in the Visigothic kingdom, a Gothic count was installed at Arles to represent the king and supervise the city's military, fiscal, and judicial affairs.[274] For the most part, however, the administration of the city and its territory remained in the hands of the local aristocracy and bishop. The town council and its magistrates continued to be responsible for collecting the taxes, repairing roads and public buildings, and keeping the peace. For his part, the bishop continued to run the church. Although from time to time, especially under Euric, he faced interference from the Visigoths, who professed the Arian creed, there are no grounds for postulating the systematic persecution of Catholic Christians.[275] In fact, the most important disadvantage from which the bishop of Arles suffered as a result of the events of the 470s was the division

---

[269] Wolfram, *Goths*, 150–88.

[270] *chronica Gallica a. DXI*, 657, ed. T. Mommsen, *MGH AA*, IX, 665; *chronicorum Caesaraugustanorum reliquiae*, a. 473, ed. T. Mommsen, *MGH AA*, XI, 222.

[271] Sidonius, *ep.* VII. 7. 1–2. On this complex issue, see C. E. Stevens, *Sidonius Apollinaris and his Age* (Oxford, 1933), 207–11.

[272] *consularia Italica, auctarii Havniensis ordo prior* 476. 1, ed. T. Mommsen, *MGH AA*, IX, 309; M. Rouche, *L'Aquitaine des Wisigoths aux Arabes, 418–781* (Paris, 1979), 41–42.

[273] Euric died there in 484, Isidore, *historia Gothorum* 35, ed. T. Mommsen, *MGH AA*, XI, 281.   [274] Wolfram, *Goths*, 214–15.

[275] K. Schäferdiek, *Die Kirche in den Reichen der Westgoten und Suewen bis zur Errichtung der westgotischen katholischen Staatskirche* (Berlin, 1967), 18–31.

of his metropolitan territory into two parts: the dioceses north of the Durance, which fell into Burgundian hands, and the dioceses south of the river, which were administered by the Visigoths. This division prevented the bishop of Arles from exercising his metropolitan rights anywhere north of the Durance, and allowed Bishop Hesychius of Vienne (*c.* 474–*c.* 490) to exercise a *de facto* control over six dioceses belonging to the Arlesian portion of Viennensis,[276] three dioceses belonging to Narbonensis II,[277] and two dioceses belonging to Alpes Maritimae.[278] Under Pope Anastasius (496–98), Hesychius's son and successor Avitus (*c.* 490–518), "the most outstanding bishop in Gaul,"[279] succeeded in depriving Aeonius of Arles of his *de jure* rights to these provinces.[280] In 500, however, Aeonius recovered these rights (although not his *de facto* rights) under Anastasius's successor Symmachus.[281] But the dispute did not end there: conflict over metropolitan rights continued for Caesarius's entire career as bishop.

This was the political situation that awaited Caesarius in Arles when he arrived from Lérins in *c.* 495. With the exception of occasional travel, he was to spend the remainder of his life in the *civitas*. It was in its city streets[282] and on its country roads,[283] in its cramped private houses[284] and well-appointed villas,[285] and in its basilicas[286] and village churches[287] that he endeavored to carry out his responsibilities as deacon, priest, abbot, and ultimately bishop. To understand his rapid rise to the episcopacy and in particular his self-fashioning as a reformer, we turn now to an account of his early career in Arles.

---

[276] St. Paul, Vaison, Orange, Carpentras, Avignon, Cavaillon. Viviers belonged to the Goths (*CIL* XII. 2700), and thus to the province of Arles.

[277] Gap, Sisteron, Apt.   [278] Embrun, Digne.

[279] Ennodius, *vita Epiphani* 173.   [280] *ep. Arel.* 23.   [281] *ep. Arel.* 24.

[282] *vita* II. 30.   [283] *vita* I. 47.   [284] *vita* II. 2.   [285] *vita* I. 50.

[286] *vita* I. 43.   [287] *vita* II. 20.

Chapter 3

THE MAKING OF A REFORMER

When he arrived in Arles, Caesarius made contact with members of the city's secular and ecclesiastical elite. The most important of these local nobles was Bishop Aeonius, Caesarius's relative and fellow citizen (*vita* I. 10). It is difficult to believe, as the authors of the *vita* suggest, that neither man was aware of his relationship to the other before their first meeting in Arles. Caesarius's biographers are likely to have endorsed this fiction in order to enhance the drama of his arrival in the city, to suppress the suggestion that he went to Arles to exploit his kinship with its bishop, and in general to de-emphasize the importance of his remaining ties with relatives he was supposed to have left behind in the "world."[1] Indeed, their entire account of Caesarius's career in Arles before 502 (*vita* I. 8–14) is dominated by an effort to create the impression that despite his re-entry into the world he remained a monk faithful to the customs of Lérins (*vita* I. 11).[2]

Besides Aeonius, Caesarius was introduced to members of the lay aristocracy in Arles, two of whom are explicitly named in the *vita*: Firminus, a *vir illustris*, and his relation (*proxima*), perhaps his wife, the *illustrissima* Gregoria (*vita* I. 8). Nothing is known of Gregoria, but Firminus's aristocratic connections are well known.[3] He was a correspondent of Sidonius Apollinaris,[4] a friend of Sidonius's son Apollinaris,[5] and a relative and correspondent of Magnus Felix Ennodius.[6] He may also have been related to

---

[1] The fact that virtually the same story occurs in *vitas patrum Emeretensium* IV. 3. 1–6 indicates that later hagiographers found it similarly useful.

[2] For other examples of this hagiographical topos, see Venantius Fortunatus, *vita Germani* 40–41; *vita Leobini* 54.

[3] M. Heinzelmann, "Gallische Prosopographie, 260–527," *Francia* 10 (1982), 531–718: 609; Stroheker, *Der senatorische Adel*, no. 156; *PLRE* II, 471.

[4] Sidonius Apollinaris, *ep.* IX. 1, 16.   [5] Ibid., *ep.* IX. 1. 5.

[6] Ennodius, *ep.* II. 7 is addressed to Firminus. Moreover, Ennodius's father may have been named Firminus, *PLRE* II, 471; Heinzelmann, "Gallische Prosopographie," 596.

Caesarius's biographer of the same name.[7] It was no doubt through Firminus and Gregoria that Caesarius became acquainted with other members of the local aristocracy,[8] whose assistance would prove valuable to him in his future career. Firminus's literary interests are also well known. It was to him that Sidonius dedicated the ninth book of his *epistolae*, and addressed the first and last letters of the book.[9] Ennodius called him "a learned author."[10] As such, he was in a position to introduce Caesarius to an eminent local rhetor, Julianus Pomerius, who was to have a profound effect on his education (*vita* I. 9).

A dedicated follower of Augustine,[11] Pomerius had originally won his reputation in Mauretania, but fled Africa, very likely because of Vandal persecution.[12] He then took up residence in Arles, where he remained despite efforts by Ruricius of Limoges and Ennodius to bring him to their towns.[13] He was eventually ordained a priest in Gaul,[14] probably by Aeonius, that is, before 502.[15] That he was also an ascetic is indicated by Ruricius's reference to the "narrow and difficult path" of spirituality that he traveled,[16] and by pseudo-Gennadius's statement that he lived a life worthy of God and was of a "fitting profession and rank."[17] He was the author of several works: the *de natura animae*, in eight books, of which fragments survive;[18] the *de virginibus instituendis*, which is lost; the *de contemptu mundi ac rerum transiturarum*, also lost; and the *de vita contemplativa*, in three books, which survives in full.[19] No dates can be assigned to these works, but it is likely that he wrote the *de vita contemplativa* after becoming a priest.[20] He probably died early in the sixth century.[21]

The authors of the *vita* tell us disappointingly little about Caesarius's relations with Pomerius. They simply report that

---

[7] Malnory, 17.

[8] E.g., Ennodius's sister Euprepia (Ennodius, *ep.* VII. 8), her son Fl. Licerius Firminus Lupicinus (Ennodius, *ep.* II. 23), another sister (name unknown), and her son Parthenius (Ennodius, *ep.* V. 12).   [9] *ep.* IX. 1, 16.   [10] Ennodius, *ep.* I. 8.

[11] *vita contempl.* III. 31. 6; M. J. Suelzer (ed.), *Julianus Pomerius. The Contemplative Life* (Westminster, Md., 1947), 11.   [12] Ps.-Gennadius, *vir. ill.* 99; Malnory, 16.

[13] Ruricius, *ep.* II. 9; Ennodius, *ep.* II. 6.   [14] Ps.-Gennadius, *vir. ill.* 99.

[15] A. Solignac, "Julien Pomère," *DS* (Paris, 1974), col. 1594, *pace* Riché, *Education and Culture*, 32, who suggests ordination after 503.   [16] Ruricius, *ep.* I. 17.

[17] "Conversatione Deo digna vivit, apta professione et gradu," ps.-Gennadius, *vir. ill.* 99.

[18] Edited by A. Solignac, "Les fragments du De natura animae de Pomère," *Bulletin de littérature ecclésiastique* 75 (1974), 41–60.

[19] Ps.-Gennadius, *vir. ill.* 99; Isidore, *vir. ill.* 12; *PLRE* II, 896; R. W. Mathisen, "*PLRE* II: Suggested Addenda and Corrigenda," *Historia* 31 (1982), 364–86: 382.

[20] Suelzer, *Julianus Pomerius*, 8.   [21] Solignac, "Julien Pomère," col. 1595.

Caesarius had a dream which convinced him to resist Pomerius's efforts to refine his "monastic simplicity" by instruction in classical rhetoric.

When he had grown weary from a vigil, he placed on his bed under his shoulder the book that the teacher had given him to read. When he had fallen asleep on it, he was soon struck with a terrible vision of divine inspiration. During his brief nap, he saw the shoulder on which he was lying and the arm with which he had been resting on the book being gnawed by a serpent winding itself around him. Terrified by what he had seen, he was shaken out of his sleep, and began to blame himself more severely for wanting to ally the light of the rule of salvation with the foolish wisdom of the world. And so he at once condemned these preoccupations, for he knew that those endowed with spiritual understanding possessed the adornment of perfect eloquence. (*vita* I. 9)

While clearly modeled on Jerome's famous dream,[22] Caesarius's dream makes a narrower point: that the true ascetic ought to shun the teachings of classical rhetoric in favor of the eloquence that comes from a pure heart and an upright way of life. But Caesarius's dream constitutes no more accurate a description of his view of classical rhetoric than Jerome's dream constituted of his view of classical literature.[23] Rather than condemning classical rhetoric as such, the dream was intended to make a positive statement about Christian culture. In fact, it hints at a debate that had been going on in Gaul throughout the fifth century over the proper style of life for the Christian clergy, their methods of pastoral care, and in particular their use of language as a strategy of christianization. The authors of the *vita* were, however, much mistaken in their suggestion that Pomerius and Caesarius stood on opposite sides of this debate. For, as his *de vita contemplativa* demonstrates, Pomerius's ideas about church reform, themselves influenced by Augustine, were to exercise a profound influence on Caesarius's own program of reform and christianization. To understand that program, we must therefore examine its antecedents in Pomerius, as well as in the writings of other like-minded Gallic reformers. These include the priest Salvian of Marseille,

---

[22] Jerome, *ep.* 22. 29. 6, ed. I. Hilberg, *CSEL* 54. See in general P. Antin, "Autour du songe de S. Jérôme," in *Recueil sur Saint Jérôme*, Coll. Latomus 95 (Brussels, 1968), 71–100. See also N. Adkin, "Some Notes on the Dream of St. Jerome," *Philologus* 128 (1984), 119–26; and E. Rice, *St. Jerome in the Renaissance* (Baltimore, 1985), 3ff.

[23] For Caesarius's use of classical rhetoric, see Arnold, 84–87; Prinz, *Frühes Mönchtum*, 475–76; E. Auerbach, *Literary Language and its Public in Late Latin Antiquity and in the Middle Ages*, trans. R. Manheim (London, 1965), 91–95.

who composed his *ad ecclesiam* and *de gubernatione dei* in the second quarter of the fifth century[24] and the anonymous priest from southern Gaul, very possibly Gennadius, who composed the list of canons known as the *statuta ecclesiae antiqua c.* 476–85.[25] There are also analogous reform ideas in the *de septem ordinibus ecclesiae*, likewise written by a priest, but the dating and provenance of this anonymous document are still too uncertain to justify its use.[26]

POMERIUS AND CHURCH REFORM

In his *de vita contemplativa*, Pomerius laid the foundation for a program of radical reform in pastoral care, which was based on the proposition – deeply Augustinian in inspiration – that bishops and their clergy should live more like monks and less like aristocrats.[27] Pomerius opened Book I by redefining the contemplative life. In his view, this was not the life of a monk who had retreated from the world to contemplate God. Rather it was that future life in which the redeemed would see God.[28] Yet at the same time Pomerius believed that the contemplative life could be anticipated on earth by an ascetic style of life, which he redefined to include both active and contemplative virtues. He therefore advised bishops who wished to pursue the contemplative life to keep their minds constantly on God (I. 8), study the scriptures (I. 8, 13. 1), and separate themselves from secular entanglements (I. 8, 13. 1), but at the same time to feed the hungry, clothe the naked, and redeem captives (I. 12. 1, 25. 1). Thus, for Pomerius the active life was not an alternative to the contemplative life or its opposite, but a component of it in its imperfect earthly form and an essential

[24] G. W. Olsen, "Reform after the Pattern of the Primitive Church in the Thought of Salvian of Marseille," *Catholic Historical Review* 68 (1982), 1–12.

[25] Ed. C. Munier, *Les Statuta Ecclesiae Antiqua* (Paris, 1960). On date and authorship, see esp. 107–24, and 209–36.

[26] Ed. W. Kalff, "Ps.-Hieronymi, 'De septem ordinibus ecclesiae'" (diss., University of Würzburg, 1935). On its reform ideas, see Munier, *Les Statuta*, 162–64, 193–97. The work may have been written in southern Gaul in the early fifth century, or in northern Spain in the late sixth or early seventh century. For a survey of the evidence, see L. A. Van Buchem, *L'Homélie pseudo-eusébienne de Pentecôte* (Nijmegen, 1967), 223–34. For more recent arguments in favor of a later date and Spanish origin, see R. E. Reynolds, "The Pseudo-Hieronymian 'De septem ordinibus ecclesiae': Notes on its Origins, Abridgments and Use in Early Medieval Canonical Collections," *RBen* 80 (1970), 238–52.

[27] G. Ladner, *The Idea of Reform* (Cambridge, Mass., 1959), 378–424, especially 389–90.

[28] *vita contempl.* I. 1. 1. Cf. Augustine, *civ. dei* XIX. 19; F. Cayré, *La Contemplation augustinienne* (Paris, 1927).

preparation for it in its perfect heavenly form (I. 12). In fact, bishops who preferred "leisured study" to the "burdensome work of administration" were to be condemned (III. 28. 1).

As Robert Markus has argued, Pomerius's thinking amounted to a "drastic modification of the ascetic ideal," akin to John Cassian's, which made the ascetic life more accessible to clerics who were not monks.[29] At the same time, however, it raised the standards of behavior that clerics could be expected to meet. Pomerius's redefinition of the contemplative life thus allowed him to censure bishops who did not pursue it. Such bishops were sinners in his view, who neglected their congregations (I. 15), extended the boundaries of their estates (I. 13. 2), devoted themselves to gluttony and drunkenness (I. 15), allowed the rich to oppress the poor (I. 15), and pursued secular wisdom (I. 13. 1). Far from redefining the contemplative life in order to make it easier for aristocratic bishops to appropriate the prestige of asceticism without giving up the prerogatives of an aristocratic lifestyle,[30] Pomerius tried to convince bishops that the ascetic ideals he promoted required far-reaching changes in behavior (I. 17). Having established that the contemplative life was, in effect, the equivalent of the proper Christian life, Pomerius closed his first book with a series of positive steps by which bishops could begin to lead a contemplative life, that is to function as "good" bishops. These included preaching to the congregation in sermons that were understandable to all (I. 23); correcting sinners by word and example, even when they were powerful aristocrats (I. 21. 1); and protecting the congregation against oppression by the rich (I. 21. 3).

In Book II of the treatise Pomerius set out to discuss the nature of a bishop's practical life (*vita actualis*), and specifically how he should exercise authority over his clerics and congregation. He began by providing concrete suggestions for correcting the faults of the congregation (II. 1–8) and maintaining the harmony of the diocese (II. 3. 2). Next, he set about answering the question whether the bishop and his urban clergy should give up their wealth and live together as monks, as Augustine's clergy did in Hippo, or whether they should continue to own property, receive salaries from the church, and live separately, as did the vast

---

[29] Markus, *Ancient Christianity*, 189–92.
[30] *pace* Heinzelmann, *Bischofsherrschaft*, 200.

majority of the clergy in Gaul.[31] Pomerius strongly favored a communal life for the clergy. The church, he said, should possess wealth and use it for the benefit of the poor (including bishops and clerics), but bishops and clerics themselves should give away their wealth out of love of perfection and in imitation of monk-bishops like Paulinus of Nola and Hilarius of Arles (II. 9. 1). In addition, where possible, they should live together under the bishop's supervision (II. 11, 16. 1, 16. 4). Those who could not give up all their possessions should at least return to the church the support they received, so as not to deprive the truly poor of their sustenance (II. 12). In the final section of Book II, Pomerius discusses in more detail, under the general heading of abstinence, the proper style of life for clerics living in common, for he maintained that renunciation of possessions was of no value unless the individual will was also renounced (II. 17. 2). Amidst the expected admonitions to abstain from excess food and drink (II. 22–23), Pomerius alluded to other virtues normally emphasized in monastic rules, such as humility and charity (I. 21).

In the third book of the treatise, Pomerius discussed the bishop's proper moral message to his congregation. In Book I he had emphasized the requirement that bishops not only preach to their congregations, but do so in easily intelligible language (I. 23). In Book III he gave a practical example of the content of that preaching, at the same time reminding preachers that their words meant nothing if they were not matched by an upright way of life (III. 14. 1).[32] Having presented bishops with a compendium of moral advice with which they might address their congregations and by which they might themselves live, Pomerius closed his book with a brief conclusion.

Many of the charges of greed, abuse of power, neglect of pastoral care, and "secular" habits of life that Pomerius leveled against bishops had already been made in Gaul, not as often by bishops themselves as by lower-ranking clerics who sought to

---

[31] II. 9, 16. J. C. Plumpe's interpretation of these passages is crucial, "Pomeriana," *Vigiliae Christianae* 1 (1947), 227–39: 233–37. Examples of clerics living apart from their bishops can be found in Sidonius Apollinaris, *ep.* VII. 15, and Beck, 81–84.

[32] Not surprisingly, his moral system owes a great deal to Augustine, particularly his condemnation of pride as the root of all other vices (III. 2–10), his interpretation of charity as a well-ordered love (III. 13–15), and his insistence on the role of grace in man's accomplishments (III. 1. 4, 18. 3: see C. Tibiletti, "La teologia della grazia in Giuliano Pomerio," *Augustinianum* 25 [1985], 489–506). The monastic character of these admonitions is also clear, as seen in Pomerius's repeated insistence on perfection (III. 15. 1, 3. 18. 1, etc.) and chastity (III. 6–7).

reform the episcopate. Such charges were usually based on the belief that unqualified candidates had become bishops: aristocrats chosen directly from the laity who had not undergone any preparation before ordination and refused to change their lives after ordination. At the beginning of the fifth century, Sulpicius Severus complained that "episcopal offices are now sought out of wicked ambitions."[33] The most common complaint about men who had obtained bishoprics by these means was their refusal to carry out standard episcopal duties, like preaching and caring for the poor. Pope Celestine (422–32) reproached Gallic bishops, particularly those recently ordained from the laity, for permitting their priests to preach while not preaching themselves.[34] More serious was the charge that lay aristocrats continued to oppress the poor even after ordination or ascetic "conversion." Among other complaints about the rich, Salvian condemned clergy and religious who "abstain from their own wives but not from the invasion of other people's property."[35]

Three competing solutions were usually proposed for this problem, which amounted to three different "profiles" of the ideal episcopal candidate; these profiles can be termed clerical, monastic, and lay.[36] Bishops of Rome repeatedly demanded that bishops be selected from among deacons or priests who had proven their worth in the local clergy.[37] Founded above all on the need of the church to base status on office-holding, this solution rejected lay aristocrats on the grounds that their status was based on inherited wealth and privilege, and rejected monks on the grounds that their status was derived from personal achievement.[38] Individual Christian communities, however, continued to favor the appointment of monks as well as lay aristocrats to episcopal office. Monks were recommended by their reputation for asceticism, generosity, wonder-working, and probity,[39] and aristocrats by their ability to look out for the community's material and political interests.[40] Communities often tried to satisfy both sets of needs by choosing candidates who combined spiritual talent with

[33] *chron.* II. 32.   [34] "Apostolici verba" 2, *PL* 50: 529.   [35] *gub. dei* v. 10. 54.
[36] The choices are clearly outlined in Sidonius Apollinaris, *ep.* VII. 9. See further, E. Griffe, *La Gaule chrétienne à l'époque romaine*, 2nd edn., II (Paris, 1966), 219–26.
[37] Zosimus, "Exigit dilectio" 1, *PL* 20: 670; Celestine, "Cuperemus quidem" 7, *PL* 50: 434–35.
[38] Celestine, "Cuperemus quidem" 2, *PL* 50: 430–31; Zosimus, "Exigit dilectio" 1, *PL* 20: 670; Sidonius Apollinaris, *ep.* VII. 9. 12.
[39] Sulpicius Severus, *vita Martini* 9.   [40] Sidonius Apollinaris, *ep.* VII. 9. 9.

impressive aristocratic connections, such as many of the monks of Lérins.[41] In response to such expectations, some aristocratic candidates for the episcopacy, although not monks themselves, nevertheless aspired to live as ascetics, aware that a reputation for ascetic living constituted a powerful additional source of authority and prestige. Once they became bishops, without disavowing the privileges of aristocratic birth, such men sought to distinguish themselves by typically ascetic activities like fasting, eating simple foods, wearing rough clothing, and reading the scriptures.[42]

In response to the problem of qualifications for episcopal office, Pomerius and other reformers proposed a solution that transcended the usual models of the ideal bishop, while at the same time incorporating elements from each. Calling upon bishops to take the most radical step aristocrats could take, they urged them to renounce their property and live a life of voluntary poverty with their fellow clergymen. Such a decision would also have meant in many cases relinquishing the very basis on which their authority and suitability for office were thought to rest.[43] Far from presenting the renunciation of property as the most honorable of a number of honorable options,[44] Pomerius implied that bishops who were too "weak" to give up their property were lacking in ardor for the contemplative life.[45] The *statuta ecclesiae antiqua* attempted to make clerics even more like monks by recommending that even those "educated in the word of God" (can. 79) earn their own keep by farming or practicing a trade rather than accepting a salary from the church (can. 29); those who did not know a trade were told to learn one (can. 45).[46]

As part of the renunciation of wealth and private life, Gallic reformers expected bishops to eschew all the entertainments of an

---

[41] Prinz, *Frühes Mönchtum*, 59–62.

[42] Sidonius Apollinaris, *ep.* VI. 12. 3 (Patiens of Lyon); Gregory of Tours, *vita patrum* 7. 2 (Gregory of Langres); Constantius of Lyon, *vita Germani* 3–4 (Germanus of Auxerre). The epitaph of Eutropius of Orange is comprehensive (*ILCV* 1065. 9–10):
> huic victus tenuis et dur[a cubilia membris]
> et vestis tegimen hisp[ida semper erat].

[43] Pomerius, *vita contempl.* II. 9–16; Salvian, *gub. dei* III. 3. 14–15; *ad eccl.* II. 4. 14; 9. 37–43.

[44] Among the options, in addition to the total renunciation of private property with all of its revenues, Faustus of Riez suggested in a letter to Ruricius of Limoges the management of one's property by sons or bailiffs, and the renunciation of ownership with the retention of usufruct, *ep.* 8.   [45] *vita contempl.* II. 12.

[46] Together with the advice that bishops treat their priests as colleagues "within the house" (can. 2), these provisions suggest that the author of the *statuta* had in mind both a voluntary poverty for the clergy and a form of communal living.

aristocratic lifestyle and revert to an exclusively Christian, ascetic culture.[47] The compiler of the *statuta ecclesiae antiqua* recommended that bishops wear inferior clothes, use plain dinner ware, eat simply (can. 4), and live in a small house near the church (can. 1). Rather than caring for property, he urged them to devote themselves to reading, prayer, and preaching the word of God (can. 3). In addition, he prohibited them from reading pagan books, and permitted them to read heretical books only if necessary (can. 5). The difference between these views – impractical as they were – and the more moderate attitudes of most bishops are immediately evident if we examine Sidonius's portrayal of the Gallic aristocrat Vettius, whom he holds up as a model for ascetic bishops.[48] Although a layman, Vettius frequently read the scriptures, abstained from wild meats, and administered his household as though he did not own it.[49] At the same time, however, he enjoyed hunting, wore refined clothing, and could fairly be considered "second to none in training horses, judging dogs, and in carrying hawks about."[50] For his part, Pomerius would not have portrayed a man like Vettius as the ideal "contemplative" bishop. Indeed, he criticized "those who deny themselves the enjoyment of lustful passion and allow their will the license of windy vanity. They refrain from the disgrace of sexual intercourse, but give in to ambition. They enjoy delicacies of all sorts and garments carefully tailored to serve their ostentation, boys with neatly curled hair and powerful horses for their pageants, hawks and well-fed hounds for the hunt, and frequent hunting parties to show off their magnificence."[51]

But it was not only a disagreement over the wealth and proper style of life for bishops that divided Pomerius and his fellow reformers from other churchmen. It was also a basic disagreement about the bishop's responsibility for preaching God's word to the people. Pomerius in particular argued that the bishop's main role as pastor was not to look out for the material welfare of his congregation, but rather to promote its spiritual welfare in word and deed, chiefly by his own good example and preaching (I. 20. 1). On this point he would have found widespread agreement.[52]

---

[47] Pomerius, *vita contempl.* I. 13.
[48] *ep.* IV. 9. 5; Heinzelmann, *Bischofsherrschaft*, 207.   [49] *ep.* IV. 9. 3–4.
[50] *ep.* IV. 9. 2, trans. W. B. Anderson, Loeb Classical Library (Cambridge, Mass., 1965).
[51] *vita contempl.* III. 17, trans. adapted from Suelzer. Although directed against laymen, Pomerius's criticism clearly applies a fortiori to bishops.
[52] Celestine, "Apostolici verba" 2, *PL* 50: 528–29.

Where he took issue with other churchmen was in the proper style
of a bishop's preaching, which he argued should be clearly
understandable to all. "Such should be the simplicity and
straightforwardness of the bishop's language: though this may
mean less good Latin, it should be restrained and dignified so that
it prevents no one, however ignorant, from understanding it but
descends with a certain charm into the heart of all who hear it."[53]
It was the social meaning of rhetoric in late Roman Gaul that gave
this standard of preaching its novelty and importance. The spoken
word not only communicated information, but also defined social
rank. The ability to compose and deliver complex and elegant
speeches required many years of education and great expense to
perfect. Because this skill was generally available only to members
of the aristocracy, it served as a mark of aristocratic birth and
carried with it a series of powerful associations. The refined speech
of an aristocrat was calculated to reinforce feelings of solidarity
with his peers, evoke a sense of deference in his inferiors, and
demonstrate to everyone his knowledge and capacity for leadership. Thus, bishops who addressed their congregations in the
highly ornate style of a Sidonius Apollinaris[54] or an Avitus of
Vienne[55] did so not to confuse their congregations, but to establish
their credentials as aristocrats, to reinforce their authority as
leaders, and to demonstrate their status as spiritual experts.[56] Those
who advocated a simpler style of public speaking, like Pomerius
and later Caesarius, did so not only to ensure communication of
the bishop's message to the entire congregation, but also to define
his authority as a teacher and a leader in a radically different way.
"Not in the splendor of his words," as Pomerius wrote, "but in
the power of his deeds, let [the bishop] place all his confidence in
preaching."[57] In this view, a bishop's authority was not to be based

[53] *vita contempl.* I. 23, trans. adapted from Suelzer.
[54] See the sermon in Sidonius Apollinaris, *ep.* VII. 9. On Sidonius's prose style, see A.
Loyen, *Sidoine Apollinaire et l'esprit précieux en Gaule aux derniers jours de l'empire* (Paris,
1943), 124–64.
[55] On his style, see H. Goelzer and A. Mey, *Le Latin de Saint Avit* (Paris, 1909), 692–726.
Although the style of sermons delivered on important occasions such as church
dedications can be expected to have been more ornate and obscure than usual (I. N.
Wood, "The audience of architecture in post-Roman Gaul," in *The Anglo-Saxon
Church*, ed. L. A. S. Butler and R. K. Morris [London, 1986], 74–79), Avitus's more
popular sermons, such as those delivered at Rogation ceremonies, do not appear much
easier for an unlettered audience to understand. See further, I. N. Wood, "Avitus of
Vienne," 145–47.   [56] Pomerius, *vita contempl.* I. 23. 1.
[57] Ibid., I. 23, trans. adapted from Suelzer.

primarily on birth, wealth, or superior education (although many would have claimed these as well), but rather on episcopal office itself, an upright way of life, and a solid Christian faith. As the *statuta ecclesiae antiqua* states: "A bishop...should seek the authority of his office in faith and the merits of his life."[58]

Pomerius and the other exponents of church reform in Gaul made the case for reform forcefully and articulately over the course of the fifth century. As priests and monks, they stood to gain from a set of standards for episcopal office that valued clerical office and an exemplary way of life over aristocratic birth and wealth. But a reform movement among priests, even including the likes of Pomerius and Salvian, whom Gennadius once described as "a teacher of bishops,"[59] did not have the slightest chance of succeeding without support from bishops, who alone had the power to enact such reforms. What was important about the group of reformers to which Pomerius and the author of the *statuta ecclesiae antiqua* belonged was the fact that they managed to attract the attention of the man who was about to become bishop of the most powerful see in southern Gaul. It was Caesarius's sympathy for the reform ideas advanced by, among others, his teacher Pomerius that would give these ideas the best chance they would have of succeeding for a long time, for, as we shall see in the following chapters, he would later enact reforms so close to those proposed by Pomerius that Riché could wonder whether it was not Caesarius who influenced Pomerius,[60] and so close to those proposed in the *statuta ecclesiae antiqua* that Caesarius could plausibly (though incorrectly) be thought to be its author.[61]

"THE BURDEN OF THE EPISCOPACY"

It was probably not long after Caesarius arrived in Arles that Aeonius began to think of him as a possible successor. His young relative already possessed a number of qualifications for the position, including native ambition, a good education, and, most importantly, impressive ascetic credentials from the monastery

---

[58] "Ut episcopus...dignitatis suae auctoritatem fide et vitae meritis quaerat," *stat. eccl. ant.*, can. 4. The same concerns for moral and doctrinal rectitude appear in the preface to the *statuta*, which lists the requirements for episcopal ordination.

[59] Gennadius, *vir. ill.* 68.

[60] Riché, *Education and Culture*, 92. Although not impossible, the age difference between the two men makes such an influence unlikely. Apart from similarities between Pomerius and Caesarius, Riché presents no evidence for his view.

[61] Malnory, 50–58.

that had already supplied Arles with two of its most successful bishops. He therefore saw to it that Caesarius acquired as many additional qualifications for the position as possible. After securing his release from Porcarius's authority, an act of courtesy that would later be required by local church law,[62] he ordained Caesarius into the clergy of Arles, first as deacon, then as priest (*vita* I. 11), offices in which he could begin to demonstrate his capacities for leadership and pastoral care.

Shortly afterwards, when the abbot of the men's monastery in Arles died around 498/99,[63] Aeonius decided to appoint Caesarius to succeed him. The promotion made it possible for Caesarius to enhance his reputation as an ascetic and further develop his leadership credentials. We know very little about the three years Caesarius spent as abbot of the monastery. The only achievement for which his biographers chose to praise him during this period was the monastery's survival to their own day: "through daily perseverance and the divine office he organized the monastery so well that it is preserved there...even today" (*vita* I. 12). It was not during his tenure as abbot, but much later, as de Vogüé has shown, that Caesarius composed a rule for the monks of this monastery.[64]

Shortly before his death, Aeonius took his final step in promoting Caesarius's candidacy for bishop. He "addressed the clergy and citizens, and through messengers asked the [Visigothic] masters of the city that after he had, God willing, departed to Christ, they choose none other than holy Caesarius to succeed him" (*vita* I. 13).[65] Among his reasons for promoting Caesarius's candidacy, according to the *vita*, was the expectation that Caesarius would reform the local church, whose discipline had been weakened during the bishop's illness; the prospect that his eternal reward would be increased by leaving behind a worthy successor; and the hope that Caesarius would continue to support Aeonius's dogmatic and political positions as an ally (*vita* I. 13). The passage concludes with the mention of Aeonius's death and the implication that Caesarius's election as bishop followed as a matter of course. "And so, with all these things faithfully ordered by divine providence, and certain of his successor, the blessed Aeonius departed to the Lord" (*vita* I. 13).

---

[62] Agde (506), can. 27.   [63] *vita* I. 12.

[64] A. de Vogüé, "La Règle de Césaire d'Arles pour les moines: un résumé de sa Règle pour les moniales," *Revue d'histoire de la spiritualité* 47 (1971), 369–406.

[65] For the identification of *ipsos dominos rerum* as the Visigoths, see Krusch, 461, n. 3.

As we have demonstrated elsewhere, Aeonius died in 501 or 502, probably on August 16.[66] Yet Caesarius was not elected to the see of Arles until December 502.[67] Such an interval, whether of four or sixteen months, strongly suggests a contested election. This impression is confirmed by other evidence. The very fact that Aeonius felt compelled to influence the choice of his successor as he did indicates that there must have been considerable uncertainty about Caesarius's ability to win the episcopacy on his own. Reasons for this uncertainty are not difficult to suggest. In the first place, Caesarius was a close relative who had only recently arrived in the diocese. His progress through the ecclesiastical *cursus honorum* had already been unusually rapid as a result of Aeonius's patronage. Even if the appointment of a relative as bishop was not yet illegal in Gaul,[68] such a move was bound to add to the feelings of jealousy and resentment that must already have existed among Caesarius's fellow clerics, especially those whose competence, seniority, and experience would normally have made them suitable candidates for the episcopacy. Second, if Caesarius's biographers are correct in stating that Aeonius promoted Caesarius as a reformer, and did not simply retroject to the time of Aeonius anachronistic conclusions about Caesarius's career, he would have been far from popular with clerics who did not wish to live the sort of common life that "reform" entailed, at least in the Augustinian/Pomerian sense. Third, Aeonius must have had his own opponents within the city, against whom he wished to have Caesarius as an ally (*vita* 1. 13). They too can be expected to have opposed the choice of Caesarius or anyone else who might have continued Aeonius's policies.

Aeonius's doubts about Caesarius's chances for success were strong enough to motivate him to bypass the normal procedure for choosing a bishop. According to church law and custom, the selection of a bishop's successor was supposed to take place after his death and to include as participants the local clergy, aristocracy, and people. Bishops who chose their own successors before death stood in violation of this principle,[69] whose purpose was to create at least the perception that bishops were chosen by a *consensus*

---

[66] W. E. Klingshirn, "Church Politics and Chronology: Dating the Episcopacy of Caesarius of Arles," *REAug* 38 (1992), 80–88: 85–86.   [67] Ibid., 84–85.

[68] The first mention in Gaul of a prohibition against nepotism appears at the Council of Paris (614), can. 3. An earlier prohibition appears in *canones apostolorum* 76, ed. F. X. Funk, *Didascalia et Constitutiones Apostolorum*, I (Paderborn, 1905), 586–89.

[69] E. Loening, *Geschichte des deutschen Kirchenrechts* (Strasburg, 1878), II, 194–96.

omnium, and to prevent the imposition of an unsuitable bishop on an unwilling congregation. Although many bishops violated (or tried to violate) this principle,[70] they ran the risk in doing so of producing resentment among those who felt cheated of their rightful participation in the election process (even if it was only a formality in many cases), undermining community consensus, and creating a state of permanent conflict within the diocese.[71]

Opposition to Aeonius's choice of a successor may also have influenced his decision to seek confirmation of his choice from the Visigothic "masters of the city." It is not certain whether such confirmation was required by the Visigoths,[72] as it later would be by the Franks.[73] Although Alaric II was by all accounts much more accommodating to the Catholic hierarchy than his father had been, he still had an interest in approving the admission of new bishops into that hierarchy. Even if such a step was not required, Aeonius was certainly prudent to consult the Visigoths in advance. But the very process by which Caesarius was chosen raises the possibility that Aeonius also approached the Visigoths because he needed their backing to ensure that, in the face of local opposition, Caesarius would in fact succeed him. With the approval of the Visigothic king behind Caesarius, rival candidates would have stood a reduced chance of success. In return for the favor, the Visigoths would have gained as a potential ally the bishop of the most strategically important city in their Gallic realm, who would have been indebted to them for his position.

Despite Aeonius's efforts to ensure a smooth succession for Caesarius, at whatever subsequent cost, there is a strong possibility that the arrangements he had made were undone at his death and that a rival candidate succeeded in having himself consecrated instead of – or in addition to – Caesarius.[74] The oldest manuscript of the episcopal *fasti* for the church of Arles, dating to around 900, lists a Bishop Johannes between Aeonius and Caesarius.[75] His name has usually been considered an interpolation, as it was by Duchesne,[76] since the *vita*, in making no mention of Johannes,

---

[70] Gregory of Tours, *hist.* IV. 36; V. 42; VI. 9. Gregory himself thwarted one such attempt, *hist.* VI. 15.

[71] Augustine's selection of Antoninus as bishop of Fussala provides a notorious example of what could go wrong when the proper consultations did not take place, *ep.* 209 and 20*.   [72] Schäferdiek, *Die Kirche*, 54–55.   [73] Orléans (549), can. 10.

[74] Mathisen, *Ecclesiastical Factionalism*, 276, n. 9.

[75] Duchesne I, 249–50. The MS is a sacramentary of the church of Arles (Paris, B. N. lat. 2812).   [76] Duchesne I, 253.

strongly implies (although it does not actually say) that Caesarius succeeded Aeonius directly. The silence of the *vita* on this point should certainly not be rejected lightly, especially since its authors do not elsewhere shrink from describing the political and doctrinal controversies in which Caesarius was involved.[77] But if a rival candidate was elected to the bishop's throne, Caesarius's biographers would have had good reasons for omitting to mention him. We cannot therefore completely reject the possibility that the *fasti* correctly listed Johannes as Aeonius's successor. Although earlier sections of the *fasti* can be shown to contain numerous errors, later sections appear more reliable, particularly the sequence of bishops beginning with Heros (408–11) and ending with Johannes (*fl.* 660). Of the twenty bishops in this sequence, Duchesne provided external corroboration for sixteen.[78] Owen Chadwick argued for the authenticity of another, long considered an interpolation.[79] Of the three remaining names – Johannes, Presaius, and Paschasius – only the last can be proven to be an interpolation.[80] There is no evidence for or against Presaius, and the only evidence against Johannes is his omission from the *vita*. If Johannes does in fact belong on the list, he must have been consecrated just after Aeonius's death by a party of bishops and local clergy opposed to Aeonius. A hint of the discord that his consecration produced may be evident in a letter written in the late fifth or early sixth century by Ruricius of Limoges to Capillutus,[81] an elderly man residing in Arles, who was later ordained a priest and carried letters on Caesarius's behalf.[82] Referring to an election of some sort, Ruricius wrote that he could not disapprove of a man whom *communis consensus* had chosen, but that Capillutus ought to advise him to "be zealous for the truth, not falsehood, peace, not destruction, teaching, not discord, the public good, not self-aggrandizement, justice, not rapacity." If the letter refers to the election of a bishop in Arles in 501/2, as seems plausible,[83] the new bishop could be identified with Caesarius, as Krusch suggested,[84] or perhaps even better, with Johannes. In either case, Ruricius's

---

[77] E.g., *vita* I. 21–24, 29–31, 36, 60. [78] Duchesne I, 255–60.

[79] O. Chadwick, "Euladius of Arles," *JTS* 46 (1945), 200–205. But see the doubts expressed by R. A. Markus, *Ancient Christianity*, 177–79.

[80] Gregory of Tours, *hist.* IX. 23. [81] Ruricius, *ep.* II. 31.

[82] A. Engelbrecht, *Patristische Analecten* (Vienna, 1892), 63–65. Capillutus turns up again in Ruricius, *ep.* II. 21, 33, 40, and Caesarius, *ep.* 4.

[83] *pace* Engelbrecht, who argued unconvincingly that ordination to secular office was meant instead, *Patristische Analecten*, 61–63. [84] *MGH AA*, VII, lxiv.

misgivings about the candidate and the tenor of his advice to Capillutus suggest a far from harmonious succession, despite the public declaration of *communis consensus*. As it happened, however, Johannes's tenure would have been brief, whether he died in office or was deposed, for, as we have seen, Caesarius was finally consecrated in December 502.

The existence of a rivalry within the city over Aeonius's successor, whether or not a rival candidate was ever consecrated, would explain very well the serious internal political problems Caesarius faced in his first years in office, which we shall examine shortly. It would also lend a greater polemical weight to the story in the *vita* that he tried to avoid consecration by hiding himself in a cemetery (presumably in the vicinity of the monastery).[85] Caesarius might of course have truly sought to avoid consecration by this gesture, as Maximus of Riez was reported to have done in a similar situation by fleeing into the woods.[86] More likely, however, this is an example of the familiar panegyrical topos of "refusing power" so as not to appear to seize it, but rather to receive it from others.[87] Caesarius might well have decided to "act out" this topos as a way of generating support for his consecration. By retreating into a cemetery, he might either appear to "die" there or, as it happened, to be sought all the more eagerly as bishop. In the end Caesarius succeeded in creating the impression that he "took up the burden of the episcopate under compulsion" (*vita* I. 14). And so it was that shortly before Christmas, at the age of thirty-two or thirty-three, he became bishop of Arles.

[85] *vita* I. 14.   [86] Eusebius Gallicanus, *hom.* 35. 8.
[87] J. Béranger, "Le refus du pouvoir," *Museum Helveticum* 5 (1948), 178–96.

Chapter 4

VISIGOTHIC ARLES AND ITS BISHOP

ASCETIC, PATRON, AND PASTOR

Late antique bishops who came to power in the face of local opposition often had to spend the early years of their episcopacy trying to restore harmony and consensus to their faction-ridden cities. When Honoratus of Lérins became bishop of Arles, according to his biographer, "his first concern was harmony and his chief task was to knit together again into one brotherhood of mutual affection those who had been separated, by passions still at white heat, over the choice of a bishop."[1] In such circumstances, bishops often found it helpful to devote more than ordinary attention to playing the part of the "good bishop." They did so by leading conspicuously holy lives, providing for the well-being of their congregations, protecting their cities, and fulfilling the many other expectations generated by public opinion and late Roman traditions of patronage and public service.[2] So, as soon as he was consecrated, Honoratus brought an ascetic "discipline" to the church and began to spend its funds on the needy.[3] Likewise, immediately after a contested election, Avitus of Clermont (571–c. 594) "showed his greatness in every respect, offering justice to the people, alms to the poor, relief to widows, and all possible assistance to orphans."[4]

Caesarius's earliest initiatives in office can in part be interpreted in the light of these examples. He first acted to reassure his congregation that despite his election as bishop, he remained a monk and an ascetic at heart. He continued to live the austere life

---

[1] Hilarius, *vita Honorati* 28. 1, trans. F. W. Hoare, *The Western Fathers* (London, 1954).

[2] J. Gaudemet, *L'Eglise dans l'empire romain* (Paris, 1958), 345–46.

[3] Hilarius, *vita Honorati* 28. 3.

[4] Gregory of Tours, *hist.* IV. 35. For the background, see I. N. Wood, "The Ecclesiastical Politics of Merovingian Clermont," in *Ideal and Reality in Frankish and Anglo-Saxon Society*, ed. P. Wormald (Oxford, 1983), 34–57.

of a monk by eating simply (*vita* I. 37), shunning comfortable clothing (*vita* II. 42), and devoting himself to prayer and spiritual reading (*vita* I. 15). Moreover, he was careful at the outset to take on only those episcopal duties that appeared compatible with a monastic way of life, such as preaching (*vita* I. 16–17), compassion for the sick (*vita* I. 20), and the protection of paupers and captives (*vita* I. 20). He distanced himself from the local church's extensive landholdings by assigning the day-to-day management of church property to his subordinates, as Augustine had done and Pomerius had advised.[5] Most importantly, he tried to conform as well as he could to the ideal of total voluntary poverty advocated by Pomerius and Augustine. To be sure, Caesarius did not renounce all personal property, for in his will he bequeathed a number of possessions to fellow clerics and the local church.[6] Nonetheless, in comparison with other bishops of his time – even other reputedly ascetic bishops – Caesarius possessed very little indeed. This can be verified by comparing his will with that of Remigius, bishop of Reims (*c.* 460–*c.* 520), described as an ascetic in his *vita*: "generous in almsgiving, attentive in keeping vigils, dedicated in prayer, perfect in charity, lavish in kindness, distinguished in teaching, well-versed in speech, and most holy in his way of life."[7] The bequests listed in Caesarius's will consisted only of a male slave named Bricianus,[8] a female slave named Agritia,[9] and assorted items of clothing, including ceremonial vestments,[10] a tunic,[11] a belt,[12] and several woolen cloaks.[13] By contrast, Remigius's bequests consisted of more than fifteen parcels of property, forty-eight tied tenants and slaves (not counting the thirty-four dependents he manumitted), eighty-five *solidi*, and an assortment of pigs, silver spoons and vases, and articles of fine clothing.[14] The

[5] *vita* I. 15; Possidius, *vita Augustini* 24; Pomerius, *vita contempl.* I. 8, 13. 1.

[6] The very fact that Caesarius composed a will at all sets him apart from Augustine, who, according to Possidius, made no will because he had no property to bequeath, *vita Augustini* 31.

[7] *vita Remedii* 2, ed. B. Krusch, *MGH AA*, IV. 2, 64–65. On the worth of this document, see K. Schäferdiek, "Remigius von Reims: Kirchenmann einer Umbruchszeit," *Zeitschrift für Kirchengeschichte* 94 (1983), 256–78 : 256–58. On Remigius's reputation for sanctity, see also Gregory, *hist.* II. 31; *glor. conf.* 78.

[8] *test.*, Morin II, 289, line 9.   [9] Ibid., 289, line 10.   [10] Ibid., 284, line 15.

[11] Ibid., 284, line 16.   [12] Ibid., 289, line 8.

[13] Including a *casula villosa melior* (*test.*, 284, line 16), a *birrus* (285, line 1), two *manta* (289, line 6, 289, line 8), and a *gaunapes* (284, line 16).

[14] Remigius, *test.*, ed. B. Krusch, *MGH SRM*, III, 336–39. On its authenticity, see A. H. M. Jones, P. Grierson, and J. A. Crook, "The Authenticity of the 'Testamentum S. Remigii'," *Revue belge de philologie et d'histoire* 35 (1957), 356–73.

estate of a truly wealthy bishop like Sidonius Apollinaris would have been even larger (at least before the Visigoths confiscated his property[15]). Against this background of wealth, Caesarius's personal poverty must have stood out clearly, confirming his status as an ascetic.

At this juncture, however, Caesarius's asceticism clearly differed from the asceticism he had practiced at Lérins. This had been entirely monastic in its significance. Undertaken in pursuit of spiritual perfection, it was judged accordingly. By contrast, the ascetic regimen Caesarius practiced as bishop was intended as much for the benefit of his clergy and congregation as for himself. Its immediate purpose was to smooth over the controversy surrounding his election by elevating him to a realm of prestige beyond politics and criticism. A reputation for asceticism was also important because it carried with it implications of generosity, a time-honored tactic for winning favor with the population. "Frugal in the midst of abundance," reads the epitaph of Bishop Sergis of Tarragona (*fl.* 540), "he lived a life of generosity for the needy."[16]

It is thus no surprise that Caesarius also appealed to his congregation and clergy by explicitly Christian forms of patronage. He supplied the poor and captives with assistance, and opened a hospital near the cathedral, where the sick could be cared for at the same time as they listened to the singing of the divine office (*vita* I. 20).[17] It may also have been at this time that Caesarius obtained from Alaric an immunity from taxation for church lands in Arles.[18] By increasing the wealth available to the church, this privilege improved its capacity for helping the poor, maintaining

---

[15] Sidonius Apollinaris, *ep.* IX. 3. 3–4.

[16] "parcus in abundantia, locuplex egentibus vixit," *ILCV* 1091. 10. There are numerous parallels. For Gaul, see Hilarius, *vita Honorati* 28. 3; *ILCV* 1073. 10, 15 (Sacerdos of Lyon); *CE* 698. 15 (Pantagarius of Vienne), and *Die christlichen Inschriften der Schweiz vom 4.–9. Jahrhundert*, ed. E. Egli (Zurich, 1895), no. 21, lines 16–17 (Marius of Avenches); for Italy, see *CE* 312. 6 (Celestine of Rome) and *ILCV* 986. 5 (Felix IV of Rome); and for Africa, see *ILCV* 1103. 3–5 (Alexander of Tipasa).

[17] Whether this was a hospital in the later Byzantine sense is doubtful, T. Miller, *The Birth of the Hospital in the Byzantine Empire* (Baltimore, 1985), 3–11.

[18] *vita* I. 20; *test.*, Morin II, 287, lines 8–10. Cavallin suspected that this and other passages of the *vita* were interpolated by the copyist of codex Paris. B. N. lat. 5295 (or its ancestor), because they are absent from other codices, *Studien*, 100–4. Krusch retains these passages, 456; Morin brackets them, but indicates that C. Lambot viewed them as genuine, Morin II, 294. Whatever the rightful status of this portion of *vita* I. 20, the tax immunity itself is unaffected, since it is also attested in the *testamentum*, although without mention of Alaric or any other indication of date.

its buildings and furnishings, and supporting the clergy. It would have pleased laymen and clerics alike.

In addition to these actions, Caesarius also tried to put into effect a number of the reforms advocated by Augustine, Pomerius, and others. While these reforms may in some ways have been prompted by the political situation in which Caesarius found himself, they can better be explained by his training as a monk and his conception of the bishop's role in the local church. It was Caesarius's view that the bishop's chief responsibility was to ensure the salvation of the people entrusted to him by seeing to it that they led lives worthy of their Christian identity and the kingdom of heaven.[19] This was by no means an exceptional understanding of the bishop's role, but Caesarius acted on it with exceptional enthusiasm. Among the many pastoral strategies he employed to carry out this mission, he most favored monastic forms of "spiritual nourishment," which he believed offered the best route to perfect Christian living, even for ordinary men and women who did not live in monasteries.

In keeping with these beliefs, one of Caesarius's first reforms was to organize a portion of the cathedral clergy of Arles into an ascetic community.[20] Although rare, this was not an entirely novel arrangement:[21] a number of monk-bishops had organized similar communities in their own dioceses, both in the east, where the practice originated,[22] and in the west, where it was introduced by Eusebius of Vercelli in the 360s[23] and made famous by Augustine.[24] Like other fifth- and sixth-century monk-bishops, Fulgentius of Ruspe for example,[25] Caesarius modified his *coenobium* on the clerical community that Augustine had established in Hippo. The

---

[19] *vita* I. 18 is typical; see also *serm.* 1.

[20] It is doubtful that all the cathedral clergy lived in this community. Celibacy (or a living apart from wife and family) would certainly have been a requirement, which not all the clergy would have been willing or able to meet. The deacon Peter, for example, lived with his daughter, who kept house for him (*vita* II. 2). He may have been among those cathedral clergy who did not live in community; alternatively, he may have been attached to a parish church.

[21] See in general, D. König, *Amt und Askese: Priesteramt und Mönchtum bei den lateinischen Kirchenvätern in vorbenediktinischer Zeit* (St. Ottilien, Germany, 1985), 124–203.

[22] E.g., at Rhinocorura in Egypt, Sozomen, *historia ecclesiastica* VI. 31. 11, ed. J. Bidez and G. C. Hansen, *Sozomenus. Kirchengeschichte*, Die Griechischen Christlichen Schriftsteller der ersten Jahrhunderte (Berlin, 1960).

[23] J. T. Lienhard, "Patristic Sermons on Eusebius of Vercelli and their Relation to his Monasticism," *RBen* 87 (1977), 164–72.

[24] Possidius, *vita Augustini* 25; Zumkeller, *Augustine's Ideal*, 40–45; König, *Amt und Askese*, 133–67.   [25] König, *Amt und Askese*, 171–75.

congregatio established by Hilarius of Arles a half century earlier may also have furnished a precedent, although the evidence that the institution involved more than a fraction of the urban clergy is scanty.[26]

In his monastery, Caesarius directed the clerics of Arles to lead a simple common life under his supervision, just as monks or nuns lived together under an abbot or abbess.[27] Clerics took up residence in the bishop's house,[28] from which women were permanently excluded,[29] and shared the bishop's table for dinner and supper,[30] simple meals at which the only silverware used was spoons.[31] On these occasions, they listened to and discussed with Caesarius readings from the scriptures and other edifying works.[32] At night they rose to sing the sequences of psalms known as nocturns (*vita* II. 6).

Caesarius had a number of reasons for organizing the cathedral clergy into an ascetic community. In the first place, by founding a clerical *coenobium* in which he himself acted as superior, he sought to strengthen his control over the clergy, who could now be held to monastic standards of behavior, particularly obedience. Second, he could provide the clerics living under his roof with the kind of systematic religious instruction that only monks had hitherto received, in places like Lérins.[33] Finally, the lifestyle of the cathedral clergy could be held up as a model for the *vita perfecta* to which the Christian community as a whole was expected to aspire.

Caesarius might have hoped that the regular association of these ascetic clerics with a congregation that had previously had contact only with the monks living in the monastery outside of town would make their example all the more persuasive. It was largely to expose his congregation more intensively to monastic spirituality that he directed the clergy to celebrate the canonical hours of Terce, Sext, and None at the cathedral church of St. Stephen, instead of within the bishop's house (*vita* I. 15). When these services were added to Lauds and Vespers, already publicly

---

[26] *vita Hilarii* 10; König, *Amt und Askese,* 207–10.

[27] The analogy is explicitly made at *vita* I. 28, where Caesarius expresses the wish that the church of Arles be adorned not only with *clericorum catervis innumeris,* but also with *virginum choris.*   [28] *vita* I. 62; II. 5–6.

[29] *vita* I. 62, which may also be an interpolation, Cavallin, *Studien,* 102. Cf. Possidius, *vita Augustini* 26.   [30] *vita* I. 62; cf. Augustine, *serm.* 356. 13.

[31] *vita* I. 37; cf. *vita Augustini* 22.

[32] *vita* I. 62; II. 33; cf. *vita Augustini* 22 and *vita Hilarii* 15.

[33] G. Bardy, "Les origines des écoles monastiques en Occident," *Sacris Erudiri* 5 (1953), 86–104, with Riché, *Education and Culture,* 101, n. 3.

celebrated in the city,[34] the divine office – in Caesarius's view, one of the most powerful spiritual instruments available – became completely accessible to laymen, especially penitents, within the city.[35] It was at these services, as well as at Mass, that Caesarius instructed the laity to learn hymns and psalms, which they were to sing like clerics in antiphonal style and in their native languages, some in Greek and others in Latin (*vita* I. 19). Through preaching too Caesarius began to propagate the ideals and values he had acquired in his monastic career. "Demonstrating the impermanence of the present and the eternity of happiness, he attracted some with sweet speech and terrified others with sharper language. Some he corrected with threats, others with charm. Some he restrained from vices through love, others through threat of punishment. He warned some in general terms through proverbs, and reproached others more harshly by calling on God as a witness" (*vita* I. 17). By such measures he sought to restore harmony to a divided city, consolidate his authority over the clergy and people, and carry out his responsibilities as bishop. As it turned out, however, his efforts were not entirely successful.

EXILE AND THE *LEX ROMANA VISIGOTHORUM*

In late 504 or early 505, Licinianus, a notary in the church of Arles, brought a charge of treason against Caesarius. He reported to Alaric II that "since he had been born in [northern] Gaul, the most blessed Caesarius was trying with all his might to bring the territory and city of Arles under Burgundian rule" (*vita* I. 21). It was a plausible charge to make, not only because Caesarius had been born in Burgundian Chalon, but more importantly because, as metropolitan bishop of the province of Arles, he could easily have been suspected of working with the Burgundians to regain control over the eleven dioceses north of the Durance that had been under the *de facto* control of the bishop of Vienne since 475.[36] It was, moreover, a charge that stood some chance of being acted upon, for Alaric had already exiled one bishop of Tours for allegedly conspiring to turn his city over to the Franks, and would

---

[34] Beck, 110–14.

[35] *vita* I. 15. This was not in itself an innovation in Gaul; it had been practiced in Vienne and Orange a generation earlier (Beck, 117), and would shortly be instituted at Tours by Bishop Injuriosus (529–46), Gregory of Tours, *hist.* X. 31. 15.

[36] Schäferdiek, *Die Kirche*, 38.

shortly afterward exile his successor for the same reason.[37] Finally, it was a charge that Licinianus was particularly competent to make. As a notary, he was in an excellent position to reveal (or fabricate) correspondence that might have supported suspicions of treason. Licinianus's motives are not difficult to explain. He was very likely one member of a party of disgruntled clerics and laymen in Arles who, two or three years into Caesarius's episcopacy, still resented his accession to episcopal power ahead of better-qualified and senior candidates, and may, in addition, have objected to the "reforms" in lifestyle that were imposed upon the clergy. The aim of Licinianus and his supporters was therefore to discredit Caesarius in the hope of deposing him and electing a more acceptable bishop. A charge of treason, whether well-founded or not, would have served their intentions well. According to Gregory of Tours, it was just such a charge that drove Quintianus from the see of Rodez between 511 and 515.[38]

Notified of the charge in 505, Alaric decided as a precaution to send Caesarius into exile at Bordeaux, more likely motivated by the political threat he posed than by his anti-Arian polemic (*vita* I. 21).[39] Little is known of his stay there, apart from the fact that he met with Ruricius, bishop of Limoges, as he must have done with a number of laymen and clerics.[40] The *vita* relates only two stories about his captivity: that he preached obedience to secular authorities and condemned the Arian beliefs of the Goths (*vita* I. 23), and that he miraculously saved Bordeaux from a great fire (*vita* I. 22). Neither story helps to explain why he was allowed to return to Arles early in 506.

The most convincing explanation for his release can be found in the internal politics of the Visigothic state.[41] Thanks to good relations with the Burgundians and a peace agreement reached with the Franks in 502, Alaric found it possible in the early years of the sixth century to turn his attention to the consolidation of power over his Gallo-Roman subjects. He first acted to confirm his

---

[37] Ibid., 36. The first bishop was Volusianus, exiled about 495/96; the second was Verus, exiled shortly after the Council of Agde, Gregory of Tours, *hist.* II. 26; X. 31. 8. For the dates, see Pietri, *La Ville de Tours*, 4.

[38] *hist.* II. 36; III. 2; *vita patrum* 4. 1. On Gregory's misinterpretation and misdating of this event, see I. N. Wood, "Gregory of Tours and Clovis," *Revue belge de philologie et d'histoire* 63 (1985), 249–72: 256–57. Whatever its value otherwise, Gregory's account demonstrates that a charge of treason could drive a bishop into permanent exile.

[39] Wood, "Gregory and Clovis," 257, *pace* Rouche, *L'Aquitaine*, 46–48.

[40] Ruricius, *ep.* II. 33.   [41] Schäferdiek, *Die Kirche*, 57–59.

royal authority and Visigothic sovereignty by producing a codification of Roman law for his Roman subjects. According to one plausible theory, this was intended to match a code already in effect for his Gothic subjects, the so-called Codex Euricianus, which may in fact have been the work of Alaric rather than Euric.[42] Charged by Alaric to produce a new code for "the needs of our people," a commission of Gallo-Roman bishops and noblemen[43] met at Aire-sur-l'Adour,[44] 120 km south of Bordeaux, and made excerpts from the Theodosian code, post-Theodosian novels, and other legal writings to create a compendium of Roman law, the *lex Romana Visigothorum* or *breviarium Alarici*.[45] After its approval by bishops and selected provincials,[46] the completed codex was promulgated on February 2, 506,[47] and copies were sent to the counts of the cities for exclusive use in legal cases.[48]

The participation of Gallo-Roman bishops in the making of the *breviarium Alarici*, which reflects their status as spokesmen for the Gallo-Roman population, is evident in the inclusion of laws favorable to the local church, and the exclusion of laws unfavorable to it.[49] For instance, laws upholding the clergy's exemption from municipal duties (XVI. I. I) and the right of accused bishops to be tried by other bishops (XVI. I. 2) were retained, while the law requiring bishops to obtain papal approval before permitting anything to be done "against ancient custom," originally passed against Hilarius of Arles, was excluded.[50] But Alaric's plans for consolidating power over his Gallo-Roman subjects went beyond the favorable treatment of their church in the civil law. At the same time as work on the *breviarium* was progressing, Alaric was planning to sponsor a council of all the Gallo-Roman bishops in his realm, to be held in Agde in September 506. Held under his sponsorship and with his per-

---

[42] H. Nehlsen, "Lex Visigothorum," *Handwörterbuch zur deutschen Rechtsgeschichte*, II (Berlin, 1978), cols. 1966–79: 1967–68, and idem, "Codex Euricianus," *Reallexikon der germanischen Altertumskunde*, 2nd edn., V (Berlin and New York, 1984), 42–47; Wolfram, *Goths*, 194–97. The alternative, that the Codex Euricianus was composed under Euric and was intended for all his subjects, both Roman and Gothic, is advanced by A. d'Ors, "La territorialidad del Derecho de los Visigodos," in *Estudios Visigoticos*, I (Rome and Madrid, 1956), 91–150: 113–17, and Collins, *Early Medieval Spain*, 24–30.

[43] *exemplar auctoritatis*, lines 4–7, *Theodosiani Libri XVI*, ed. T. Mommsen and P. M. Meyer, 2nd edn. (Berlin, 1954), xxxiii–xxxiv.

[44] *subscriptio Aniani*, line 6, *Theodosiani Libri XVI*, xxxv.

[45] *praescriptio breviarii*, line 3, *Theodosiani Libri XVI*, xxxii.

[46] *exemplar auctoritatis*, line 8.   [47] Ibid., line 19.   [48] Ibid., lines 9–14.

[49] Schäferdiek, *Die Kirche*, 45–47.   [50] Valentinian, *nov.* 17.

mission, the council was to symbolize and confirm the integration of the Gallo-Roman church into the Visigothic state. It would represent the first in a series of annual "national" councils, with the next scheduled to be held the following year in Toulouse, to which Hispano-Roman as well as Gallo-Roman bishops would be invited.[51]

Caesarius was kept well informed of preparations for the *breviarium* and the Council of Agde during the winter months of his exile. In fact, he discussed the upcoming council with Ruricius.[52] He was most likely released, because, as bishop of the most influential see in southern Gaul, his support for Alaric's plans was crucial to their success.[53] In return for his cooperation and loyalty, the Visigoths were prepared to offer him an important role in the Visigothic state and in its newly defined *Landeskirche*, a role symbolized at the outset by his precedence over the other metropolitan bishops at the council.

Released under these conditions, Caesarius returned to Arles in the late winter or spring of 506. His arrival was celebrated with the customary ceremonies of *adventus*: a crowd comprising the entire Christian community, both men and women, went out to greet him, carrying candles and crosses, and singing psalms (*vita* I. 26). This was one of the rituals by which the community symbolized its return to consensus after a period of conflict and dissent.[54] The community was also moved to declare its consensus by a bloodier rite: the stoning of Licinianus to death (*vita* I. 24). It is significant that this was not the Roman but the biblical punishment for betrayal and false witness.[55] According to his hagiographers, however, Caesarius intervened to prevent this ritual of communal vengeance. In imitation of Jesus, he pardoned his betrayer, who had earlier been identified with Judas.[56] An abundant shower of

---

[51] Caesarius, *ep.* 3; Agde (506), can. 49.   [52] Ruricius, *ep.* II. 33.

[53] Schäferdiek, *Die Kirche*, 57–59.

[54] On *adventus* as a ceremonial expression of consensus, see S. MacCormack, *Art and Ceremony in Late Antiquity* (Berkeley and Los Angeles, 1981), 18, and in greater detail, "Change and Continuity in Late Antiquity: The Ceremony of Adventus," *Historia* 21 (1972), 721–52.

[55] The *vita* attributes the condemnation of Licinianus to Alaric's orders (*iussio regis*, I. 24). Arnold has pointed out, however, that the customary Roman punishment for such an offense, also included in Alaric's new code, was deportation, exile, and *infamia*, 221. In view of this and other inconsistencies in the *vita*, it is more reasonable to attribute the attempted stoning of Licinianus to the decision of a mob rather than royal command.

[56] For the bishop's traditional role in obtaining pardon for condemned criminals, see E. James, "'Beati pacifici': Bishops and the Law in Sixth-Century Gaul," in *Disputes and*

rain that fell in the midst of a crop-threatening drought was widely interpreted as a demonstration of divine approval for this course of events (*vita* I. 26).

THE COUNCIL OF AGDE

Held in the basilica of St. Andrew, just outside the walls of the port city of Agde, the sessions of the council met late in the summer of 506 and closed on Sunday, September 10.[57] As the signature list demonstrates, Caesarius presided over the council's sessions. His name appears first, followed by the names of the metropolitan bishops of Bordeaux, Eauze, and Bourges, the bishop of the royal capital of Toulouse, the bishop of the host city of Agde, the other bishops in attendance, and the priests and deacons representing absent bishops. In all, twenty-four bishops, eight priests, and two deacons attended the council from the eight Gallic provinces wholly or partly under Visigothic control.[58] Not every diocese in the Visigothic kingdom was represented at Agde. While some absences were due to vacancies or lapses in communication, others were probably due to political disputes. The bishop of Aix, for instance, refused to attend the council or to send a representative because he rejected Caesarius's claim to exercise metropolitan authority over him.[59] Ruricius of Limoges also declined to attend, ostensibly because of illness. Yet, as Caesarius pointed out, had that been the case, he could still have sent a priest or deacon in his place.[60] It is more likely that his absence was due to feelings of offended pride at having received what he considered to be an impolitely late invitation to the council.[61] Despite such absences, the churchmen who met at the council could fairly be said to have represented the hierarchy of the Gallo-Roman church in Alaric's kingdom. It was thus a measure of the success of Alaric's new policy toward the church that the council's resolutions both opened and closed with expressions of gratitude to the king and

---

Settlements: Law and Human Relations in the West, ed. J. Bossy (Cambridge, 1983), 25–46: 33–43.   [57] *CCSL* 148, 189–226.

[58] A full discussion of the signature list can be found in Schäferdiek, *Die Kirche*, 243–47.

[59] Caesarius, *ep.* 8a, Morin II, 14.   [60] Caesarius, *ep.* 3.

[61] Ruricius, *ep.* II. 33; Schäferdiek, *Die Kirche*, 57. The council reacted against such lapses in protocol by passing a law requiring suffragan bishops to attend any synod or ordination to which their metropolitan bishop invited them, unless prevented by grave illness or royal command (can. 35).

prayers for the prosperity of his kingdom, the longevity of his reign, and the welfare of his people.[62] By these signs of favor and their very participation in the council, the assembled bishops registered their approval of the king and his policies.

The primary purpose of the council was pastoral rather than doctrinal or disciplinary. As they proclaimed in the preface to the canons, the bishops met to discuss "the behavior and official responsibilities of clerics and bishops and the needs of congregations."[63] In particular they worked under Caesarius's leadership to establish for the Catholic church in Visigothic Gaul a uniform set of pastoral regulations that would govern the activities of the clergy, the administration of church property, the organization of the liturgy, the behavior of the laity, relations with the Jews, and the organization of monastic life. Towards this end, they placed much emphasis on the confirmation of existing church law. Many of the canons they approved simply restated, with only slight modifications, legislation formulated by earlier Gallic, Spanish, African, and eastern councils, often with an explicit reference to the "authority of the fathers."[64] In this way, they not only reminded clergy and laity to observe frequently neglected or violated provisions of the law, but also drew attention to the continuity of the church with its Gallo-Roman past and to its solidarity with the universal church. But reassurances about the council's conformity to the "authority of the fathers" also made it possible for it to approve a substantial body of new legislation without seeming to depart from church tradition. In aiming at what Ladner has described as "improvement on the basis of a return to original perfection,"[65] the bishops assembled at Agde could justify both the confirmation of existing legislation and the creation of new legislation for changing conditions.[66] At the same time they could proceed with the reform initiatives advanced by Caesarius, not only in the passage of new legislation, but also in the confirmation of existing legislation, since they consciously included under this rubric, in addition to previous councils and

---

[62] *CCSL* 148, 192, 212.

[63] "de disciplina et ordinationibus clericorum atque pontificum vel de ecclesiarum utilitatibus tractaturi," *CCSL* 148, 192. On the history of the concepts of *utilitas populi* and *utilitas ecclesiae*, see M. H. Hoeflich, "The Concept of Utilitas Populi in Early Ecclesiastical Law and Government," *ZRG KA* 67 (1981), 36–74.

[64] can. 4, 7, 22, 24, 35, 36, 43, and 49; Schäferdiek, *Die Kirche*, 60, n. 188.

[65] Ladner, *Idea of Reform*, 48, 298–303.

[66] Cf. the preface to the Council of Orleans (538), *CCSL* 148A, 114.

collections of canons, the *statuta ecclesiae antiqua*, itself a reform document.[67]

The council concerned itself first of all with the behavior of the clergy, since every program of pastoral care depended on their competence. They were to be set apart from the laity by their simple, chaste, and sober way of life. Clerics were advised to wear clothing, shoes, and hair that suited their profession.[68] Priests, deacons, and subdeacons, to whom marriage was forbidden after ordination, were prohibited from attending weddings and other parties where suggestive singing and dancing took place.[69] Priests and deacons who were already married were reminded to refrain from sleeping with their wives.[70] No cleric was to have contact with a woman who was not closely related to him,[71] least of all with a slave or freed woman.[72] All clerics were enjoined to avoid drunkenness.[73]

Regulations for the clergy were also intended to remind them of their subordination to the local bishop. Unlike bishops, priests were prohibited from blessing the congregation or penitents at Mass.[74] They were required to obey all reasonable commands from their bishops,[75] who had the power to admonish or sanction those clerics they judged to be insubordinate.[76] Those who appealed to secular patrons after such rebukes could be excommunicated.[77] In addition, clerics needed their bishop's permission to travel outside the diocese[78] or to bring a case in civil court.[79] In return for faithful service, they were guaranteed stipends from the church.[80]

In keeping with its interest in clerical discipline, the council also reiterated the qualifications for ordination into the clergy and promotion to higher rank. Deacons were required to have attained an age of twenty-five years[81] and priests and bishops thirty

---

[67] "In primo id placuit, ut canones et statuta patrum per ordinem legerentur," can. 1. See further, K. Schäferdiek, "Das sogenannte zweite Konzil von Arles und die älteste Kanonessammlung der arelatenser Kirche," *ZRG KA* 71 (1985), 1–19: 11–13.

[68] can. 20, based on *stat. eccl. ant.*, can. 25 and 26.

[69] can. 39, taken verbatim from Vannes (461/91), can. 11.   [70] can. 9.

[71] can. 10, based on *stat. eccl. ant.*, can. 27. Cf. also II Arles, can. 3, and *brev. Al.* XVI. 1. 6.

[72] can. 11, based on II Arles, can. 4.

[73] can. 41, an abridged version of Vannes (461/91), can. 13.

[74] can. 44, an abrogation of Riez (439), can. 4.

[75] can. 3, based on Vaison (442), can. 7, and *stat. eccl. ant.*, can. 89.   [76] can. 2.

[77] can. 8.   [78] can. 38, based on Vannes (461/91), can. 5.

[79] can. 32, based on Vannes (461/91), can. 9, and II Arles, can. 31.   [80] can. 36.

[81] can. 16, based on III Carthage (397), can. 4, ed. C. Munier, *Concilia Africae A. 345–A. 525, CCSL* 149, 329.

years.[82] Married candidates for these offices were required to live apart from their wives for a specified time before ordination.[83] Penitents[84] and men married twice or married to women married twice[85] were barred from ordination. In their dealings with men already ordained, bishops were cautioned against promoting junior clerics over senior clerics without good reason.[86] Because men who had followed a clerical career path to the episcopacy would in most cases already be older than thirty (by the principle of seniority), and would not normally be still living with their wives, rules about age limits and the separation of clerics from their wives were, where bishops were concerned, mainly intended to discourage the consecration of laymen.

The council's unusually detailed concern for the preservation and accumulation of church property was based on two factors: the church's need for larger revenues to support its expanding pastoral obligations and greater pressure on clerics and laymen to enrich themselves at the expense of an increasingly wealthy institution. As a result, donations to the church were encouraged and protected at every step of the way. Bishops who had no descendants were encouraged to designate the church as their heir.[87] Anything they received either as individuals or as representatives of the church, they were required to use for the church's benefit.[88] Clerics or laymen who interfered with donations or bequests made to the church by their relatives were to be excommunicated.[89] Once the church possessed property, it could be disposed of only under special circumstances. Real property of little value to the church, such as the extremely small fields or vineyards that the custom of partible inheritance regularly created, could be sold, exchanged, or given away by the bishop without any consultation.[90] In this category were also included persistently recalcitrant runaway slaves[91] and small gifts given to pilgrims and clerics.[92] More valuable property, including real estate, houses, slaves, and silver, was not supposed to be alienated under any conditions. When, however, a bishop judged it necessary or useful

[82] can. 17, based on Neocaesarea (314/25), can. 11, ed. J. D. Mansi, *Sacrorum conciliorum nova et amplissima collectio*, II (Florence, 1759), col. 542.   [83] can. 16.

[84] can. 43, based on *stat. eccl. ant.*, can. 84, and Toledo (397/400), can. 2, ed. J. Vives, *Concilios Visigóticos e Hispano-Romanos* (Barcelona and Madrid, 1963), 20.

[85] can. 1, based on Valence (374), can. 1, and II Arles, can. 45.   [86] can. 23.

[87] can. 33.   [88] can. 6.

[89] can. 4, based on Vaison (442), can. 4, and *stat. eccl. ant.*, can. 86.   [90] can. 45.

[91] can. 46.   [92] can. 7.

to the church to sell property or donate revenues in usufruct, he was required to obtain the signatures of two or three fellow bishops to validate the transaction.[93] Slaves who were manumitted by the church could be given a vineyard, field, or house up to a maximum value of twenty *solidi*. Anything given in excess of this amount was to be repaid by the freedman at the death of the bishop who had manumitted him.[94] For their part, bishops and clerics, whether they were attached to the cathedral or some other parish, were not permitted to sell or give away any article of church property. If they did so, they were excommunicated and required to reimburse the church to the best of their ability.[95] The same penalties were assessed against clerics who suppressed, lost, or gave away deeds or other documents affirming the church's ownership of property and thereby caused a loss of church property.[96] Petty thefts of church property by clerics were punished by a lighter penalty.[97]

Caesarius's influence on the council is particularly evident in its liturgical provisions. His first concern was the enforcement of uniform liturgical practices throughout the kingdom.[98] All "sons of the church" (a favorite phrase of Caesarius's[99]) were to follow the Roman custom of fasting on Saturdays in Lent rather than the Gallic custom that treated Saturdays and Sundays alike;[100] all churches were required to transmit the creed to baptismal candidates on Palm Sunday, a Milanese custom;[101] all laymen were required to take communion on the feasts of Christmas, Easter, and Pentecost;[102] and a uniform order of service was established for Matins and Vespers.[103] His second concern was the establishment of episcopal control over all aspects of public worship. Newly established altars were to be blessed by the bishop as well as consecrated with oil;[104] only the bishop was permitted to bless the congregation or penitents in church[105] and to preside over the ritual of public repentance;[106] and no one was permitted to leave Mass on Sunday before the bishop gave his final

---

[93] can. 7, reversing the requirement in *stat. eccl. ant.*, can. 50 that the bishop obtain the permission of his clerical subordinates before alienating property. [94] can. 7.

[95] can. 22, based on the *canones in causa Apiarii*, Carthage (419), can. 39, *CCSL* 149, 129.

[96] can. 26.

[97] can. 5. This was *communio peregrina*, by which the benefits accorded to local clerics were reduced to the level allocated to visiting clerics, Morin II, 38.

[98] Schäferdiek, *Die Kirche*, 65–66.   [99] *serm.* 134. 3; 201. 1; 230. 5.

[100] can. 12.   [101] can. 13; cf. Schäferdiek, *Die Kirche*, 65, n. 220.   [102] can. 18.

[103] can. 30.   [104] can. 14.   [105] can. 44, repealing Riez (439), can. 4.

[106] can. 15.

blessing.[107] Most significantly, while rural dwellers were permitted to attend Mass on most Sundays and feasts in private chapels (*oratoria*), they were required on the feasts of Easter, Christmas, Epiphany, the Ascension, Pentecost, and John the Baptist to attend Mass in churches under the bishop's direct control, that is, the cathedral or parish churches.[108]

The council also sought to confirm the bishop's authority over the private affairs of the laity. Men who wished to divorce their wives on the grounds of infidelity (*fornicationis causa*, Mt. 5: 32) were required to obtain a judgment against them by an episcopal commission before the marriage could be dissolved.[109] Laymen involved in long-standing feuds were to be censured by bishops for refusing reconciliation with their enemies and excommunicated if they did not subsequently make peace.[110] In addition, regulations were passed to excommunicate murderers and perjurers,[111] those guilty of malicious prosecution against the church or a cleric,[112] and those who engaged in augury.[113] Finally, the council confirmed earlier laws protecting freedmen[114] and abandoned children.[115]

Like the compilers of the *breviarium Alarici*, the bishops assembled at the council refrained from anti-Arian but not anti-Jewish polemic.[116] To avoid invidious comparisons between Christian and Jewish dietary customs, Christians were warned against eating with Jews.[117] In addition, because they were thought particularly liable to apostatize, Jews wishing to convert to Christianity were required to undergo a lengthier catechumenate than other converts before baptism.[118]

The final area of the council's interest was the regulation of monastic life. Legislation was passed to tighten the control of abbots over their monks by setting the conditions under which

---

[107] can. 47.   [108] can. 21.

[109] can. 25, providing a role for the bishop in the *probatio adulterii* mandated by Vannes (461/91), can. 2.

[110] can. 31, giving bishops a more explicit role than they had in the regulations of II Arles, can. 50.   [111] can. 37, taken verbatim from Vannes (461/91), can. 1.

[112] can. 32.   [113] can. 42, taken almost verbatim from Vannes (461/91), can. 16.

[114] can. 29, based on Nîmes (394/96), can. 7.

[115] can. 24, based on Vaison (442), can. 9.   [116] *brev. Al.* XVI. 3, 4.

[117] can. 40, taken verbatim from Vannes (461/91), can. 12, and widened – significantly – to include laymen as well as clerics. Cf. Caesarius, *sermo de esca vel potu Iudaeorum prohibendis*, Morin I, 918 (= *CCSL* 104, 967). See also B. Blumenkranz, "'Iudaeorum convivia' à propos du concile de Vannes (465), c. 12," in *Etudes d'histoire du droit canonique dédiées à Gabriel le Bras*, II (Paris, 1965), 1055–58.   [118] can. 34.

monks could enter the clergy,[119] move from one monastery to another,[120] or set themselves up as hermits.[121] In addition the council sought to strengthen the bishop's control over monks and monastic communities by requiring his permission for new monasteries,[122] and prohibiting abbots from controlling more than one monastery.[123] Finally, the council confirmed a law omitted from Alaric's *breviarium* that set a minimum age for the veiling of nuns,[124] and required women's monasteries to be built at a distance from men's monasteries.[125]

Like all church legislation, the canons passed by the Council of Agde represented the expression of an ideology more than an enforceable program of law. Nonetheless, the council represented an important and influential step in Caesarius's reform program.[126] It is true that he did not succeed in promoting the more radical pastoral reforms that he was beginning to put into effect in Arles, such as voluntary poverty, a common life, and high standards of personal spirituality for the clergy. The reasons are not difficult to discern. Decisions at Agde, as at most church councils, were reached through a process of negotiation and compromise that aimed at universal agreement rather than the endorsement of any one bishop's views.[127] Despite his position of leadership, Caesarius was still only one among many bishops at the conference. Nor did his metropolitan status contribute much to his power, since he had only entered the position a short time before and had not had time to build up a network of support through the ordination of suffragan bishops. Without widespread support from his suffragans and other colleagues, Caesarius could not carry reforms that many bishops regarded as unacceptable. Nonetheless, he did manage to win approval for a variety of important pastoral measures. We cannot determine with certainty which canons Caesarius pro-

---

[119] can. 27.   [120] can. 27, based on Angers (453), can. 8.
[121] can. 38, taken verbatim from Vannes (461/91), can. 7.   [122] can. 27.
[123] Agde, can. 38, taken verbatim from Vannes (461/91), can. 8.
[124] Agde, can. 19; Zaragoza (380), can. 8, *Concilios Visigóticos*, 16. See Schäferdiek, *Die Kirche*, 61, n. 191.   [125] can. 28.
[126] Agde was widely cited by later councils, including the Frankish national council of 511 and the Burgundian council of 517, Arnold, 231–39.
[127] For an expression of this ideology of *consensus*, see the preface to the Council of Vannes (461/91): "ut communis ex multorum collatione tractatus, consentiente in Christo spiritu, multarum sententiarum auctoritate firmetur: ne singulorum pro arbitrii sui qualitate definitio aut imperitiae decipiatur errore, aut tumore praesumptionis uel iracundiae deprauetur, et dum unusquisque sine fratrum collatione suo tantum credit arbitrio, statuat quod merito possit omnibus displicere," *CCSL* 148, 150–51. In addition, see Mathisen, *Ecclesiastical Factionalism*, 111, n. 96.

moted at the council, but an interesting pattern emerges from an examination of the council's new legislation, for it is precisely in these canons that themes characteristic of Caesarius's sermons and pastoral activity stand out: the promotion of monasticism,[128] the christianization of the peasantry,[129] the maintenance of proper decorum in public worship,[130] and the use by clerics of personal and ecclesiastical property for the sole benefit of the church.[131] Of particular interest among this group, in view of Caesarius's political problems of 505/6, are canon 2, which affirms the bishop's power to correct insubordinate clerics, and canon 32, which calls for the excommunication of laymen guilty of malicious prosecution against a cleric. These canons were clearly intended to protect bishops and other clerics from the kind of political attack that had recently sent Caesarius into exile. It is likely that Caesarius supported their confirmation by the council.

THE MONASTERY FOR WOMEN AND THE SIEGE OF ARLES

Several months after he returned from Bordeaux, and probably after the Council of Agde as well, Caesarius began to erect a monastery for women just outside the city walls of Arles (*vita* 1. 28). Thus began his involvement with an institution that would preoccupy him for the rest his life. The monastery was built for a small group of ascetic women living under the spiritual direction of Caesarius's sister Caesaria, probably in the kind of household monastery typical of female asceticism at this time.[132] That such a group existed before the official opening of the monastery in 512 can be inferred from a letter written by Caesarius to his sister "and her whole community."[133] The letter clearly predates the promulgation of Caesarius's *regula virginum*, issued at the opening of the monastery, because despite its persistent warnings against excessive "familiarity" with outsiders, particularly men, the letter makes no mention of the elaborate cloister regulations that characterized Caesarius's rule.[134] The women's community can be dated even earlier – before 508 – if we make the reasonable assumption that Caesarius would not have used a metaphor upholding the integrity of the church plate (*ep.* 21. 5) at any point after 508, when he

---

[128] can. 27, 28. [129] can. 18, 21. [130] can. 47. [131] can. 6, 7, 33.
[132] P. Brown, *The Body and Society: Men, Women, and Sexual Renunciation in Early Christianity* (New York, 1988), 263–65. [133] *ep.* 21, Morin II, 134–44.
[134] de Vogüé and Courreau, 283, although I would disagree with the date.

himself melted down altar vessels for the redemption of captives.[135] The letter probably dates therefore to late 506/early 507
when Caesarius commenced work on the monastery. Although
the monastery's exact location is unknown, it appears to have been
situated where it could be seen from the walls,[136] probably to the
south of the city, the only extensive suburban area available for
building. Benoit suggested that the structure was located on the
site of the medieval chapel of Saint-Césaire-le-Vieux in the
Alyscamps cemetery.[137] In this location, across the river and
upstream from the men's monastery, the institution would have
satisfied the condition laid out in the Council of Agde that
women's monasteries be founded at some distance (*longius*) from
men's monasteries.[138] It would also have had the advantage of
proximity to one of the holiest sites in the city, the grave of St.
Genesius.

Caesarius's decision to found a monastery in concert with his
sister was probably motivated by a variety of considerations.
Because there was as yet no women's monastery in Arles, the
foundation of such an institution allowed Caesarius, perhaps in
conscious imitation of Augustine,[139] to provide women, particularly the daughters of aristocratic households, with the same
opportunities for monastic life as he had long sought to promote
for men. Moreover, the new monastery could be made to enhance
the city's prestige by functioning as a tangible symbol of its
prosperity and status. In addition, the institution could be expected
to provide the city and its citizens with much-needed divine
protection, for as members of a "professional society of prayer,"[140]
the nuns who lived there would be obligated to pray both for their
founder[141] and for the safety of the entire community as well.[142]

---

[135] *infra*, p. 114.   [136] "Dumque laborem...everti videret et destrui," *vita* I. 28.
[137] Benoit, *Les Cimetières*, 53.   [138] Agde (506), can. 28.
[139] On Augustine's monasteries for women in Hippo, see Zumkeller, *Augustine's Ideal*,
45–46.   [140] J. M. Wallace-Hadrill, *The Frankish Church* (Oxford, 1983), 58.
[141] Caesarius mentions this obligation in the preface to his *regula virginum*: "I ask you,
consecrated virgins...that...you beg by your holy prayers to have me made a
companion of your journey, so that when you happily enter the kingdom with the holy
and wise virgins, you may, by your petitions, obtain for me that I not remain outside
with the foolish," *reg. virg.* I, trans. adapted from M. M. McCarthy, *The Rule for Nuns
of St. Caesarius of Arles* (Washington, D.C., 1960).
[142] "The man of God...formulated the idea that the church of Arles should be adorned
and the city protected not only by countless troops of clergy, but also by choirs of
virgins," *vita* I. 28. On the symbolic value of such "choirs of virgins" for cities, see
Brown, *The Body and Society*, 271: "They stood for all that was most holy and enduring
in the heart of the settled land."

The timing of the project, however, suggests that the founding of a nunnery in the city was also calculated to provide Caesarius with political advantages. By endowing the city with so highly esteemed an institution, Caesarius was acting in his capacity as chief patron of the Christian community, and especially of the families that had entrusted their women to him. Even though he spent church wealth rather than his own wealth on the project, Caesarius could, like any patron, expect his generosity to be rewarded by increased loyalty and support from his clients. In addition, he could expect his legitimate power as bishop to be confirmed, for as the Council of Agde had made clear, only bishops had the power to authorize the construction of monasteries within their dioceses.[143] Finally, he could expect the monastery to serve as an architectural focal point for consensus and civic unity in much the same way as his *adventus* had served as a ceremonial focal point for consensus. For a bishop who had only recently returned from exile and, as it turned out, still had powerful enemies in the city, these would not have been negligible assets.

The outbreak in 507 of a war between the Visigoths and an alliance of Franks and Burgundians soon put a halt to these plans. The war began with acts of aggression by Clovis, who was probably motivated by a desire for political, economic, and territorial gains rather than by the zeal of a newly converted Catholic to liberate the Roman population of Gaul from the Arians.[144] After a victory over the Alamanni in 506 and the acquisition of lands along the upper Danube in modern Bavaria,[145] Clovis turned his attention to the riches of Aquitaine, despite attempts by Theoderic to prevent the conflict.[146] In late summer of 507, the Visigoths under Alaric met Clovis near Poitiers.[147] According to Procopius, Alaric's troops forced him to fight before reinforcements could arrive from Theoderic, whose forces had been tied down in Italy by an imperial blockade.[148] The battle, which took place at Vouillé (or Voulon),[149] resulted in total Frankish victory.[150] Alaric was killed along with many Gallo-

---

[143] can. 27. [144] Wood, "Gregory and Clovis," 262–64.

[145] Cassiodorus, *var.* II. 41; James, *Franks*, 84–85. [146] Cassiodorus, *var.* III. 1–4.

[147] Gregory of Tours, *hist.* II. 37.

[148] Procopius, *de bellis* v. 12. 39; Marcellinus Comes, *chronicon* a. 508, ed. T. Mommsen, *MGH AA*, XI, 97.

[149] For Vouillé, see A. Longnon, *Géographie de la Gaule au VIᵉ siècle* (Paris, 1878), 576–87. For Voulon, see R. A. Gerberding, *The Rise of the Carolingians and the Liber Historiae Francorum* (Oxford, 1987), 41. [150] Gregory of Tours, *hist.* II. 37.

Roman nobles fighting on his side.[151] In 508, after wintering in Bordeaux, the Franks took the city of Toulouse and its Visigothic treasury,[152] but failed to capture Carcassonne, location of another Visigothic treasury, which included the spoils taken by Alaric I from the sack of Rome.[153] Clovis then decided to return to Paris by way of Tours, taking Angoulême on his way.[154]

In the meantime, probably late in 507, the Burgundians drove south, accompanied by a detachment of Franks. Tributary to Clovis since 500,[155] they may have joined his alliance reluctantly.[156] Their targets were Narbonne[157] and Arles, which they besieged.[158] With the assistance of a Gothic garrison, the Arlésiens resisted fiercely over the winter of 507/8. During the siege, the monastery for women, which had already reached an advanced stage of completion, was largely destroyed by the invaders (*vita* I. 28), who probably intended to use its building materials in their siege works.[159] It may well have been at this time that Caesaria and her sisters were sent for safekeeping to the monastery in Marseille – probably Cassian's monastery for women[160] – from which they were later recalled in 512 (*vita* I. 35).

The destruction of his monastery disturbed Caesarius deeply, but he soon found himself facing a more immediate and familiar problem. One night, a member of his clergy, who also happened to be a relative from Chalon, lowered himself over the wall and fled to the enemy camp (*vita* I. 29). Although the man's motives were described in the *vita* as purely personal ("fear of captivity" and "the capriciousness of youth"), he was widely suspected by the population of being an emissary sent by Caesarius to betray Arles to the Burgundians. Residual doubts about Caesarius's loyalty only served to reinforce these suspicions. A riot broke out among the population (*popularium seditione*), in which Jews were said to have played a prominent part,[161] and the Goths arrested Caesarius and imprisoned him in the palace. As they saw it, their first obligation was to move this powerful and dangerous adversary to a place where he could not endanger Gothic control over the city. Accordingly, they decided to smuggle Caesarius out

[151] Gregory of Tours, *hist.* II. 37.   [152] Gregory of Tours, *hist.* II. 37.
[153] Procopius, *de bellis* V. 12. 41–42.   [154] Gregory of Tours, *hist.* II. 37.
[155] Gregory of Tours, *hist.* II. 32–33.   [156] Wood, "Avitus of Vienne," 170.
[157] Isidore, *historia Gothorum* 37, *MGH AA*, XI, 282.
[158] "Etenim obsidentibus Francis ac Burgundionibus civitatem," *vita* I. 28.
[159] Arnold, 246–47.   [160] G. de Plinval, "Césarie," *DHGE* XII (1953), col. 213.
[161] *vita* I. 29.

of the city by night in a *dromo*, a fast troop ship, and, in the words of the *vita*, "either drown him at night in the depths of the Rhône or keep him prisoner in Beaucaire," located a few miles upstream (*vita* I. 29). The Burgundian blockade of the Rhône, however, was so thorough that the Goths found it impossible to launch the vessel. Instead, they took Caesarius back to the palace, and refused to disclose his whereabouts (*vita* I. 30). "This turn of events," according to *vita* I. 31, "pleased the devil and delighted the Jews, who were spewing forth shameful charges against our people everywhere, without any regard for their own treachery."

The purpose of the anti-Jewish polemic suffusing this account becomes clear when we examine the circumstances in which Caesarius was said to have been released. The story deserves to be quoted in full:

One night, one of the Jewish troops, stationed along the part of the city wall that the Jews happened to be responsible for guarding, tied a letter to a stone and threw it at the enemy, pretending to strike them. In the letter he indicated his name and religion, and invited them to set their scaling ladders at night at the place the Jews guarded, provided that in return for the favor he offered, no Jew in the city should suffer captivity or plundering. But in the morning, when the enemy had retreated a little way from the wall, some of the citizens went outside the protecting wall among the rubble, as they were accustomed to do. On finding the letter they brought it back inside and revealed its contents to everyone in the forum. Soon the traitor was brought forth, convicted, and punished. Then indeed the cruelty of the Jews that was savage to God and hateful to men was finally and openly destroyed. Soon too our Daniel, that is holy Caesarius, was led out of the lion's den, and the accusation of the satraps was disproved (cf. Dn. 6: 23–24).

As several commentators have pointed out, there are at least two serious problems with the credibility of this account.[162] First, the explicit treachery of the letter and the circumstances of its discovery are altogether suspicious. It is difficult to believe that the author of a letter like this would include so much incriminating information about himself and his plans, and then send the missive in such a way that it could be easily intercepted. It is even more difficult to believe that the Jews of Arles, who had reportedly attacked Caesarius for treasonable acts only a short time before,

---

[162] I. Lévi, "Saint Césaire et les Juifs d'Arles," *Revue des études juives* 30 (1895), 295–98: 296–97; J. Juster, *Les Juifs dans l'empire romain*, II (Paris, 1914), 213; S. Katz, *The Jews in the Visigothic and Frankish Kingdoms of Spain and Gaul* (Cambridge, Mass., 1937), 114–15.

could so quickly and completely have abandoned their loyalty to the Goths. Second, it is unclear exactly how a diversion of suspicion away from Caesarius and toward the Jews could have convinced the Goths to release Caesarius. The guilt of one party did not entail the innocence of the other. Why did the Goths not simply treat the two cases as entirely separate attempts by members of the local population to betray their city to the Burgundians?

One solution to these problems is to cast doubt on the veracity of the entire account by stressing the hagiographical purpose for which it was composed. Thus, in Katz's judgment, "the account as related by Cyprianus of Toulon, a panegyrist of Caesarius, must be accepted with caution ... Little credence can be given to any of the accounts of treason, whether ascribed to Caesarius or to the Jews of Arles."[163] But an alternative to rejecting the historicity of the whole of *vita* I. 29–31 is to treat the story as a highly selective, incomplete, and tendentious account of events that nevertheless has a core of truth at its center. The story's inconsistencies can then be resolved by making two reasonable assumptions. The first assumption is that the letter thrown over the walls was not written by a Jew at all but was forged by one of Caesarius's supporters.[164] This would explain the letter's incriminating details, the ease with which it was discovered, and the apparent contradiction between Jewish loyalty to the Goths in *vita* I. 29 and their disloyalty in *vita* I. 31. The second assumption is that the authors of the *vita* deliberately understated the role of Catholic Christians in the "sedition of the population" that broke out when the defection of Caesarius's relative was announced. By simply failing to report the full extent of opposition to Caesarius from his own congregation, his hagiographers could create the impression that it was only religious outsiders, that is Jews and Arian Christians, who condemned the bishop's actions, thus leaving the consensus of the Catholics intact to all appearances.

If we accept these assumptions, a possible connection between an accusation of treason against the Jews and Caesarius's release suggests itself. The forged letter was not intended for the Goths but for Catholic Gallo-Romans. Its purpose was to stir up hatred against the Jews as a means of consolidating support for Caesarius, which had been seriously weakened by the charges against him.[165]

[163] Katz, *The Jews*, 115; see also Lévi, "Saint Césaire," 296.
[164] Juster, *Les Juifs*, II, 213.
[165] J. Parkes, *The Conflict of the Church and the Synagogue* (New York, 1961), 321.

With the alleged treachery of the city's Jewish minority as a rallying point, an angry Christian population could be more easily manipulated into demonstrations of support in favor of their bishop's innocence. Because they badly needed citizen manpower for the defense of the city, the Goths would eventually have to have given in to the Catholic majority rather than the Jewish minority, even if they themselves still doubted Caesarius's innocence. In the end, the Visigoths released Caesarius from captivity. Although his standing had been badly shaken by events, he remained in power and, what is more, in a position to take advantage of an imminent change in the political landscape, which made the Ostrogoths masters of Provence. How Caesarius and his programs of church reform and christianization fared under their control is the subject of the next chapter.

Chapter 5

THE OSTROGOTHIC PEACE

THE RELIEF OF ARLES

Arles suffered through the siege for most of 508. Finally, in the summer of 508, freed from the pressure of a Byzantine blockade, Theoderic sent out a force of soldiers under the command of Ibba to relieve the city.[1] The army arrived in the vicinity of Arles sometime in the autumn, and defeated the Burgundians and Franks in a great battle, at which, according to Jordanes' inflated estimate, 30,000 Franks perished.[2] By the end of 508, having lifted the siege of Arles,[3] Ibba left with his army to continue operations against the Burgundians. The following year he drove them out of Narbonne,[4] and with the aid of another Ostrogothic army in the east,[5] forced them to retreat to the Durance, their former boundary with the Visigoths. Theoderic then incorporated the territory east of the Rhône and south of the Durance as the praetorian prefecture of the Gauls, abolished by the Visigoths in 476/77. The decision was symbolic as well as practical. In reestablishing the prefecture, Theoderic signaled his intention to save the region from the "barbarians" and reincorporate it into the "Roman" empire, as he had restored it.[6] In 510/11 he appointed as prefect Petrus Marcellinus Felix Liberius, a patrician and distinguished Roman official, who had most recently served as praetorian prefect of Italy (493/4–500).[7]

---

[1] Jordanes, *Getica* 302; Cassiodorus, *chronica*, a. 508, *MGH AA*, XI, 160. The mobilization date was set for June 24, 508, Cassiodorus, *var.* I. 24.

[2] Jordanes, *Getica* 302; Cassiodorus, *var.* VIII. 10. 6; Schmidt, *Ostgermanen*, 157, n. 3.

[3] For the date, see Mommsen, *MGH AA*, XII, xxxii, and W. Levison, "Zur Geschichte des Frankenkönigs Chlodowech," *Bonner Jahrbücher* 103 (1898), 42–86: 54.

[4] Cassiodorus, *var.* IV. 17.   [5] Schmidt, *Ostgermanen*, 157.

[6] Cassiodorus, *var.* III. 17, 38, 43.

[7] *PLRE* II, 677–681; J. O'Donnell, "Liberius the Patrician," *Traditio* 37 (1981), 31–72. Between 508 and 510 the conquered territory was administered by Gemellus, a *vicarius* reporting to the prefect of Italy (Cassiodorus, *var.* III. 16, 17; O'Donnell, "Liberius," 44; *PLRE* II, 499–500).

As before 476, the seat of the prefecture as well as of the vicariate was located at Arles. Provincial governors were not established, however, since the prefecture was so small.[8] Instead, Gothic counts were set over cities or groups of cities, whose internal governance remained about the same as under the Visigoths.[9] Gothic troops, under the command of military counts, were stationed in the cities and rural garrisons.[10] A string of forts along the Durance protected the territory from attack by the Burgundians,[11] who under Gundobad, and especially Sigismund, pursued an openly pro-Byzantine foreign policy.[12] The border with the Visigothic kingdom, on the other hand, was left unfortified, for in 511 Theoderic became its king as well, acting as regent for Alaric's ten-year-old son, his grandson, Amalaric. He did so after deposing the Visigoths' own choice of a king, Alaric's illegitimate son Gesalec, who was killed *c.* 513 "across the Durance."[13] It may have been in a skirmish with Visigothic supporters of Gesalec around this time that Liberius was ambushed and gravely wounded in the vicinity of Saint-Gabriel (*vita* II. 10–12).

With their consolidation of control over Provence, the Ostrogoths established a stable political framework in the region that lasted until 536, when the Franks took their place. It was during this period, largely as a result of his own political skills and a favorable secular and ecclesiastical political climate, that Caesarius achieved his greatest successes as a pastor and reformer, above all, the permanent refounding of his monastery for women and the convening of the Councils of Arles (524), Carpentras (527), Orange (529), and Vaison (529). Because specific aspects of Caesarius's pastoral work are covered in more detail in the following chapters (6, 7, 8), we shall concentrate in this chapter on the sequence of local and regional political events, both secular and ecclesiastical, that shaped his pastoral activities during this period. We shall pay particular attention to a subject of intrinsic political and religious interest, namely Caesarius's activity as a patron, especially on behalf of prisoners of war and the monastery for women. The political narrative of this chapter will proceed as far as 529, with Caesarius's success at the Council of Vaison, and will

---

[8] Schmidt, *Ostgermanen*, 347.
[9] Wolfram, *Goths*, 291.
[10] Schmidt, *Ostgermanen*, 346–47.
[11] Cassiodorus, *var.* III. 41.
[12] Wolfram, *Goths*, 312.
[13] Isidore, *historia Gothorum* 38, *MGH AA*, XI, 282; *chronicorum Caesaraugustanorum reliquiae*, a. 513, *MGH AA*, XI, 223.

resume in Chapter 9, with the loss of his political influence that gradually followed in the 530s.

THE AFTERMATH OF WAR AND THE RANSOMING OF CAPTIVES

As soon as he was able, Caesarius turned his attention to the pressing issues of post-war recovery and reconstruction. The walled city itself had not been taken (*vita* I. 34), but the surrounding countryside had been devastated: food supplies were exhausted and large numbers of peasants had been killed, enslaved, and driven into exile. In a sermon adapted from Quodvultdeus of Carthage, and probably delivered after the lifting of the siege, Caesarius recalled the miseries war had brought:

Since dire calamity struck our eyes at the time of the siege, and now afflicts them in time of death, and scarcely anyone survives to bury the dead, consider also the evils we have borne through the just judgment of God, when whole provinces were led into captivity, mothers of families were abducted, pregnant women were carried off, little children were torn from their arms and thrown into the road, half-dead, and nurses were not permitted to keep living children or to bury the dead. On all sides there was great agony and grief. (*serm.* 70. 2)

Rural areas suffered the greatest losses. In a sermon delivered to a rural congregation after 508, Caesarius compared the soul of the sinner to the devastated countryside.

This is the reason, brothers, why we suffer frequent tribulations and distress: God somehow retaliates. We are unwilling to love our own souls, which he loves; and he permits the *villa* that we love to perish. For just as our countryside has been left a wasteland because of the enemy, so our souls have been left in ruins for a long time because of many vices and sins. Therefore, because we did not love the souls that God loves, we lost everything that we loved in this world. (*serm.* 6. 6)

The afflictions of war also produced urgent requests for food, clothing, and shelter, to which Caesarius responded according to his patronal obligations (*vita* I. 20, 45; II. 8–9). Theoderic in turn, writing in the winter of 508/9, promised money for rebuilding the city walls and shipments of food from Italy as soon as the sailing season reopened in the spring.[14] In addition, in 510 he ordered a

---

[14] Cassiodorus, *var.* III. 44. On sources of food, see *var.* IV. 5, 7.

remission of taxes for the fourth indiction (September 1, 510–
August 31, 511) on behalf of "the people of Arles who, holding
out for our side, endured the impoverishment of a glorious
siege."[15]

The inhabitants of Arles and its countryside were not, however,
the only victims of the war.[16] One consequence of the Ostrogothic
victory was the enslavement of a great number of Frankish and
Burgundian warriors, who were brought back to the city and
interned in basilicas and other public buildings to await ransom
from captivity or sale into slavery.[17] Although they were enemies
of the city, and in most cases either Arian Burgundians or pagan
Franks,[18] Caesarius decided to use church wealth to ransom them
from captivity. He first melted down the silver table service that
Aeonius had left for the bishop's use. He then sold off the church's
censers, chalices, patens, and even the silver ornaments that
decorated the cathedral (*vita* I. 32). Finally, he encouraged his
congregation to contribute alms for the purpose.[19]

These actions raised fierce objections in Arles, especially among
the clergy. In the first place, many of the objects sold by Caesarius
were offerings that the pious had left to the church for the salvation
of their souls, and it was not thought proper to alienate, as it were,
the grounds of their salvation.[20] As a prefect's decree put the
matter in 483, "It is wrongful and sacrilegious that the goods
which a man has, for the sake of the poor, bestowed on the
venerable church on behalf of his own salvation or the eternal rest
of the souls of his family should be transferred to another by those
particularly entrusted with protecting it."[21] Moreover, in declining to obtain their consent for the alienation of property,
Caesarius had given the entire clergy an insulting reminder of their
lack of authority over church property, as confirmed at the
Council of Agde.[22] Finally, he had performed these intolerable

---

[15] Cassiodorus, *var.* III. 32.
[16] On Theoderic's help for the region in general, see Cassiodorus, *var.* III. 40, 42.
[17] *vita* I. 32; for a more detailed discussion, see W. Klingshirn, "Charity and Power: Caesarius of Arles and the Ransoming of Captives in Sub-Roman Gaul," *JRS* 75 (1985), 183–203.
[18] Ibid., 190. Arguments for a late (post-507) dating of Clovis's baptism and the conversion of his warriors can be found in Wood, "Gregory and Clovis" and James, *Franks*, 121–29.   [19] Caesarius, *serm.* 30. 4, 6; 35. 4; 39. 1; 146. 2.
[20] In addition to the references in Klingshirn, "Charity and Power," 185, n. 18, see Caesarius, *ep.* 21. 5.   [21] Rome (502), *MGH AA*, XII, 446–47.
[22] *supra*, p. 101, n. 93.

actions for the benefit, not of Catholics, Romans, and fellow citizens, but pagans, barbarians, and enemies.

Caesarius defended himself from these charges with a variety of arguments. To those who objected to his use of church wealth, particularly precious objects that had been donated to the church, he answered with arguments drawn largely from Ambrose's *de officiis ministrorum*.[23] He pointed out that Jesus had commanded his apostles not to possess gold or silver (Mt. 10:9), and that he had at the Last Supper dipped his bread into a ceramic dish and not a silver cup (Mt. 26:23).[24] He further asserted that since Jesus had given his life for the redemption of all mankind from sin, it was proper to use gifts dedicated to him for the redemption of individual men from captivity (*vita* I. 33). To those who objected to the ransoming of Arians and pagans, he argued that since Christ's work of salvation and liberation was meant to embrace all "rational men," man's work should be similarly universal in scope. More significantly, he suggested that those who were not ransomed might be permanently lost to the Catholic church, since they could easily be converted to Arian Christianity or Judaism by those who purchased them as slaves (*vita* I. 32). To those, finally, who objected to his ransoming of enemies, the most serious charge of all, he cited the biblical injunction that one should treat others as one would like to be treated oneself, and emphasized, as he did in many sermons, the need to love even one's enemies.[25]

The mere fact that Caesarius needed to elaborate these arguments at all indicates that his control of church property was neither as absolute nor as secure as it sometimes seemed, and could easily be challenged by critics. Caesarius was even more exposed to such criticisms than other bishops because he essentially had no wealth of his own to distribute. He therefore had to rely heavily on the resources of others for his acts of charity and patronage. In part he succeeded in soliciting necessities from outsiders. For instance, at some point between 508 and 516, when he did not have enough food to feed the captives and newly redeemed prisoners whom he supported in Arles, the Burgundian kings Gundobad and Sigismund sent three cargo ships of grain down the Rhône, probably in gratitude for Caesarius's efforts to redeem Burgundian soldiers from captivity (*vita* II. 8–9). But for the most part, Caesarius relied

---

[23] *de officiis ministrorum* II. xxviii. 136–43, *PL* 16: 139–42.   [24] *vita* I. 32.
[25] Klingshirn, "Charity and Power," 191.

on the resources of his own church. In the long run this meant relying on members of the congregation, for it was ultimately they who replenished the depleted wealth of the church. This reliance on the congregation, in turn, helps to explain the remarkably frequent references to almsgiving and tithes in Caesarius's sermons,[26] which do not so much reflect an extraordinary interest in assisting the poor as they do an extraordinary need for the means with which to assist them.

But Caesarius's reliance on his congregation for the fulfillment of his charitable ambitions should not necessarily be regarded as a weakness. By enlisting the assistance of his people in the ransoming of captives, Caesarius could increase their attentiveness to the pastoral message that his actions were meant to convey. It was a message with multiple levels of significance. In the first place, Caesarius could be seen to have practiced a form of patronage that had become, by the sixth century, one of the bishop's foremost responsibilities, widely praised in episcopal panegyric.[27] In so doing he too could win praise for his actions, thereby enhancing his personal prestige. Moreover, his actions could function as an example to others of fundamental Christian virtues such as charity, hospitality, and love of enemies. Most broadly of all, the redemption of captives could be employed as a mechanism for defining the bishop's true congregation. For in this case the recipients of the bishop's patronage were not the citizens of Arles or the members of the Catholic church in Arles. They were instead enemies and *infideles*, political and religious outsiders, who deserved redemption not only because they were fellow human beings, but more importantly because they were potential members of the *civitas dei*. Caesarius's interest in converting these captives was not only theoretical. The *vita* claims that the ransoming of captives actually resulted in conversions to the Catholic faith: "He embellished and protected the church by this action; he did not disfigure it. He made the womb of the mother open up with children; he did not cause it to be harmed" (*vita* I. 33). This is highly symbolic language, but its general meaning is clear. The "mother" represents the church,[28] and the "womb"

---

[26] For a discussion of Caesarius's encouragement of almsgiving, see A.-M. Abel, "La pauvreté dans la pensée et la pastorale de saint Césaire d'Arles," in *Etudes sur l'histoire de la pauvreté (Moyen âge–XVIᵉ siècle)*, ed. M. Mollat, I (Paris, 1974), 111–21.

[27] Klingshirn, "Charity and Power," 184–87.

[28] J. C. Plumpe, *Mater Ecclesia* (Washington, D.C., 1943).

represents the baptismal font.[29] "Making the womb of the mother open up with children" would then signify the admission of new members into the church. As we have suggested elsewhere, these converts were likely Frankish warriors who converted from paganism,[30] partly in response to Caesarius's patronage, and partly in imitation of Clovis and his nobles, probably baptized in December 508, around the same time. Thus, by his actions as a patron, Caesarius demonstrated to his people as concretely as possible the value of charity for the constitution of the Christian community, both as it was and as he hoped it would become.

THE MONASTERY FOR WOMEN

It was likewise by his patronage toward the women's monastery that Caesarius hoped to present the whole community with a model for perfect Christian living. He therefore set out to rebuild the monastery, whose nearby ruins furnished a daily reminder of the recent siege. Uncertainty about the prospects for peace, however, prompted him to relocate the institution from the exterior to the interior of the city walls. The site he selected, located in the extreme southeastern corner of the city, had as much significance for the city's Christian community as the tomb of St. Genesius outside the walls, for it was there that the city's original cathedral and "old baptistery" were located.[31] By choosing this site, Caesarius could underscore the connection between the monastery's inhabitants and the city's earliest and most heroic Christians; the nuns in turn could reaffirm the holiness of the site by their prayers and holy way of life. The monastery was dedicated on August 26, 512, a Sunday, and placed under the patronage of St. John the Baptist, probably because of its proximity to the baptistery.[32] Several years later, probably in 524,

---

[29] W. M. Bedard, *The Symbolism of the Baptismal Font in Early Christian Thought* (Washington, D.C., 1951), 17–36.

[30] Klingshirn, "Charity and Power," 199–202. Although Clovis may have been converted from Arian Christianity, as Wood has argued ("Gregory and Clovis," 266–68), he could not have been baptized as an Arian, since he would not then have required or been permitted rebaptism, Arles (314), can. 9. Similarly, the baptismal imagery used in the *vita* of Caesarius would argue against the notion that any of the newly baptized were Arians.   [31] *reg. virg.* 73; *vita* I. 35.

[32] *test.*, Morin II, 283, line 17; Benoit, "Le premier baptistère," 45. After Caesarius's death, the monastery was renamed after him, and survived until the French Revolution. For a bibliography of its later history, see *Répertoire topo-bibliographique des abbayes et prieurés*, ed. L. H. Cottineau and G. Poras, I (Macon, 1935), cols. 150–51.

Caesarius held dedication ceremonies for a basilica of St. Mary, which was to serve as the nuns' communal burial place.[33] Although the site of the church is disputed, the evidence seems stronger in favor of a location inside the walls next to the monastery rather than outside the walls in the Alyscamps cemetery.[34] The church was composed of a nave with two side aisles, whose altars were dedicated to St. John the Baptist and St. Martin.

As planned, Caesarius designated his sister Caesaria as abbess of the new monastery, a choice in keeping with precedent and with his intention to retain control over the institution during his lifetime.[35] She returned to Arles from the monastery in Marseille to which she had been sent for protection, and with a few companions entered the *coenobium* in Arles (*vita* I. 35). Around this time, Caesarius presented her with the first version of his *regula virginum*, arguably the first rule written specifically for a women's monastery in either east or west.[36]

This rule constitutes our best evidence for the organization and functioning of the women's monastery. In its present form, it can be divided into three parts. The first part (chapters 1–47) consists of the version of the rule presented to Caesaria in 512 together with amendments to the original rule made before 534. As de Vogüé has shown, this first part can be divided into three subsections on the basis of the source material Caesarius employed: (1) chapters 1–16, which were based on "eastern" sources such as Book IV of Cassian's *Institutes*, the Pachomian corpus, the *Rule of*

---

[33] *vita* I. 57. For the date of the church, see Benoit, "Le premier baptistère," 41–42; for its dedication to the Virgin Mary, see A. de Vogüé, "Marie chez les vierges du sixième siècle: Césaire d'Arles et Grégoire le Grand," *Benedictina* 33 (1986), 79–91.

[34] Arguments against locating the basilica within the walls rest primarily on the view that Caesarius would not have violated the Roman tradition of burials *extra muros*, Hubert, "La topographie religieuse," 24–25, and de Vogüé and Courreau, 106–7. But this view does not take into account the pastoral strategy by which Caesarius hoped to replace precisely such Roman customs of civic self-definition with Christian alternatives. Moreover, archaeological excavations within the walls in the monastery complex have uncovered at least one example of a sixth-century burial, F. Benoit, "Les reliques de saint Césaire, archévêque d'Arles," *Cahiers archéologiques* I (1946), 51–62: 51, and "Le premier baptistère," 45. Finally, it is unlikely that Caesarius would have risked building another monastic structure outside the city walls so soon after the destruction of his earlier attempt. On the other hand, locating the burial church inside the walls also presents difficulties, de Vogüé and Courreau, 106–11. Ultimately, only excavation can solve this complicated topographical problem.

[35] Pachomius had given control over his monastery for women to his sister (*vita tertia Graeca* 42, *Sancti Pachomii Vitae Graecae*, ed. F. Halkin, Subsidia Hagiographica 19 [Brussels, 1932]), as had Augustine (Possidius, *vita Augustini* 26) and Romanus and Lupicinus (*vita patrum Iurensium* 60).   [36] de Vogüé and Courreau, 68–69.

the *Four Fathers* and the *Second Rule of the Fathers*; (2) chapters
17–35 and 43, which were based on the *ordo monasterii* and
praeceptum of Augustine; and (3) chapters 36–47, which were based
on original legislation by Caesarius.[37] The second part of the rule
(chapters 48–65 and 72–73) was issued on June 22, 534 as a
recapitulatio of chapters 1–47. It was meant to summarize
Caesarius's final changes to the rule, and to conclude the process of
revision and experimentation that had gone on before 534. The
third part, consisting of an *ordo psallendi* (chapters 66–70) and an
ordo convivii (chapter 71), was inserted into the rule as an appendix
in 534, but was probably composed earlier.[38]

It is unfortunately impossible to determine exactly what portion
of chapters 1–47 constituted the original version of the rule as
presented to Caesaria in 512. Apart from a reference to the
"basilica of saint Mary" in *reg. virg.* 45, which must be dated to a
period after the erection of the church in 524, no section of
chapters 1–47 can be dated to a particular year. Although de
Vogüé has convincingly argued that the three main sub-sections of
this part were composed in chronological sequence, it is difficult to
be certain about his dating of these sections, which rests on the
premise that Caesarius did not have direct access to the Augustinian
rules until the 520s. Nevertheless, it is possible to differentiate
between the version in effect before 534 (chapters 1–47, 66–71) and
the full version in effect after 534 (chapters 1–73). We shall employ
this distinction in the discussion that follows, first describing the
monastery as it function in the period before 534 and later, in
Chapter 9, noting the significant changes to the rule made in 534.

The most distinctive feature of the *regula virginum* – although
not, as it happens, an entirely novel feature[39] – was its provision
for a strictly regulated cloister. Until the day of their death, nuns
were absolutely prohibited from leaving the monastery for any
reason (*reg. virg.* 2). Entrance by outsiders into the cloistered
sections of the monastery was strictly regulated as well, with
exceptions made only for the monastery's male steward (*provisor*),
who supplied the monastery with necessities from the outside (*reg.
virg.* 36); bishops and clergymen who celebrated Mass in the
oratory (*reg. virg.* 36); bishops, abbots, and other religious laymen
who wished to pray in the oratory (*reg. virg.* 38); religious women
of suitable virtue who were invited to dinner (*reg. virg.* 39, 40);

---

[37] Ibid., 45–66, 88–98.   [38] Ibid., 95.   [39] Ibid., 71–81.

and workmen and slaves brought in to make repairs (*reg. virg.* 36). Relatives wishing to visit the nuns were permitted to meet them in the *salutatorium*, under the supervision of a senior nun (*reg. virg.* 38, 40).

The severity of these restrictions, unparalleled in Caesarius's *regula monachorum* or other rules for monks, reflects the bishop's belief that male and female ascetics required different rules (*reg. virg.* 2). Far more than men, he believed, women who sought "the cool refuge of chastity"[40] required protection from the outside world, in particular from sexual aggression by men, temptations to immodesty, and a loss of reputation.[41] Although some of the sisters were widows or married women who had left their husbands (*reg. virg.* 5), most were unmarried women and girls, some as young as six or seven years of age (*reg. virg.* 7). Having left the watchful care of their families ("relictis parentibus suis," *reg. virg.* 2), they required another form of protection.[42] A strictly cloistered monastery, from which men could be almost completely excluded, was ideal for the purpose. Such an institution could serve as a "Noah's ark" to protect from the "storms and tempests" of the world those who had resolved to live in the monastic family, under Caesarius, their "father" and Caesaria, their "mother" (*vita* I. 35). Cloister regulations served another practical purpose as well: by emphasizing the self-contained status of the monastery, they reinforced its image of self-sufficiency and independence, and helped to protect it from outside interference, a goal toward which Caesarius devoted extraordinary effort, as we shall see in greater detail shortly.[43]

Life within the monastery was based on the fundamental principles of the *vita communis* that Caesarius had become acquainted with at Lérins, but with many innovations of his own design. At the head of the institution stood the abbess (*abbatissa*), the "mother of the monastery" (*reg. virg.* 27, 35, 47). She alone was responsible for the spiritual well-being of the sisters, the material workings of the monastery, and relations with outsiders

---

[40] Caesarius, *ep.* 21. 2.

[41] Note, for instance, Caesarius's references to *fama* (*reg. virg.* 36), *pudicitia* (*reg. virg.* 23), and *honestas* (*reg. virg.* 46).

[42] On family protection of virgins in the fourth century, see Brown, *The Body and Society*, 263–64.

[43] D. Hochstetler, "The Meaning of Monastic Cloister for Women according to Caesarius of Arles," in *Religion, Culture, and Society in the Early Middle Ages*, ed. T. F. X. Noble and J. J. Contreni (Kalamazoo, Mich., 1987), 27–40.

(*reg. virg.* 27); she was not put under the close supervision of a male cleric. She was assisted by a prioress (*praeposita*), who functioned as second-in-command (*reg. virg.* 27, 35), and by senior nuns (*reg. virg.* 30) in charge of various departments and activities within the monastery.[44] Obedience to the abbess, the prioress, and all of their subordinate officers was strictly required, as was absolute faithfulness to the rule.[45]

As we would expect in a rule so much influenced by Augustine, charity and unanimity were highly prized, as was personal poverty. The nuns, who had entered the monastery from rich and poor families alike (*reg. virg.* 7, 21), were advised to maintain "one soul and one heart in the Lord" and to hold all things in common (*reg. virg.* 20). Private property in all its forms was absolutely prohibited, and detailed regulations were included to govern its disposition (*reg. virg.* 5, 6, 21). Sisters were not to have private rooms, but instead slept in separate beds in a single dormitory (*reg. virg.* 9). All were to live in harmony and mutual respect (*reg. virg.* 21) without quarrels or violence (*reg. virg.* 26, 33). The common property of the monastery was to be dispensed from storerooms on the basis of need, not individual desires, and was to include only simple clothing, food, drink, and utensils (*reg. virg.* 44, 71). Gifts that were too elegant for the monastery, such as silks, paintings, or objects of silver and gold, were to be sold or used for the basilica of St. Mary (*reg. virg.* 45). Work was also shared in common. All sisters, except the abbess and the prioress, were obliged to take turns at cooking (*reg. virg.* 14), weaving (*reg. virg.* 16), and other daily tasks (*reg. virg.* 14) like copying manuscripts (*vita* I. 58).

The whole daily routine of the monastery, including intervals of work (*reg. virg.* 22), was designed to encourage devotion to prayer (*reg. virg.* 40). The day's main structure was provided by the common prayer of the divine office, which consisted of an unusually lengthy schedule of prayers, hymns, and psalms.[46] In addition, the first two hours of the day were to be spent in spiritual reading (*reg. virg.* 19); for this reason all nuns were required to learn how to read (*reg. virg.* 18). During the third hour of the day, just before Terce, one of the nuns read while the rest worked (*reg.*

---

[44] E.g., novices (4, 35, 42), the choir (35, 42), the entrance (25, 43), the storerooms (30, 32, 40, 42), the infirmary (32, 42), and wool working (27, 30).

[45] *reg. virg.* 18, 29, 35, 47.

[46] *reg. virg.* 66–70. I am indebted to Sr. Mary Kiely for this point.

virg. 20). Reading also took place at meals (*reg. virg.* 18), which occurred once daily in periods of fasting and twice daily at other times (*reg. virg.* 71). Self-denial also played an important role in the monastery's spiritual routine. Besides fasting, the sisters kept silence (*reg. virg.* 19, 20), and abstained in general from baths (*reg. virg.* 31), meat, poultry, and fine wine (*reg. virg.* 30, 71).

For Caesarius, this society of sisters represented the ideal Christian community in Arles, their monastic regime the very image of perfect Christian living. Although they lived in a form of isolation from the rest of the city, their community and way of life could still serve as an example to all – made known by Caesarius and other clerics and religious in contact with the monastery (*reg. virg.* 36, 38, 39), by relatives who visited their sisters, daughters, or other relatives there (*reg. virg.* 38, 40), and by the poor begging at the gates, who received alms from the steward (*reg. virg.* 42). Even in death, the sisters continued to serve as an example to the population as a whole. After prayers in the monastery, their bodies were conducted by the bishop to the basilica of St. Mary outside the cloister (*reg. virg.* 70). There they were interred in stone sarcophagi arranged along the floor of the basilica in rows, just like the beds the women had occupied in their dormitory (*reg. virg.* 9, 51). For, as Caesaria the Younger later wrote, "God wanted us to possess a single place of burial, just as we made up a single sheepfold in life."[47] Open to the public, as the monastery itself was not, the burial church served as a place of veneration for the holy bodies of the sisters and, as many thought, a setting for further instruction through answered prayers and miracles.

In addition to providing his sister and her companions with living quarters and a rule, Caesarius also sought to make them self-sufficient and independent of outside control. Although the sisters cooked and made clothes for themselves, they could not support themselves by their labor alone. They still required an income from outside sources to pay for food, building maintenance, and other necessities, the need for which could only grow as the population of the monastery increased. It was therefore important to the monastery's survival that it be provided with an adequate endowment on which to draw for its needs. Some proportion of this endowment, perhaps a large proportion, would have been provided by affluent citizens of Arles and wealthy entrants into the

---

[47] *statutum de iure sepulturae servando*, Morin II, 129.

monastery, who were encouraged in the rule to give their property to the abbess for the common good (*reg. virg.* 21). Yet these gifts were not sufficient to endow the monastery, and Caesarius, as patron, was required to make up the difference. As we have seen, however, Caesarius had no family fortune with which to endow the monastery. He was therefore forced to take a step that would once again create dissension within the ranks of the local clergy and set him at odds with the civil authorities.

In order to provide the women of his monastery with an adequate endowment, Caesarius decided to draw again upon the resources of the local church. Because he had spent all the church's reserves of silver on the ransoming of captives, however, the only asset that remained available to him was ecclesiastical real estate. His control over this was much more limited than his control over movable resources. By the provisions of the Council of Agde, a bishop was permitted to alienate on the basis of his own authority only small properties of low value;[48] properties of greater value could be sold or granted in usufruct only if necessity required it, and then only with the written approval of two or three local bishops.[49] Caesarius appears to have paid scrupulous attention to these regulations. In his will, written in part before 512 and largely dedicated to justifying and confirming the measures he had taken for the endowment and protection of the monastery, he asserted that he had sold for the benefit of the monastery only church property that was "of little use to the church and unprofitable" and had done so, moreover, with the signed consent of his fellow bishops.[50] If this claim was true, Caesarius's actions were irreproachable under the terms of Gallic church law.

Yet even if it was canonically legal, the sale of church lands for the benefit of Caesarius's monastery was likely to have further disquieted those clerics who still harbored feelings of resentment over his use of church wealth in the ransoming of captives. Indeed, the sale of church lands was even more objectionable than the sale of church plate, for in reducing the landholdings of the church, he threatened the very basis of the clergy's own support.[51] It is in this context that we must explain the move made late in 512 to have Caesarius arrested by the Ostrogoths.[52] It is usually assumed that

---

[48] Agde (506), can. 45.   [49] can. 7.   [50] *test.* 6, Morin II, 286, lines 2–5.
[51] E. Lesne, *Histoire de la proprieté ecclésiastique en France*, I (Lille, 1910), 39–40.
[52] M.-J. Delage, "Le séjour de Césaire d'Arles en Italie," *Studia Patristica* 23, ed. E. A. Livingstone (Louvain, 1989), 103–10: 104.

he was charged on this occasion with collaboration with the Burgundians, as he had been in his two previous encounters with the Visigoths.[53] This may be true: sometime before 511 the bishop of Aosta had been accused of the same crime, although Theoderic later found him innocent.[54] But it may be significant that the *vita*, which cited charges of treason in the two earlier cases, makes no mention of such charges in this instance. Instead, it explicitly associates Caesarius's arrest with his "zeal" for the women's monastery (*vita* 1. 36). It is therefore possible that Caesarius was accused of a crime for which there was better proof. While his alienation of church lands for the benefit of the women's monastery conformed to the strictest letter of Gallic church law, it flagrantly violated provisions adopted by the Roman church for itself in November 502.[55] These had been given a wider, civil application in 507 by a decree of the Roman Senate and a letter of King Theoderic.[56] As confirmed by the king, these regulations prohibited the alienation of all rural lands owned by the church, whether large or small, to any persons whatever (although the usufruct of rural estates could be granted to clerics, captives, and pilgrims). Other real property, such as houses in towns and movable property without liturgical or ornamental value to the church, such as gold, silver, jewels, and clothing, could be disposed of by sale, donation, or exchange. Unable to prosecute him in Gaul under canon 7 of the Council of Agde, Caesarius's opponents in the clergy of Arles may well have decided to charge him with an offense against the much stricter provisions of Roman church (and now civil) law, a charge for which plenty of evidence was available. In the end, whatever the charge, the local authorities arrested Caesarius and sent him under guard to King Theoderic in Ravenna.

RAVENNA

Caesarius probably arrived at the court of Theoderic in spring or summer of 513. His retinue included the notary Messianus (*vita*

---

[53] Malnory, 102; Schmidt, *Ostgermanen*, 343; G. Bardy, "L'attitude politique de saint Césaire d'Arles," *Revue d'histoire de l'église de France* 33 (1947), 241–56: 250; Wolfram, *Goths*, 313.   [54] Cassiodorus, *var.* I. 9.   [55] *MGH AA*, XII, 449–51.
[56] *praeceptum regis Theoderici*, MGH AA, XII, 392. For commentary, see G. Pfeilschifter, *Der Ostgotenkönig Theoderich der Grosse und die katholische Kirche* (Münster-in-Westphalia, 1896), 227–29.

I. 40), whose eyewitness account of the journey was incorporated into the *vita*.[57] According to this account, Caesarius made a splendid impression on the king.

He entered the palace and under the guidance of Christ approached King Theoderic to greet him. When the king saw the fearless and venerable man of God, he reverently stood up to greet him. When he had removed the royal insignia from his head, he greeted him again very cordially. First he questioned him about the difficulties of his journey, and then affectionately inquired about his Goths and the people of Arles. After the holy bishop had gone out of his sight, the king addressed his courtiers: "Let God not spare those who have without just cause subjected this innocent and holy man to so long a journey. I recognized what sort of man he was by the fact that when he came in to greet me I trembled all over. I see," he said, "the face of an angel; I see an apostolic man. I consider it wrong to suppose any evil of so venerable a man." (*vita* I. 36)

It is difficult to deduce much from Messianus's report about Caesarius's vindication from the charges he faced. More light is shed on these events by the letter of congratulations that Magnus Felix Ennodius sent Caesarius in reply to his own report of success.[58] Written shortly before Ennodius's consecration as bishop of Pavia,[59] the letter attributes Caesarius's vindication to divine protection and Theoderic's respect for his monastic way of life, humility, spiritual learning, and good example. There was of course no need for Ennodius to mention his own support, which the correspondence with Caesarius strongly suggests. In his own defense, Caesarius might also have employed the theme of holiness that runs through Messianus's account and Ennodius's letter. He certainly could not deny that he had sold church plate to pay for the ransoming of captives or alienated church lands for the endowment of the monastery. But he could attempt to justify these actions by arguing that "holy" motives lay behind them, such as compassion for prisoners or zeal for the monastic life. Convinced by this defense, impressed by the level of patronage mobilized on Caesarius's behalf, and – perhaps most importantly – eager to win and retain the support of the Roman population in his new praetorian prefecture, Theoderic set Caesarius free. He

---

[57] The word "inquiunt" in *vita* I. 37 and elsewhere indicates reported speech. For an explanation, see W. E. Klingshirn, *The Life, Testament, and Letters of Caesarius of Arles* (Liverpool, forthcoming).   [58] Ennodius, *ep.* IX. 33 = Caesarius, *ep.* I.
[59] F. Vogel, *MGH AA*, VII, xxv.

then more concretely expressed his esteem for the bishop by sending a silver bowl weighing sixty pounds (and worth about 300 *solidi*) along with 300 additional *solidi* to the inn where Caesarius was staying (*vita* I. 37). To these he added a message: "Your son the king asks that your blessedness worthily accept this vessel as a gift, and use it in his memory" (*vita* I. 37). Yet, instead of keeping the bowl, as Theoderic had expected he would, Caesarius had it sold and with the proceeds began to ransom captives (*vita* I. 37). The fact that Theoderic excused this act of *lèse-majesté* suggests that he really was convinced of Caesarius's right to use gifts given for one purpose – even by a king – for a completely different purpose. Indeed, Theoderic's approval of Caesarius's actions stimulated a parallel generosity on the part of the court and local aristocracy. According to the *vita*, "all the senators and leading men in attendance at his palace competed in wishing for the blessed man to distribute the price of their gifts with his right hand" (*vita* I. 38). By conveying gifts to Caesarius, donors could hope to share in his access to the power of God, to win for themselves the influence of his prayers, and in view of the competitive framework of late antique gift-giving, to draw public attention to their own generosity, and thereby to enhance their status. By receiving these gifts, Caesarius could not only obtain the resources for further acts of charity, but also strengthen his ties with royal and aristocratic donors, which in turn enabled him to exercise a correspondingly more effective patronage. With the proceeds he received, Caesarius concentrated on ransoming all the captives whom the Ostrogoths under Mammo had seized from Burgundian territory north of the Durance in 508.[60] Prominent among these were many of the inhabitants of Orange, which had been almost totally enslaved (*vita* I. 38). He then supplied the liberated captives with provisions, horses, and wagons and sent them on their way.

Caesarius earned his reputation as an "apostolic" man not only by his asceticism and generosity, but also by what were perceived as acts of miraculous power. Like Germanus of Auxerre, who had performed miracles on behalf of high court officials in Ravenna when he journeyed there in the middle of the fifth century,[61] Caesarius was reported to have performed miracles for the benefit of individuals with close connections to the court. In one incident,

---

[60] Schmidt, *Ostgermanen*, 157.   [61] Constantius of Lyon, *vita Germani* 37–39.

he healed a "young man serving in the office of the prefect" from a terminal illness (*vita* I. 39–40). In the other he freed the house of the deacon and physician Helpidius, a frequent visitor to Theoderic's court,[62] from a demonic "infestation" whose most annoying feature was the occurrence of frequent showers of stones inside his house (*vita* I. 41).

It was, according to the *vita*, by such acts of generosity and wonder-working that Caesarius's reputation reached the city of Rome where "the Senate, the leading men, the pope, the clergy, and the people began…to yearn [for his arrival]" (*vita* I. 38). Caesarius himself had important reasons for visiting the city, not the least of which was a need to work out with Pope Symmachus arrangements for endowing his monastery that would not subject him to further threats of arrest and deportation. He probably arrived in early autumn of 513.

ROME

In order to advance their own claims to primacy, the bishops of Rome had long welcomed provincial bishops who sought to obtain their assistance in such enterprises as advancing claims to regional supremacy or appealing the unfavorable decisions of local synods.[63] In return for an acknowledgment of papal primacy, popes had often been willing to take sides in such disputes, and their assistance, while not always decisive, often proved helpful. Following the example of a number of his predecessors, Caesarius decided while in Italy to seek the pope's assistance on a number of matters. He brought with him to Rome[64] a written petition that listed four points of church law on which he sought papal confirmation.[65] His first point was, under the circumstances, the most urgent. He asked Symmachus to prohibit the alienation of ecclesiastical lands in Gaul, but to allow such alienation in cases where monasteries would benefit from the transaction. By securing Symmachus's assent on this point, he hoped to win special treatment for his own monastery as well as to establish the grounds on which to defend himself from future charges of illegal

---

[62] *PLRE* II, 537.　　　[63] Mathisen, *Ecclesiastical Factionalism*, 44–68.
[64] Morin II, 10. The absence from this document of the names of letter-carriers (such as are found on another of Caesarius's petitionary letters, Morin II, 13–14) suggests that Caesarius brought the document to Rome himself.　　　[65] *ep.* 7a, Morin II, 12.

alienation. Caesarius also requested a ruling against three violations of church law that he had failed to prevent. First, he asked the pope to prohibit laymen who had held public office from being ordained as clerics or bishops, unless they first underwent a long probationary period as *conversi*. Second, he requested that professed widows and nuns be prohibited from marriage, whether voluntary or forced. Finally, he asked the pope to condemn simony. In a letter of November 6, 513, Symmachus responded to these requests.[66] He approved the last three requests *in toto*, but gave only partial support to the first. While he approved the prohibition against alienation of church lands, he refused to grant any special exemption for monasteries. At most, carefully observing the terms of the law on alienation that he himself had sponsored in 502,[67] he allowed the usufruct of church property to be granted to monasteries, as well as to deserving clerics and pilgrims. He cautioned, however, that the term of this arrangement was to be temporary, not permanent, lasting only as long as the usufructuary lived.[68] Although Caesarius was certainly disappointed by this decision, Symmachus could not have acted otherwise. He had sponsored the law of 502 as part of a strategy for protecting himself from the supporters of Laurentius, the recently deposed "anti-pope" of 498/99. In an attempt to depose Symmachus in favor of their own candidate, they had charged him with violating the law of 483 that prohibited the alienation not only of landed property belonging to the church but also church plate and other precious objects.[69] Symmachus was exonerated from these charges at the council of November 6, 502 when the law of 483 was declared invalid on the grounds that it had not been approved by the bishop of Rome.[70] It was at this point, in order to protect himself from future charges of wrongdoing, that Symmachus promoted a law on church property that was much more favorable to his own interests.[71] In

---

[66] Symmachus, "Hortatur nos" (= Caesarius, *ep.* 7b), Morin II, 10–11.

[67] *MGH AA*, XII, 449.

[68] It is true, as L. Ueding observed (*Geschichte der Klostergründungen der frühen Merowingerzeit* [Berlin, 1935], 57), that this last provision made less sense in the case of an institution than it did in the case of an individual, but in defining the length of the arrangement as he did, Symmachus was simply spelling out the maximum term of *ususfructus* in Roman law; see Klingshirn, "Caesarius's Monastery," 458, n. 63.

[69] See the Laurentian fragment, *LP* I, 44.   [70] *MGH AA*, XII, 447–48.

[71] C. Pietri, "Le sénat, le peuple chrétien et les partis du cirque à Rome sous le pape Symmaque (498–514)," *Mélanges d'archéologie et d'histoire de l'Ecole Française de Rome* 78 (1966), 123–39: 135–39.

these circumstances, Symmachus could hardly have violated at Caesarius's request a law that meant so much to his own political survival. Indeed, Symmachus's political interests conflicted with Caesarius's on this point, and it was the latter who had to yield. But on another more important point, their political interests intersected, and an agreement was reached that proved to be favorable to both bishops.

Ever since the beginning of his episcopate, like his predecessor Aeonius, Caesarius had been unable to exercise his metropolitan rights in the Burgundian territories across the Durance. Since 490 these had been exercised by Avitus of Vienne. In leaving intact the southern border of the Burgundian kingdom, the Ostrogothic victories of 508 had not altered this state of affairs. Caesarius was therefore reduced to making symbolic claims over the dioceses that lay in the hands of his rival, a good example of which was his recent freeing of captives from dioceses north of the Durance.[72] In asking Symmachus to confirm his metropolitan rights, Caesarius could not hope to alter Avitus's *de facto* control over the disputed dioceses. But he could act to prevent Avitus from trying to transform *de facto* control into a form of *de jure* control, as he had already succeeded in doing, albeit temporarily, under Pope Anastasius. On November 6, 513, at Caesarius's request, Symmachus confirmed his metropolitan rights in the same terms as Pope Leo had in 450, by assigning the dioceses of Valence, Tarentaise, Geneva, and Grenoble to Vienne, and the rest of the dioceses in the province to Arles.[73]

Like many of his fifth-century predecessors, however, Caesarius aspired to control more than just the province of Viennensis. In leaving unspecified the exact composition of the province of Arles, Symmachus had given him the opportunity to define his province as widely as the current state of ecclesiastical politics would allow. Caesarius therefore wasted no time in seeking the pope's confirmation of the metropolitan rights he also claimed over the province of Narbonensis II. In a petition delivered to Symmachus in the spring of 514, Caesarius requested that he warn the bishop of Aix that "when the metropolitan bishop of Arles has called him to a council, or when divine religion demands his presence at an ordination, he not refuse to come," in other words that he cede his

---

[72] Klingshirn, "Charity and Power," 192–95.
[73] Symmachus, "Sedis apostolicae" (= Caesarius, *ep.* 6), Morin II, 9–10.

metropolitan rights over Narbonensis II to Caesarius.[74] Symmachus confirmed these claims in a letter of June 11, 514.[75]

Yet Symmachus did more than reconfirm Caesarius's metropolitan rights over most of Viennensis and the whole of Narbonensis II. He also decided to name Caesarius the papal vicar (*vicarius*) of Gaul,[76] the first in a long series of bishops of Arles to be given such an honor.[77] Symmachus chose to symbolize the vicar's status by the *pallium*, a band of wool decorated with crosses and worn about the shoulders.[78] He granted Caesarius the exclusive right to wear this vestment "throughout Gaul."[79] As papal vicar, Caesarius's main responsibility was to oversee papal interests in Gaul by convening councils to take care of problems of concern to Rome, referring to Rome conflicts that could not be resolved at the local or regional level, and furnishing clerics traveling to Rome with letters of introduction (*litterae formatae*) to ensure that only authorized reports on Gallic affairs reached the Roman see.[80] Although some of the duties incumbent on the papal vicar of Gaul resembled those previously conferred by bishops of Rome on bishops of Arles,[81] the role differed markedly – in Roman eyes, at least – from the much more loosely defined

[74] Caesarius, *ep.* 8a, Morin II, 13–14. That Caesarius's request pertained to his authority as a metropolitan rather than as papal vicar is indicated by his demand that the bishop of Aix attend ordinations, the supervision of which was a metropolitan rather than vicarial responsibility. That this request required the bishop of Aix to cede his metropolitan rights is clear from the procedure for episcopal ordinations. Except in cases where a metropolitan bishop was to be ordained, the only bishops required to attend episcopal ordinations were those from the same province. Metropolitans had no authority to summon other metropolitans on these occasions.

[75] Symmachus, "Qui veneranda" (= Caesarius, *ep.* 8b), Morin II, 13.

[76] On the terminology, see Mathisen, *Ecclesiastical Factionalism*, 50, n. 37. Caesarius's right to the title of "vicar" cannot be disputed, despite the fact that vicarial status as such was not expressly granted to a bishop of Arles until 545. Cf. *ep. Arel.* 41, and G. Langgärtner, *Die Gallienpolitik der Päpste im 5. und 6. Jahrhundert. Eine Studie über den apostolischen Vikariat von Arles* (Bonn, 1964), 149–50.

[77] Langgärtner, *Gallienpolitik*, 149–83.

[78] In the east this garment was worn by all bishops, but in the western church it was worn only by the pope and those bishops he specially permitted to wear it, J. Braun, *Die liturgische Gewandung im Occident und Orient* (Freiburg im Breisgau, 1907), 620–76. For the possibility that this (Roman) *pallium* was preserved among Caesarius's relics along with a Gallic *pallium*, see Benoit, "Les reliques," 57–61, and H.-I. Marrou, "Les deux palliums de Saint Césaire d'Arles," in his *Christiana Tempora* (Rome, 1978), 251–52.

[79] Symmachus, "Hortatur nos" (= Caesarius, *ep.* 7b), Morin II, 11, lines 35–6; *vita* I. 42.

[80] Symmachus, "Qui veneranda" (= Caesarius, *ep.* 8b), Morin II, 13.

[81] Letters of introduction, *ep. Arel.* 1; appeal to Rome, *ep. Arel.* 18.

position of favor held by such bishops as Patroclus,[82] Leontius,[83] and Aeonius.[84] From Caesarius's time on, vicars of Gaul were required to supervise not just their own metropolitan province, however widely that might be defined, but the whole of Gaul as well.[85] Moreover, their status was given official recognition in the form of the *pallium*, an indication of papal favor that was not conferred on the fifth-century bishops of Arles. In addition, the official duties of vicars were standardized, remaining essentially the same throughout the sixth century.[86] Finally, the honor was institutionalized, passing for the rest of the sixth century, with papal and imperial (or royal) permission, to whatever bishop happened to occupy the *cathedra* of Arles.[87]

The policy of appointing papal vicars was first developed at the beginning of the fifth century in response to the transferral of the eastern part of the prefecture of Illyricum, consisting of the civil dioceses of Dacia and Macedonia, to the control of the eastern emperor.[88] In order to keep ecclesiastical control over the region from slipping away to the patriarch of Constantinople, Pope Innocent named Rufus, the bishop of Thessalonica, as vicar over the whole of eastern Illyricum.[89] The vicariate was then conferred *ex officio* on future bishops of Thessalonica. A similar policy was employed under somewhat different conditions later in the fifth century to assert papal primacy over Spain, which had by then fallen into Visigothic hands. First, in 469/83 the bishop of Seville, metropolitan capital of Baetica, was made vicar of the whole of Spain;[90] later, in 521, the vicariate was split between the bishops of Seville and Elche.[91]

Symmachus established a vicariate for Gaul under analogous conditions. By establishing a papal vicar for a region under

[82] Mathisen, *Ecclesiastical Factionalism*, 40–68; W. Völker, "Studien zur päpstlichen Vikariatspolitik im 5. Jahrhundert," *Zeitschrift für Kirchengeschichte* 46 (1928), 355–80: 355–69. [83] Mathisen, *Ecclesiastical Factionalism*, 228–34. [84] *ep. Arel.* 22.

[85] This did not always mean that vicars in fact exercised such wide supervision. In Caesarius's case, vicarial authority proved no more able to cross political boundaries than metropolitan authority. [86] *ep. Arel.* 41, 43; Gregory the Great, *ep.* v. 58.

[87] E.g., *ep. Arel.* 51. According to T. Klauser, *Der Ursprung der bischöflichen Insignien und Ehrenrechte* (Bonn, 1948), 18–19, imperial permission was required because the *pallium* was originally one of the imperial insignia.

[88] C. Pietri, *Roma christiana*, II (Rome, 1976), 1089–93.

[89] Innocent, "Lectissimo et gloriosissimo," *Collectio Thessalonicensis* V, ed. C. Silva-Tarouca (Rome, 1937), 21–22.

[90] Siricius, "Plurimorum relatu," Thiel I, 213–14.

[91] Hormisdas, "Fecit dilectio tua," Thiel I, 787–88; idem, "Suscipientes plena," Thiel I, 979–80.

"barbarian" control (with the exception of Provence, arguably still in "Roman" hands), Symmachus found a way of asserting his claim to territories over which he had no other form of control. His choice of the bishop of Arles to play the part was based on the city's status as capital of the praetorian prefecture, its location along important communication routes, the history of cooperation between its bishops and the bishops of Rome, and, perhaps most important, confidence in the competence and loyalty of a bishop whose style of leadership and patronage, seen most recently in his activities as a redeemer of captives, so closely mirrored Symmachus's own.[92]

As a result of Symmachus's decision, Arles was to be honored as a miniature Rome, "Gallula Roma Arelas," in a sense that Ausonius could not have foreseen. Not only was its bishop granted permission to wear the *pallium*, in imitation of the bishop of Rome, but the deacons of Arles were given the right to wear *dalmaticae*, white tunics worn exclusively by the deacons of Rome.[93] The year 513 thus marked the beginning of a close relationship between Arles and Rome that would endure until the end of the sixth century. It was a relationship founded on mutual interests. The bishops of Rome gained a source of information in Gaul, a voice in Gallic affairs, and a legitimation of their primacy; the bishops of Arles gained a new source of prestige that could be used in their own political initiatives.

ARLES: 513–23

Caesarius returned to Arles in a much stronger political position than he had been in just a few months earlier. Far from being deposed, as his opponents had hoped, he had managed through a combination of good fortune and political skill to win the enthusiastic backing of Theoderic and Symmachus. In addition, through his charitable and "miraculous" achievements he had succeeded in forging new links of patronage and support in Ravenna and Rome. These gains confirmed his standing as the leading prelate in Ostrogothic Gaul, and made his position in Arles incalculably more secure. Above all they permitted him to resume

---

[92] Klingshirn, "Charity and Power," 198–99.
[93] *vita* I. 42. On *dalmaticae*, see Braun, *Die liturgische Gewandung*, 249–302.

his program of pastoral reform, which had been interrupted by the war of 507/9. Since Caesarius's pastoral initiatives will themselves be the subject of Chapters 6, 7, and 8, we shall devote the remainder of the present chapter to his other activities in the same period, which provide a context for his pastoral achievements.

Shortly after returning to Arles, Caesarius turned his attention to the two groups of clients that always had the greatest claim on his patronage: prisoners of war and the sisters of his monastery. Drawing on a surplus of 8,000 *solidi*, over 100 pounds of gold, that had been given to him in Italy, he went to redeem captives in the vicinity of Carcassonne, besieged by the Franks in the recent war.[94] He also sent "abbots, deacons, and clerics" to "different places" for the same purpose (*vita* I. 44). Around the same time, perhaps in 515, Caesarius also decided to seek the help of the bishop of Rome in guaranteeing the financial and administrative independence of his monastery.[95] Symmachus had died in July 514, and was succeeded a week later by Hormisdas, his choice as successor,[96] who continued Symmachus's policy of cooperation with the vicar of Gaul. Among other matters, Hormisdas informed Caesarius of his consecration as bishop,[97] and described negotiations to end the Acacian schism between the churches of Rome and Constantinople.[98] Caesarius in turn sought two favors from the pope.

First, he requested that Hormisdas confirm the monastery's independence by prohibiting future bishops of Arles from interfering in its internal affairs.[99] A council of Arles in the early 450s had conferred similar privileges on the monastery of Lérins, ruling that the abbot was responsible for the whole "lay multitude," while the bishop was responsible for all "clergy and ministers of the altar."[100] Caesarius's willingness to seek such privileges from the bishop of Rome clearly signals the closeness of his ties to the apostolic see; his decision not to call a council of his fellow bishops to consider the question may have been due to his general unwillingness to convene councils in the period between

---

[94] Procopius, *de bellis* V. 12. 41; *vita* I. 44.
[95] For the date, see de Vogüé and Courreau, 341–42.
[96] E. Caspar, *Geschichte des Papsttums*, II (Tübingen, 1933), 129.
[97] Hormisdas, "Quamvis ratio" (= Caesarius, *ep.* 9), Morin II, 14.
[98] Hormisdas, "Iustum est" (= Caesarius, *ep.* 10), Morin II, 14–17. Avitus of Vienne in turn received news of these negotiations by way of clerics from Arles, *ep.* 41.
[99] Hormisdas, "Exulto in domino" (= Caesarius, *ep.* 18), Morin II, 126.
[100] *CCSL* 148, 133–34; de Vogüé and Courreau, 343–44.

506 and 524, the reasons for which we shall consider shortly.[101]
Hormisdas for his part was only too happy to fulfill a request that
provided so important a validation of Roman claims to universal
authority. He ruled, in the earliest of many papal confirmations of
such privileges,[102] that none of Caesarius's successors "should ever
dare to appropriate for himself any power in the monastery. The
only exception is that in the pious exercise of their pastoral
responsibilities, the bishop and his clerics may visit the household
of Christ the Lord that dwells there, [provided they do so] with
sincere intentions and at convenient times, in keeping with what is
fitting."[103]

In his second request, Caesarius asked Hormisdas to approve a
donation he had recently made to the women's monastery of
profits accruing from the sale of church lands.[104] It was a sign of his
new-found political strength that Caesarius did not seek Hormisdas's prior approval of the transaction this time, but simply his
confirmation of a *fait accompli*. He softened the impact of this
breach of church law by assuring the pope that he would never
presume to carry out such illicit alienations in the future.
Hormisdas approved his sale of church lands, but cautioned him
against such transactions in the future. Indeed, he suggested that
instead of allowing them to use their money to purchase church
property, Caesarius should have encouraged the buyers to donate
their money directly to the monastery: "It is fitting that a good
deed be performed without payment. The reward of upright zeal
ought to be hoped for rather than demanded, to prevent the
remuneration of charity from being diminished through the
advantage of a sale."[105]

Caesarius sought to strengthen the authority of this letter by
soliciting the consensus of his suffragan bishops for its contents.
Seven bishops from the province of Arles signed the document, by
which they indicated their approval of Hormisdas's decision and
their willingness to uphold its provisions.[106] The letter thus
became a kind of conciliar document as well as a pronouncement
by the bishop of Rome. As such, it became part of a dossier of
documents intended to protect the women's monastery. Its only

---

[101] *infra*, p. 136.
[102] E. Ewig, "Beobachtungen zu den Klosterprivilegien des 7. und frühen 8. Jahrhunderts," in his *Spätantikes und fränkisches Gallien*, II, 411–26: 414.
[103] Hormisdas, "Exulto in domino" 2, Morin II, 126.   [104] Ibid., 3, Morin II, 126.
[105] Ibid.   [106] Morin II, 127.

surviving copy is found, along with the *regula virginum* and other documents concerning the monastery, in the ninth-century codex lat. Monacensis 28118, which also contains the *codex regularum* of Benedict of Aniane.[107]

The signatures on Hormisdas's letter indicate the small number of suffragan bishops willing or able to acknowledge Caesarius's metropolitan authority in the period between 513 and 523. Of the five bishops whose sees can be identified with reasonable certainty, one came from the civil province of Viennensis (Cyprianus of Toulon) and the remainder came from Narbonensis II (Johannes of Fréjus,[108] Contumeliosus of Riez) and Alpes Maritimae (Marcellus of Senez, Severus of Vence[109]). The sees of the remaining bishops – Montanus and Petrus – are unknown, but it is probable that neither came from Marseille or Aix, whose bishops still disputed control over Narbonensis II with Caesarius, but rather from Uzès, Glandève, or Antibes. The rest of the bishops whom Caesarius claimed as his suffragans were located in territories north of the Durance. He received a sharp reminder of his lack of authority over this region in 517, when Avitus of Vienne and Viventiolus of Lyon convened a council of the Burgundian kingdom at Epao, probably the modern Albon, located in the Rhône valley between Vienne and Valence.[110] Unlike the Councils of Agde (506) and Orléans (511), this council was not convened at the behest of a German king,[111] but rather on the suggestion of Pope Hormisdas.[112] It cannot therefore be considered a "national" council in the same sense as the Councils of Agde and Orléans, despite the fact that a "Catholic" Burgundian kingdom had come into being in 516 with the accession of Sigismund, recently converted to Catholic Christianity.[113] Almost all of the bishops in the kingdom either attended or sent a representative: four bishops came from the ecclesiastical province of Lyon,[114] eight bishops from the province of Vienne,[115] two

---

[107] Ibid., 100, 125.   [108] de Vogüé and Courreau, 273.   [109] Ibid., 358, n. 14.

[110] J. Gaudemet, "Concile d'Epaone," *DHGE* XV (1963), cols. 524–45: 524. The text of the council can be found in *CCSL* 148A, 20–37.

[111] Loening, *Geschichte des deutschen Kirchenrechts*, I, 567, n. 3; Gaudemet, "Concile d'Epaone," col. 525.   [112] Avitus, *ep*. 90.

[113] Wood, "Avitus of Vienne," 227.

[114] Viventiolus of Lyon, Silvester of Chalon, Gregorius of Langres, and Praumatius of Autun.

[115] Avitus of Vienne, his brother Apollinaris of Valence, Victorius of Grenoble, Constantius of Martigny, Sanctus of Tarentaise, Maximus of Geneva, Seculatius of Die, and Venantius of Alba/Viviers.

bishops from the province of Besançon,[116] one bishop from the province of Sens,[117] and, most vexing to Caesarius, nine bishops and a priest from the province of Arles.[118] Shortly after Avitus's death in 518, his successor Julianus joined Viventiolus of Lyon in holding another council at Lyon, which two of Caesarius's suffragans attended.[119]

In contrast to his colleagues in the Burgundian and Frankish kingdoms, Caesarius had not held a council in his province since 506, perhaps as a form of protest against what he viewed as a usurpation of his metropolitan rights.[120] That changed in 523 when the expansion of Ostrogothic territory in Gaul brought control over the disputed dioceses back to him. Relations along the heavily fortified frontier between the Ostrogoths and the Burgundians had been tense since the war of 507/9, but relatively peaceful nonetheless.[121] In 522, however, after the death of his first wife, Theoderic's daughter, Sigismund had their son Segeric killed on suspicion of treason.[122] Clovis's son Chlodomer took advantage of the unrest to invade the Burgundian kingdom from the west in revenge for the murder of his mother's parents by Sigismund's father.[123] In 523 he captured Sigismund and put him to death,[124] but was himself killed the following year by Sigismund's brother Godomar at the battle of Vézeronce.[125] Theoderic meanwhile, seeking to avenge the death of his grandson,[126] as well as to cushion Provence from the Frankish advance,[127] sent an army under Tuluin into Burgundy,[128] which succeeded in winning a broad stretch of territory north of the Durance, probably as far as

---

[116] Claudius of Besançon who, although technically a metropolitan bishop, was not accorded metropolitan standing, and Bubulcus of Windisch.

[117] Tauricianus of Nevers.

[118] Gemellus of Vaison, Valerius of Sisteron, Catolinus of Embrun, Iulianus of Carpentras, Constantius of Gap, Florentius of Orange, Florentius of Saint-Paul-Trois-Châteaux, Fylagrius of Cavaillon, Praetextatus of Apt, and the priest Peladius, a delegate from Bishop Salutaris of Avignon.

[119] These were Florentius of Orange or Saint-Paul-Trois-Châteaux and Fylagrius of Cavaillon, *CCSL* 148A, 38–41.

[120] O. Pontal, *Die Synoden im Merowingerreich* (Paderborn, 1986), 51.

[121] Wolfram, *Goths*, 311–13.

[122] Gregory of Tours, *hist.* III. 5; Marius of Avenches, *chronicon*, a. 522, *MGH AA*, XI, 234; Schmidt, *Ostgermanen*, 162, n. 2.   [123] Gregory of Tours, *hist.* III. 6.

[124] Ibid.; Marius of Avenches, *chron.*, a. 523, *MGH AA*, XI, 235.

[125] Gregory of Tours, *hist.* III. 6; Marius of Avenches, *chron.*, a. 524, *MGH AA*, XI, 235; Agathias, *hist.* I. 3. 3.   [126] Schmidt, *Ostgermanen*, 353.

[127] R. Buchner, *Die Provence in Merowingischer Zeit* (Stuttgart, 1933), 3, n. 7.

[128] Cassiodorus, *var.* VIII. 10. 8; Wolfram, *Goths*, 312.

the Isère.[129] By this turn of events, Caesarius's metropolitan province was finally unified under a single power, for the first time since the 470s.

THE COUNCILS OF 524–29

Caesarius acted quickly to consolidate his control over the dioceses returned to him by the Ostrogothic expansion. In June 524 he invited the twenty-one bishops of his newly unified province to attend a provincial council in Arles.[130] The initiative was a success. Eighteen bishops were represented in all, including bishops of eight of the dioceses represented at Epao in 517,[131] and two of the dioceses represented at Lyon in 518/23.[132] Among the bishops in attendance was Maximus of Aix, who had until this point refused to relinquish his claim to metropolitan control over the province of Narbonensis II. The appearance of his signature to the council's resolutions in order of seniority rather than at the head of the list indicates that he was not only forced to attend the council but also to give up his claims to metropolitan status, as commanded by Symmachus in 514.[133] A similar placement of his signature at the Councils of Orange (529),[134] Vaison (529),[135] and Marseille (533)[136] indicates that he remained in this subordinate position for as long as Caesarius continued to hold councils.

The political gains of 524 were further consolidated by subsequent councils. Caesarius pointedly convened the next three of these in dioceses formerly controlled by the bishop of Vienne:[137] in November 527 at Carpentras, in July 529 at Orange, and in November 529 at Vaison. These councils were attended by a majority of the bishops in his extended province. Moreover, by 527 Caesarius had asserted metropolitan control over the province

---

[129] Schmidt, *Ostgermanen*, 163, n. 2.   [130] *CCSL* 148A, 43.

[131] Apt, Carpentras, Cavaillon, Orange, Avignon, Saint-Paul, Gap, Embrun.

[132] Orange or Saint-Paul, Cavaillon.

[133] *CCSL*, 148A, 45, line 10. Except for the Council of Orléans (533), whose signature lists appear to rank some metropolitan bishops by seniority, all other Gallic councils of the first half of the sixth century at which more than one metropolitan was present listed them together before listing their suffragan bishops. It is thus reasonable to suppose that Caesarius's councils of 524–33 would have done the same if any other metropolitan besides himself had been present. The appearance of Maximus's signature among the rest of Caesarius's suffragans would seem to indicate that he could not assert his metropolitan status.

[134] Ibid., 64, line 10.   [135] Ibid., 80, line 9.

[136] Ibid., 85, line 27.   [137] Pontal, *Synoden*, 51.

of Alpes Maritimae as well as Narbonensis II. Gallicanus of Embrun, who had not attended the Council of Arles, not only attended the Council of Carpentras, but also agreed to sign simply in order of seniority.[138]

The councils of 524–29 were not of course convened merely to demonstrate Caesarius's political control, but more importantly to transact pressing church business. Through them, Caesarius sought to promote his program of pastoral reforms outside his own diocese, discipline recalcitrant suffragans, and carry out his responsibilities as papal vicar of Gaul. He first devoted himself at the Council of Arles to restating and modifying the rules for ordaining deacons, priests, and bishops. An increase in the number of parishes and the clergy required to man them (can. 2) had encouraged bishops to relax the standards set up at Agde by ordaining men below the minimum age limits, men who had married twice, men who had married women married twice, penitents, and above all men who had not previously held clerical rank. The council responded by restating the minimum ages for ordination set down at Agde (can. 1) and reiterating its prohibitions against ordaining penitents, twice-married men, and the husbands of twice-married women (can. 3). But it also modified the policy for admitting laymen into the clergy by permitting them to be ordained as bishops, priests, or deacons after they had lived as *conversi* for only a year (can. 2) rather than the longer period (*multo tempore*) envisioned in 513. In addition, the council attempted to prevent a bishop's existing clergy from escaping his control by prohibiting other bishops from giving them assistance when they fled from their own dioceses (can. 4). By such provisions the council aimed at increasing the number of men qualified and available to serve as clerics in any particular diocese.

When they came to the Council of Arles, the bishops of Provence also took part in the solemn dedication of the basilica of St. Mary, which Caesarius had built to serve as the burial place for the sisters of his monastery (*vita* 1. 57). It was not long after the council, perhaps in 525, that Caesaria the Elder died, and was buried in the basilica next to the tomb reserved for Caesarius (*vita* 1. 58). She was succeeded as abbess by Caesaria the Younger, perhaps Caesarius's niece. Around the same time, it has been plausibly suggested, Caesarius's nephew, the deacon Teridius, was

---

[138] *CCSL* 148A, 49, line 11.

named steward of the monastery.[139] By these appointments, control over the institution was retained in the hands of Caesarius's family.

At Caesarius's next council, held in Carpentras in November 527 and attended by fifteen bishops, two questions were decided. First, Caesarius succeeded in persuading his fellow bishops to reprimand Bishop Agroecius of Antibes, one of the most senior bishops in the province.[140] He was barred from saying Mass for a year on the grounds that he had ordained Protadius to the priesthood before he had lived as a *conversus* for the required length of time.[141] Although his representative had agreed to this regulation at the Council of Arles,[142] Agroecius clearly felt no compunction about ignoring it. His violation of the canon is one indication of the opposition Caesarius faced in trying to impose an ascetic way of life on the clergy. Agroecius's seniority made this opposition all the more serious, for it threatened to sway the support of other bishops for Caesarius. To uphold his threatened authority, Caesarius asked Pope Felix to confirm the council's decision. In his reply of February 3, 528, Felix upheld the requirement for a probationary period before ordination.[143] Whether Agroecius heeded this ruling is entirely unknown. He did not appear at any subsequent church councils, and by the Council of Orléans (541) Antibes had a new bishop. This was not the last time, however, that Caesarius would appeal to the bishop of Rome for help in supporting his authority as metropolitan.

The council's second achievement was the ruling that rural parishes had the right to keep property given them by donors for the sustenance of their clergy and the upkeep of their churches.[144] Bishops were only permitted to draw on these resources when revenues from their own property holdings were too small to cover their expenses; even then, real estate (*de facultatola*) and objects of divine service (*de ministerio*), such as sacred vessels, vestments, and books, were not to be alienated, and the parish was to be left with sufficient resources for its own needs.[145] By this

---

[139] Morin, "Le prêtre," 259–60. On *c.* 525 as the date of his appointment, see de Vogüé and Courreau, 405.

[140] Agroecius had been a bishop since at least 506 when he signed the resolutions of the Council of Agde, *CCSL* 148, 213, line 30.

[141] *CCSL* 148A, 50–51. For the exact charge, see C. J. Hefele and H. Leclercq, *Histoire des conciles*, II, part 2 (Paris, 1908), 1076, n. 1.   [142] *CCSL* 148A, 45, lines 17–18.

[143] Felix, "Legi quod" (= Caesarius, *ep.* 11), Morin II, 17–18.

[144] *CCSL* 148A, 48.   [145] Lesne, *Histoire de la propriété*, I, 64.

resolution, as we shall see in more detail in Chapter 8, the council took an important step toward giving local parishes the autonomy they needed to serve as effective centers of christianization in rural areas.

At the conclusion of their meeting, the bishops assembled at Carpentras agreed to meet in November of 528 at Vaison.[146] This meeting was postponed until November of 529, however, after a decision was reached to hold a council at Orange in July 529 to take up the problems of grace, predestination, and free will that had exercised the minds of Gallic churchmen since they first came into contact with Augustine's anti-Pelagian writings in the early fifth century.[147] Postponement of the Council of Vaison suggests that the decision to hold the Council of Orange was influenced by developments unforeseen by Caesarius and his fellow bishops in November 527. The most likely explanation for this change of plans was the occurrence of the Council of Valence, probably held in 528,[148] which challenged the orthodoxy of Caesarius's teachings on grace (*vita* I. 60). The council was convened by Julianus of Vienne, and brought together bishops from the ecclesiastical province of Vienne and (probably) Lyon ("antistites Christi ultra Eseram consistentes," *vita* I. 60). Although we cannot deny that Julianus convened the council to solve a genuine theological problem,[149] it is difficult not to imagine political motives as well, since just five years earlier he had seen most of his suffragans transferred to Caesarius's province. Caesarius was invited to the council, along with other bishops of his province, but he declined to attend, claiming illness. In his place he sent among other clerics his most loyal ally, Cyprianus of Toulon (*vita* I. 60).

Because the canons of Valence are no longer extant, we cannot be certain about its precise views on grace, predestination, and free will. But it is clear from the report of the proceedings in the *vita*, the definition of faith passed at Orange in 529, and its confirmation by Pope Boniface in 531, that the bishops assembled at the council upheld in general the "anti-predestinarian" orthodoxy that had

---

[146] *CCSL* 148A, 48.

[147] For a history of the "semi-Pelagian" conflict in Gaul, see G. de Plinval, "L'activité doctrinale dans l'église gallo-romaine," in *Histoire de l'église*, ed. A. Fliche and V. Martin, IV (Paris, 1948), 397–419. For a useful account of the Council of Orange, see G. Fritz, "Orange," *DTC* XI. 1 (1931), cols. 1087–1103.

[148] For the date, see Krusch, 442, and D. M. Cappuyns, "L'origine des 'Capitula' d'Orange 529," *Recherches de théologie ancienne et médiévale* 6 (1934), 121–42: 122, n. 2.

[149] *pace* Arnold, 346.

prevailed in Gaul since the mid-fifth century.[150] The most important point at issue was the role of "prevenient grace" in the acquisition of faith in Christ. The majority held the opinion that faith had its origins not in grace, but in nature.[151] Cyprianus and other supporters of Caesarius, on the other hand, argued that "no one could make any advance in divine progress on his own unless he had first been called by the intervention of God's grace."[152]

Despite their arguments, Cyprianus and his supporters failed to carry the day, and Caesarius decided to convene another council to defend his orthodoxy and settle the controversy. In making this decision, he was no doubt also influenced by a renewed interest in condemning Pelagian ideas that arose *c.* 520 in Rome, Constantinople, and Sardinia, as a consequence of pressure from the so-called "Scythian monks."[153] Indeed, it was from Rome that Caesarius had received the collection of *capitula* that would furnish the basis for the twenty-five canons of Orange.[154]

The Council of Orange was held on the occasion of the dedication of a basilica that Liberius, praetorian prefect of Gaul, had given to the city. Fourteen bishops from Caesarius's province assembled for the meeting, along with eight high-ranking laymen (*viri illustres*), whose presence demonstrated the strong aristocratic (and royal) support that Caesarius could rely upon to settle this dispute. Besides Liberius, the highest ranking Ostrogothic official in Provence, the list included Namatius, later governor of Provence under the Franks and thereafter bishop of Vienne (*c.* 552–59),[155] and Pantagatus, probably identical with the bishop of Vienne of the same name (538–547/49).[156] The other five aristocrats – Syagrius, Cariattho, Opilio, Marcellus, and Deodatus – cannot be further identified. On July 3, 529 these men joined the bishops of Provence in signing the council's resolutions, which consisted of a brief preface, twenty-five canons, and a definition of

---

[150] For the development of this prevailing orthodoxy, see R. Markus, "The Legacy of Pelagius: Orthodoxy, Heresy, and Conciliation," in *The Making of Orthodoxy: Essays in Honour of Henry Chadwick*, ed. R. Williams (Cambridge, 1989), 214–34.

[151] "Indicas enim, quod aliqui episcopi Galliarum…fidem tantum, qua in Christo credimus, naturae esse velint, non gratiae," Boniface II, "Per filium" I, *CCSL* 148A, 66 (= Caesarius, *ep.* 20. 1).

[152] "nihil per se in divinis profectibus quenquam arripere posse, nisi fuerit primitus dei gratia praeveniente vocatus," *vita* I. 60.   [153] Markus, "Legacy," 223–26.

[154] *CCSL* 148A, 55.

[155] Namatius 5, Heinzelmann, "Gallische Prosopographie," 655.

[156] Pantagatus 3, Heinzelmann, "Gallische Prosopographie," 662.

faith.[157] The canons themselves were based almost verbatim on the *capitula* that Caesarius had received from Rome.[158] The preface and definition of faith, on the other hand, were original compositions, probably by Caesarius. Taken together, these documents promoted a moderate Augustinianism. On the one hand, the council followed Faustus of Riez and other anti-predestinarians by rejecting the most extreme Augustinian positions, both explicitly, as in the case of predestination to evil,[159] and implicitly, as in the case of predestination to salvation. On the other hand, without ever condemning Faustus by name, it followed Augustine in strongly affirming the prior and essential role of divine grace in the acquisition of faith[160] and the performance of good works.[161] It was a compromise that owed much to Caesarius's own theological sympathies, which were divided between the "semi-Pelagianism" of Lérins and the Augustinianism of Pomerius, whose influence on Caesarius's concept of grace was profound.[162]

The solution proposed at Orange also answered Caesarius's need for a pastorally useful definition of grace, a definition that would communicate the importance of grace in human belief and action without conveying the impression that people were predestined to good or evil no matter what they actually did. Accordingly, the council offered the reassuring view that "all the baptized, if they are willing to labor faithfully, with Christ's help and cooperation, can and should fulfil what belongs to the soul's salvation."[163] In the simplified interpretation Caesarius offered in his sermons, this amounted to the view that salvation was available without restriction to all those who faithfully carried out the practices recommended by the church, especially almsgiving and charity (*serm.* 60. 1). The contrast with Augustine's more nuanced view is most evident in sermons Caesarius adapted from Augus-

---

[157] *CCSL* 148A, 64–65.
[158] Cappuyns, "L'origine," 124–25. The first eight canons were drawn from the *capitula sancti Augustini*, an anonymous *florilegium* from fifth-century Gaul, ed. Fr. Glorie, *CCSL* 85A, 243–73. The remainder were derived from the *liber sententiarum ex operibus sancti Augustini delibatarum* by Prosper of Aquitaine, Fritz, "Orange," col. 1090.
[159] *definitio fidei, CCSL* 148A, 63, lines 209–12. [160] Ibid., 63, lines 222–23.
[161] Ibid., 63, lines 213–18. [162] Tibiletti, "La teologia della grazia," 489–506.
[163] "omnis baptiszati Christo auxiliante et cooperante, quae ad salute animae pertinent, possint et debeant, si fideliter laborare voluerint, adimplere," *definitio fidei, CCSL* 148A, 63, lines 206–8, trans. J. Patout Burns, *Theological Anthropology* (Philadelphia, 1981), 119.

tine.[164] For instance, in concluding a sermon on the value of voluntary poverty and almsgiving, Caesarius departed from his model, Augustine's *Sermon 85*, in a passage that clearly implies that salvation is achievable by a man's own efforts: "Brothers, if we think intently about the unique and outstanding medicine of almsgiving and, as far as our resources permit, if we give to the poor either in food or in clothing, we shall deserve to obtain not only the forgiveness of our sins, but also our eternal reward" (*serm.* 153. 4). A more striking assertion of the same view can be seen in Caesarius's conclusion to another sermon, modeled on Augustine's *Sermon 49*. Exhorting his congregation to imitate St. Stephen's love of his enemies, Caesarius quotes a passage from St. Matthew: "If you forgive other men their sins, your heavenly father will forgive you your sins" (Mt. 6: 14). He then concludes:

Observe, brothers, the mercy of our Lord: he has placed in our power how we shall be judged on the day of judgment. If we forgive sins, they will be forgiven us; if we do not forgive, we shall not be forgiven. Let us therefore, beloved brothers, love not only our friends, but also our enemies, so that before the tribunal of the eternal judge we might come with a secure conscience, saying, "Give, Lord, because we gave; forgive, because we forgave; we have done what you ordered; now you fulfill what you promised." (*serm.* 220. 3)

The addition of the formula "with the grace of God" in an almost identical passage from another sermon (*serm.* 219. 2) does little to restore Augustine's subtlety on this point.

The theological achievement of the Council of Orange was equalled a few months later by the pastoral achievement of the Council of Vaison.[165] Meeting in November 529, Caesarius and eleven of his suffragans reached agreement on five canons. In the last three canons, which dealt with liturgical matters, they decided to require that the Kyrie Eleison be recited at Matins, Vespers, and Mass, and that the Sanctus be sung at every Mass (can. 3); that the words "Sicut erat in principio" be added to the Gloria Patri (can. 5); and that the name of the bishop of Rome be mentioned in liturgical prayers (can. 4). The purpose of these reforms was both to bind the churches of Provence more closely to Rome and other churches (an intention mentioned in all three canons and

---

[164] W. M. Daly, "Caesarius of Arles. A Precursor of Medieval Christendom," *Traditio* 26 (1970), 1–28: 20–22.   [165] *CCSL* 148A, 77–81.

fully in line with Caesarius's political leanings) and to legitimate the more radical reforms of the council's other two canons. The first of these directed parish priests to educate young unmarried lectors in their own homes, and the second gave priests and deacons the right to preach. The radical nature of these canons lay in their assault on the episcopal prerogatives of teaching and preaching. It is significant that Caesarius could convince only eleven of his suffragans to agree to them, in contrast with the seventeen suffragans who had signed the more moderate reform resolutions of Arles (524). The failure of some of his strongest supporters to sign the canons of Vaison, including Fylagrius of Cavaillon, Praetextatus of Apt, and Aletius of Vaison, all of whom had signed the canons of Orange a few months earlier and would sign (or have a representative sign) the canons of Marseille in 533, provides an indication of just how difficult it was for bishops to accept these canons. The absence of Aletius's signature or that of a representative is all the more remarkable in view of the fact that the council met in his own city. In "abstaining" from a vote on the canons of Vaison, whether by refusing to sign them or declining to attend the council, Aletius and his colleagues could express their disagreement with Caesarius's reforms without blocking them completely. They therefore allowed the reforms to go forward, albeit with reduced support.

Given this resistance to reform, the most surprising fact about the councils of 524–29 is not that Caesarius's reform efforts went no further, but that they went as far as they did. Caesarius owed this achievement to the support he received from a solid core of loyal suffragans. The most prominent among these was Cyprianus of Toulon, who demonstrated his support for Caesarius not only by defending Caesarius's views on grace at the Council of Valence and composing his biography, but also by signing all five of Caesarius's councils after Agde, as well as the two documents that Caesarius submitted to his fellow bishops for approval: the letter of Hormisdas and *recapitulatio* of the *regula virginum*. No other suffragan supported Caesarius as consistently over as long a period, but there were other, less senior bishops who signed or had a representative sign as many of the councils of 524–29 as took place during their tenure. They included Constantius of Gap,[166]

---

[166] Arles (524), *CCSL* 148A, 45, lines 21–22; Carpentras (527), *CCSL* 148A, 49, line 7; Orange (529), *CCSL* 148A, 64, lines 5–6; and Vaison (529), *CCSL* 148A, 80, lines 6–7.

Heraclius of Trois-Châteaux,[167] and Vindimalis of Orange.[168] It was with the help of these men (about whom, unfortunately, nothing else is known) that Caesarius promulgated reforms at the councils of 524–29 that were intended above all to promote the christianization of Provence. But it was within his own diocese, unchallenged by any cleric of equal status, that Caesarius exercised the most direct control over this process. By examining his efforts of christianization in the city and countryside of Arles, where his program could be implemented more fully than anywhere else, we may discover the upper limits of its decidedly mixed success. We turn first to the sermons, ceremonies, and rites of healing and exorcism by which Caesarius attempted to promote christianization in his diocese and at the same time to define the authority by which he did so.

---

[167] Carpentras (527), *CCSL* 148A, 49, line 5; Orange (529), *CCSL* 148A, 64, line 17; and Vaison (529), *CCSL* 148A, 81, line 9.
[168] Carpentras (527), *CCSL* 148A, 49, line 18 and 51, line 39; Orange (529), *CCSL* 148A, 64, line 21; and Vaison (529), *CCSL* 148A, 80, line 15.

Chapter 6

CHRISTIAN RHETORIC AND RITUAL ACTION

As they entered the Christian episcopate in increasingly large numbers over the course of the fifth and sixth centuries, Gallic aristocrats found it possible to redefine their local authority and prestige in a new ideology largely of their own making.[1] Toward the end of the fifth century, however, reformers such as Pomerius and the author of the *statuta ecclesiae antiqua* challenged the increasingly aristocratic character of this redefinition, arguing that episcopal authority should be based more on the bishop's exemplary faith and ascetic way of life than on his birth, wealth, or superior education. How closely Caesarius abided by these reform ideas can best be seen in the displays of word and action by which he attempted to establish his own authority as bishop and to mobilize that authority for the inculcation of Christian values. Because Caesarius himself thought it most important, we begin this chapter with his authority as a preacher, and then proceed to consider the equally potent non-verbal sources of his authority: his performance of church ritual and his reputation as a holy man, which led to a belief in his miraculous powers.

THE ART OF PREACHING

At the heart of Caesarius's work as a pastor lay the conviction that the bishop's primary responsibility was to instill in his people the values, beliefs, and practices that would ensure for them a place in the kingdom of God (*serm.* 4. 4; 230. 5). Living in a culture in which the spoken word still carried great authority,[2] and disposed by his social class and education to trust the power of rhetoric, Caesarius simply took it for granted that preaching provided the

---

[1] Van Dam, *Leadership*, 141–56.
[2] This was the case despite the widespread importance of writing in the early middle ages, R. McKitterick, "Conclusion," in *The Uses of Literacy in Early Mediaeval Europe*, ed. R. McKitterick (Cambridge, 1990), 319–33: 320.

most effective means of accomplishing his pastoral objectives.[3] For
him, a bishop's sermons were meant to work like the terrifyingly
powerful trumpets that brought down the walls of Jericho and
penetrated the city: they could destroy the hardiest of sins and lay
bare a man's soul (*serm.* 115.5–6). Like the prophets of ancient
Israel, Caesarius felt obligated to wield these potent weapons of
instruction, warning, and persuasion. Like Isaiah, he believed that
he was commanded by God to "cry out unceasingly; lift up your
voice like a trumpet blast and announce to my people their sins"
(Is. 58: 1).[4] Failure to do so would have brought God's retribution
upon him: "If you do not tell the wicked man of his sin, I shall
hold you responsible for his death" (Ez. 3: 18).[5] Accordingly, he
preached in the urban cathedral and rural parishes alike (*vita* II. 20),
and delivered sermons on Sundays and feast days, as well as at the
daily offices of Matins and Vespers.[6] Such devotion to preaching
was not in itself unusual in Gaul. Bishops were regularly praised
for their preaching,[7] and their responsibility to carry it out was
widely acknowledged.[8] Although Pomerius and Caesarius criticized bishops who rarely or never preached,[9] most bishops
probably took this responsibility seriously, for the right to preach
was itself a powerful source of authority. This right became all the
more powerful when it was regularly exercised, for preaching
offered bishops the opportunity to demonstrate their superior
education, moral authority, and spiritual expertise. It was because
they considered it a powerful source of prestige and authority that
bishops jealously guarded the right to preach: most bishops
refused to share this prerogative with their diocesan clergy, for fear
of diluting or undermining their own authority.

Where Caesarius differed from many of his colleagues was not
so much in the act of preaching (although he may have preached
more often than most bishops), but rather in the art of preaching,
which set his authority as a preacher on a different footing. Unlike
preachers such as Sidonius Apollinaris and Avitus of Vienne,

---

[3] This was a widespread assumption. For instance, after ordering their colleagues to
preach, the bishops assembled at the Council of Valencia in 549 declared that, "we
know that people have been drawn to the faith by hearing the preaching of bishops,"
can. I, *Concilios Visigóticos,* 61.

[4] *serm.* I. 3; 4. 2; 5. I; 57. I; 80. 2; 115. 5; 183. I; 230. 3.

[5] *serm.* 4. 2; 5. I; 57. I; 145. I; 183. I; 217. 3; 225. 4.

[6] *vita* I. 59. *Serm.* 118, for example, was delivered at the morning office, and *serm.* 76 at
the evening office.   [7] Heinzelmann, *Bischofsherrschaft,* 118–22; Beck, 259–61.

[8] Avitus, *hom.* 16, *MGH AA,* VI. 2, 125.

[9] Pomerius, *vita contempl.* I. 18–21; Caesarius, *serm.* I. 10–17.

147

Caesarius preached in a deliberately simple and direct Latin style as advised by Augustine and Pomerius.[10] It was "lowly speech," a true *sermo humilis*,[11] often modeled on the Bible,[12] with the pronunciation, morphology,[13] and diction[14] of the vernacular Latin spoken by his audience. Caesarius preferred this "ordinary, everyday, rustic speech" (*serm.* 1. 20; 86. 1; 114.2) to the "elegant and luxuriant worldly eloquence" (*serm.* 1. 20) that bishops like Sidonius and Avitus employed, because he believed it could be understood by the whole congregation, whereas the latter could be appreciated by only a few cultivated persons (*serm.* 1. 20). As a result, when he adapted sermons from other preachers, as he frequently did, Caesarius simplified these in accord with his own principles, abbreviating complex theological arguments, eliminating irrelevant details, and rephrasing complicated syntax. As he said at the beginning of one sermon, "If we offered explanations of the sacred scriptures in the same order and with the same eloquence with which they are offered by the holy fathers, only a few cultivated persons would be nourished by this teaching, and the ren   multitude would be left hungry" (*serm.* 86. 1). The use of simple language to address peasant audiences was not in itself unprecedented, especially among bishops with a monastic background or ascetic sympathies.[15] Yet even for most such bishops, sermons delivered on important occasions such as the ordination of a bishop or the dedication of a church,[16] or sermons

---

[10] Augustine, *doctr. christ.* IV. x. 24; Pomerius, *vita contempl.* I. 23.

[11] Auerbach, *Literary Language*, 27–66, esp. 53; C. A. Rapisarda, "Lo stile umile nei sermoni di S. Cesario d'Arles. Giustificazioni teoriche e posizioni polemiche," *Orpheus* 17 (1970), 115–59; D. Norberg, *Manuel pratique de latin médiéval* (Paris, 1968), 93–104; Delage I, 175–208; E. Clerici, "Il sermo humilis di Cesario d'Arles," *Rendiconti dell'Istituto Lombardo. Classe di lettere, scienze morali e storiche* 105 (1971), 339–64.

[12] I. Bonini, "Lo stile nei sermoni di Cesario di Arles," *Aevum* 36 (1962), 240–57: 240–42.

[13] On pronunciation and morphology, see Wright, *Late Latin*, esp. 45–103. Although much in this book remains controversial, Wright has clearly shown how changes in the pronunciation of later Latin could have reflected changes in morphology without affecting orthography, thus leaving a developing vernacular invisible in the texts of those who still knew how to spell "properly." For further discussion, see M. Van Uytfanghe, "Histoire du latin, protohistoire des langues romanes et histoire de la communication," *Francia* 11 (1983), esp. 595–613; R. McKitterick, *The Carolingians and the Written Word* (Cambridge, 1989), 7–12; and the essays collected in *Latin and the Romance Languages*, ed. Wright.

[14] G. Morin, "Quelques raretés philologiques dans les écrits de Césaire d'Arles," *Bulletin du Cange* 11 (1936), 5–14; A. Ernout, "Du latin aux langues romanes," *Revue de philologie* 43 (1969), 7–14: 11–13; A. Vaccari, "Volgarismi notevoli nel latino di S. Cesario di Arles (†543)," *Archivum Latinitatis Medii Aevi* 17 (1943), 135–48.

[15] Arnold, 122.   [16] Wood, "The Audience of Architecture," 74–75.

delivered on any occasion when men of their own class were present to judge them, demanded a more cultivated style. So we are informed of Hilarius of Arles that, "If there were no cultivated men in the audience, he nourished the hearts of the peasants with simple speech. But whenever he saw that educated men had come in, he was stimulated to an unaccustomed level of gracefulness in speech and appearance: he appeared larger than life."[17] Caesarius, by contrast, uniformly gave preference to the least well-educated members of his audience: "And because uncultivated and simple folk are unable to climb the same heights as cultivated persons, the latter should deign to bend down to their ignorance. For well-educated persons can understand what is said to the simple, but simple persons are entirely incapable of understanding what is preached to the cultivated" (*serm.* 86. 1). Having dispensed with an authority based on secular rhetorical training, Caesarius relied on a different form of authority, an authority based on "faith and the merits of his life."[18] As Pomerius explained, "A bishop's teaching should be none other than his life. His listeners will draw sufficient profit if what they see their teachers perform in a spiritual fashion they also hear preached to them in a simple fashion...From this it should be understood that a teacher of the church should not glory in the display of an elaborate style, for otherwise he might seem not to wish to edify the church of God, but rather to show off the great extent of his learning. He should place his entire confidence in his preaching, therefore, not in the brilliance of his words, but in the power of his deeds."[19]

Caesarius's rejection of "worldly eloquence" did not of course prevent him from employing a wide array of rhetorical techniques in his sermons, many based on Augustine's *de doctrina christiana*. But he restricted these techniques to the most severely practical, which had as their sole function "the edification of the church of God." As Augustine had advised, Caesarius preached "first and foremost to be understood."[20] His delivery was exemplary, for like any good orator, he was aware of the principle well expressed by Quintilian that "All emotional appeals will inevitably fall flat, unless they are given the fire that voice, look, and the whole carriage of the body can give them."[21] He always spoke in a loud, clear voice (*vita* I. 54), and varied his gestures and facial expressions

---

[17] *vita Hilarii* 14.   [18] *stat. eccl. ant.*, can. 4.   [19] Pomerius, *vita contempl.* I. 23.
[20] *doctr. christ.* IV. viii. 22.
[21] Quintilian XI. 3. 2, trans. H. E. Butler, Loeb Classical Library.

to suit the content of his message and the disposition of his audience (*vita* I. 17). Moreover, unlike his predecessor Hilarius, who had been known to harangue his weary congregation for as long as four hours,[22] Caesarius normally spoke for less than half an hour (*serm.* 76. 3). This suited the attention span of his audience (*serm.* 195. 4), and encouraged the attendance of the poor, whose work prevented them from participating in long services (*serm.* 76. 3; 91. 8; 100. 1B). Brevity also made his sermons easier to remember, as Caesarius himself noted (*serm.* 22. 1; 23. 2). This was supremely important, since the bishop believed that by storing what it had learned from biblical stories, sermons, figural images, and other sources of edification, an individual's memory served as a repository of moral exemplars and thus a kind of template for Christian living.[23] Indeed, Caesarius explicitly linked the memory of his sermons with the performance of good deeds. In a sermon on the love of enemies, he promised to narrate stories from the Old and New Testament "so that you might be able to retain such outstanding love in your memories and with the help of God carry it out in your actions" (*serm.* 36. 1μ). At the close of a sermon delivered in a rural parish, he instructed the congregation "to memorize this reading in your hearts so that in the future you may deserve to receive eternal rewards" (*serm.* 19. 6). And in a sermon on almsgiving and the Last Judgment, he advised his audience "always to remember this gospel reading, and labor mightily with God's help, so that you can avoid eternal flames and happily reach the kingdom of heaven" (*serm.* 158. 6).

Caesarius worked hard to deliver sermons that were clear, convincing, and above all memorable. To this end, he accommodated his rhetorical style to his pastoral intentions. In a redefinition of Cicero's three levels of style, Augustine had recommended that preachers employ a subdued style for teaching, a moderate style for praising and blaming, and a grand style for persuading their audiences.[24] He warned speakers not to use one style exclusively within a sermon, but to alternate among styles for variety and maximum effect.[25] Caesarius largely followed this advice. He favored an emotionally neutral, relatively unadorned, "subdued" style most of the time, but rose as necessary to the

[22] *vita Hilarii* 14–15.
[23] On the moral value of a well-trained memory in antiquity and the middle ages, see Carruthers, *The Book of Memory*, 12–13, 71.   [24] *doctr. christ.* IV. xix. 38.
[25] Ibid., IV. xxii. 51.

moderate and grand styles, characterized by more impassioned language and the increased use of rhetorical figures. To make his sermons lively, dramatic, and memorable, he used figures at every level of style, especially figures of parallelism, repetition, and sound.[26] He maintained a pleasing rhythm based on stress accent by the consistent use of *clausulae*, brief rhythmic sequences at the ends of sentences.[27] In addition, he employed more colloquial features, such as rhetorical questions, exclamations, vivid metaphors from agriculture, commerce, and other aspects of daily life,[28] and dialogue between himself and fictitious interlocutors from the audience, a technique borrowed from Augustine for anticipating and then refuting objections.[29] Most importantly, to lend authority and eloquence to his preaching, he frequently quoted or paraphrased the scriptures, which like Augustine's ideal preacher[30] he knew well (*vita* I. 16, 52), both in the Vulgate and the Vetus Latina.[31]

But the impact of a sermon did not depend only on memorable content, an appealing style, or persuasive delivery. Much of its authority came from the architectural setting in which it was delivered and the ritual performance to which it belonged, both of which reinforced its message with messages of their own. Although these conditions of setting and performance played a part whenever and wherever Caesarius preached, their persuasive impact was potentially at its greatest when he preached in his cathedral church on Sundays or feast days. For it was there and then that architecture and ritual were most impressively combined to enhance the authority of the bishop and the appeal of his message.

SACRED SPACE AND TIME

Although little is known of the appearance of the basilica of St. Stephen in Arles, the floor plan of the eleventh-century church of Saint-Trophime that replaced it suggests that the cathedral resembled fifth-century basilicas found in Rome, Ravenna, and

---

[26] Bonini, "Lo stile," 243–57.   [27] Delage I, 206–7.

[28] *vita* I. 16; A. Salvatore, "Uso delle similitudini e pedagogia pastorale nei Sermones di Cesario di Arles," *Rivista di cultura classica e medioevale* 9 (1967), 177–225.

[29] On Augustine's use of this figure, see M. I. Barry, *St. Augustine, the Orator: A Study of the Rhetorical Qualities of St. Augustine's Sermones ad Populum* (Washington, D.C., 1924), 149–51.   [30] *doctr. christ.* IV. v. 7.   [31] Delage I, 116–17.

elsewhere.[32] It included a rectangular nave topped by windows and probably flanked by lower side aisles, with an atrium at its entrance (*vita* II. 29). Inside, long rows of columns running along the nave focused attention on the apse, where the centers of ritual action were situated: the *ambo*, from which the scriptures were read; the altar, surrounded by a chancel railing (*vita* I. 32), where the bishop celebrated the sacrifice of the Mass; and the *cathedra*, the bishop's chair from which he delivered his sermons.[33] Adorned, as were its counterparts elsewhere, with mosaics and frescoes,[34] the church was a place of shimmering sun light and lamp light, bright silver ornaments (*vita* I. 32), brilliant tapestries, and gleaming marble surfaces.[35] Those who entered it were reminded of paradise, as in the fifth-century cathedral in Clermont, where, according to Gregory of Tours, "people feel the fear of God and a great brightness, and the pious often notice a very sweet aroma coming toward them as though of spices."[36]

Even when no ritual was being conducted in it, the basilica was meant to instruct and inspire. Its structure symbolized the regularity and hierarchy of the Christian cosmos. Its decorations prefigured the splendor and beauty of the world to come. Its mosaics and frescoes recalled the milestones of salvation history.[37] Its relics transmitted the healing power of Christ and his saints.[38]

---

[32] R. Krautheimer, *Early Christian and Byzantine Architecture*, 3rd rev. edn. (Harmondsworth, 1981), 177–78, provides a general description of the fifth-century basilica in the west. See also A. Marignan, *Etudes sur la civilisation française*, II (Paris, 1899), 135–82, and J. Hubert, *L'Art pré-roman* (Paris, 1938), 45–50.

[33] The pre-Romanesque church beneath the present Saint-Trophime is discussed in L. H. Labande, "Etude historique et archéologique sur Saint-Trophime d'Arles du IVe au XIIIe siècle," *Bulletin monumental* (1903), 459–97: 478–81; J.-M. Rouquette, *Provence romane*, I, *La Provence rhodanienne* (La Pierre-qui-Vire, 1974), 269–71; and J. Thirion, "Saint-Trophime d'Arles," *Congrès archéologique de France* 134 (1976), 360–479: 369–71.

[34] For accounts of mosaics and frescoes in Gallic churches, see Gregory of Tours, *hist.* II. 16; VII. 22; *glor. mart.* 21, 22, 61; *vita Genovefae* 56, ed. B. Krusch, *MGH SRM*, III, 237–38; Marignan, *Etudes*, II, 175; H. Woodruff, "The Iconography and Date of the Mosaics of La Daurade," *Art Bulletin* 13 (1931), 80–104; and R. Markus, "The Cult of Icons in Sixth-Century Gaul," *JTS* 29 (1978), 151–57: 152–53.

[35] For comparison, see Gregory of Tours, *hist.* V. 45; Venantius Fortunatus, *carm.* 3. 7; Sidonius Apollinaris, *ep.* II. 10. 4; A. Grabar, *Christian Iconography: A Study of its Origins* (Princeton, 1968), 99.

[36] *hist.* II. 16. The fragrance of incense, candles, and flowers contributed to the effect; see also *hist.* II. 31, and Marignan, *Etudes*, II, 163.

[37] For a survey of the educational potential of these images, see H. L. Kessler, "Pictorial Narrative and Church Mission in Sixth-Century Gaul," in *Pictorial Narrative in Antiquity and the Middle Ages*, ed. H. L. Kessler and M. S. Simpson (1985), 75–91.

[38] Van Dam, *Leadership*, 230–55.

When the basilica was used as a stage for the performance of the liturgy, these features served to enhance the dignity, grandeur, and intelligibility of the ceremony as well as the status of the bishop who conducted it. In particular, the bishop's place of honor in the basilica's hierarchically arranged space favored his claims to authority and demands for obedience. His association with the basilica's holy relics validated his own claims to sanctity. Most significantly, the association of the basilica with paradise strengthened his self-proclaimed status as a representative of Christ and gave divine sanction to his preaching. "It is," as Augustine once said in a sermon, "Christ who teaches; he has his *cathedra* in heaven."[39]

Truly, the basilica appeared an awesome and holy place. Speaking one Sunday at the dedication of a renovated basilica, Caesarius paraphrased the exclamation that Jacob had uttered after dreaming of the ladder to heaven (Gn. 28: 17): "How terrifying this place is! Here is the house of God and the gate of heaven, and it will be called the court of God."[40] Many preachers had chosen to explain this phrase by emphasizing the role of the basilica as a *porta caeli*, a gateway to heaven.[41] This was an explanation that Caesarius implicitly rejected, for he felt that no physical place, but only the crucified Christ could be said to perform this mediating function (*serm.* 87. 3). He concentrated instead on what he saw as the dual significance of the phrase "house of God." In one sense, he said, it referred to the house of paradise that Christians could inherit by prayer and good works;[42] in another sense it referred to God's dwelling in individuals.[43] In another sermon, Caesarius conflated these two interpretations.

[This] temple [is] made of wood and stone in order that the living temples of God may gather [here] and come together into one temple of God. A single Christian is one temple of God and many Christians are many temples of God...Now these temples of Christ, that is, devout

---

[39] *sermo de disciplina christiana* 15, PL 40: 678.

[40] "Terribilis est locus iste; hic est domus dei et porta celi et vocabitur aula dei," A. Höfer, "Zwei unbekannte Sermones des Caesarius von Arles," *RBen* 74 (1964), 44–53: 49, lines 23–4 (attributed without explanation to pseudo-Caesarius in *PLS* 5, 159). The same verse was inscribed on the arch over the altar in the church of St. Martin in Tours, *Inscriptions chrétiennes de la Gaule antérieures au VIIIe siècle*, ed. E. Le Blant (Paris, 1856–65), no. 177.   [41] Van Dam, *Leadership*, 243–45.

[42] Höfer, "Zwei unbekannte Sermones," 49–50, lines 24–33.

[43] Ibid., 50, lines 34–6; see 1 Cor. 3: 16–17.

Christian souls, are scattered throughout the world, but when Judgment Day comes, they will all be gathered together and will form one temple in eternal life. (*serm.* 229. 2)

In this and other sermons,[44] Caesarius maintained that the holiness of the basilica did not depend so much on the innate sanctity or subsequent "sanctification" of the materials of which it was composed, on the holy relics enshrined there, or even on God's "dwelling" in the sanctuary, as much as on the collective activity of worship that went on there. In Caesarius's view, it was essentially the "people of God" – both clergy and laity – who collaborated in the sanctification of place and time by their ritual activity. Through their efforts, the basilica was made into a sacred space, simultaneously a recollection of Eden and an anticipation of the kingdom of God, which stood outside the coordinates of routine social space just as Sundays and feast days stood outside the coordinates of ordinary "agricultural" time.[45]

It was at this time and place, in this "place of peace and charity" (*serm.* 224. 1) that the "whole people" (*serm.* 152. 1) was expected to act out in ritual form its devotion to God, its obedience to the bishop, and the love of its members for one another. This ritual enactment of Christian perfection was designed not only to *express* the Christian beliefs and values of the population, but also to *promote* those beliefs and values, by affirming the reality of the Christian world view and providing a model for Christian living in the everyday world. As J. Z. Smith has explained, "Ritual is a means of performing the way things ought to be in conscious tension to the way things are in such a way that this ritualized perfection is recollected in the ordinary, uncontrolled order of things."[46] The music people heard at Mass, the images they saw, the ritual actions they witnessed and performed, their very participation itself – all were meant to reinforce the message Caesarius proclaimed in his sermons, and to do so in a "language" that was all the more convincing for being implicit and non-verbal. It is this function of the liturgy as a ceremony of "ritualized perfection" that explains Caesarius's extraordinary concern with the way people prepared for it and behaved during it, for, as everyone knew, exterior appearances reflected inner states (*vita* I. 46; II. 35).

---

[44] *serm.* 152. 1; 228. 1.   [45] Van Dam, *Leadership*, 291–94.
[46] J. Z. Smith, *Imagining Religion: From Babylon to Jonestown* (Chicago, 1982), 63.

To make their souls as bright as the new clothes they wore (*serm.* 14. 1) and as luminous as the basilica itself (*serm.* 229. 3), Caesarius required the members of his congregation to undergo certain rites of preparation for the Mass. They were urged to give alms to the poor,[47] settle disputes,[48] confess their sins,[49] and, on the day of the service, bring offerings of bread or wine for communion,[50] and when possible, tithes of the harvest.[51] The whole of the day was to be reserved for prayer and worship, and "secular pursuits" were to be avoided (*serm.* 116. 6), including agricultural work[52] and sexual relations,[53] for such pursuits were seen as activities incompatible with the "state of nature" represented by the myth of Eden and replicated by ascetic practice.[54] Powerful sanctions awaited those who violated these taboos. "If a man has sexual relations with his wife…on Sunday or on any other feast day, the children conceived at that time will be born as lepers or epileptics, or possibly even possessed by the devil. Lepers are usually produced not by wise people who remain chaste on feast days and other prescribed days, but rather by rustics (*rustici*) who do not know how to restrain themselves" (*serm.* 44. 7).

For Christians who planned to receive communion, taboos were even more restrictive, for the ritual placed them in a state of union with God and fellow Christians. To prepare for it, they had to avoid sexual relations for several days,[55] and eradicate their sins through prayers, fasts, and alms.[56] The smallest residual sin could doom the Christian as he took communion at the altar (*serm.* 187. 4), and Caesarius often reminded his congregation of St. Paul's warning that "whoever eats the body and blood of the Lord unworthily will be guilty of profaning his body and blood" (1 Cor. 11 : 27).[57] In addition, men were required to wash their hands before receiving communion, and women, whose purity was more difficult to ensure, were obliged to cover their hands with a linen cloth (*serm.* 227. 5; 229. 4). It seems to have been largely

---

[47] *serm.* 14. 2; 16. 2; 86. 5; 188. 6; 198. 1; 225. 5.
[48] *serm.* 14. 2; 16. 2; 188. 6; 224. 4; 229. 4.
[49] Höfer, "Zwei unbekannte Sermones," 50, line 30. [50] *serm.* 13. 2; 14. 3; 19. 4.
[51] *serm.* 229. 4. [52] Orléans (538), can. 31. [53] *serm.* 44. 7.
[54] Van Dam offers a stimulating Lévi-Straussian discussion of these taboos, *Leadership*, 285–88.
[55] *serm.* 187. 4; 188. 3. See also *serm.* 16. 2 and 19. 3, delivered on parish visits.
[56] *serm.* 202. 4; 227. 2; Höfer, "Zwei unbekannte Sermones," 50, lines 29–32.
[57] *serm.* 44. 6; 202. 4.

because these taboos were so restrictive that people rarely participated in the ritual of communion, and had to be required to do so at the critical feasts of Christmas, Easter, and Pentecost.[58]

In the same way, Caesarius attempted to regulate behavior at the Mass itself, for improper, irreverent, and rude behavior threatened not only the person who engaged in it, but the entire assembly as well: "Anyone who engages in unsuitable and unfitting gossip in church offers a kind of poison or sword to other people, since he neither hears the word of God himself nor permits others to hear it" (*serm.* 77. 6).[59] In contrast to the highly structured language of the Mass and Caesarius's sermons, "gossip" was random and shapeless talk which had to be suppressed not only because it distracted the audience's attention, but also because its very individuality thwarted the group consensus the Mass was supposed to achieve.[60] Caesarius considered this sort of behavior so threatening to the integrity of the ceremony that he warned the congregation that it would lead to the invasion of the devil, whose presence was all the more to be feared at moments of contact between the normally separated human and divine orders.[61]

The devil, dearest brothers, has grown accustomed to assault us especially when he knows that we have taken precautions against him by means of spiritual weapons. Because he is not able to drive us away physically from the assembly of the church, he tries to involve us in fruitless thoughts and idle talk in the church itself. In this way he can eliminate the benefits of the reading and the remedies of prayer through empty, vain, or perhaps even bitter conversations and sordid thoughts. (*serm.* 77. 7)

In fact, no one could realistically deny this possibility, since demon possession was not an uncommon occurrence at Mass. At least three such incidents occurred during Caesarius's career. Once during a celebration of Mass in a rural parish church, an eight-year-old boy in clerical dress (probably a lector) began to exhibit symptoms of possession just after the homily (*vita* II. 20). On another occasion, a man became possessed in the basilica of St. Stephen during Sunday Mass (*serm.* 79. 1). In yet another incident, a woman shouting and frothing at the mouth burst into the cathedral upon the terrified congregation (*vita* I. 43). Besides producing general terror, these incidents effectively verified

[58] Agde (506), can. 18; Beck, 150–54.
[59] See also *serm.* 50. 3; 55. 4; 72. 1; 80. 1; and N. Adkin, "A Problem in the Early Church: Noise During Sermon and Lesson," *Mnemosyne* 38 (1985), 161–63.
[60] I owe this point to Raymond Van Dam.   [61] For example, Easter, *serm.* 98. 1.

Caesarius's characterization of the world as a battleground between demonic and divine forces. They also suggested a link between the aimless talk of gossiping Christians and the uncontrollable ravings of possessed persons, and reinforced Caesarius's pleas for polite attention with images of the exorcist's "quieting" of the demoniac. Caesarius thus demanded that the congregation concentrate on singing, praying, and listening to the scriptures in unison[62] rather than gossiping as individuals, so that their "holy shouting" might confuse the devil and drive him out of church (*serm.* 80. 2).

Caesarius did not direct his attention to verbal activity alone. He also insisted that the congregation observe the rules of decorum by wearing appropriate clothing to church (*serm.* 224. 2), and exhibiting the proper gestures of deference, including genuflecting,[63] bowing and nodding,[64] and standing up instead of lying on the floor of the church "as if in bed."[65] By insisting on these standards of respect, Caesarius demonstrated the great symbolic, practical, and ideological importance of posture, expression, and gesture in the inculcation of moral and cultural values. Pierre Bourdieu explains: "The principles embodied in this way are placed beyond the grasp of consciousness, and hence cannot be touched by voluntary, deliberate transformation, cannot even be made explicit; nothing seems more ineffable, more incommunicable, more inimitable, and, therefore, more precious, than the values given body, *made* body by the transubstantiation achieved by the hidden persuasion of an implicit pedagogy."[66] The ideology Caesarius advocated is tellingly revealed in an analogy he repeatedly used in his sermons, that people should behave in church exactly as they would in the presence of a powerful person: "As for those who neither genuflect nor bow their heads, I would like to know if they were seeking something important for themselves from a king, a judge, or another powerful person, whether they would demand it standing with head erect in a careless and casual fashion " (*serm.* 77. 3).

This was a society in which structures of hierarchy, domination, and dependence were taken completely for granted.[67] It was a

---

[62] *serm.* 75. 3; see also *vita* I. 19.   [63] *serm.* 76. 1; 77. 1.   [64] *serm.* 77. 1.

[65] *serm.* 78. 1.

[66] P. Bourdieu, *Outline of a Theory of Practice*, trans. R. Nice (Cambridge, 1977), 94.

[67] For instance, *serm.* 225. 3: "Therefore, let each and every one of you cry out on behalf of chastity, peace, justice, and truth...If a more powerful person is persecuting the truth, humbly beg him [to stop]. If it is your equal who despises justice, advise him to

society in which the bishop's biographers could praise him for
moderation in prohibiting his slaves and free-born servants from
receiving more than thirty-nine lashes in a single day (*vita* I. 25), a
limit based on biblical authority (Dt. 25: 3; I Cor. 11: 24). It was,
as a result, a society in which relations with the divine could
plausibly be said to resemble or replicate the unequal relations
between human beings, and where God could be preeminently
conceived of as a powerful man or patron. So Caesarius frequently
made analogies between the Christian's duty of obedience and
reverence toward God and the duties of slaves[68] and tenants[69]
toward the powerful,[70] kings,[71] lords,[72] and nobles.[73]

What is more, because the bishop claimed to represent Christ in
his role at Mass, demands for deference toward God could be
translated into demands for deference toward the bishop as well
(*serm.* 16. 2). And because the bishop, unlike Christ, stood at the
center of a system of authority and domination that required
continual legitimation and validation from below, gestures of
deference made at Mass could be interpreted equally well as
expressions of communal consensus for the bishop or acts of public
reverence for God. But in neither of these cases was it enough for
the congregation to behave with decency and respect; community
participation had to be complete. Caesarius therefore urged
Christians to attend Sunday and feast day Masses regularly,[74] to
arrive on time,[75] and, what is more, to remain for the entire
ceremony,[76] or, for those not taking communion, at least until the
episcopal blessing at the end of the Pater Noster.[77] In this context,
absence or departure from the assembly represented more than a
refusal to participate in the service; it also represented a withholding or withdrawal of consensus for the bishop's claim to
authority. By contrast, the full participation of the community
granted him a visible legitimacy, and expressed in ritual form the
ideal hierarchical relationship between the bishop and his congregation. At no time did this ritual expression of consensus matter
more than at the bishop's sermon, for by consenting to remain in

---

give up his sin ... If it is a person subservient and inferior to you who does not do what
is right, chastise him, rebuke him, and if you have the power, punish him with
severity." [68] *serm.* 12. 5; 15. 2; 32. 3; 44. 2; 64. 3; 157. 6.
[69] *serm.* 7. 3; 33. 1; 44. 2. [70] *serm.* 72. 3; 73. 3; 227. 3. [71] *serm.* 73. 3.
[72] *serm.* 47. 3. [73] *serm.* 187. 2.
[74] R. Etaix, "Deux nouveaux sermons de saint Césaire d'Arles," *REAug* 11 (1965), 9–13:
12, lines 22–7; *serm.* 74. 3. [75] *serm.* 72. 1. [76] *serm.* 73; 74.
[77] *serm.* 73. 2; Agde (506), can. 47; Orléans (511), can. 26; Orléans (538), can. 32.

church for the sermon, the congregation not only indicated its willingness to consider the bishop's message, but more fundamentally acknowledged his right to define and promote a system of values and beliefs in the first place. It was in recognition of the symbolic significance of the bishop's sermon as well as its pedagogical value that the author of the *statuta ecclesiae antiqua* had recommended excommunication for anyone leaving church during the sermon.[78] On one occasion, when his authority to preach was called into question by a premature departure from church, as it frequently was (*serm.* 73. 1), Caesarius was said to have taken more direct action:

One day, as he looked down from the altar after the reading of the gospel, Caesarius saw some people leaving the church who particularly refused to listen to the word, that is the sermon, of the blessed man. Immediately he ran down and cried out to the people: "What are you doing, my children? Why are you being led outside? Have wicked thoughts overcome you? Stay here for a word of advice on behalf of your souls and listen carefully! You will not be allowed to do this on Judgment Day!" ... Because of this he very often had the doors shut after the reading of the gospel until those who had once been deserters rejoiced by God's will at their chastisement and spiritual progress. (*vita* 1. 27)

Although it is similar to a passage in the *vita Hilarii*,[79] this anecdote probably does not represent a retelling of that incident. All bishops faced the possibility that individual members of their congregation might walk out of church, "gossip" among themselves, or refuse in some other way to participate in the ceremony. The withdrawal of consensus that such acts implied constituted a direct threat to their authority and had to be met with direct action whenever possible. Closing the doors of the church was an act of coercion that, apart from its practical effects, also demonstrates Caesarius's faith in the capacity of ceremonial behavior, even if forced or manipulated, not only to reflect but also, eventually, to affect the mentality of individuals.

MIRACLES AS COMMUNICATION

In his effort to promote a Christian system of values and beliefs, Caesarius did not confine himself to the formal, public ceremonies over which he presided as bishop. For, as Augustine and Pomerius

[78] *stat. eccl. ant.*, can. 31.   [79] *vita Hilarii* 18.

had repeatedly emphasized, it was a bishop's whole character and way of life that influenced his congregation, not just what he said in his sermons or did at Mass.[80] To a large extent of course this sort of advice was intended to curb the vices and abuses of power to which bishops were prone. But it was also intended to draw attention to the more personal forms of authority and influence that bishops could project – through such public manifestations of holiness as dress, appearance, and demeanor. Everyone knew, for instance, even a Frankish stranger, that Caesarius wore mere "rags" rather than linen (*vita* II. 42). His whole aspect in fact was that of a holy man: "His appearance revealed his inner self. For he was always of a placid and angelic countenance, and in the words of scripture (cf. Prov. 15: 13), his face shone because of his joyful heart" (*vita* I. 46; see also II. 35). Most impressive and well-known of all was his conduct toward others (*vita* I. 45). This was made especially clear by his acts of charity for the sick and the poor (*vita* I. 20), the hungry (*vita* II. 8–9), and captives and strangers (*vita* I. 44; II. 23–24).

It was by all these outward signs that Caesarius was thought to exemplify the Christian ideals he preached: "He did not teach in words what he did not fulfill by example" (*vita* I. 46). In so doing, he laid the foundation upon which a reputation for holiness could be built. For by leading what had come to be known as the *vita apostolica*,[81] a life in imitation of the asceticism, probity, and missionary zeal of the apostles, bishops could be esteemed as "living images" of their own holiness. As such, by virtue of their "merits," they could be sought out, like Jesus and his apostles, to perform cures, exorcisms, and other wonders. In Gaul, the most influential example of this apostolic ideal was provided by Martin of Tours – not the "historical" Martin, but the Martin created by Sulpicius Severus and refined by later hagiographers.[82] As a result of their efforts, Martin appeared to have become a "man filled with God" by means of his ascetic, monastic, and charitable accomplishments.[83] Thus did he possess *auctoritas* and *gratia*,[84] which shone out in remarkable acts of resuscitation, healing, exorcism, and control over nature, making him not only *sanctus*,

---

[80] Augustine, *doctr. christ.* IV. xxvii. 59; Pomerius, *vita contempl.* I. 17.

[81] K. S. Frank, "*Vita apostolica.* Ansätze zur apostolischen Lebensform in der alten Kirche," *Zeitschrift für Kirchengeschichte* 82 (1971), 145–66.

[82] R. Van Dam, "Images of Saint Martin in Late Roman and Early Merovingian Gaul," *Viator* 19 (1988), 1–27.

[83] "vir Deo plenus," Supicius Severus, *vita Martini* 3. 1.   [84] Ibid., 10. 2.

but "powerful also and truly apostolic."[85] Widely disseminated over Gaul,[86] this image of Martin created a set of expectations and standards for bishops in the minds of clergy and laity alike. Henceforth any bishop who was reckoned to lead a conspicuously holy and "apostolic" life might raise the expectation among his people that God would favor him with the same powers as Martin. Such expectations could not of course have arisen without the widespread belief that under the right conditions God's power could be validly and visibly exercised by men.[87] The question was not, therefore, whether bishops could function as wonder-workers, but whether any given bishop had met the conditions for doing so.

In the opinion of his hagiographers, Caesarius had fulfilled precisely the right conditions: "He had so many gifts bestowed on him by divine grace ... that he has not been crowned for only one merit, but because of his shimmering merits, he is now encircled by such great and numerous crowns that he is completely transformed into a crown of glory" (*vita* I. 59). Accordingly, like Martin, he was described as a "man filled with God" (*vita* II. 18) and an "apostolic man" (*vita* I. 21, 36, 38,), and credited with the performance of miraculous deeds, which constituted further evidence for his holiness.[88] It is these miracles we wish to examine more closely, for to the extent that beliefs about them were already current during Caesarius's lifetime, they can tell us something about the role that his actions and his reputation as a holy man played in his promotion of a Christian value system.

As they are found in the *vita*, the stories of Caesarius's miracles represent the final stage in the creation of his image as a wonderworker. But the miracle stories in the *vita* can also be used to document an earlier stage in the life of this image, for it is clear that a number of these stories were already in circulation as oral narratives while Caesarius was still alive, long before they were written into the *vita*. News of a miracle he worked in Ravenna, for instance, "traveled not only through the city, but also through the whole province, because of the prayers and reports of the faithful" (*vita* I. 40). "Almost the whole city" knew the details of Liberius's wounding across the river Druentia, and his remarkable recovery

---

[85] "potens etiam et vere apostolicus," ibid. 7. 7.

[86] E. Ewig, "Le culte de saint Martin à l'époque franque," in his *Spätanikes und fränkisches Gallien*, II, 355–70.

[87] P. Brown, *The Making of Late Antiquity* (Cambridge, Mass., 1978), 11–18.

[88] E.g., *vita* I. 22: "After this miracle, everyone in Bordeaux admired him so much that they regarded him not only as a bishop, but also as an apostle."

in Caesarius's presence (*vita* II. 10). Furthermore, "many people" in Arles knew the story of how the fire that threatened the women's monastery turned back at Caesarius's prayers (*vita* II. 26). Told and retold over the years, such stories contributed to Caesarius's image as a holy man during his own lifetime. Those who heard such stories, together with those who had originally witnessed the incidents that gave rise to explanations of wonder-working in the first place, constituted the audience for the multiple messages that miracles carried.

The miracles attributed to Caesarius in the *vita* can be divided into two categories, those he worked in person, and those worked by his relics, both before and after his death. Each represents a different mode of access to divine power.[89] Miracles in the first category represent a highly centralized system of therapy. They could only be performed by the bishop, who used only approved techniques. In contrast, miracles in the second category represent a more decentralized system of therapy. Although Caesarius's clergy controlled access to most – but not all[90] – of his relics, they could not and did not control the use of those relics. Thus relic miracles could be performed by anyone with access to a relic. To use an analogy from ancient medicine, the miracles that the bishop performed were like the cures worked by a trained physician (*vita* I. 49), whereas the miracles produced by relics were like the cures worked by herbs and potions: although prescribed by experts, they could be applied by patients on their own. On the basis of these differences, miracles in each category served to communicate Christian values and beliefs in different ways.

Of the thirty-three miracle stories in the *vita*, sixteen recount miracles performed by Caesarius in person and one a miracle performed at his urging by another bishop. It is reasonable to assume that many if not all of these stories had their roots in Caesarius's practice of visiting, blessing, anointing, and praying for those who were sick, possessed by demons, or stricken with misfortune. Indeed, in his sermons, Caesarius directly advised the sick to "run to church, and receive the body and blood of Christ, and be anointed with holy oil by the priests and ask the priests and deacons to pray over them in Christ's name" (*serm.* 19. 5).[91] Because Caesarius himself was responsible for these performances,

[89] This explanation is based on Brown, *Cult of the Saints*, 113–18, with important corrections supplied by Van Dam, *Leadership*, 128–33.
[90] E.g., *vita* II. 10–12, 25. [91] See also *serm.* 13. 3; 50. 1; 184. 5.

most of them followed a similar ritual pattern, consisting of five stages: a request for Caesarius's help, his response, his diagnosis of the problem, performance of the appropriate ritual actions, and announcement of a successful outcome.

Nearly every miracle story begins with a request. There are two reasons for this. First, Caesarius was reluctant to act on his own initiative, since the perception that he did so might have led to charges of pride, arrogance, and vainglory, which could quickly have destroyed his reputation for holiness.[92] Second, no one could presume that Caesarius would take on his case. Since he had the power to reject cases, his help had to be appropriately requested, often with the gestures of supplication addressed to all powerful men, such as kneeling or falling prostrate at his feet (*vita* I. 39; II. 2, 18, 28, 29). Such expressions of humility were not only designed to represent the humility of petitioners before Caesarius; they could also be interpreted as ritual anticipations of Caesarius's humility before God as he prayed for a cure.

People sought Caesarius's help for three kinds of problems: demon possession, physical illness, and natural threats, particularly fire. That petitioners chose Caesarius to intervene in these problems indicates their belief in his competence. As Peter the deacon says in the *vita*, "Have pity on my old age, servant of Christ; come and pray for my daughter, for I believe that the Lord will deny you nothing" (*vita* II. 2). Belief in Caesarius's competence suggests in turn the degree to which petitioners assented to the doctrines he preached and the practices he advocated. Requesting his help in cases of demon possession, for instance, indicated a belief in the church's definition of demons and demon possession. Seeking cures of physical illness from the bishop instead of a local folk healer signaled a willingness to follow Caesarius's advice to the sick: "Anyone who runs to church in sickness will receive both bodily health and forgiveness of sins. Since we can find a double advantage in church, why do wretched people bring multiple evils upon themselves through enchanters, through springs, trees, and diabolical amulets, or through sooth-sayers, *haruspices*, diviners, and fortunetellers?" (*serm.* 13. 3).

---

[92] P. Brown, *Society and the Holy in Late Antiquity* (Berkeley and Los Angeles, 1982), 242. Caesarius is represented as acting on his own in only two instances, both unusual. The first involves an exorcism performed on the road to Lérins when he was nineteen years old, before he had a reputation for holiness to protect (*vita* I. 5). The second involves an exorcism he performed secretly in the forum. Because not even his attendants knew about it, it could not have been imputed to arrogance on his part (*vita* II. 30).

Caesarius's first response to these requests, as recorded in the *vita*, was often to refuse them, in order to avoid charges of pride (I. 39; II. 20). "But although it is always customary for the servants of God to refuse to perform miracles, this servant of Christ in particular, even when he was confident at the time because the Lord suggested it that an opportunity for him to perform a miracle was at hand, did not want to be overbold in seizing it, but tried carefully to avoid it" (*vita* II. 5). Moreover, when other bishops were present, he always yielded to them, so as not to appear too eager to display his own powers (*vita* I. 47; II. 16). In the end, however, unless someone else performed the miracle first (*vita* I. 47), Caesarius always consented to fulfill the request, at least in the miracle stories told by his biographers.

The next stage in the performance of a miracle was a professional diagnosis of the problem, which Caesarius either performed himself (*vita* II. 21, 29) or delegated to subordinates (*vita* II. 19). Sometimes he visited the homes of the afflicted to do so (*vita* I. 39; II. 2), but more often they were brought to him (*vita* II. 18, 20, 29). When demon possession or physical illness was suspected, he reached his diagnosis, like any good physician, by asking questions (*vita* II. 18, 29), inspecting the patient (*vita* II. 21), and comparing the case at hand with others he had seen (*vita* II. 21).

Once the nature of the problem had been determined, Caesarius turned to the ritual procedures for solving it. These varied according to each case, but never consisted of any other than ecclesiastically approved techniques: praying, anointing with consecrated oil, blessing with holy water, laying on hands, or making the sign of the cross. The actions Caesarius took were normally performed in the presence of other people, such as members of the household (*vita* I. 40; II. 2, 19), the congregation at Mass (*vita* I. 43; II. 20), other bishops (*vita* I. 47; II. 16), and crowds of people (*vita* I. 22; II. 21). The presence of these observers was essential to the success of cures and exorcisms since as a group they reinforced the patient's belief in Caesarius's competence with their own expectations.[93] At the same time they constituted the audience for which Caesarius performed, whose expectations he attempted to satisfy, and who in turn communicated his actions to others as eyewitnesses. After performing the appropriate rituals, it

---

[93] C. Lévi-Strauss, "The Sorcerer and His Magic," in his *Structural Anthropology*, trans. C. Jacobson and B. Grundfest Schoepf (Garden City, N.Y., 1967), 161–80: 162.

was then Caesarius's practice either to leave the scene immediately, before any effects were noticed (*vita* I. 40), or to send the patient back home as quickly as possible (*vita* II. 21). According to his hagiographers, the purpose of this practice was to counteract any impressions of arrogance that might have arisen if he waited for the cure to occur in his presence (*vita* II. 3).

The final stage in the process was a successful outcome, often accompanied by expressions of gratitude from beneficiaries (*vita* I. 40; II. 4, 16), communication of the news to the whole community (*vita* I. 40), and the narrator's assurances that the affliction never returned (*vita* I. 43; II. 19, 20, 21). To avoid charges of arrogance, Caesarius was careful never to attribute any of these successes to his own efforts, but rather to God's power (*vita* I. 40; II. 3, 20). In fact, he played an important part, along with patients and observers, in creating the conditions under which a successful outcome could be expected, largely by establishing and maintaining the framework of belief in which this could occur, and by acting in accord with the expectations of participants and observers. The high degree of success he enjoyed in the *vita* is, however, deeply misleading. It does not mean that all his performances as a wonder-worker were successful, but rather that his biographers selected only successful performances to write about. There may have been many occasions when not even they could maintain that Caesarius's efforts had been successful. In such cases, his habit of assigning responsibility for miracles to God rather than himself would have made it easier for him to deflect the responsibility for failures, thus preserving his reputation and the possibility of future success.

Because they represented face-to-face encounters with his people, occasions of miracle-working offered Caesarius the opportunity to communicate with them by means of persuasive actions and gestures. In particular, they enabled him to symbolize, reinforce, and promote adherence to the church's system of values and beliefs. For instance, by stimulating divine action, Caesarius could show firsthand the reality, omnipotence, and beneficence of the Christian God. Moreover, by demonstrating his access to divine power, he could act out his self-proclaimed role as mediator between God and man, and so legitimate his authority as bishop. Furthermore, by presiding over rituals designed to "set things right" within the community, such as reintegrating sick and possessed persons or restoring the normal balance of nature,

Caesarius could turn occasions of miracle-working into celebrations of community consensus.[94] In addition, by remedying
individual cases of sickness or misfortune, Caesarius could validate
the church's doctrine of suffering: that for citizens of the heavenly
city, suffering was a temporary, and (under the right conditions)
even reversible, inconvenience of bodily existence, not an essential
feature of the human condition. Finally, Caesarius could underscore the point that healing was to be performed by God and his
appointed ministers using approved techniques, not by folk healers
using amulets, herbs, potions, and spells. In his efforts as a
wonder-worker, then, Caesarius offered something even more
satisfying than the solution of immediate problems: he offered a
symbolic system of order and meaning that was not simply
proclaimed in church, but acted out in the community for all to see
and so to believe.

In contrast to the miracles he was reputed to have worked in
person, Caesarius had no control over the miracles attributed to his
relics. Indeed, it is difficult to see how he could have considered the
use of these relics fully legitimate, since they appeared to provide
unregulated access to divine power, an objection that informed his
opposition to many ostensibly "pagan" practices as well.
Although he is not known to have denounced the use of relics – his
own or anyone else's – Caesarius exhibited at best a lukewarm
enthusiasm for the practice. He did not, to be sure, reject the role
that the cult of the saints in general could play in legitimating his
authority, solidifying community consensus, and communicating
the values and beliefs of the Christian religion.[95] Indeed, he
employed the myth of St. Trophimus's mission to Arles to bolster
the prestige of his city,[96] took part in liturgical celebrations
honoring St. Genesius,[97] and delivered numerous sermons on
the veneration and imitation of locally important saints, including
Honoratus (*serm.* 214) and Stephen (*serm.* 219, 220). But at the
same time, he was never depicted as actively engaged in the
business of saints' cults, in building shrines, transferring relics, and
all the other activities bishops are seen carrying out in the pages of
Gregory of Tours. Moreover, unlike the hagiographical writings

---

[94] Van Dam, *Leadership*, 264–72.   [95] See in general Brown, *Cult of the Saints*.
[96] Caesarius, *de mysterio trinitatis* 17, Morin II, 179; L. Levillain, "La crise des années
507–508 et les rivalités d'influence en Gaule de 508 à 514," in *Mélanges offerts à Nicholas
Iorga* (Paris, 1933), 537–67: 551–55.
[97] *passio sancti Genesii Arelatensis* 5; Gregory of Tours, *glor. mart.* 68.

of Gregory, Caesarius's sermons on martyrs and saints emphasized their role as models of Christian behavior and intercessors at the Last Judgment rather than wonder-workers (*serm.* 214–26). For these reasons, it is best not to interpret the stories of relic miracles in the *vita* as evidence of Caesarius's attempts to promote his own sanctity through the dissemination and veneration of his relics. Rather we should see in these stories a reflection of his reputation for sanctity in the eyes of others, a continuing effort by his supporters to further promote this reputation, and the determination of members of his congregation to acquire for themselves the remedies for their afflictions.

There are sixteen stories of relic miracles in the *vita*, five of which relate *post-mortem* miracles. While some of these miracles were attributed to the spontaneous eruption of divine energy in the presence of Caesarius or his relics (*vita* I. 26, 30, 50; II. 17, 36, 44), most resulted from the direct efforts of individuals to solve their problems. Having obtained access to a relic, it was they and not Caesarius or his clerics who controlled the order of events. Relic miracles, therefore, followed no fixed ritual pattern, but did share certain characteristics with one another, since they all took place within a similar framework of expectations and beliefs.

The uses for which people sought relics of the bishop were essentially the same as those for which they sought his help in person: illness, demon possession, and the imbalances of nature. The first step in the resolution of these problems was acquiring an appropriately potent relic. In only a single case was Caesarius asked directly for one of these, a piece of cloth as it happened. He underscored his attitude to relics by ordering it to be placed under an altar overnight before being used (*vita* II. 14). On other occasions relics were used without his knowledge or permission. They included his body or anything that had come into contact with it: a cloak he wore (*vita* II. 12), his saddlecloth (*vita* II. 25), bottles of oil he had blessed (*vita* I. 51), the official staff that was carried for him on journeys (*vita* II. 22, 27), the water and linens used to prepare his body for burial (*vita* II. 39–42), and the beds he slept in (*vita* I. 30, 50).[98] Because they managed the bishop's domestic arrangements, organized his travels, and supervised preparations for his burial, the clerics closest to Caesarius, preeminently Messianus and Stephanus, were the most reliable source

---

[98] As *loci* for divine power, the beds of saints were considered equivalent to the tombs in which they "slept," Van Dam, *Leadership*, 192.

of relics (*vita* II. 13–15, 22, 27, 41, 42). They were eager to supply these to anyone who wanted them, even if some dissimulation was required (*vita* II. 13–15), for in so doing they promoted Caesarius's reputation for holiness. In this sense they were engaged in fashioning the image of Caesarius as a saint long before composing his *vita*. Indeed, their composition of the *vita* can be seen as simply an extension of their "saint-making" efforts during the bishop's lifetime; the *vita* was simply another relic.

Different kinds of relics were accorded different properties: for instance, the water used to wash Caesarius's body after death and the linens used to dry it were considered particularly useful in cases of fever (*vita* II. 39, 40, 41, 42), whereas the clothes he wore could stop cases of uncontrollable bleeding (*vita* II. 10–12, 13–15). In recognition of these specialized qualities, people often went to a great deal of trouble to procure just the relic they thought they needed. Liberius's wife Agretia, for instance, coaxed Stephanus into stealing one of the cloths that Caesarius warmed at the fire to use as a hot compress at night (*vita* II. 13). Years later, a Frank demanding a piece of Caesarius's clothing was disappointed to receive only a piece of the linen used to dry his corpse instead (*vita* II. 42).

Once obtained, relics were deployed in a variety of ways: directly applied to affected parts of the body (*vita* II. 12), soaked in water which was then drunk (*vita* II. 39, 40, 41, 42), fastened to the wall of a building (*vita* II. 22), or fixed into the earth (*vita* II. 27). Although people were expected to treat them with a certain amount of veneration (*vita* I. 51; II. 15, 42), no additional prayers or rituals were required to trigger their efficacy. Thus, when put into place, they normally took effect within a short time "statim": *vita* II. 22, 25, 40, 42; "in eadem hora": *vita* II. 12, 42).

Like the miracles worked by Caesarius in person, miracles worked by his relics depended for their efficacy on the beliefs and expectations of those who employed them, as corroborated by the attitudes of others. Even though many of the cures took place in private, they would have been inconceivable without affirmation from the larger group. A good example of the conjunction between individual and group belief can be seen in the following miracle story, one of two in the *vita* in which a bed used by Caesarius was credited with exacting a punishment for sin:[99]

---

[99] In the other miracle, a Gothic soldier occupying the bishop's house was stricken after sleeping in Caesarius's bed, *vita* I. 30.

While the holy man was making the rounds of his parishes, he was welcomed at the villa of Launico by its owners. After his departure, in the room in which he had slept, and on the covers [of his bed], a dissolute physician named Anatolius sought out the services of a prostitute. He was to be very sorry for such a sin, for he was soon seized with trembling in public by the devil that had incited him. In the sight of everyone he was knocked to the ground, and in the process of acknowledging the power (*virtus*) of the servant of God, he publicly confessed the audacious crime for which he had been seized. (*vita* I. 50)

Anatolius's seizure was clearly thought to have been catalyzed by the recent presence of Caesarius, whose power transformed a private, guilty act into a spectacle of public shame, and thereby made it possible for an externalized sin to be forgiven and "driven out" by means of a public act of confession. It was the same drama of "authority," "confession," and "reintegration" that took place in cases of exorcism.[100] But what is especially important to note is that without Anatolius's consciousness of guilt and the availability of a credible forum for its externalization, Caesarius's *virtus* would have had no effect on him at all. So this story not only provides a demonstration of the social conditions required for the production of miracles, but more specifically emphasizes the importance of the individual's socially-conditioned belief.

Like the miracles Caesarius performed in person, then, relic miracles both depended on and further confirmed an existing framework of belief. Moreover, they conveyed a similar series of messages. Both kinds of miracles thus helped to reinforce in the most concrete and immediate possible terms the values, practices, and beliefs that Caesarius taught more abstractly through preaching and the liturgy. At the same time, because such miracles took place in the community itself, and required the initiative and trust of patients for their success, and the participation and affirmation of onlookers for their credibility, they also to help to illustrate the transformation of Christianity in late antique Arles from an organized into a community religion. A society where such events and procedures could be widely esteemed as miraculous was a society in which the population was well on its way toward adapting the Christian religion to their own aims and traditions. In non-romanized regions of northern Europe, where such shared perceptions were lacking, miraculous actions could not be

100 Brown, *Cult of the Saints*, 106–13.

recognized as such, and missionaries sought to persuade by other forms of ritual.[101]

[101] I. N. Wood, "Pagans and Holy Men, 600–800," in *Irland und die Christenheit: Bibelstudien und Mission*, ed. Próinséas Ní Chatháin and M. Richter (Stuttgart, 1987), 347–61 : 355.

Chapter 7

CHRISTIANITY AS A COMMUNITY RELIGION

The "model for living" that Caesarius proposed to his audiences consisted of a system of interrelated beliefs, values, and practices elicited by specialists from the Christian scriptures over the course of several centuries. As we have seen, it was quintessentially an "organized" religious system which, unlike paganism, had not arisen from the community itself. Yet Christianity also aspired to function as a "community" and a "local" religion, conforming to the religious needs, traditions, and expectations of the local community, just as traditional paganism had always done. Since these were demands to which the Christian religion was in many respects deeply ill-suited, it comes as no surprise that commitment to the Christian value and belief system promoted by Caesarius was "differentially" distributed among the people of the *civitas* of Arles.[1] At the periphery were those who refused allegiance to any form of Christianity, either openly or secretly, such as Jews and pagans, or those who refused allegiance to "orthodox" Christian theology, such as Arians. At the center were those who accepted, in principle at least, the whole of Caesarius's religious program, mainly clergymen, monks, nuns, and lay ascetics. Finally, between center and periphery were those who acted to accommodate the Christian religious system to their own family and community needs. In some cases this meant retaining traditional pre-Christian beliefs, practices, and values for which Christianity provided no suitable substitute. In other cases it meant adopting or adapting acceptable features of Caesarius's program. The diversity of religious practice that resulted was in fact the price to be paid for organizing a system of religion that saw itself called to encompass the entire community. It is this diversity toward which we now turn our attention, specifically the ways in which Christianity was perceived and practiced as a community religion. In the present

---

[1] P. Worsley, *The Trumpet Shall Sound*, 2nd edn. (New York, 1968), xxiv.

chapter we discuss the practices and beliefs of those nearer the Christian center, primarily but not exclusively the urban population. In the following chapter, we move toward the geographical, social, and religious periphery to examine the beliefs and practices of those further from the center, primarily the rural population.

DEFINING THE CHRISTIAN COMMUNITY

A community religion presupposes a community, and, as we saw in Chapter 2, the *civitas* of Arles consisted of a number of communities throughout antiquity. Unfortunately, it is as impossible to compose an ethnography of these communities in the sixth century as in previous centuries. What we can offer is a fragmentary portrait of the Christian population of the diocese, and a discussion of the means by which Caesarius attempted to define the meaning of a Christian community.

The continuing position of Arles as a center of commerce meant that its population would continue to be diverse. In the sixth century, it consisted of Goths, Franks, Greeks, Syrians (a generic term for all those of eastern Mediterranean origin), Jews, and finally Gallo-Romans, who were themselves a far from homogeneous group.[2] Caesarius's congregation in turn was made up mostly of Greeks and Gallo-Romans. The only two languages known to have been used in his church were Latin and Greek (*vita* I. 19), and the names of members of the congregation, although not certain indicators of ethnic origin, are consistent with a Greco-Roman population. The occupations of Christians in Caesarius's congregation was likewise diverse and reflective of the city's commercial role. Caesarius mentions businessmen (*negotiatores*),[3] salesmen (*institores*),[4] goldsmiths (*aurifices*),[5] craftsmen (*fabri*),[6] physicians (*medici*),[7] and artisans (*artifices*).[8] In urging his people to give tithes to the church, he cites as their sources of revenue agriculture, commerce, manufacturing, and *militia*, which in-

---

[2] In 589, for instance, the council held at nearby Narbonne legislated for a population that consisted of "Goths, Romans, Syrians, Greeks, and Jews," can. 4, *CCSL* 148A, 254–55. On Greeks in Arles, see *vita* I. 19; on Syrians, see P. Lambrechts, "Le commerce des 'Syriens' en Gaule du Haut-Empire à l'époque mérovingienne," *L'Antiquité classique* 6 (1937), 35–61; on Jews, see *vita* I. 29, 31; II. 49.
[3] *serm.* 6. 2; 7. 1; 8. 1; 43. 7; 72. 1.   [4] *serm.* 72. 1.   [5] *serm.* 72. 1.
[6] *serm.* 72. 1.   [7] *serm.* 5. 5.   [8] *serm.* 72. 1; 76. 3.

cluded all forms of government service.[9] Unfortunately, however, closer acquaintance with the Christians of Arles is nearly impossible. Only names, social ranks, and fragments of the life stories of Caesarius's parishioners emerge from the sources. From *vitae*, for instance, we learn that his congregation included high-ranking aristocrats (*viri illustres*) like Parthenius,[10] Liberius and his wife Agretia,[11] Firminus and Gregoria,[12] Martianus,[13] and Salvius;[14] other noble men and women such as Ferreolus[15] and Eucyria;[16] lower-ranking officials such as Desiderius, the public archivist;[17] and ordinary free persons like Johannes[18] and Vincentius,[19] who owned houses in Arles. From the *testamentum*, we hear of Caesarius's slaves Agritia,[20] Bricianus,[21] and the anonymous servants employed in his household.[22] For the clergy we likewise have only names, ranks, and isolated stories: the priests Lucius,[23] Jacob,[24] Messianus the biographer, and Leo;[25] the deacons Didimus,[26] Peter,[27] and Stephanus the biographer; the subdeacon Augustus;[28] and the notary Licinianus, who may have been a cleric.[29] Finally, funerary inscriptions tell us little more about the laity than the names, ages, and dates of death of those whose relations could afford to commemorate their demise: Eustasia, who died at age 36 on September 3, 501 or 502;[30] Eulogios, who died at about age 50 on July 25, 524;[31] Antonina, who died at age 30 on January 10, 525;[32] Paul, who died at age 44 on January 4, 529;[33] Peter, son of the late Asclipius, who died at age 43 on January 18, 530;[34] Apriles, who died at age 40 in 530;[35] Secolasia, who died at age 46 in the year 531;[36] and Thaumasta, who died at age 60 on November 30, 532.[37]

While we cannot know much about individual members of the community of Arles in the early sixth century, we can say more about the ways in which its leaders attempted to define the community in Christian terms. In the fifth century, as we have seen, the city's growing christianization was symbolized by the development of an explicitly Christian topography and by the

[9] *serm.* 33. 1. [10] *vita* I. 49. [11] *vita* II. 10–15. [12] *vita* I. 8. [13] *vita* II. 41. [14] *vita* II. 40. [15] *vita Apollinaris* 10. [16] *vita* II. 18. [17] *vita* II. 39. [18] *vita* II. 26. [19] *vita* II. 28. [20] *test.*, 289, line 10. [21] *test.*, 289, line 9. [22] *test.*, 289, line 12. [23] *vita* II. 19. [24] *vita* II. 24. [25] *test.*, 289, line 7. [26] *vita* II. 19. [27] *vita* II. 2–4. [28] *test.*, 285, line 6. [29] *vita* I. 21. [30] Le Blant, *Inscriptions*, no. 510. [31] CIL XII. 933. [32] *Nouveau recueil des inscriptions chrétiennes de la Gaule antérieures au VIIIe siècle*, ed. E. Le Blant (Paris, 1892), no. 162. [33] CIL XII. 934. [34] CIL XII. 936. [35] CIL XII. 935. [36] CIL XII. 937. [37] Le Blant, *Inscriptions*, no. 530.

introduction of Christian festivals of consensus and protection. Such changes continued into the sixth century. To be sure, Arles remained in many ways a recognizably Roman city. Its forum was still at the center of civic life (*vita* II. 30) and its citizens still entertained themselves by watching races at the circus,[38] spectacles at the theater,[39] and wild beast hunts at the amphitheater.[40] But at the same time, the city was taking on an increasingly Christian identity. Through his construction of the monastery for women and its adjacent burial church, Caesarius continued Bishop Hilarius's policy of transforming the urban topography. Not only did he contribute further to the development of the ecclesiastical quarter in the southeastern section of the city; he also attempted to alter the definition of the city in a more fundamental way. For, by permitting nuns to be buried in the basilica of St. Mary, located within the city walls, rather than in the city's traditional burial grounds outside the walls, Caesarius acted consciously against the longstanding Roman custom of burial *extra muros*. This was a highly significant gesture: it is difficult to imagine a more deliberate contrast with the burial practices, and hence the communal self-identity, of the Roman city. Although there is some evidence in Aix and Riez for the burial of bishops *intra muros* before this time,[41] this may be the earliest well-dated example of the burial of other privileged Christians within the walls, which was permitted in anticipation of Caesarius's burial in the same place.[42] Caesarius's action did not of course spell the end of traditional burial practices; the rest of the Christian population continued to be buried outside the city walls.[43] Nor did it spell the

---

[38] *serm.* 61. 3; Procopius, *de bellis* VII. 33. 5.   [39] *serm.* 61. 3.

[40] *serm.* 12. 4; 31. 2; 89. 5; 150. 3. For some idea of the variety of animals available, see *serm.* 152. 3, where Caesarius poses the analogy of a "spiritual amphitheater" with its "savage forest" of vices: "I see in our character the anger of lions, in our emotions the savagery of bears, in our minds the inconstancy of panthers, in avarice the rapacity of wolves, in concupiscence the thirst of wild asses, in our senses the filth of vultures, in our memories the forgetfulness of deer, in lies the cunning of foxes, in hatred the poison of vipers, in fasting the slowness of cattle, in our hearts the awkwardness of calves, in pride the boldness of bulls, in shamelessness the impudence of rams, in frivolity the fickleness of wild goats, in our flesh the callousness of boars, in our thoughts the slough of pigs, on our tongues the envy of wild boars, in our consciences the spots of tigers, in anger the swelling necks of serpents, in our sins the great weight of elephants."

[41] J. Guyon, "L'évolution des sites urbains en Provence (Antiquité et Haut Moyen Age). L'example de Marseille, Aix, Arles, et Riez à la lumière des recherches et fouilles récentes," *Ktema* 7 (1982), 129–40: 136–38.

[42] This would modify a view expressed by Février, "Arles," 81.

[43] Sintès, "Les necropoles," 95–99.

end of traditional burial churches. Before his death in 530, a certain Peter erected the church of Saints Peter and Paul in the Alyscamps cemetery to serve at his burial place.[44] Yet Caesarius's construction of a burial church inside the walls should not be interpreted as an isolated occurrence, since it took place at the same time as other changes in the city's definition of its public space, evidently part of a larger process of "de-romanization."

A hint of this new state of affairs has been uncovered in recent excavations of the circus. Exploring the foundations of the structure, archaeologists discovered evidence of permanent habitations dating from the end of the fourth to the middle of the sixth century, when the circus appears to have been systematically demolished.[45] The habitations were located in the arcades that supported the outside wall of the circus. At some point in the late fourth century, these spaces were sealed off at the top and extended outward by stone walls and tile roofs. Walls built inside each of the enclosed arches created multi-room apartments that originally measured approximately 100 m², but were subdivided in the first half of the sixth century into units of about one third the original area.[46] Since we know that the circus was in use up to the time of its demolition,[47] the presence of these dwellings must not have been incompatible with its continuing operation.[48] That these dwellings were erected at the same time and by a central authority is clear from the consistency with which they were built, the careful leveling of the site beforehand, and the construction of a road to serve the area and a wall to divide it from the nearby necropolis.[49] The population of the site is uncertain, but in its more densely populated phase in the first half of the sixth century perhaps as many as 500–700 inhabitants lived there.[50] They were not isolated from the rest of the city, but were connected by the first-century road that ran from the forum, which had become a

[44] *CIL* XII. 936. In the middle ages the church became Saint-Pierre-de-Mouleyrès. Although much of its surrounding cemetery was destroyed in the nineteenth century by the construction of railway yards, a number of ancient sarcophagi can still be seen protruding from the hillside beneath the church in the cross-cut left by the railroad line, Février, "Arles," 84.

[45] C. Sintès, "Le cirque romain: Les fouilles récentes," in *Du nouveau sur l'Arles antique*, ed. C. Sintès, 63–65; idem, "Le site aux IVᵉ et Vᵉ siècles: une tentative de reconstitution," in *Carnets de fouilles d'une presqu'île*, *Revue d'Arles* 2 (Arles, 1990), 59–62; Gauthier, "Informations archéologiques" (1986), 394–97.

[46] Sintès, "Le site," 59.   [47] Procopius, *de bellis* VII. 33. 5.

[48] Hallier, "Le cirque romain," 61.   [49] Sintès, "Le site," 59–60.

[50] C. Sintès, letter to the author, July 29, 1992.

dirt track by the fifth century.[51] Along this road, under the modern Hôpital Van-Gogh, were located other late dwellings in use between the early fifth and the mid-sixth century.[52]

The circus habitations do not offer the only example in late antique Arles of the private use of public space. At some point in the first half of the fifth century, part of the portico of the forum appears to have been demolished to make room (and provide building materials) for a house.[53] The decision of the city's civil authorities to allow such encroachments indicates not only that Arles faced a housing shortage in the fifth and sixth centuries, but more importantly that perceptions of the city's identity had significantly changed. The encroachment of private dwellings into Roman public structures anticipates the development of "medieval" cities, in which well-constructed buildings that no longer served their original purpose were converted to other uses, when they were not mined for *spolia*.[54] These early examples in Arles of the privatization of public space suggests that its identity as a Roman city, with the lavish provision of secular, public spaces which that identity implied, was beginning to disintegrate in the fifth and sixth centuries. This made it easier for Arles to take on the identity of a Christian city.

To compensate for the loss of secular, public space, the inhabitants of Arles found new uses for Christian space. They began, for instance, to use the cathedral as a meeting place on Sundays and feast days. While Mass was going on inside, men met in the atrium, the porticoes, or in the street just outside (*serm.* 74. 3) to carry on business with their neighbors, which included talking, quarreling among themselves, and "pleading and hearing lawsuits" (*serm.* 16. 3; 55. 1, 3).[55] While in one sense practices of this kind reveal a lack of participation in the religious life of the

---

[51] Jacob *et al.*, *Gallia Informations* (1987–88), part 2, 233.

[52] C. Sintès, "Les fouilles de l'Hôpital Van-Gogh," in *Du nouveau sur l'Arles antique*, ed. C. Sintès, 44–48.   [53] Jacob *et al.*, *Gallia Informations* (1987–88), part 2, 233–34.

[54] B. Ward-Perkins, *From Classical Antiquity to the Middle Ages: Urban Public Building in Northern and Central Italy, AD 300–850* (Oxford, 1984), 206–18. See *brev. Al.* XV. 1. 1 (= *CTh* XV. 1. 9), whose *interpretatio* states: "If any of those living in a city erect houses for themselves in public places, they should be permitted to possess these without disturbance."

[55] It is very unlikely that this last phrase refers to any official judge or court. Episcopal courts were clearly not involved (Gaudemet, *L'Eglise*, 246), and *CTh* II. 8. 1 and *CTh* II. 8. 19 had prohibited secular courts from hearing cases on Sundays and certain feast days; these rulings were followed in barbarian codes (*brev. Al.* II. 8. 1, 2, and *edict. Theod.* 154). What the activity in Arles probably represents is the informal, private settling of legal disputes in the presence of powerful local patrons, e.g., *serm.* 55A. 2:

community, in another sense they represent the centrality that the basilica and its religious services had come to take on in the community's secular life, a strong indication of the continuing progress of christianization in the city.

At the same time as these changes were occurring, a new community religious festival was introduced into the city: an annual Rogation festival celebrated around the Ascension. Mamertus of Vienne was credited with organizing this ritual of communal penance *c.* 470 when his city suffered from an alarming series of portents and emergencies.[56] The practice soon spread from Vienne to other parts of Gaul.[57] It generally involved three days of fasting, prayers, sermons, and processions to holy places.[58] In Arles this form of Rogations took place on Wednesday, Thursday, and Friday, probably just before or just after the Ascension,[59] and involved two hours of services each day in the basilica (*serm.* 208. 3). Like other Rogation services held irregularly at times of need, these Rogations responded to a variety of emergencies affecting both the city and countryside: siege,[60] plague,[61] barbarian occupation,[62] warfare, hail, drought, and famine.[63] In early sixth-century Arles, ceremonies were held one spring to put a stop to excessive rains and flooding (*serm.* 207. 3) and, on another occasion, to bring an end to drought (*serm.* 208. 2). For such rituals of communal protection to work most effectively, the participation of the entire community was required. In the Frankish kingdom slaves were supposed to be released from work so that the "whole people" could request protection from common dangers.[64] By the same logic, Caesarius argued forcefully for universal attendance and participation in these ceremonies (*serm.* 207. 2; 208. 3; 209. 4).

Yet in Arles, the Catholic Christian religion did not command the loyalty of the entire population. The presence of religious "others" within the city not only prevented Christian ceremonies

"There are also some judges and powerful men who wish to plead or hear cases on saints' days or other feasts."

[56] Sidonius Apollinaris, *ep.* v. 14. 2; VII. 1. 3–6; Gregory of Tours, *hist.* II. 34; W. Pax, "Bittprozession," *RAC* II (Stuttgart, 1954), cols. 422–29.

[57] In addition to Sidonius, *supra*, see Orléans (511), can. 27.

[58] The ceremonies are described in Gregory of Tours, *hist.* IX. 6 (Paris) and Avitus of Vienne, *hom.* 6, *MGH AA*, VI. 2, 110–11 (Vienne).

[59] *serm.* 209. 4; Beck, 105.   [60] Sidonius Apollinaris, *ep.* VII. 1. 2.

[61] Gregory of Tours, *hist.* IV. 5 (Clermont); IX. 21 (Marseille); X. 30 (Tours, Nantes).

[62] Eusebius Gallicanus, *serm.* 25. 2.   [63] Ibid., *serm.* 25. 1.

[64] Orléans (511), can. 27.

from expressing a universal consensus; it also raised important questions about the city's Christian identity, for the community was defined not only by who belonged to it, but also by who did not. To Caesarius, there were only three categories of religious outsiders: pagans, Jews, and heretics (*serm.* 154. 5; 157. 4; 180. 1; 181. 2). He had essentially two reasons for discussing these groups: first, to prevent his congregation from taking up unauthorized practices from them, and second, to define more clearly what it meant to be an orthodox Christian by defining what it meant to be something other than an orthodox Christian. He rarely spent much time discussing heresy, mainly Arianism, because its following, at least in Arles, was confined to Gothic soldiers and officials, whose religious influence on the local population would have been minimal. What few references Caesarius did make to heretical sects were mainly intended to sharpen his definition of orthodox Christianity.[65] Paganism and Judaism, on the other hand, posed serious threats to the Christian identity of his people, so Caesarius spent far more time drawing distinctions between these religious systems and the Christian religion. Leaving aside a discussion of paganism until Chapter 8, we shall discuss Judaism here.[66]

There is no doubt that Caesarius favored the conversion of Jews, but whether he spent much effort pursuing this ideal is a more difficult question to answer. It is likely that he approved of the recommendation in the *statuta ecclesiae antiqua* that Jews, along with pagans and heretics, be permitted to hear the word of God at Mass up to the dismissal of the catechumens (can. 16). Those who heard his sermons would often have heard him discuss the shortcomings of Judaism and argue for the superiority of Christianity.[67] Yet few Jews are likely to have attended Christian services, and those who did were probably already leaning in the direction of conversion. A more indirect, but possibly more effective method of conveying his message to Jews involved

---

[65] *serm.* 96. 5; 110. 1; 118. 4; 123; 175. 4; 176. 5.

[66] A thorough discussion of the Jews of sixth-century Arles is available in A. Saint-Saëns, "Césaire d'Arles et les Juifs," (Mémoire de Maîtrise, University of Strasburg, 1979), which the author very kindly permitted me to read. A published version is forthcoming from the Mellen Research University Press. For a more general discussion of Jews and Christians in the early middle ages, see B. Blumenkranz, *Juifs et chrétiens dans le monde occidental* (Paris, 1960).

[67] J. Courreau, "Saint Césaire d'Arles et les Juifs," *Bulletin de littérature ecclésiastique* 71 (1970), 92–112.

asking his parishioners to report what he had said to their neighbors (*serm.* 78. 5), even those who were not yet Christians (*serm.* 180. 1). For instance, on one occasion, after a long discussion of Old Testament "prefigurations" of the superiority of the Christian church to the synagogue, Caesarius told his audience: "If, as we trust, you wish to remember all of this, you will be able to explain clearly the mystery of the Christian religion whenever the situation or opportunity presents itself, not only to Jews, but also to pagans" (*serm.* 104. 6). Ideally, such messages would be accompanied by the persuasive impact of good example (*serm.* 104. 6). In one sermon, adapted from Augustine's *Sermon* 178 with the telling substitution of Jews for pagans, Caesarius warned his congregation of the theological consequences of stealing from Jews: "When you, a Christian, steal from a Jew, you prevent him from becoming a Christian. And perhaps you will respond at this point, 'I do not penalize him from any hatred, but rather discipline him out of love, so that through this harsh and saving discipline I might make him a Christian.' I would understand and believe you if what you took from a Jew you gave to a Christian."[68]

This "grim caricature" of Augustine notwithstanding,[69] the main purpose of Caesarius's preaching about the Jews was not to convert them. It was rather to differentiate between Judaism and Christianity for those who were already Christians (*serm.* 96; 104; 107; 163), and to appropriate themes from the Hebrew Bible for Christian uses.[70] In addition, Caesarius acted to prevent his congregation from adopting Jewish practices, such as Sabbath observance or strict conformity to dietary laws, which had appealed to Christians in Gaul in the fifth century,[71] and continued to do so into the following century.[72] To distinguish the Christian Sunday from the Jewish Sabbath, Caesarius required fasting on Saturdays as well as other weekdays in Lent. By making Saturday like every other weekday, he took away a special privilege it had retained as the Sabbath.[73] To prevent Christians from following

---

[68] Caesarius, *serm.* 183. 6, adapted from Augustine, *serm.* 178. 5.
[69] P. Brown, "St. Augustine's Attitude to Religious Coercion," in his *Religion and Society in the Age of Saint Augustine* (London, 1972), 260–78: 277.
[70] For example, see Caesarius's redefinition of Christians as the Chosen People, Daly, "Caesarius of Arles," 9–20.
[71] Vannes (461/91), can. 12; *stat. eccl. ant.*, can. 83.
[72] Orléans (538), can. 14, 31; Macon (581/83), can. 15.
[73] Agde (506), can. 12; C. J. Hefele and H. Leclercq, *Histoire des conciles*, II, part 2, 986, n. 1.

the laws of *kashrut*, Caesarius prohibited them from attending Jewish social functions (*convivia*) or inviting Jews to theirs.[74] He reasoned that since Christians and Jews did not share the same ideas of what it was proper to eat, Christians might seem inferior to Jews if they ate foods Jews regarded as unclean. Such regulations were in themselves difficult to enforce. But Caesarius made enforcement even more difficult by publicly admitting his high regard for Jewish piety, particularly almsgiving (*serm.* 1. 8) and abstinence from work on the Sabbath (*serm.* 13. 3 ; 73. 4).

Despite their status as religious outsiders in Arles, Jews appear to have been generally regarded as members of the civil community.[75] Their legal status as Roman citizens was confirmed by the *Breviary* of Alaric (II. 1. 10) and, as far as we know, largely respected in practice. During the siege of 507/8, for instance, Jews served in the local militia, albeit with a separate section of the fortifications to defend (*vita* I. 31).[76] To be sure, religious tensions sometimes ran high, making it easy for the Christian majority to accept accusations of Jewish treachery fabricated by Caesarius's supporters during the siege (*vita* I. 31). But despite these and other efforts to isolate the Jews from their Christian neighbors and cast doubt on their loyalty to the "Christian" city, Jews could still be conceived in the first half of the sixth century as members of the civil community. When Messianus and Stephanus recalled the universal grief that fell over the city at Caesarius's death, they listed those who mourned his passing in pairs of universalizing opposites: "Everyone – good and evil, just and unjust, Christians and Jews, those leading and those following the procession – called out together ... " (*vita* II. 49). To be sure, the participation of Jews in ceremonies of consensus is a commonplace of biography, hagiography, and panegyric.[77] But far from detracting from the value of such testimony, this fact should inspire confidence in it. For by including the Jews in an ideal description of the *consensus omnium*, the authors of the *vita* explicitly included the Jews in the community of those whose consensus was thought to matter. The fact that the Jews are associated in this series with the evil and the

---

[74] Vannes (461/91), can. 12; Agde (506), can. 40. See Blumenkranz, "'Iudaeorum Convivia.'"   [75] Katz, *The Jews*, 82.

[76] Military service by Jews had been prohibited by several laws in the Theodosian code and Sirmondian constitutions (XVI. 8. 16, 24; Sirm. 6), but none of these was taken up into the *Breviary*, which only restricted Jews from holding public office (*nov.* 3).

[77] B. Blumenkranz, "Die Juden als Zeugen der Kirche," *Theologische Zeitschrift* 5 (1949), 396–98.

unjust, and opposed to the good, the just, and Christians did not necessarily bar them from membership in the Christian city. As a committed Augustinian, Caesarius believed that during its pilgrimage on earth the Christian church was composed of both good and evil souls (*serm.* 120. 4; 156. 5). No one could tell who would eventually be saved: even those outside the church – Jews, heretics, or pagans – might eventually believe (*serm.* 180. 1). Since bishops could not impose standards of Christian perfection on even the membership of the church, it stood to reason that they could not hope to do so for the larger, more heterogeneous community. As long as this interpretation of the church prevailed and Judaism continued to thrive (or at least survive) in Arles, the boundaries of the civil community could never be made perfectly identical with the boundaries of the Christian community. But even if they could have been, the practical results might have been the same, for the definition of what it meant to belong to a Christian community was itself in dispute between Caesarius and his congregation.

THE SPECTRUM OF CHRISTIAN RELIGIOSITY

Like Augustine, Caesarius believed that the ideal Christian life was fundamentally a social life.[78] At the same time, he believed that the only community in which the Christian could be truly at home, which in the ancient world meant to be truly a citizen, was in the city of God, his rightful *patria* (*serm.* 7. 2). Until he reached the heavenly Jerusalem, the Christian lived in the world as a pilgrim, a traveler, and a stranger, no longer a citizen of the earthly city nor yet a citizen of paradise (*serm.* 151). Yet, while he followed Augustine in refusing to identify the city of God with any human institution, Caesarius still sought to create the best possible approximation of the *civitas dei*, although necessarily a deeply imperfect version of it, in the *civitas Arelatensis*. His model for this Christian community was the monastery, which stood for him, as it had for Augustine, as an image of the city of God on earth.[79] As we have seen, Caesarius employed this model in his efforts to organize and reorganize the lives of monks, nuns, and clerics in Arles. But he also, characteristically, attempted to impose it on his lay congregation, supplementing minimum standards of belief

---

[78] *civ. dei* XIX. 5.
[79] Zumkeller, *Augustine's Ideal*, 154, and Markus, *Ancient Christianity*, 78–82.

and behavior with a much stricter biblical and monastic regimen of religious devotion and social behavior.[80]

We begin with religious devotion. Caesarius recommended that his people, like monks, fast and keep watch (*serm.* 10. 3; 44. 4; 72. 1), especially in Lent (*serm.* 196. 1; 198. 5) and before the baptism of themselves or their children (*serm.* 84. 6; 225. 6). He also advised them to pray at every opportunity, not just on Sundays and feast days, but every day (*serm.* 100. 4), and not just in public, but privately as well (*serm.* 198. 5). It was for this purpose that he had added the services of Terce, Sext, and None to Matins and Vespers at the cathedral (*vita* 1. 15), at which he urged frequent attendance (*serm.* 86. 5; 196. 2). For the same reasons, following a provision of the *Rule of the Four Fathers*,[81] he prohibited work on the Lord's day, and directed that the time be devoted to God (*serm.* 13. 3).[82] At these regular prayer sessions, he urged his people to pray for others in addition to themselves – even for enemies (*serm.* 72. 5) – and to ask not just for temporal goods like health, peace, and prosperity, which he asserted were of secondary importance, but above all for eternal life (*serm.* 146. 3).

No doubt there were some in Arles who tried to follow this advice by fasting, keeping vigils, and saying their prayers at every opportunity. But to sustain the level of religious devotion that Caesarius demanded would have been impossible for the majority of the population. Even Caesarius admitted that many found it difficult to fast and keep vigils (*serm.* 30. 1, 2; 37. 1). In addition, not many Christians in the city, perhaps only the rich and the very poor, would have had the leisure regularly to attend services in the cathedral throughout the day. It was difficult enough for the "working poor and craftsmen" to spare a half hour for Matins early in the morning, and even Caesarius recognized their eagerness to leave at the usual hour (*serm.* 76. 3). As a "professional" Christian, it was hardly fair of him to argue that if he, with all his responsibilities, could find the time to provide spiritual nourishment to his people, they should be able to find the time to accept it (*serm.* 76. 3). Likewise, giving up work on Sundays to devote the time exclusively to God was often not a matter of choice for laborers in the city, let alone peasants in the countryside, who, unlike the rich, could not live without working and, unlike

---

[80] See in general, P. Christophe, *Cassien et Césaire, prédicateurs de la morale monastique*, (Gembloux, Belgium, 1969), 48–73.   [81] *RIVP* 9.

[82] Christophe, *Cassien et Césaire*, 62.

monks, nuns, and clerics, could not rely on the wealth of the church for support. As for the content of their prayers, in a world fraught with insecurity, the suggestion that people spend most of their time praying for eternal life simply contradicted what they perceived their own needs to be. Good health, peace, and prosperity cannot have been of secondary importance to most of the people of Arles, who must have prayed for many of the same things Avitus of Vienne once rebuked his congregation for praying for: "the happiness of worldly life, the death of enemies, an increase in wealth, a long life, the prestige of secular office."[83]

Caesarius's suggestion that laymen devote their time to spiritual reading produced the same gap between ideal and reality. It is difficult to exaggerate the importance that he placed on reading the Bible and other religious texts.[84] For him, the scriptures were "letters of invitation" from the Christian's true homeland, the city of God. Refusing to read them was like a bailiff refusing to read a letter of instructions from his master: such an offense deserved imprisonment (*serm.* 7. 3). Caesarius thus instructed his congregation to listen carefully to the scriptures in church and then to reread them at home (*serm.* 7. 1), especially during the long winter nights when he thought three hours was not too much to spare (*serm.* 6. 2). There were, however, objections. Some maintained that there was no time available for spiritual reading. They were urged to read the Bible instead of gambling (*serm.* 198. 3) or attending "extravagant luncheons which occupy us until evening" or "dinners which sometimes keep us up ... to the middle of the night" (*serm.* 6. 1; see also *serm.* 8. 2).

Others protested, more fundamentally, that they did not know how to read (*serm.* 6. 2; 8. 1). This was a problem that affected a substantial proportion of the population, not just the peasants to whom *Sermon* 6 was addressed, but also the urban population.[85] While Caesarius took it for granted that bailiffs could read the instructions sent by their masters (*serm.* 7. 3), he also mentions illiterate merchants who hired intermediaries to keep their

---

[83] Avitus, *hom.* 7, *MGH AA*, VI. 2, 117.

[84] See now A. Ferreiro, "*Frequenter legere*: The Propagation of Literacy, Education, and Divine Wisdom in Caesarius of Arles," *Journal of Ecclesiastical History* 43 (1992), 5–15.

[85] The extent of literacy in late antiquity is in dispute. For a low estimate, see W. V. Harris, *Ancient Literacy* (Cambridge, Mass., 1989), 285–322; for a higher rate, as measured by the "testamentary habit," see E. A. Meyer, "Literacy, Literate Practice, and the Law in the Roman Empire, A.D. 100–600," (Ph.D. diss., Yale University, 1989), esp. 32–72, 205–7, and 342–46.

accounts and read to them (*serm.* 6. 2; 8. 1).[86] Furthermore, it is clear from his *regula virginum* that not all of the women entering the urban monastery could be expected to know how to read upon their arrival;[87] the same holds true for the men who entered Bishop Aurelianus's monastery in Arles after 547.[88] To such illiterate Christians, Caesarius suggested that they either listen to others read the scriptures or hire intermediaries to do so (*serm.* 6. 2; 8. 1). Apparently, there were "poor men" available to perform this service; they may have been clerics (*serm.* 8. 1).

Certainly, some members of Caesarius's congregation may have followed this advice. The example of Servulus, an indigent paralytic whom Gregory the Great was later to observe begging in the portico of S. Clemente in Rome, is instructive.[89] Although completely illiterate, Servulus purchased codices of the scriptures for himself (presumably from the alms he received), and had visitors read them aloud to him.[90] But even if manuscripts of the Bible were as easily acquired in Arles as Caesarius assumes,[91] and as the story of Servulus suggests for Rome,[92] it would be rash to assume that the scriptures were widely read by the lay population. Gregory's story, for instance, lays great stress on Servulus's exemplary piety, which included constantly thanking God despite his paralysis and dedicating his days and nights to giving praise and singing hymns.[93] Preoccupied by the need to work, most Christians did not enjoy as much free time as such activities, including reading, seemed to require. "I am a peasant," said one member of Caesarius's audience, "and I am completely occupied in working the land; I am not able to listen to or read the scriptures" (*serm.* 6. 3).

Against such objections, Caesarius suggested that peasants memorize some of the texts they heard in church, including the Creed and Lord's Prayer, selected antiphons, and the fiftieth and ninetieth psalms, which they could then recite while they worked (*serm.* 6. 3).[94] He advised others to memorize the same list (*vita* I. 19; *serm.* 130. 5), with the addition of passages from the Old and

---

[86] On the use of intermediaries, see Harris, *Ancient Literacy*, 33–35.
[87] *reg. virg.* 18.   [88] Aurelianus, *regula ad monachos* 32.   [89] *dial.* IV. 15. 2–5.
[90] *dial.* IV. 15. 3.
[91] "Is it possible that someone who knows how to read cannot find books in which he can read divine scripture?" (*serm.* 6. 1).
[92] G. Cavallo, "Libro e pubblico alla fine del mondo antico," in *Libri, editori e pubblico nel mondo antico*, ed. G. Cavallo (Rome and Bari, 1975), 81–132: 113–16.
[93] *dial.* IV. 15. 3.   [94] See also *serm.* 13. 2; 16. 2; and 19. 3.

New Testaments and the apocrypha (*serm.* 15. 2; 158. 1, 6; 196. 2). The verbatim memorization of religious texts, especially the psalms, was of course precisely the sort of task Caesarius expected clerics[95] and religious[96] to undertake, not so much for their intellectual training as for their moral improvement.[97] As he told a group of monks, "The psalms are the weapons of God's servants; whoever knows them by heart does not fear his adversary" (*serm.* 238. 2). Yet for those with untrained memories, verbatim memorization was exceedingly difficult.[98] Indeed, several monks complained to Caesarius that they could not do it: "One says that he is not capable of memorizing; another says, 'I want to do it, but I have a bad memory'" (*serm.* 238. 1). If such a task was difficult for literate monks, it must have been far more difficult for illiterate laymen, especially peasants, not only because they were unable to check their memories against a written text, but also because they lived in a culture in which memory for things mattered far more than verbatim memory.[99] Caesarius, however, insisted that what he demanded was not difficult: "No one should say, 'I cannot remember anything that is read in church.' Without doubt you can if you wish" (*serm.* 6. 3). Indeed, he seems to have thought that the simple repetition of texts in church was enough to ensure their eventual memorization. Referring to Psalm 103, he said at the beginning of one sermon, "This psalm, dearest brothers, which is recited at vigils in both churches and monasteries throughout the whole world is so well known to almost all men that the greatest portion of the human race knows it by heart" (*serm.* 136. 1). The bishop's confidence in his congregation's ability to memorize such texts appears to have been based on his own observations of peasant culture, in particular the songs that peasants sang. "How many peasant men and women," he asked, "remember and sing shameful and diabolic love songs? Are they able to learn and remember what the devil teaches and not remember what Christ teaches?" (*serm.* 6. 3; see also *serm.* 130. 5). Despite the fact, however, that songs, oracles, and poems are sometimes remembered word for word in oral cultures,[100] we should not underestimate the obstacles to verbatim

[95] Vaison (529), can. 1.   [96] *serm.* 238. 1.
[97] Riché, *Education and Culture*, 115–16; Carruthers, *The Book of Memory*, 12–13, 71.
[98] Riché, *Education and Culture*, 464.
[99] J. Goody, *The Interface Between the Written and the Oral* (Cambridge, 1987), 167–90.
[100] Ibid., 176.

memorization for Caesarius's audience. Even non-verbatim memorization was difficult for many of them, as the bishop himself acknowledged when he asked people to remember the gist of his sermon in order to pass it on to others:[101] "And if someone cannot remember the whole sermon, he should remember three or four passages, and provided that one tells another what he has heard, by relating the whole to one another in turn, you will not only be able to hold it in your memory, but also carry it out in deeds, with the help of Christ" (*serm.* 6. 8). That lay audiences required this alternative is not surprising if we compare them to Caesarius's clergy, many of whom found it difficult to summarize for the bishop brief stories read to them just minutes or hours before (*vita* I. 62; II. 31).

Yet, as much as he wanted them to live like clerics and religious in the world, Caesarius recognized that it was deeply undesirable, not to say impossible, for even a large fraction of his congregation to renounce their possessions, abandon their productive roles, and dedicate themselves to a life of poverty (*serm.* 37. 1). Not only would this have undermined the existing social and economic system; it would also have eliminated the continuing income from the laity on which the church depended. Their support was especially important in Arles, where it was Caesarius's expectation that the local clergy, as well as monks and nuns, would renounce their property to live off the charity of the congregation. As Julianus Pomerius had written, reflecting Cassian,[102] "And so God ordained that tithes and first fruits, first born and sin offerings, and gifts that he commanded to be offered to himself should be distributed to the bishops and ministers in order that, while a most devoted people furnish them the necessaries of life, they themselves might minister to their creator and shepherd with undisturbed minds..."[103] Caesarius therefore proposed an attenuated form of monastic renunciation, which produced spiritual benefits for the donor and at the same time ensured the church's financial security.[104] He urged members of his congregation to give up their superfluous possessions (*serm.* 30, 34), defined as what remained after family, kinsfolk, slaves, taxes, and other obligations had been taken care of (*serm.* 34. 2–3). Gifts were solicited in the form of tithes, which constituted a literal tenth of produce or income

[101] *vita* I. 61; *serm.* 74. 4; 78. 5; 104. 6.   [102] *conl.* 21. 2.
[103] *vita contempl.* II. 16. 3, trans. adapted from Suelzer.
[104] Christophe, *Cassien et Césaire*, 55–56.

(*serm.* 33. 1), and alms (*serm.* 25–27), which included all other gifts, such as gold, silver, clothing, grain, wine, olive oil, and ransom for captives (*serm.* 19. 2; 25. 1; 33. 1; 35. 4; 38. 5; 158. 5). Both forms of gift-giving were strictly voluntary. They were to be used not only for the involuntary poor, but for the voluntary poor as well, that is, abbots, monks, clerics, and other servants of God (*serm.* 14. 3; 27. 1, 3). Tithes and alms in turn benefited the donor by serving to redeem his sins. Giving them was even better than private fasting or keeping vigils, for those practices were insufficient without almsgiving, while almsgiving was sufficient without them (*serm.* 199. 2). Indeed, those who complained that they could not fast or keep watch, read or pray were advised to give alms instead (*serm.* 30. 1, 2). Almsgiving was especially recommended to the rich, because of their greater capacity to give and their disinclination to perform other works of piety (*serm.* 27. 3). Yet even those with few or no possessions could give alms: a scrap of bread, a drink of cold water, or a spiritual gift such as forgiveness of an injury (*serm.* 25. 3; 28. 3; 30. 3; 38. 5; 39. 1). In the latter sense, almsgiving was like love (*serm.* 37. 1; 38. 5): because it came from the heart, it was open to all Christians. Similar benefits were produced by other traditional works of mercy, such as welcoming pilgrims and strangers, visiting the sick and prisoners, and reconciling rivals and enemies (*serm.* 14. 2; 64. 2; 68. 1; 157. 5; 198. 3).

It is likely that members of Caesarius's congregation reacted to these norms in different ways. For the rich, giving alms and tithes to the bishop for him to distribute meant relinquishing the patronage value of those gifts, specifically the right to receive goods and services from clients in return. In exchange for giving up this right, the upper classes of Arles were promised spiritual benefits and social prestige. There is no doubt that at least some of those who could afford it exercised such charity – Caesarius could not have ransomed as many captives as he did without substantial gifts from aristocrats – but they probably did not abandon traditional forms of patronage to do so. As a result, because it almost certainly complemented rather than replaced traditional patronage,[105] the almsgiving and tithing of the rich probably did not reach the heights of liberality it might have without other

---

[105] For the co-existence of patronage with charity and public benefaction, see P. Garnsey and G. Woolf, "Patronage of the Rural Poor in the Roman World," in *Patronage in Ancient Society*, ed. A. Wallace-Hadrill (London, 1989), 153–70: 154.

competing forms of generosity. For those who were not rich, gift-giving was a different matter altogether. To the extent that it coincided with local traditions of mutual assistance, almsgiving was probably common.[106] Indeed, Caesarius once commended an audience that included a number of the working poor for its generosity in almsgiving (*serm.* 31. 1). Tithes, however, appear to have been widely resisted, as is clear from attempts first made in the sixth century to render them obligatory.[107] The motives behind this resistance are not difficult to imagine. Gifts of one tenth of a family's income were a heavy financial burden for those who were already required to pay steep rents to their landlords and taxes to the king.

The unwillingness and inability of Caesarius's congregation to perform the same religious devotions as monks should not of course detract from the routine acts of devotion that they did perform, such as attending Mass (*serm.* 14. 1; 44. 1; 72. 1), having their children baptized (*de gratia*, Morin II, 162), and teaching them to live as Christians (*serm.* 130. 5). But their reluctance to follow many of Caesarius's religious prescriptions suggests an even greater independence in following the social obligations he enjoined. Indeed, many decided for themselves which of Caesarius's values to accept, reject, or modify.

CHRISTIAN VALUES AND SOCIAL BEHAVIOR

Many of Caesarius's sermons upheld values widely accepted in the community, such as civic harmony, peace, and justice. Likewise, many of the practices that Caesarius condemned, such as devious trade practices and oppression of the poor, would also have been widely condemned in the community. Indeed, most of the "mortal sins" (*crimina capitalia*) against which Caesarius preached (*serm.* 179. 2) were already prohibited in the Roman law of the time, including sacrilege,[108] homicide,[109]

---

[106] For the extent to which Caesarius took such local traditions for granted, see *serm.* 1. 8 (Delage): "if a bishop ... is unable to ... disburse food for the body, a layman will give it, or even a pagan, or sometimes even a Jew."

[107] Lesne, *Histoire de la propriété*, I, 15–16, 186–90; Tours (567), *CCSL* 148A, 198. In 585, the Council of Macon, declaring that the practice of paying tithes was widely neglected, ordered the faithful to pay their tithes on pain of excommunication, can. 5.

[108] *Sacrilegium* was a very broad term relating to violations of the imperial sanctity as well as the sanctity of church possessions, doctrines, practices, and officers. For prohibitions, see *CTh* VI. 5. 2 = *brev. Al.* VI. 1. 2; XVI. 2. 2 = *brev. Al.* XVI. 1. 1.

[109] *CTh* IX. 10. 1 = *brev. Al.* IX. 7; Valentinian, *nov.* 19 = *brev. Al., nov.* 3.

adultery,[110] perjury,[111] theft,[112] and rape.[113] But Caesarius could not count on such support for all the values and practices he recommended, particularly those "counsels of perfection" that he had modeled on monastic living. As we shall see, what was most at issue was not the refusal of his congregation to abide by monastic standards they already held, but their unwillingness to espouse many of these standards in the first place.

We begin with charity, *perfecta caritas* (*serm.* 23. 3; 35. 3), the pre-eminent Christian and monastic virtue, the "bond of social cohesion" (*vinculum societatis, serm.* 24. 4).[114] Without it, Caesarius said, other devotions were insufficient (*serm.* 38. 5; 39. 4), and even if no other devotions were practiced, it would suffice (*serm.* 37. 1; 38. 5; 39. 2). Up to a point, the ideal of charity was probably widely accepted in the community. In a face-to-face society like Arles, disagreements over land ownership, debts, water and grazing rights, and other goods and privileges could serve as continuing sources of conflict, disharmony, and violence if not promptly resolved (*serm.* 35. 5). It was not uncommon for neighbors to refuse to speak to one another for days, months, or years as the result of even an insignificant quarrel (*serm.* 36. 7). In such situations, the image of charity provided a model for the settlement of disputes that was based on negotiation and consensus rather than litigation and conflict.[115] Often the bishop himself acted as mediator;[116] at other times members of the community were urged to do so.[117] Interpreted in this practical sense, the ethic of charity meant a willingness to forgive injuries, submit to arbitration, and come to terms with one's adversaries (*serm.* 39. 4). These were steps that many were probably willing to take for the sake of peace and good order. When called upon to love their enemies unconditionally, however, Caesarius's congregation resisted. Not only did they fall short in practicing this ideal, as Caesarius's repeated admonitions on the subject demonstrate; they also rejected the ideal itself as impractical (*serm.* 35. 2; 37. 2).

[110] *CTh* III. 16. 1 = *brev. Al.* III. 16. 1; *edict. Theod.* 54.
[111] *CTh* XI. 39. 10 = *brev. Al.* XI. 14. 5.　　[112] *CTh* IX. 2. 5.
[113] *CTh* IX. 24 = *brev. Al.* IX. 19. 1; *edict. Theod.* 17. 19.
[114] See also *serm.* 22. 2; 23. 4; 29. 1.
[115] J. Bossy, "Postscript," in *Disputes and Settlements*, ed. J. Bossy, 287–93: 288. On Caesarius's preference for negotiation over litigation, see *serm.* 35. 1.
[116] *stat. eccl. ant.*, can. 54; *vita* I. 45. See further James, "'Beati pacifici.'"
[117] *serm.* 14. 2; 16. 2; 19. 2; 60. 4; 64. 2; 86. 5; 188. 6; 198. 3; 204. 3; 224. 4; 225. 5; 229. 4.

Even more difficult for Caesarius's congregation to accept and practice was the virtue of chastity (*serm.* 41. 2), in its most rigorous form, permanent sexual renunciation. As we have seen, Caesarius did not expect the majority of his congregation to commit themselves to so exacting a standard for their entire lives. Like Augustine and other church leaders,[118] he considered marriage an "honorable estate" whose main purpose, as the marriage agreement clearly indicated, was the production of legitimate offspring (*serm.* 44. 3). According to Caesarius, married persons who remained faithful to one another, engaged in sexual relations solely for the procreation of children, gave alms together, and kept the commandments were assured of a future with Job, Sara, and Susanna in the world to come (*serm.* 6. 7). Nonetheless, permanent sexual renunciation remained the standard against which other forms of behavior were measured: "There are three *professiones* in the holy Catholic church: virgins, widows, and married people. Virgins produce one hundred-fold, widows sixty-fold, and married persons thirty-fold" (*serm.* 6. 7). In keeping with this belief, Caesarius sought to enforce a high degree of sexual continence among members of his congregation, sometimes in the same language with which he exhorted monks and nuns to maintain their state of chastity.[119] Married men were advised to abstain from sex in a wide range of situations: for the first three days of marriage;[120] during Lent and periods of penitence;[121] for several days before Sundays, Christmas, martyrs' feasts, or holy days;[122] while their wives were pregnant (and thus unable to conceive),[123] or menstruating;[124] and, for catechumens, just before and after their baptism.[125] Those who violated these taboos were threatened with the prospect of conceiving defective children (*serm.* 44. 7).[126] Despite such dire threats, the frequency with

---

[118] A. Zurek, "L'etica coniugale in Cesario di Arles: rapporti con Agostino e nuovi orientamenti," *Augustinianum* 25 (1985), 565–78.

[119] Delage II, 284–85, nn. 1–3.

[120] *vita* I. 59. The practice goes back to the Vulgate text of Tb. 6: 18, 22. See P. J. Payer, "Early Medieval Regulations Concerning Marital Sexual Relations," *Journal of Medieval History* (1980), 353–76: 365. [121] *serm.* 68. 2; 199. 7.

[122] *serm.* 44. 3, 7; 187. 4; 188. 3, 6; 199. 7; 225. 5; 229. 4.

[123] *serm.* 44. 7; J. T. Noonan, *Contraception. A History of its Treatment by Catholic Theologians and Canonists* (Cambridge, Mass., 1965), 77.

[124] *serm.* 44. 7. The prohibition was based on Lv. 15: 24; 18: 19; 20: 18.

[125] *serm.* 200. 4.

[126] Gregory of Tours relates the story of a blind and crippled boy whose mother confessed to having conceived him on a Sunday night, *virt. Mart.* II. 24.

which Caesarius repeated himself on this point suggests that his congregation found it difficult, to say the least, to accept such restraints on their marital sexual behavior.[127]

Sexual relations outside marriage were condemned a fortiori, not only because they were motivated by *libido* (*serm.* 44. 3), for this could occur within marriage as well, but also because they were normally temporary, and not directed toward the procreation of children (*serm.* 42. 4).[128] As a result, Caesarius urged the married men in his congregation to avoid relations with slave girls, whether their own (*serm.* 41. 5) or their neighbors' (*serm.* 41. 3), and other married or unmarried women (*serm.* 41. 3; 42. 2; 43. 6). They needed a good deal of convincing, however. Not only was a man who had sexual relations with his slaves not punished, said Caesarius; instead, he was congratulated by his peers: "Talking to one another with joking and stupid laughter, they compare who has done this more often" (*serm.* 42. 3). Women too were cautioned against sexual relations outside of marriage, but unlike men they were also punished for it by the community (*serm.* 42. 3; 43. 3).

Even more threatening to Caesarius's ideals of matrimony than these temporary liaisons was the widespread custom of concubinage. As practiced in the Roman world, it normally involved a socially recognized and long-lasting relationship of cohabitation between partners who were either unwilling or unable to contract a legitimate union, usually because of differences in social status.[129] Provided that neither partner was married, it was not illegal in sixth-century Arles,[130] and there was no dishonor attached to the relationship (*serm.* 43. 4), unlike prostitution, which could be a source of shame if publicly revealed (*serm.* 45. 2). Caesarius does not seem to have concerned himself with those who took concubines because they were legally barred from contracting legitimate marriages; these were mostly slaves and freedmen for whom concubinage served as a *de facto* form of marriage,[131] which Augustine at least had been prepared to accept as valid.[132] Caesarius rather concentrated on members of the upper class for whom, like the young Augustine, concubinage was normally practiced in the

---

[127] Payer, "Early Medieval Regulations."   [128] Beck, 227.

[129] S. Treggiari, "Concubinae," *Papers of the British School at Rome* 49 (1981), 59–81: 59–64.   [130] *CJ* v. 26. 1 (326).

[131] E. Rawson, "Roman Concubinage and Other *de facto* Marriages," *Transactions of the American Philological Association* 104 (1974), 279–305.   [132] *de bono coniugali* 5.

interval between the end of boyhood and legitimate marriage to a social equal (*serm.* 43. 2, 4) or after the death of a spouse (*serm.* 42. 5). Among such men, the custom was not generally considered sinful (*serm.* 32. 4; 42. 5). Indeed, it was so widely practiced that offenders were too numerous to excommunicate (*serm.* 42. 5; 43. 5). Caesarius therefore tried to eradicate the practice by other tactics. After first appealing to the authority of the scriptures (*serm.* 42. 4; 43. 2), he pointed out the "double standard" implicit in the practice of concubinage.

I would like to know, however, whether those who are not married and who before marriage were not afraid or ashamed to commit adultery, would want their brides to be violated by adulterous relations before coming to marriage. For, since there is no man who would endure this, why does each and every man not preserve the pledge for his bride that he wants her to preserve? Why does he want to take a virgin as his wife when he is himself corrupted? (*serm.* 43. 2)

Against the belief that different moral codes applied to men and women, Caesarius asserted, like Augustine,[133] that men and women were equal in the eyes of God (*serm.* 32. 4; 42. 3; 43. 3), although this should not be interpreted too broadly, since he stressed their fundamental inequality in other contexts.[134]

Caesarius further maintained that, according to Roman law, the children born of concubines were themselves born into slavery (*serm.* 42. 5). This statement indicates that the concubines of upper class men in Arles were normally slaves themselves, since in Roman law the status of a child born outside of legitimate marriage was derived from its mother.[135] Even when subsequently freed, Caesarius added, children born of slaves were not permitted by law to receive an inheritance from their fathers.[136] The conclusion of this passage makes it even clearer that the argument was aimed at the propertied classes of Arles: "And now consider whether it is not sinful when the ornament of noble blood is so

[133] Augustine, *serm.* 9. 4.

[134] *serm.* 43. 1; 120. 1. See S. F. Wemple, *Women in Frankish Society. Marriage and the Cloister, 500–900* (Philadelphia, 1981), 24–25.

[135] Ulpian, *liber singularis regularum* v. 9, ed. J. Baviera, *FIRA* II, 268–69.

[136] *serm.* 42. 5. A law of Constantine had permitted concubinage to be subsequently legitimated, and the offspring of a concubine to inherit the name, status, and property of its father, either *ex testamento* or *ab intestato*, but only if the woman was free-born, *CJ* v. 27. 5. If she was not, the offspring of the relationship were permitted to receive at most a fixed proportion of the family property, *CTh* IV. 6. 7. See P. M. Meyer, *Der römische Konkubinat nach den Rechtsquellen und den Inschriften* (Leipzig, 1895, repr. Aalen, 1966), 133–42.

humiliated that slaves are born from men of great nobility"
(*serm.* 42. 5). It was precisely these "noblemen" who would often
have endured a lengthy interval between the end of boyhood and
the arrangement of a properly advantageous marriage. Their ease
of access to slave girls might have strongly predisposed them to
live in concubinage for the duration. Concubinage was thus the
byproduct of a marriage strategy in which young men delayed
marriage, in Caesarius's words, "to find wives more noble and
richer than they are" (*serm.* 43. 4). Indeed it is likely to have been
these very noblemen who criticized Caesarius for his views on the
matter: he concluded several sermons on the topic with the
unusual request that people not become angry at him (*serm.* 32. 4;
42. 6; 43. 9). Because the custom of concubinage coincided so well
with the social practices and values of wealthy men in the
community, who would normally have been among the most
influential public supporters of the Christian value system, the
practice proved particularly resistant to episcopal pressure.

Unable to excommunicate such highly placed individuals *en
masse*, Caesarius resorted to a weaker ecclesiastical remedy. He
declared that he would follow Roman custom and refuse to give
the customary nuptial blessing to bridegrooms who were no
longer virgins.[137] This strategy was designed to motivate Christians through their individual consciences as well as their concern
for social standing. First, the denial of a public blessing could be
thought to constitute a fair indication of a man's chances at the Last
Judgment: "What sort of sentence at the future judgment will be
applied to the man who was not considered worthy while in the
world of receiving a blessing with his bride?" (*serm.* 43. 5).
Second, such a denial could affect a man's reputation, but only to
the extent that community standards coincided with those
advanced by the bishop. A similar tension between episcopal and
community standards is evident in Caesarius's condemnation of
prevailing methods for regulating family size.

Motives for limiting family size in Arles varied according to
individual circumstances, of course, but economic and demographic factors must have remained primary.[138] Poor parents had

[137] *serm.* 42. 5; 43. 5; *vita* I. 59; *stat. eccl. ant.*, can. 101. For a history of the practice, see L.
Anné, *Les Rites des fiançailles et la donation pour cause de mariage sous le Bas-Empire*
(Louvain, 1941), 137–231.
[138] E. Eyben, "Family Planning in Antiquity," *Ancient Society* 11–12 (1980–81), 5–82:
79–81.

to balance the labor value of additional children against the cost of bringing them up. Wealthy parents, on the other hand, concerned themselves more often with maintaining the family's standard of living in succeeding generations, since the family estate was normally divided among all the children. Ultimately, for rich and poor families alike, the limitation of family size was a demographic necessity; left unchecked for several generations, population growth could easily outdistance the sustenance capacity of local economies.[139] For these reasons, the ideal family size in late antique Arles remained at two or three children (*serm.* 52. 4), as it had been throughout antiquity.[140] To achieve these results, a variety of methods for controlling family size were practiced in Arles, including sexual abstinence, contraception, abortion, infanticide, and child abandonment; how widely and with what success these were practiced is a matter of dispute.[141] Caesarius believed that the limitation of family size was immoral on two counts, first because he thought the desire itself was based on greed (*serm.* 52. 4), and second, because he found most of the methods in use to be morally reprehensible. He therefore condemned the practice vehemently:

No woman should take potions for the purpose of abortion, nor should she kill children who have been conceived or already born...nor should women take those diabolical potions that prevent them from conceiving. Any woman who does this should know that she is guilty of as many cases of homicide as children she could have borne. I would like to know, however, if a free-born woman who took deadly potions to prevent conception would want her slave girls or female tenants to do the same. And therefore, just as each slave owner wants slaves born for herself to serve her, so she should rear or give to others to rear all the children she conceives. (*serm.* 44. 2)[142]

As this passage demonstrates, the only permissible method of disposing of unwanted children was to give them away to others

[139] F. Braudel, *Civilization and Capitalism, 15th–18th Century*, I, *The Structures of Everyday Life*, trans. S. Reynolds (New York, 1981), 33.

[140] Eyben, "Family Planning," 75, n. 232.

[141] On family planning in general, see Eyben, "Family Planning." On sexual abstinence and its effects, see E. Patlagean, "Sur la limitation de la fécondité dans la haute époque byzantine," *Annales ESC* 24 (1969), 1353–69. On contraception, see K. Hopkins, "Contraception in the Roman Empire," *Comparative Studies in Society and History* 8 (1965), 124–51, and Noonan, *Contraception*. On abortion, see E. Nardi, *Procurato aborto nel mondo grecoromano* (Milan, 1971). On infanticide, see L. Williamson, "Infanticide: An Anthropological Analysis," in *Infanticide and the Value of Life*, ed. M. Kohl (Buffalo, N. Y., 1978), 61–75. On abandonment, see J. Boswell, *The Kindness of Strangers: The Abandonment of Children in Western Europe from Late Antiquity to the Renaissance* (New York, 1988). [142] See also *serm.* 51. 4.

to rear, a reference to abandonment, widely practiced in the ancient and medieval world.[143] But this was not in Caesarius's view the best course of action, for as he saw the matter it was far better to avoid having unwanted children in the first place. He therefore offered a more highly valued and equally effective means of limiting family size, practiced in other societies as well,[144] which also conformed well to the Christian ideal of chastity. "You do not now wish to have a child? Sign a religious agreement with your husband. Let childbirth cease as a result of chastity; abstinence alone should be the reason for the sterility of a pious woman" (*serm.* 52. 4).[145]

Yet at the same time, the existence of strong pressures to limit family size in this society did not eliminate the need or the desire for children: "Some married men and women are liable to become overly despondent when they reflect on the fact that they have no children. What is worse, they are sometimes so impatient that they think they can have children not from God, but from sacrilegious medicines or the sap of trees" (*serm.* 51. 1). Again, economic and demographic factors predominated. While poor families needed children for their value as laborers and as sources of security in old age, it was often the destiny of the family fortune that concerned wealthy families without children (*serm.* 51. 2). Just as for those who desired no more children, Caesarius was prepared to recommend an ascetic lifestyle to couples who could not have children.

Let no one be sad or lament his sterility when he sees so many clergymen, monks, and nuns remain in God's service without earthly children until the end of their lives ... Let those who have bodily sterility preserve a spiritual fertility, and let those who cannot have children of flesh try to give birth to spiritual offspring. All good works are our children; whoever does good works daily will not cease to have spiritual children. (*serm.* 51. 3)

But there was more at stake here than a personal salvation obtained through the "spiritual children" of almsgiving and good works. The institutional church stood to gain as well, since childless couples could bequeath a greater proportion of their wealth to the church than couples with children. Indeed, it has recently been suggested that such considerations influenced attempts by the church in late antiquity and the early middle ages to

---

[143] Boswell, *The Kindness of Strangers.*
[144] Williamson offers examples, "Infanticide," 63.   [145] See also *serm.* 1. 12.

"encourage...heirlessness by disallowing the use of collaterals, adopted sons, and other means to plug the succession gap."[146] Yet, although Caesarius probably did not hesitate to take advantage of existing gaps in succession in order to add to the wealth of the church,[147] he did not oppose attempts to find alternative heirs. His objections to prevailing methods of stimulating fertility were largely based on their pagan, magical, or folk character (*serm.* 51. 4). Likewise, his opposition to concubinage was primarily based on moral grounds; like Augustine he probably would have been satisfied to legitimate illicit relations through marriage,[148] an act that also legitimated illegitimate children (provided the mother was free-born).[149] The elimination of heirs, if it happened at all, would have been inadvertent. For Caesarius, in fact, the inability of a concubine's offspring to receive the inheritance of their father was an argument against concubinage (*serm.* 42. 5). His intervention in the sexual and reproductive activities of members of his congregation did not issue therefore from a desire to acquire property for the church, but from a desire to impose monastic habits of sexual abstinence and renunciation on the laity.[150] The real conflict between the bishop and his community did not erupt over competing material interests, but rather over control of marriage, sexuality, and fertility.

A similar conflict can be observed in Caesarius's attacks on customs of conviviality, particularly heavy drinking and eating, dancing, and the telling of obscene stories, poems, jokes, and songs. For participants, of course, these were the essential features of *convivia*. Heavy drinking, for instance, was a widespread custom, practiced by clergy and laity alike.[151] Far from being considered sinful by the population (*serm.* 46. 1), it was an integral element in the fabric of hospitality and social intercourse. "My friend will be

[146] J. Goody, *The Development of the Family and Marriage in Europe* (Cambridge, 1983), 100. A critical review can be found in B. Shaw and R. P. Saller, "Close-Kin Marriage in Roman Society?" *Man* n.s. 19 (1984), 432–44.

[147] This can be deduced from *serm.* 60. 1–2 in which Caesarius urged testators to bequeath to the church the equivalent of one child's portion, as Augustine had also recommended, *serm.* 355. 3–4. See Gaudemet, *L'Eglise*, 294–9.

[148] Augustine, *de bono coniugali* 17.   [149] *CJ* v. 27. 5.

[150] M. Verdon, "Virgins and Widows: European Kinship and Early Christianity," *Man*, n.s. 23 (1988), 488–505.

[151] *serm.* 46. 8; 47. 4; 55. 4; Agde (506), can. 41. On the Gallic passion for wine, see also Diodorus v. 26. 3. For a variety of anthropological approaches, see *Constructive Drinking: Perspectives on Drink from Anthropology*, ed. M. Douglas (Cambridge, 1987), and *Beliefs, Behaviors, and Alcoholic Beverages: A Cross-Cultural Survey*, ed. M. Marshall (Ann Arbor, Mich., 1979).

angry," said a member of Caesarius's congregation, "if I invite him to a party, and do not give him as much to drink as he wants" (*serm.* 46. 4). At the same time, hosts might be offended by their guests' refusal to consume appropriate amounts of drink (*serm.* 47. 2). Drinking also constituted a communal affirmation of solidarity and manhood: "Whenever those unhappy drunkards gorge themselves on too much wine, they ridicule and disparage those who drink sensibly and moderately. 'You should be ashamed of yourselves,' they say. 'Why aren't you drinking as much as we are?' For they say that the others are not men" (*serm.* 47. 1). Drinking in fact provided opportunities for competitive displays of virility: "Larger cups are provided and a contest takes place according to an established law of drinking; whoever can defeat the others earns praise for the offense" (*serm.* 46. 3).

Caesarius attacked these customs on numerous grounds, citing the physical effects of excessive drinking, the violent quarreling it caused, and its incitement of adultery and homicide (*serm.* 46. 3). He also criticized heavy drinkers for wasting resources they could have given their families or the poor (*serm.* 46. 4). In this connection, he particularly condemned the behavior of peasants at local festivals.

It is said that some of the *rustici*, when they have either gotten wine or made other drinks for themselves, invite their neighbors and kin for a drinking party as though it were a wedding feast. They keep their guests for four or five days and overwhelm them with excessive drinking. Their guests do not return home from their deplorable drinking until their host has completely drained out all the drink he had; in four or five days he consumes in lamentable and shameful drinking what could have refreshed him and his family for two or three months. (*serm.* 47. 7)

Extravagant feasting like this is characteristic of the competition for honor and status in many societies. It often seems economically wasteful to outsiders who misunderstand the symbolic, social purposes of food and drink. That the custom persisted in the face of criticism from the church can be attributed to its central role in the local community, and to the lack of any suitable Christian alternative.

Not only did the custom of protracted communal feasting persist in its traditional form; it was also extended to the celebration of Christian festivals, such as martyrs' feasts (*serm.* 55. 2; 225. 1, 5), Christmas (*serm.* 188. 5), and Easter (*serm.* 201. 1). Although Caesarius repeatedly urged his congregation to conduct these celebrations "in a frugal and sober fashion" (*serm.* 188. 5), to invite the poor in addition to relatives and friends (*serm.* 188. 4), and not to force the newly baptized at Easter to drink too much (*serm.* 201. 2), it is clear that to the people of Arles the proper celebration of these special occasions demanded an abundance of feasting, dancing, and drinking. Indeed, even at ordinary times feasting might take on religious aspects, for instance when toasts were offered to the angels and saints. At certain parties, Caesarius complained,

[guests] begin to drink to various names, not only of living people, but also of angels and other saints of old. They think that they are offering them a great honor if they overwhelm themselves with drunkenness at their names, but are unaware that no one does so grave an injury to the holy angels and saints as those who, by drinking in their names, try to kill their own souls ... If pagans, who are unaware of God, do these things, it is no wonder and not something to be lamented, because they have no hope in God and are preserving the ancient custom of their ancestors. But why do Christians ... still imitate the shameful drunkenness of pagans after they have been found worthy of being freed, by God's grace, from their lack of faith? (*serm.* 47. 5)[152]

While it may have originated in pagan religion, the custom of drinking at religious celebrations in Arles should not be interpreted as an expression of paganism, but rather as an alternative form of Christian piety. Other aspects of communal celebration can be interpreted in the same way. For instance, Caesarius routinely condemned the singing, dancing, and telling of stories and jokes that often took place at feasts, and especially at Christian religious festivals. "What kind of Christian is the man who ... drinks until he vomits and, after he is drunk, gets up to dance and leap like a madman in diabolical fashion, and sings shameful, bawdy, and wanton verses?" (*serm.* 16. 3).[153] In a society where sickness and death were never far away, and in an agricultural system where bursts of intense labor were followed by long periods of underemployment, we should not underestimate the value these rituals had as highly prized forms of entertainment. But such rituals went far beyond mere amusement. In addition to transmitting community values, and affirming cultural solidarity, jokes, stories, and songs also carried a genuinely religious significance. Those who celebrated martyrs' feasts by dancing and singing in front of churches (*serm.* 13. 4; 55. 2) were not rejecting

[152] See also *serm.* 55. 3.   [153] See also *serm.* 1. 12; 13. 4; 19. 3; 46. 3; 55. 2; 225. 5.

Christianity in favor of paganism, as Caesarius charged, but were rather adapting Christian ceremonies to their own patterns of religious expression. Caesarius of course did not understand these celebrations in such terms. Instead, as in the case of concubinage and the control of family size, he proposed "sobering," ascetic, and essentially unappealing ecclesiastical alternatives to his audiences. To counteract the largely non-verbal and oral expressions of celebration that eluded his control, he proposed that periods of leisure be dedicated to spiritual reading (*serm.* 6. 1), and that prayers and psalms replace "diabolical and shameful love songs" (*serm.* 6. 3). Moreover, so that thoughts could be reinforced with deeds, he argued that resources given over to extravagant feasting should be given as alms instead (*serm.* 47. 6), and asserted that resisting the pressure of friends and masters to drink constituted a form of martyrdom (*serm.* 47. 2).

But these efforts were effectively checked by distinctions in religious culture that were gradually arising between religious specialists, such as clergymen, monks, nuns, and pious aristocrats on the one hand, and everyone else in the diocese on the other. Christian ethics could not be practiced in the same way by both groups. There were, to begin with, fundamental differences between the quantities of leisure time available to each group for the performance of religious obligations.[154] By the early sixth century, religious specialists obtained most of their support from the laity – both rich and poor – in the form of tithes, donations of treasure and land, and the labor of slaves and tenants on monastic or ecclesiastical estates.[155] They thus had a freedom from productive labor which most lay people did not. Their alienation from the existing subcultures of production, whether rural or urban, led in turn to a corresponding freedom from the ceremonies, customs, and social necessities inherent in those subcultures. Moreover, as communities of celibate monks and nuns were formed, and as a discipline of celibacy was gradually imposed upon the clergy, religious specialists ceased to have need of the same inheritance strategies as other men and women. Freed from the pressure of production and reproduction, monks, nuns, and clergymen were thus much more capable of practicing the ethics and religious duties preached by their bishops than the rest of the Christian population. For the majority of Christians, on the

---

[154] Van Dam, *Leadership*, 297–98.
[155] Lesne, *Histoire de la propriété*, I, 110–11, 343–52.

other hand, the distance remained wide between what bishops like Caesarius were coming to require and what was socially imaginable, feasible, and desirable. No amount of rhetoric could much increase the willingness or the ability of the laity to imitate religious specialists beyond the level that their social, economic, and cultural routine already permitted, whatever their individual inclinations to piety might have been.

To raise the issue of these distinctions is to confront directly the question of "elite" and "popular" religion in late antiquity and the early middle ages. We may take it for granted that, despite Caesarius's efforts, there were some men and women in Arles who aspired to religious perfection and many who did not, and that those who did aspire to such perfection practiced a different sort, perhaps a different "level," of Christianity than those who did not. But were distinctions in attitude and practice between these groups based simply on different degrees of religious commitment, or on fundamentally different cultures and mentalities, as Le Goff and others have argued?[156] This question is difficult to answer on the basis of the evidence we have examined in this chapter, for we have intentionally limited ourselves to attitudes and behaviors that did not suggest a fundamental disloyalty to the Christian religion, although they may have challenged the bishop's authority on specific points of practice. The question comes into clearer focus when we examine the religious behavior that Caesarius characterized as pagan, for it is on this that arguments for "a relatively hermetic stratification on two cultural levels"[157] have been based. Did this behavior represent a superficially christianized form of paganism or a valid and coherent "alternative" Christianity? It is to answer this question that we turn to the religious system accepted, practiced, and experienced at the periphery of society, to some degree within Arles itself, but mostly in the countryside, among the peasants.

[156] J. Le Goff, *Time, Work and Culture in the Middle Ages*, trans. A. Goldhammer (Chicago, 1980), 153–58; J.-C. Schmitt, "'Religion populaire' et culture folklorique," *Annales ESC* 31 (1976), 941–53; M. Lauwers, "'Religion populaire', culture folklorique, mentalités: notes pour une anthropologie culturelle du moyen âge," *Revue d'histoire ecclésiastique* 82 (1987), 221–58. For criticism of this framework of interpretation, see J. Van Engen, "The Christian Middle Ages as an Historiographical Problem," *American Historical Review* 91 (1986), 519–52, and J. M. H. Smith, "Oral and Written: Saints, Miracles, and Relics in Brittany, c. 850–1250," *Speculum* 65 (1990), 309–43.

[157] Le Goff, *Time, Work and Culture*, 158.

Chapter 8

THE LIMITS OF CHRISTIANIZATION

It was in confrontation with the attitudes and practices he condemned as "pagan" that Caesarius's program of christianization met its most severe test. Like "superstition" and "magic," "paganism" was not a label that its practitioners applied to their own activities; it was rather a Christian term of opprobrium for the (deficient) religion of others.[1] To Caesarius, as to other church leaders, "paganism" designated all religious behavior and belief that he could not ascribe to Christianity or Judaism.[2] In addition to the phenomena of Gallo-Roman religion, it included all other ritual activity that evaded his control, much of which was arguably Christian or religiously neutral in intention, if not in appearance. So broadly defined a set of attitudes and practices could not have been confined to the countryside, and we must be careful not to equate "pagans" (*pagani*) with peasants (*rustici*), as the speakers of late Latin appear to have done.[3] *Rusticitas*, as Caesarius understood it, was above all an ideological or behavioral category, and not a sociological one. As Peter Brown has observed, "*rusticitas* overlapped with the habits of the rural population; but it by no means coincided exclusively with them."[4] In other words, the acts which made people pagan in Caesarius's eyes could be observed as easily in the center of the city as deep in the countryside (*serm.* 52. 2). Still, it makes sense to discuss these diverse "pagan" phenomena together and to do so primarily in the context of the countryside, since it is in these manifestations

---

[1] On superstition, see D. Grodzynski, "Superstitio," *REA* 76 (1974), 36–60. On magic, see D. E. Aune, "Magic in Early Christianity," *ANRW* II. 23. 2 (1980), 1507–57, and C. R. Phillips, "The Sociology of Religious Knowledge in the Roman Empire to A.D. 284," *ANRW* II. 16. 3 (1986), 2677–2773, esp. 2711–32. On the origins of the term "pagan," see C. Mohrmann, "Encore une fois: Paganus," *Vigiliae Christianae* 6 (1952), 109–21.

[2] As Vigilius, bishop of Thapsus, wrote in *c.* 500: "There are three religions in the world, that of Jews, pagans, and Christians," *dialogus contra Arianos* I. 15, *PL* 62: 157D.

[3] Le Goff, *Time, Work and Culture*, 92–93.   [4] Brown, *Society and the Holy*, 231.

of behavior among the peasants of Arles that we can most clearly see both the effects of Caesarius's program of christianization and its limits. We therefore begin with a discussion of the material and cultural background to Caesarius's efforts in the countryside. We then proceed to the diverse behaviors Caesarius regarded as pagan, his strategies of christianization and depaganization, and the emergence of a community Christianity for the peasantry.

PEASANT SOCIETY AND CULTURE

As in the city of Arles itself, the end of the fifth century and beginning of the sixth century brought signs of "de-romanization" to the countryside, as landlords and peasants began to return to pre-Roman patterns of rural settlement and social organization. In their disruptive effects, these changes provided bishops like Caesarius with both a problem and an opportunity: a problem because the stripping away of Roman culture exposed and strengthened the more ancient religious loyalties, beliefs, and behaviors that had long defined a peasant's life in Provence, but also an opportunity because, as some anthropological studies of conversion suggest, it was at just such moments of political and cultural change that new religious loyalties, beliefs, and behaviors could be introduced and confirmed.[5] Although we cannot specify exactly how these cultural changes might have affected peasant religion, we can at least suggest the possibility that the two seemingly incompatible religious trends that we can observe in Caesarius's sermons – the growth of peasant Christianity and continued loyalty to traditional religion – constituted two related and equally explicable responses to the same process of cultural change.

Several hints of a process of de-romanization are evident in patterns of rural settlement. To begin with, along with the continuing occupation of villages (*vici*) from the Roman period,[6]

[5] Horton, "African Conversion"; R. Horton, "On the Rationality of Conversion," *Africa* 45 (1975), 219–35, 373–99; Peel, "Conversion and Tradition."

[6] For example, at Vitrolles, a cemetery excavated in 1981 was found to contain thirteen graves dating between the fifth and seventh centuries (Gauthier, "Informations archéologiques" [1986], 456). At St.-Jean-de-Garguier many late antique structures have been identified, with burials as well (Euzennat, "Informations archéologiques" [1967], 403; Salviat, "Informations archéologiques" [1974], 509–10; and Salviat, "Informations archéologiques" [1977], 517). Late burials have also been found at Fos-sur-Mer (Salviat, "Informations archéologiques" [1972], 519, and Gauthier, "Informations archéologiques" [1986], 410–11), and at Berre-l'Etang (Gauthier, "Informations

there is good evidence for a reoccupation in the fifth and sixth centuries of Iron Age hilltop fortresses (*oppida*) that had been largely abandoned during the Roman period. This change took place on many sites throughout Provence, and appears to suggest a return to pre-Roman settlement patterns, although caution is required, since reoccupation could have had many different causes, some purely local.[7] Numerous examples are available from the *civitas* of Arles. At Velaux, for instance, 11 km east of the Etang de Berre, excavations conducted since 1983 have demonstrated that the *oppidum* of Saint-Propice, occupied during the second century BC, was reoccupied sometime between the fifth and seventh centuries AD.[8] At the *oppidum* of Saint-Blaise, excavations undertaken between 1980 and 1985 in the northern part of the site have revealed occupation layers containing a notably high density of materials (amphoras, animal bones, shellfish, coins, glass, and over 60,000 potsherds), which date between the late fifth and seventh century AD and rest directly on pre-Roman strata.[9] At Evenos (Var), in a region that belonged to the *civitas* of Arles until the mid-fifth century when it became part of the *civitas* of Toulon, the upland site of Saint-Estève was occupied between the Neolithic period and the first century BC, utterly deserted during the Roman period, and then "massively reoccupied" toward the end of the fourth or beginning of the fifth century AD.[10] Its inhabitants covered the five-hectare site with dwellings and a small chapel (5 m × 11·25 m), and left behind hundreds of potsherds, metal fragments, and pieces of glass.[11]

Concurrently with the reoccupation of *oppida*, caves occupied during pre-Roman times were permanently reoccupied in late antiquity.[12] A good example in the *civitas* of Arles is provided by the cave of La Fourbine, located about 15 km east of Arles.[13] Careful excavation in one corner of the cave, which was already

archéologiques" [1986], 405). At Roquefort-la-Bedoule, pottery of the third to sixth centuries has been found (Gauthier, "Informations archéologiques" [1986], 448) and at Saint-Blaise, burials and vestiges of the early Christian period have been discovered (Euzennat, "Informations archéologiques" [1967], 413, and idem, "Informations archéologiques" [1969], 435).   [7] Février, "Problèmes de l'habitat," 222–27.
[8] Gauthier, "Informations archéologiques," 455–56.   [9] Ibid., 447–48.
[10] J.-P. Brun, "L'habitat de hauteur de Saint-Estève (Evenos, Var)," *Revue archéologique de Narbonnaise* 17 (1984), 1–28.   [11] Ibid., 25.
[12] Gagnière and Granier, "L'occupation des grottes," 225–39.
[13] G. Congès et al., "Un dépotoir de la fin de l'Antiquité dans la grotte de la Fourbine, Saint-Martin-de-Crau (B.-du-Rh.)," *Revue archéologique de Narbonnaise* 16 (1983), 347–64.

known to have been inhabited during the Bronze Age, has revealed the presence of two more recent phases of occupation: a phase of intermittent use during the second half of the fourth century AD and a more permanent phase during the sixth and seventh centuries AD. The second phase appears to represent a more permanent occupation because of the presence of large amounts of pottery for cooking, domestic metal objects like locks, and over 620 animal bones, the majority of which came from sheep and goats.[14]

The reasons for the reoccupation of such pre-Roman sites during late Roman or post-Roman times remain obscure. Certainly, increased military activity in the *civitas* during the fifth and early sixth centuries posed a threat to peasants on outlying farms, especially when the protection of the government or the aristocracy was unavailable. In particular, the wars of 471/76 and 507/9 had caused widespread loss of life, destruction of farmland and crops, and famine.[15] Under such conditions, caves were a natural place of refuge.[16] In addition, nucleated settlements like *oppida* could also offer collective protection from government officials and local aristocrats, especially if the entire community placed itself under the protection of a single powerful patron.[17]

A related example of de-romanization may be found in the decreasing number of villas in the *civitas* occupied during the fifth century. While some villas continued in operation throughout the fifth and sixth centuries,[18] others were permanently abandoned in the fourth or fifth centuries.[19] There is so far no evidence for the building of new villas. Of course, given the incomplete state of archaeological knowledge, we must be cautious.[20] Nonetheless, a

---

[14] Ibid., 361.   [15] Sidonius Apollinaris, *ep.* VI. 12; Caesarius, *serm.* 70. 2.

[16] Ammianus Marcellinus XXVIII. 6. 4.

[17] L. Harmand, *Le Patronat sur les collectivités publiques des origines au bas-empire* (Paris, 1957), 448–61, 473–84.

[18] One example is furnished by the large villa at Martigues under excavation since 1975. Built around 25/30 AD, it remained in use, with some interruptions, into the late sixth century (Gauthier, "Informations archéologiques," 432–36). Another example is the villa of Launico, which Caesarius visited (*vita* I. 50).

[19] For instance, at Martigues (Benoit, "Informations archéologiques" [1964], 585–86; Salviat, "Informations archéologiques" [1974], 519; and idem, "Informations archéologiques" [1977], 525), Nôtre-Dame-d'Amour (Benoit, "Informations archéologiques" [1964], 588–90), Vitrolles (Salviat, "Informations archéologiques" [1977], 530; Gauthier, "Informations archéologiques," 456), and Maussane (Euzennat, "Informations archéologiques" [1967], 405).

[20] For example, because complete sequences of datable pottery types are not yet available for late antique Provence, previous dates for abandonment might be incorrect, or later

decline in the number of villas in use during the fifth and sixth centuries in Provence would seem to match similar developments in other parts of Gaul, where the widespread abandonment of villas began in the north and center during the third century and continued in the south during the fourth and fifth centuries.[21] Agreement on the causes of this decline has not yet been reached; the specific political and economic conditions of each region must certainly have played their part.[22] One reason may have been that villas were abandoned when the properties on which they were situated were taken over by wealthy landowners in the vicinity, who no longer needed the original villa buildings because they administered their newly enlarged estates from a central location.[23] That this was occurring in the middle of the fifth century is clear from Salvian, who condemned the mechanisms by which large landowners acquired the properties of their poorer neighbors.[24] A sermon by Caesarius reveals that landowners were still practicing the same tactics a century later:

Someone desires another man's villa, and he says, "That villa of my neighbor's is a good one. I wish it were mine! I wish I could acquire it, and join this estate (*fundus*) to that one!" ... If his neighbor is a poor man (*pauper*) who has been put in the position of having to sell or who can be pressured and forced into selling, his eye turns in that direction, and he hopes that he can take away either the villa or the tenant farm (*colonica*) of his poor neighbor. He therefore inflicts troubles on him. For example, he secretly convinces those in power to have tax collectors entangle him or to adlect him to some ruinous public office. Because of the many debts he incurs from these actions, the unfortunate man would have to sell his small property (*casella*), by which he and his sons are supported. Driven

levels of occupation misdated, Février, "Problèmes de l'habitat," 224–27, 234–35. Moreover, the apparent lack of evidence for new construction may be due to a change to more perishable building materials, such as wood or clay, or to a tendency on the part of owners to leave behind fewer datable objects, Wightman, *Gallia Belgica*, 243–62.

[21] In Belgica, there is evidence of a decline at the end of the second century, Wightman, *Gallia Belgica*, 243–50, and at Lyon, in the third century, S. Walker, "La campagne lyonnaise du 1er siècle av. J.C. jusqu'au 5ème siècle ap. J.C.," in *Récentes recherches en archéologie gallo-romaine et paléo-chrétienne sur Lyon et sa région* (Oxford, 1981), 279–325: 309–12. In the south, the countryside of Béziers appears to have still been thriving into the fourth and fifth centuries, M. Clavel, *Béziers et son territoire dans l'antiquité* (Paris, 1970), 612–16. Cf. in general, M. Le Glay, "La Gaule romanisée," in *Histoire de la France rurale*, ed. G. Duby and A. Wallon, I, *La Formation des campagnes françaises* (Paris, 1975), 281–83. [22] Walker, "La campagne lyonnaise," 312.

[23] Wightman, "Peasants and Potentates," 111–14.

[24] Salvian, *gub. dei* IV. 20, 30–31; V. 38–39.

by necessity, he goes to the rich man through whose wickedness he is being oppressed and afflicted, and ignorant of the fact that he is suffering because of his actions, says to him: "I ask you lord to give me a few *solidi*, for I am in need; I am beset by creditors." And the rich man replies, "I do not have the money right now." He says this so that the other man, misled by this falsehood, will have to sell. Finally when the poor man tells him that he is forced to sell his villa because his troubles are too great, the rich man immediately replies: "Although I do not have money of my own available, I am eager to borrow the money from somewhere else so as to help my friend. If necessary I shall even sell my silver, so that you do not suffer any hardship." When the poor man seeks this favor, the rich man claims not to have it. But when he says that he will sell his land, the rich man says that he will help his so-called friend ... And for the property (*casella*), for which he previously offered, say, 100 *solidi*, the rich man agrees to give only half the price when he sees the poor man's straitened circumstances. (*serm.* 154. 2).

By describing the ways in which the rich increased their landholdings in sixth-century Arles, this story points to connections between changing settlement patterns and social organization. The "poor man" of the story was in fact a small landholder of curial status. The price of 100 *solidi* that Caesarius speculates might have been offered originally for his estate suggests that its size was more than adequate to support his family and to qualify him for curial burdens. Depending on the location of the land, quality of the soil, and type of crops grown, it may have measured as much as fifty or a hundred *iugera* (12·5–25 ha).[25] When he found himself burdened by fiscal and curial expenses, his first inclination was to seek a loan from his wealthy neighbor. It was only after he failed to obtain this that he decided to sell his land in order to satisfy his obligations. At that point, his wealthy neighbor not only bought his property, but made him a client as well, by "rescuing" him from a difficult situation.

It was by such stratagems that large landowners increased their holdings and further consolidated their patronage and control over a population that had been growing increasingly dependent since the fourth century. By Caesarius's time, it is likely that the

---

[25] For the sale near Faenza in 539 of an "orchard or olive yard" of twenty *iugera* for 110 *solidi*, see *Die nichtliterarischen lateinischen Papyri Italiens aus der Zeit 445–700*, ed. J.-O. Tjäder, II (Stockholm, 1982), P. 30, with commentary in Jones, *LRE* II, 822. For properties worth 100 *solidi* in Gaul, see the will of Bertram of Le Mans as analyzed by Jones, *LRE* II, 783.

social pyramid of the countryside was even more steeply pitched at the apex than it had been two centuries earlier, with a small group of extremely wealthy landowners dominating local society much as in pre-Roman times.[26] Below them were smaller landowners like the "poor man" in Caesarius's sermon, moderately well off in comparison with landless peasants, but vulnerable to harassment, domination, and expropriation by their wealthy neighbors. Still lower on the pyramid were those peasants who either did not own any land or did not own enough to feed their families. They earned their living as tenants (*coloni*) of other men's lands, and at peak times as casual laborers.[27] *Coloni* fell into three broad categories: those who had been hereditarily tied to the land by the fiscal laws of the fourth century, and were subsequently deprived of most of their personal rights; those who had been tied to the land by other mechanisms, and except for freedom of movement retained their rights as persons; and those who, like the *coloni* of the early empire, were personally free and held their tenancies at will.[28] Finally, at the bottom of the pyramid were slaves,[29] who were used in agricultural labor as well as domestic service.[30] They differed legally from tied *coloni* in having no personal rights whatever, but in practical terms it was (and is) often difficult to distinguish between the two groups.[31]

As a result of these changes, most of the land in the sixth-century *civitas* of Arles was owned by those who did not work it: individual lay and clerical landlords, Gothic (and later, Frankish) kings, who had acquired imperial property, and the Christian church, including local parishes,[32] monasteries,[33] the cathedral church,[34] and by the end of the sixth century at the latest, the church of Rome.[35] Throughout the *civitas*, however, the principal

---

[26] Wightman, "Peasants and Potentates," 114–16.

[27] Precisely ranked after relatives (*parentes*) and higher-status clients (*amici*), but before slaves (*mancipia*), the *clientes* of *vita* I. 61 were in fact tenants, L. Bieler, "Zur Mosella des Ausonius: 'cliens' in der Bedeutung 'colonus,'" *Rheinisches Museum* 86 (1937), 285–87.   [28] Jones *LRE* II, 801–3.   [29] *vita* I. 61.

[30] For instance, in his will Remigius mentions slaves working as vine-dressers, including Albovichus and Enias, *test.*, *MGH SRM*, III, 337, lines 15, 22. On the controversial question of agricultural slavery in late antiquity, see R. MacMullen, "Late Roman Slavery," *Historia* 36 (1987), 359–82, and R. Samson, "Rural Slavery, Inscriptions, Archaeology and Marx: A Response to Ramsey MacMullen's 'Late Roman Slavery,'" *Historia* 38 (1989), 99–110.

[31] See *serm.* 44. 2 for the equation of an *ancilla* and a *colona*. Remigius disposes of *servi* and *coloni* in virtually identical terms, e.g. *test.*, 336, line 25–337, line 1.

[32] Carpentras (527), can. 1.   [33] *vita* I. 48; II. 11; *test.*, 287–88.

[34] *test.*, 287–88.   [35] Gregory the Great, *ep.* VI. 6, 51.

unit of labor remained the individual peasant household, whether it was composed of slaves, *coloni*, or smallholders. On a property owned by the nunnery in Arles, for instance, the hunting of wild boars by Gothic officers and soldiers so troubled "the people of that household" that they came and complained to Caesarius (*vita* I. 48). At the same time, in northern Gaul, Remigius mentioned numerous peasant families in his will,[36] and Palladius a century earlier assumed the participation of families of men, women, and children in agricultural work.[37]

In Caesarius's day, as earlier, the peasants of Arles raised livestock in the Crau;[38] fished, bred horses, and processed salt in the Camargue;[39] and in the more fertile areas of the *civitas* produced the Mediterranean triad of grain, wine, and olive oil.[40] It is hardly necessary to point out that their lot was a difficult one. Caught between the demands of the government and the landlord on the one hand and the needs of their families on the other, and faced with the apparently random hostility of nature, peasants had to eke out a living from what were usually very meager resources. Starvation was the penalty for failure; subsistence the reward for success.[41] But peasants had through long experience fashioned a culture for themselves that ordered their lives and mitigated the hardships they had to endure.[42] It was not a completely separate culture from that of the city: the peasant society of sixth-century Arles was a "part-society" with a "part-culture,"[43] sharing the language, government, economy, and increasingly the religion of the city. Where peasant culture diverged from urban culture was

---

[36] For instance, the swineherd Mellovicus and his wife Pascasiola (337, lines 23–24), and the slave Merumvas, his wife Meratena, and their sons Marcovicus and Medovicus (338, lines 3–4).

[37] E. Frézouls, "La vie rurale au Bas-Empire d'après l'œuvre de Palladius," *Ktema* 5 (1980), 193–210: 200.   [38] Gregory of Tours, *hist.* IV. 44.

[39] It may have been on its plains that Symmachus's Spanish horses spent the winter of 399/400, and his buyers searched for Gallic horses "outstanding in swiftness and breeding," Symmachus, *ep.* IX. 20.

[40] Sidonius, *ep.* V. 20. 4; Caesarius, *serm.* 7. 4; 27. 3.

[41] Jones, *LRE* II, 808–12; C. E. Stevens, "Agriculture and Rural Life in the Later Roman Empire," in *The Cambridge Economic History of Europe*, 2nd edn., I, ed. M. M. Postan (Cambridge, 1966), 92–124: 122–24; P. Garnsey, *Famine and Food Supply in the Graeco-Roman World: Responses to Risk and Crisis* (Cambridge, 1988), 43–68.

[42] K. Dobrowolski, "Peasant Traditional Culture," in *Peasants and Peasant Societies*, ed. T. Shanin (Harmondsworth, 1971), 277–98; R. Redfield, *Peasant Society and Culture* (Chicago, 1956); and for the Mediterranean world specifically, *Mediterranean Countrymen*, ed. J. Pitt-Rivers (Paris, 1963).

[43] A. L. Kroeber, *Anthropology* (New York, 1948), 284.

above all in its traditional way of life, which survived because of its proven value for success. This was passed down orally and visually from generation to generation. As Caesarius keenly observed in a sermon delivered at a rural parish, " Who has shown you how to prune your vines and when to plant new shoots? For unless you have seen or heard or asked expert farmers, who can show you how to cultivate your property?" (serm. 6. 4). The peasant's way of life consisted of the whole body of knowledge, relationships, attitudes, strategies, and rituals that was passed down in this way.[44] It included not only traditional farming practices,[45] but also relationships within the family,[46] rituals of celebration,[47] techniques of healing,[48] and the knowledge embodied in proverbs, folklore, songs, and humor.[49] Among the most important aspects of peasant culture were the traditional rituals and beliefs by which peasants sought to explain, predict, and control the forces of nature. For although everyone in this pre-industrial society depended on the processes of nature, peasants were clearly more dependent than anyone else, since they were not as well insulated from the failures of nature as townsfolk.[50] Their great dependence on nature, in turn, reinforced belief in a traditional cosmology, which both accounted for their insecurity and provided ritual protection from it. And so a close relationship was established between the agricultural rhythms of life as experienced by the peasant and an intricate pattern of festivals, rites, myths, and customs, whose purpose was to reduce the manifold insecurities of rural existence, and to guarantee every year, as far as possible, another year's survival.[51] It was this religious and cultural system that Caesarius endeavored to disrupt by his programs of christianization and depaganization.

PEASANT RELIGION

It is only because Caesarius chose to attack the traditional religious practices and beliefs of the peasants of Arles in his sermons that we have any evidence at all about religion outside the urban center.

[44] Dobrowolski, "Peasant Traditional Culture." For the survival of much of this tradition as folklore, see A. Varagnac, *Civilisation traditionelle et genres de vie* (Paris, 1948), 9–38.
[45] Surveyed in Stevens, "Agriculture and Rural Life," 92–108.
[46] For a traditional division of labor within the peasant household, see Gregory of Tours, *glor. conf.* 30.   [47] *serm.* 47. 7.   [48] *serm.* 50–52.   [49] *serm.* 6. 1, 3.
[50] Jones, *LRE* II, 810–11; Dölger, "Christliche Grundbesitzer," 298.
[51] M. P. Nilsson, *Greek Folk Religion* (Philadelphia, 1940), 3–41.

But this evidence is more difficult to interpret than the evidence we examined in the previous chapter. This is partly because, as an aristocrat, a cleric, and an urban resident, Caesarius knew far less about peasants than about his fellow townsmen. What information he did acquire about peasants and pagan practices often came to him indirectly from the reports of landowners and rural clergy, and must frequently have been incomplete and inaccurate.[52] Moreover, Caesarius shared traditional feelings of contempt for the intelligence of peasants, further biasing his reports of their behavior.[53] But the most serious barrier to our interpretation of Caesarius's sermons against paganism is their indiscriminate polemic. It was (and is) difficult enough for an outsider to deduce religious intentions from observed or reported behavior. But Caesarius further obliterated distinctions in religious intention, and hence religious loyalty, by the wide range of behavior and belief that he condemned as pagan: from the sacrifices and dedications of traditional Gallo-Roman religion to such activities as bathing in rivers on the feast of John the Baptist (*serm.* 33. 4) and exchanging presents on New Year's Day (*serm.* 192. 3; 193. 3), activities which had either been adapted to Christian purposes,[54] or drained of their religious content.[55] Modern readers of Caesarius's sermons have often accepted his condemnations of paganism at face value, detecting "superstitions" and "pagan survivals" at every level of peasant religious practice.[56] Yet an analysis of Caesarius's sermons reveals a complicated diversity of religious intentions behind the behavior that he so monotonously and formulaically condemned. Although we can never be certain of the "true" religious intentions of those he criticized for pagan activities – any more than he could be certain of them – we can use this analysis to propose a portrait of peasant religiosity in sixth-century Arles.[57]

To begin with, we can divide the peasants of Arles into three

---

[52] "audivimus," *serm.* 13. 5; 53. 1; "multorum relatione," *serm.* 54. 1; 184. 5; "hoc pervenit ad me," *serm.* 54. 6.

[53] "Quis enim hominum quamvis rusticus non intellegat et agnoscat...," *serm.* 136. 2. See further, Le Goff, *Time, Work and Culture*, 87–97.

[54] P. Audin, "Césaire d'Arles et le maintien de pratiques païennes dans la Provence du VIe siècle," in *La Patrie Gauloise d'Agrippa au VIème siècle* (Lyon, 1983), 327–38: 332–33.

[55] R. Manselli, "Resistenze dei culti antichi nella pratica religiosa dei laici nelle campagne," in *Cristianizzazione ed organizzazione ecclesiastica*, I, 57–108: 64, n. 13.

[56] E.g., R. Boese, *Superstitiones Arelatenses e Caesario collectae* (Marburg, 1909); G. Konda, *Le Discernement et la malice des pratiques superstitieuses d'après les sermons de s. Césaire d'Arles* (Rome, 1970).   [57] See now R. Markus, *Ancient Christianity*, esp. 1–17.

broad categories of religious affiliation: those who identified themselves as practitioners of traditional religion, those who identified themselves as Christians in the bishop's sense of the term, and those who identified themselves as Christians in their own sense of the term, who continued to engage in a wide variety of pagan and Christian practices.[58] But determining the religious affiliation of those whom Caesarius condemned for paganism is not a simple task. Unfortunately, the most obvious index of Christian affiliation and one that Caesarius mentions frequently, the reception of baptism, is also the least useful. Although infant baptism was becoming increasingly common by the sixth century,[59] many self-professed Christians continued the earlier practice of deferring baptism until old age, remaining catechumens for most of their lives.[60] At the same time, many of those who had been baptized, whether as children or adults, continued to regard themselves as practitioners of traditional religion. As Caesarius informed one rural audience: "All those who have been baptized should avoid profane observances ... No one should refuse to work on Thursdays in honor of Jupiter. No man or woman, brothers, should observe this custom at any time, lest the Lord judge those who sacrilegiously transfer to Jupiter's day what they ought to observe on the Lord's day to be pagans rather than Christians" (*serm.* 19. 4). This sermon indicates that there was no necessary link between baptism and religious practice.[61] A better indication of Christian affiliation was attendance at Mass, for this obligation could not be as easily imposed on an unwilling population as baptism, and was required of all Christians, whether baptized or not (at least up to the "prayer of the people" after the sermon when catechumens and penitents were dismissed[62]). As Ambrose's teacher Simplicianus replied to Marius Victorinus, who claimed to have converted to Christianity, "I shall not consider you a Christian until I see you in a church of Christ."[63] Although social pressures in these face-to-face communities were potentially strong enough to force reluctant villagers to attend Mass,[64] we can suppose that most of those whose pagan practices Caesarius

---

[58] P. Audin employs essentially the same categories in "Césaire d'Arles," 337.
[59] Beck, 161; Caesarius, *de gratia*, Morin II, 162; *serm.* 84. 6; 225. 6.
[60] Beck, 163; Caesarius, *serm.* 70. 2; 129. 5; 200. 4–5.
[61] Manselli, "Resistenze dei culti antichi," 59–61.   [62] Beck, 143.
[63] Augustine, *conf.* VIII. ii. 4.
[64] G. Le Bras, *L'Eglise et le village* (Paris, 1976), 186.

condemned at Mass at least professed to being Christians, for example the audience of *Sermon* 53:

It is gratifying to us, dearest brothers, and we give great thanks to God, that we see you faithfully coming to church... We are sad nevertheless, and lament the fact that we know that some of you are frequently going to the ancient worship of idols, like godless pagans bereft of the grace of baptism. We have heard that some of you are making vows at trees, praying at springs, and practicing diabolical divination. (*serm.* 53. 1)

Furthermore, when Caesarius attacked the pagan practices of those whose attendance at Mass cannot be deduced from the context, he sometimes provided other evidence for their Christian affiliation: some made the sign of the cross before eating sacrificial meat (*serm.* 54. 6); others acquired amulets from members of the clergy (*serm.* 50. 1).

Such indications make it clear that there were two categories of those who practiced what Caesarius called paganism: those who identified themselves as Christians and those who did not. Because Caesarius's sermons were above all addressed to those present to hear them, it is not surprising that most of his attacks on paganism were aimed at Christians. But because he also expected his audience to carry his message to their relatives, friends, neighbors, *coloni*, and slaves (*vita* 1. 61; *serm.* 33. 4; 74. 4; 78. 5), some of whom may not have been Christians, we hear from time to time of pagan behavior that shows no signs of sympathy for Christianity. In *Sermon* 53, for instance, after condemning members of his congregation, as we have seen, for offering vows and prayers at trees and springs, and observing rituals of divination, Caesarius turned to condemn others for what he said was far worse:

There are unhappy and wretched people... who not only are unwilling to destroy the shrines of the pagans, but are also not afraid or ashamed to rebuild those which have been destroyed. And if anyone thinking of God wants to burn down the trees next to shrines or to scatter and destroy these diabolic altars, they become angry, insane, and inflamed with excessive fury. As a result they dare to beat those who are trying to overturn these idols because of their love for God, or perhaps they do not hesitate to think about murdering them. (*serm.* 53. 1)

This was clearly not the same kind of behavior as offering prayers at springs, and it is most unlikely that those who engaged in it considered themselves Christians. Caesarius did not address them as though they were present in the congregation. In fact, he dedicated the rest of his sermon to convincing those with influence or power over them to correct them by persuasion or coercion, to prevent them from rebuilding rural shrines, and to continue to destroy those altars and sacred trees that still existed (*serm.* 53. 2). Several details in the sermon – for example the degree of coercion it envisions – make it clear that Caesarius was speaking mainly to the landowners in his audience about their tenants and slaves, who, though baptized, were still ardent pagans. Another deliberate rejection of Christianity appears in the behavior of at least some of those men and women who honored Jupiter by refusing to work on Thursdays. In addition to this gesture of pagan reverence, Caesarius accused them of doing the same work on Sundays that they refused to do on Thursdays (*serm.* 13. 5). If Caesarius's accusation was correct, the religious preferences of these individuals would seem to be clear. Every village, villa, and town must have had at least some such persons in their midst, who rejected Christianity and remained loyal to their traditional religion.[65]

Yet, the evidence of Caesarius's sermons suggests that most of those Caesarius accused of pagan practices found themselves in a more complicated relationship to Christianity and traditional religion, with strong loyalties to both systems.[66] Many peasants, for instance, did not find it difficult to practice traditional rituals alongside Christian rites. Making a living off the same land as their ancestors and working by the same agricultural calendar, they continued to practice the same rituals that had long assured success: prayers, libations, animal sacrifices, and dedications of food, clothing, and tools.[67] They performed these rituals at places in the landscape revered long before Celts, Greeks, or Romans arrived in Provence: groves of trees, springs, shrines, and rural altars of stone or earth.[68] Trees were considered especially sacred, as Martin of Tours discovered when a crowd of peasants stood by while he tore down a pagan temple, but attacked him when he tried to cut down the sacred pine tree next to it.[69] In Arles, when sacred trees fell or were cut down, peasants refused to take the

---

[65] See *serm.* 52. 2: "not only in other places, but even in this city (*in hac ipsa civitate*), there are still said to be some unfortunate women who neither spin nor weave on Thursdays in honor of Jupiter." [66] James, *The Origins of France*, 93–96.

[67] Gregory of Tours, *glor. conf.* 2; Caesarius, *serm.* 1. 12; 14. 4; 19. 4; 53. 1; 54. 5, 6.

[68] *serm.* 1. 12; 13. 3; 14. 4; 53. 1, 2; 54. 5; *vita* 1. 55.

[69] Sulpicius Severus, *vita Martini* 13.

wood home for their fireplaces, a gesture of reverence that amazed Caesarius (*serm.* 54. 5). Ceremonies at these sites were often accompanied by feasts at which the food and drink offered in sacrifices was consumed in common (*serm.* 19. 4; 54. 6).

It is difficult to argue that such activities were compatible with Christian orthodoxy. A long Jewish and Christian tradition classified such practices as idolatrous, and Caesarius was not alone in condemning them on these grounds. From the fifth century until well into the eighth, Christian authorities repeatedly condemned peasants in Gaul for performing similar rituals.[70] Reaction to these condemnations cannot be gauged, but we need not suppose that Christian peasants were unaware of an inconsistency in their performance of pagan rituals. For instance, in order to excuse their participation in sacrificial feasts, some in Caesarius's congregation told him, "I make the sign of the cross and then I eat" (*serm.* 54. 6). The ambivalence of this gesture was significant. It affirmed the Christian identity of the one who made it, and acknowledged an inconsistency between that identity, and the act of eating sacrificial meat, perhaps even a dangerous inconsistency that required protection. But at the same time, it did not rule out the inconsistent behavior. Caesarius attributed the consumption of sacrificial food to "simplicity, ignorance, or most plausibly, gluttony" (*serm.* 54. 6), but those who ate this food and crossed themselves before doing so appear to have acted out of a belief in two separate religious systems, each of which they employed for different purposes. By this interpretation, traditional rituals performed at holy places and times did not constitute a substitute for Christian rituals or a challenge to them, but rather a parallel system of belief and practice. This system was principally useful in situations where Christianity offered no credible alternative or where the stakes were so high that traditional rituals could not risk being abandoned. Not having evolved as a local, community religion designed with the needs of peasants in mind, Christianity was slow to develop rituals for agricultural success that could rival the proven capacities of traditional rituals. At the same time, traditional methods of explanation, prediction, and

---

[70] E. Vacandard, "L'idolatrie en Gaule au VIe et au VIIe siècle," *Revue des questions historiques* 65 (1899), 424–54; R. Markus, "From Caesarius to Boniface: Christianity and Paganism in Gaul," in *Le Septième Siècle: changements et continuités. The Seventh Century: Change and Continuity*, ed. J. Fontaine and J. N. Hillgarth (London, 1992), 154–72.

control appeared best suited to the most traditional aspects of peasant life. By thinking and more importantly acting in this way, Christians could continue to practice rituals which even they, if they gave the matter any thought, might acknowledge to be inconsistent with their Christian identity. Such dual religious loyalties would not seem to be unusual. To this day in northern New Mexico, for instance, as a result of a long and complicated process of acculturation, the Pueblo peoples of the upper Rio Grande Valley continue to practice traditional "pagan" dances, ceremonies, and rituals side by side with an enthusiastic Roman Catholicism – so enthusiastic, in fact, that converts to Protestantism have been expelled from several pueblos.[71]

As we have seen, Christian authorities in Gaul condemned all parallel systems of "idolatry." But many forms of ritual behavior presented more complicated dilemmas of interpretation.[72] What, for instance, were bishops to make of the custom of blowing horns and ringing bells at lunar eclipses and new moons (*serm.* 13. 5; 52. 3)? Like Maximus of Turin before him,[73] Caesarius condemned this practice as a "vain pagan superstition" (*serm.* 52. 3), perhaps reflecting its origins in traditional religion,[74] but how much religious content did the practice retain for its participants? Did the ritual signify a belief that demonic forces had stolen away the moon,[75] or did it merely constitute a collective response to an alarming astronomical phenomenon? A similar problem was posed by the practice of waiting for auspicious days of the week to begin a journey or return home (*serm.* 54. 1). Calling this a "sacrilegious custom of pagans" (*serm.* 1. 12), Caesarius claimed that the laymen and clerics who engaged in it were in effect honoring the divinities for whom the days of the week were named: the sun, moon, Mars, Mercury, Jupiter, Venus, and Saturn (*serm.* 52. 2; 54. 1; 193. 4). But since he leveled the very same charge against those who even *called* the days of the week by these names, we need to question either the accuracy of Caesarius's charge of paganism or his definition of the term, for the use of

---

[71] E. P. Dozier, "Rio Grande Pueblos," in *Perspectives in American Indian Culture Change*, ed. E. H. Spicer (Chicago, 1961), 94–186, esp. 175–78; S. D. Gill, *Native American Religions* (Belmont, Calif., 1982), 142–50.

[72] Markus, "From Caesarius to Boniface."   [73] *serm.* 30.

[74] According to Polybius v. 78. 1, the Galatians (also Celts) interpreted lunar eclipses as ill-omened.

[75] D. Harmening, *Superstitio. Überlieferungs- und theoriegeschichtliche Untersuchungen zur kirchlich-theologischen Aberglaubensliteratur des Mittelalters* (Berlin, 1979), 250.

pagan names to designate the days of the week would appear to have long been devoid of religious significance. Despite objections to this nomenclature by generations of Christian preachers,[76] and frequent proposals to rename the days according to the order of their creation in the Book of Genesis,[77] Portuguese was the only Romance language to adopt the Christian nomenclature.[78]

Evidently some of the practices Caesarius labeled as pagan were religiously neutral in content and intention. This appears to be the case for the songs that peasants learned by heart (*serm.* 6. 3; 130. 5) and sang at communal celebrations. Although Caesarius characterized them as "diabolic," he seems to have objected principally on moral grounds, calling them "shameful" (*turpia*),[79] "bawdy" (*amatoria*),[80] "lewd" (*luxuriosa*),[81] and "inimical to chastity and honor."[82] It is unlikely that those who sang such songs did so from motives Caesarius would have recognized as religious.

A connection between paganism and immorality appears particularly strong in Caesarius's criticism of the Kalends of January, whose popularity had made it a traditional target for episcopal disapproval. This three-day festival celebrated the end of the old civic year and the beginning of the new.[83] By the fourth century AD numerous rituals – both public and private – had crystallized around it, all in some way taking advantage of the potency associated with the annual renewal of time. The festival was enthusiastically celebrated in both the city and countryside of Arles (*serm.* 192. 3). Among its components was a wide variety of acts symbolically performed at the beginning of the year so as to be valid for the remainder of it. "On the night before New Year's," according to Caesarius, "some of the *rustici* also arrange their own tables so that they are full of many necessary foods. They want the table to be arranged in this way all night because they believe that the Kalends of January can make it possible for

---

[76] Augustine, *enarrationes in Psalmos* 93. 3, *PL* 37: 1192–93; Martin of Braga, *de correctione rusticorum* 8–9; W. von Wartburg, "Les noms des jours de la semaine dans les langues romanes," in his *Von Sprache und Mensch* (Bern, 1956), 45–60.

[77] Endorsed by Caesarius in *serm.* 54. 1; 193. 4.

[78] Perhaps under the influence of Martin of Braga in the late sixth century, S. McKenna, *Paganism and Pagan Survivals in Spain up to the Fall of the Visigothic Kingdom* (Washington, D.C., 1938), 93–94; M. Meslin, "Persistances païennes en Galice, vers la fin du VIe siècle," in *Hommages à Marcel Renard*, II (Brussels, 1969), 512–24: 516–17.

[79] *serm.* 6. 3; 33. 4.   [80] *serm.* 6. 3; 16. 3.   [81] *serm.* 13. 4; 33. 4.

[82] *serm.* 33. 4.

[83] M. Meslin, *La Fête des kalendes de Janvier dans l'empire romain* (Brussels, 1970), provides a full discussion of the festival from its origins through late antiquity.

their meals to remain in such abundance throughout the entire year" (*serm*. 192. 3). There were also those who refused to share their hearth with neighbors on the eve of the Kalends, on the grounds that this would damage the integrity of the family fire at a critical juncture in time (*serm*. 192. 3; 193. 3).[84] The implausibility of Caesarius's charge that this denial represented a selfish withholding of favors from the needy is demonstrated by the subsequent exchange of presents, which were intended to renew friendship and harmony for another year (*serm*. 192. 3; 193. 3). Feasts were also held in Arles, as we can gather from Caesarius's accusations of "carnal and luxurious celebration," heavy drinking, and "sacrilegious" dancing (*serm*. 192, 193).

Although the bishop could argue that the Kalends of January was intrinsically pagan because of its connection with the Roman god Janus (*serm*. 192. 1), it is difficult to see any pagan intentions in these activities. This would even seem to hold true for the notorious masquerades of the Kalends, in which men put on the skins and heads of stags and heifers and "soldiers" dressed as prostitutes.[85] The wearing of deer masks and skins in particular was liable to be condemned as pagan because of its connections to Cernunnos, the Celtic stag god.[86] Yet participants denied that there was anything pagan in the ritual. "This is not the pursuit of sacrilege," objects a character in one of Peter Chrysologus's sermons on the Kalends, "but a wish for sportive enjoyment. It is the joy over a new era, not the folly of the old; it is the beginning of the year, not a pagan outrage."[87] Caesarius's congregation would seem to have agreed. They believed these observances to be minor sins or no sins at all (*serm*. 192. 3), and Caesarius found it necessary to warn them that those who engaged in such behavior were "raging with madness rather than engaging in joyful celebration" (*serm*. 193. 2). Indeed, Caesarius mainly objected to the festival on grounds other than paganism. He denounced the

---

[84] Ibid., 72. Compare the Greek practice of restricting the worship of Zeus Ktesios, protector of house and property, to close family members only, Isaeus 8:15–17, a reference I owe to Michael Jameson.

[85] *serm*. 13. 5; 192. 2; 193. 1. For a full discussion of these ceremonies, see R. Arbesmann, "The 'cervuli' and 'anniculae' in Caesarius of Arles," *Traditio* 35 (1979), 89–119, and Meslin, *La Fête*, 79–93.

[86] M. P. Nilsson, "Studien zur Vorgeschichte des Weihnachtfestes," *Archiv für Religionswissenschaft* 19 (1916–19), 50–150: 71–76; Arnold, 172; Meslin, *La Fête*, 87–89; Arbesmann, "The 'cervuli' and 'anniculae'," 117.

[87] Peter Chrysologus, *serm*. 155. 5, trans. adapted from Arbesmann, "The 'cervuli' and 'anniculae'," 112–13.

excessive drinking, profane songs, and obscene dancing of the festival as immoral, and condemned its beast mimicry and transvestism for blurring divinely ordained boundaries between human and animal, and male and female bodies.[88] Those acts he did not find immoral he faulted for evading church control. He criticized as "diabolic," for instance, the exchange of New Year's gifts, or *strenae* (*serm.* 192. 3; 193. 3). If we can deduce his motivations from the sermons of his predecessors, his objection was not to gift-giving as such, but to a form of gift-giving that evaded the church's rules. For it was customary at the Kalends that rich and poor alike give presents, not to those in need but to fellow citizens, especially to those whose friendship and support mattered most. The motive was thus not love or generosity, but the maintenance of ties of friendship and clientship. Maximus of Turin explains the result:

The poor man is forced to give what he does not own and to offer a gift in return for which he leaves his own children in debt. But the rich and those who are generous in this gift-giving are not themselves to be considered immune from sin. For a rich man who bestows a *solidus* on some other rich man refuses to give a *denarius* to a beggar; and the man who hurries on the Kalends to the house of a friend loaded down with gold arrives empty-handed at church on Christmas. You see, therefore, that among most men there is a greater concern for present adulation than future remuneration.[89]

Not only did this custom confirm the existing social structure;[90] it also permitted donors to bypass the church's mechanism for alleviating poverty, that is, the giving of alms. As Augustine advised, "Do not mix yourselves with pagans by similarity of customs or deeds: they give New Year's gifts; you should give alms."[91] The Kalends of January clearly threatened the church by more than its paganism. In fact, it had become an essentially "secular" festival that offended church officials more because of its "worldly" emphasis on prosperity and celebration than because of any religious deviance it might have exhibited.

Like traditional rituals of celebration, traditional techniques of prediction and control, such as divination and healing, continued to be practiced in the diocese of Arles. They too drew Caesarius's

---

[88] Brown, *The Body and Society*, 432. [89] *serm.* 98. 2.
[90] Meslin, *La Fête*, 101–4. [91] Augustine, *serm.* 198. 2.

condemnation for paganism. But even if they can be attributed in part to a "neutral technology" of Mediterranean living,[92] they cannot be deprived of all religious content, for they continued to rely on a traditional and essentially religious understanding of the cosmos for their perceived efficacy.[93] Because the bishop's version of Christianity did not authorize any forms of divination and only a limited and impractical range of healing techniques, there was little chance of eradicating these traditional practices. But at the same time, the lack of suitable alternatives within the Christianity preached by Caesarius made it possible for traditional techniques of divination and healing to be incorporated into local versions of Christian practice.

Many men and women in the diocese of Arles consulted soothsayers with a variety of titles: *harioli*,[94] *haruspices*,[95] *praecantatores*,[96] *cara(g)ii*,[97] *divini*,[98] and *sortilegi*.[99] It is unfortunately impossible to connect these titles with particular techniques of predicting the future. Not only did Caesarius not spell out the practices of each specialist, but he frequently used the same titles for healers as he did for soothsayers. Apart from the interpretation of bird songs (*serm.* 54. 1), sneezes (*serm.* 54. 1), the length of belts or bandages (*serm.* 52. 5; 184. 4), and the other "auguries" that Caesarius mentions (*serm.* 1. 12; 12. 4; 52. 1; 53. 1; 54. 1, 3, 5), diviners in Arles probably relied on a wide range of traditional methods, including the casting of lots, the observation of birds in

---

[92] P. Brown, "Art and Society," in *Age of Spirituality: A Symposium*, ed. F. Weitzmann (New York, 1980), 17–37: 23.

[93] I would thus disagree with the description of these religious activities as "magical" in V. I. J. Flint's very interesting *The Rise of Magic in Early Medieval Europe* (Princeton, 1991). There are serious methodological problems with any use of "magic" as a fundamental category for the study of christianization. By implying that even in late antiquity rituals of healing, divination, control over nature and the like were merely neutral techniques of manipulation, which lacked religious "reverence" (8) and were thus easily detached from traditional religion, this approach bypasses the most important problem posed by christianization: how and with what effects Christianity replaced paganism as the primary *religious* loyalty of the population. Moreover, treating the whole range of pagan religious practice as magical from the start is itself covertly christianizing: it demeans traditional religion by denying it status as a "true" religion and it anticipates the Christian incorporation of "pagan"/"magical" practices by assuming that those practices were already devoid of religious content.

[94] *serm.* 52. 5.   [95] *serm.* 13. 3; 50. 1; 52. 1; 54. 5.

[96] *serm.* 1. 12; 12. 4; 13. 5; 14. 4; 19. 4, 5; 50. 1; 52. 1; 54. 1; 184. 4; R. Etaix, "Nouveau sermon pascal de Saint Césaire d'Arles," *RBen* 75 (1965), 201–11: 209, line 166.

[97] *serm.* 1. 12; 12. 4; 13. 3, 5; 19. 4, 5; 54. 1, 3, 5; Etaix, "Nouveau sermon pascal," 209, line 167.   [98] *serm.* 1. 12; 13. 3, 5; 19. 4, 5; 50. 1; 54. 1, 3, 5; 184. 4.

[99] *serm.* 12. 4; 13. 3; 50. 1; 52. 5; 54. 1.

flight, and the like. People sought them out for such purposes as determining the length of their lives (*serm.* 18. 4)[100] or locating thieves and stolen property (*serm.* 184. 4).[101] No one doubted their effectiveness, not even Caesarius: "But perhaps someone says, 'What do we do about the fact that these auguries and soothsayers and diviners frequently announce true things to us?' Scripture appeals to us and warns us about this very subject when it says ... 'The Lord Your God tests you to discover whether you fear him or not' (Dt. 13: 1–3)."[102]

Yet because he believed that in a Christian universe knowledge of the future was the prerogative of God alone, Caesarius condemned the practice of divination (*serm.* 54. 1), as countless apologists and preachers had done before him.[103] At the same time, however, the growing popularity of expressly Christian forms of divination such as the *sortes biblicae* and the *sortes sanctorum* indicates the strength of the practice. In the *sortes biblicae*, long practiced in the church, books of the Bible were opened at random for advice and prediction of the future.[104] The *sortes sanctorum* involved the random selection of oracular responses from a collection designed for the purpose,[105] much like the *sortes Sangallenses*, extant in a palimpsest copy of the late sixth or early seventh century. In this text, a series of questions was followed by twelve responses each; the correct response was discovered by throwing dice.[106] Although both forms of divination were practiced and tolerated by clerics in Caesarius's day, including bishops, they were also condemned by church leaders. The Councils of Vannes (461/91) and Agde (506) condemned both practices;[107] the Frankish Council of Orléans (511) condemned only the *sortes sanctorum* – tellingly, for the *sortes biblicae* appear to have been highly favored by the Frankish nobility.[108] Despite

---

[100] See also Gregory of Tours, *hist.* v. 14. [101] Idem, *hist.* VII. 44.
[102] *serm.* 54. 3. [103] Augustine, *doctr. christ.* II. xx. 30–xxiv. 37.
[104] Sulpicius Severus, *vita Martini* 9; Augustine, *conf.* VIII. xii. 29; *ep.* 55. 37.
[105] R. Ganszyniec, "Les Sortes Sanctorum," *Congrès d'histoire du Christianisme. Jubilé Alfred Loisy*, III, *Annales d'histoire du Christianisme* 3 (1928), 41–51.
[106] A. Dold (ed.), "Die Orakelsprüche im St. Galler Palimpsestcodex 908 (die sogenannten 'Sortes Sangallenses')," *Österreichische Akademie der Wissenschaften*, Philosophisch-historische Klasse, Sitzungsberichte 225, Band 4, Abhandlung (1948), with commentary in R. Meister (ed.), "Die Orakelsprüche im St. Galler Palimpsestcodex 908 (die sogenannten 'Sortes Sangallenses'): Erläuterungen," *Österreichische Akademie der Wissenschaften*, Philosophisch-historische Klasse, Sitzungsberichte 225, Band 5, Abhandlung (1951). [107] Vannes (461/91), can. 16; Agde (506), can. 42.
[108] Gregory of Tours, *hist.* IV. 16; v. 14.

these condemnations, the practices continued — clear indications of the ways in which Christianity might be adapted to meet the expectations of local populations.

Closely related to techniques for predicting the future were procedures for controlling it. Often the same specialists offered both services to their clientele.[109] Caesarius spoke chiefly against remedies for sickness, which included herbs and potions,[110] incantations,[111] and amulets composed of organic material (herbs, amber),[112] or written spells (*caracteres*)[113] that were suspended from the body[114] or bound to it.[115] Like techniques of prediction, these procedures were widely acknowledged to be effective.

But again you say, "Meanwhile, sometimes, in the absence of enchanters (*praecantatores*), many people slip dangerously close to death, from a snake bite or some other ailment." It is true, my dear brothers, that God permits this to the devil, just as I said above, in order to test the Christian people. The result is that, when people are sometimes able to receive remedies for their illnesses through these sacrileges, and recognize some truth in them, they more easily believe in the devil afterwards. (*serm.* 54. 3).[116]

In fact, practices of divination and healing posed many of the same problems for a Christian bishop. Both depended for their effectiveness on a traditional understanding of the cosmos. The attribution of predictive powers to the songs of birds, or healing powers to amulets, charms, and incantations presupposed a cosmos in which beings, objects, and times were closely connected by diffuse unseen forces and accessible to manipulation by those with special knowledge. Even the medicinal use of traditional herbs and potions, whose "objective" effectiveness has been recognized by modern science, often depended for their "subjective" effectiveness on belief in the divinity of mother earth who provided them,[117] and on the performance of proper rituals of collection and application.[118] A regulation from late sixth-century Galicia acknowledged as much: "In the collection of medicinal herbs, let

---

[109] Isidore, *etymologiae* VIII. 9. 30, ed. W. M. Lindsay (Oxford, 1911).

[110] *serm.* 51. 4.

[111] R. Etaix, "Les épreuves du juste. Nouveau sermon de Saint Césaire d'Arles," *REAug* 24 (1978), 272–77: 275, lines 85–87. [112] *serm.* 13. 5; 14. 4.

[113] *serm.* I. 12; 13. 5; 14. 4; 50. 1; 51. 4; 52. 5; 184. 4. [114] *serm.* 52. 5; 184. 4.

[115] *serm.* I. 12; 19. 4; 50. 1; 51. 4; Harmening, *Superstitio*, 235–47.

[116] See also *serm.* 50. 1. [117] Pliny, *hist. nat.* XXIV. 1.

[118] A survey can be found in A. Delatte, *Herbarius: Recherches sur le cérémonial usité chez les anciens pour la cueillette des simples et des plantes magiques*, 3rd edn. (Brussels, 1961).

it not be permitted to perform any rituals or incantations except the Creed and the Lord's Prayer, so that only God may be honored as creator and lord of all things."[119] Moreover, both diviners and "folk" healers could be esteemed as alternative figures of authority in the community. The fact that many of them were women made them doubly threatening to the organized church.[120] As Caesarius warned his congregation: "The Christian is someone who, in this persecution [by the devil], does not desert God, nor send for the soothsayer, nor make bindings, nor bring in any enchantresses. When a woman recites an incantation, a serpent recites it."[121]

To counteract these healing practices and reinforce the authority of the church hierarchy, Caesarius offered an ecclesiastical form of therapy. In accordance with biblical teaching,[122] he urged the sick to "run to church, receive the body and blood of Christ, be anointed with holy oil by the priests, and ask the priests and deacons to pray over them in Christ's name" (*serm.* 19. 5).[123] This was the procedure that Caesarius's own reported cures followed. But these attempts at centralization ran directly contrary to the tradition of "medical pluralism" characteristic of ancient society, a tradition in which the sick could opt for various strategies of healing on the basis of their income, social status, residence, and the nature and gravity of their affliction.[124] For peasants, folk healers of all kinds were usually the first specialists consulted. Churches were often far away, and, in the case of many illnesses, the remedies offered by the church may have been perceived as less effective than what was locally available. When assistance was sought from a bishop or saint, it was often as a last resort, after *harioli*, *sortilegi*, and other traditional practitioners had failed.[125] The "upright art of physicians," which Caesarius also recommended (*serm.* 52. 5), was expensive, scarce – being available only in larger towns and substantial villas[126] – and subject to the same culturally perceived limits of success as any other strategy of healing.[127] It is no surprise that when their children fell ill, the

---

[119] Braga (572), can. 74, *Concilios Visigóticos*, 103.
[120] Note the *herbaria* in *serm.* 52. 5 and the female soothsayers in Gregory of Tours, *hist.* v. 14; VII. 44.   [121] Etaix, "Les épreuves du juste," 275, lines 85–87.
[122] Jm. 5: 14–15.   [123] See also *serm.* 13. 3; 52. 5; 184. 5.
[124] Brown, *The Cult of the Saints*, 114–15; A. Rousselle, "Du sanctuaire au thaumaturge: La guérison en Gaule au IVᵉ siècle," *Annales ESC* 31 (1976), 1085–1107. On the interpenetration of these healing traditions, especially in pharmacology, see G. E. R. Lloyd, *Science, Folklore, and Ideology* (Cambridge, 1983), 119–49.
[125] E.g. Gregory of Tours, *virt. Mart.* I. 26; IV. 36; *virt. Iul.* 46a.
[126] Note *vita* I. 50.   [127] Flint, *The Rise of Magic*, 251–53.

mothers of Arles said to one another: "Let us consult that *hariolus* or *divinus*, that *sortilegus*, that *herbaria*. Let us sacrifice the clothing of the sick boy, his belt should be examined and measured; let us offer some magical spells, let us attach some charms to his neck" (*serm.* 52. 5).[128] So widespread in fact was this attitude that those who did not make use of reputable local healers, and who continued to suffer from ill health or bad luck, were liable to receive advice from their fellow villagers.

It can happen, brothers, that a persecutor comes from the devil's side to someone who is sick, and says: "If you had summoned that *praecantator*, you would be well right now; if you had been willing to hang those spells from yourself, you could have regained your health by now." ... Perhaps someone else comes and says, "Send to that *divinus*; send him your belt or your bandage, let him measure and examine it; and he will tell you what you will do or whether you can escape." And another says, "That man really knows how to smoke out spirits (*fumigare*). Whenever he did this for anyone, things got better immediately, and every evil departed from his house." (*serm.* 184. 4, adapted from Augustine, *serm.* 286. 7)

It was the variety and reliability of these old remedies, their widespread availability, and their wide social acceptance that promoted their use among country people. Healing specialists could be found in any large village, and herbs or charms were locally available. Not even dedicated Christians could afford to spurn these accessible and effective sources of healing.

Occasionally there are women with sick children who behave as though they were wise Christian women, and who respond to their nurses or other women through whom the devil has suggested these things by saying, "I don't get mixed up in that sort of thing myself, because the verse read in church says, 'You cannot drink from the cup of the Lord and the cup of the demons; you cannot share the table of the Lord and the table of the demons' (1 Cor. 10: 20–21)." And yet, when she has said this as if to excuse herself, she then says, "Go and do what you know how to do; no resource from the storeroom is to be denied to you." (*serm.* 52. 6)

Given the attitude of ordinary Christians to these practices, it comes as no surprise that many clerics and religious, who had access to relics and copies of the scriptures, went into the business of producing amulets that contained these sacred objects (*serm.*

[128] See also *serm.* 50. 1.

50. 1). Although he condemned the practice, Caesarius could do little about it. Like Christian forms of divination, such as the *sortes biblicae* or *sortes sanctorum*, the making of Christian amulets and the recitation of Christian prayers at the collection and application of medicinal herbs arose out of an interest in accommodating the Christian religion to existing practice.

This process went on at the same time as the complementary process by which peasants adapted traditional forms of piety to Christian practice. According to Caesarius, there were people, particularly in the countryside,[129] who celebrated the feasts of the martyrs "by getting drunk, dancing, singing shameful songs, performing choral dances, and pantomiming in devilish fashion ... While they should be doing the work of Christ, they are attempting to carry out the service of the devil" (*serm.* 55. 2). Although Caesarius identified this behavior as pagan (*serm.* 13. 4), it was clearly no more than an alternative form of Christian devotion, as we have seen,[130] for it was performed at Christian holy places ("ante ipsas basilicas sanctorum," *serm.* 13. 4), on Christian holy days ("in sanctis festivitatibus," *serm.* 13. 4), and in honor of Christian holy men and women ("ad natalicia martyrum," *serm.* 55. 2). The recording of similar complaints from sixteenth-century Spain would seem to confirm the essentially Christian character of these ceremonies: "The report of Huecas, in respect to the annual visit of the town to the shrine of Mary Magdalen ... comments sourly that the people when at the shrine on St. Mark's day 'dance with too much enthusiasm' ('bailan con demasiado negocio')."[131]

Sometimes adaptation to Christian practice endowed an old ritual with new meaning. This occurred on the birthday of John the Baptist, celebrated on June 24, a feast the Gallic church considered as important as Easter, Christmas, and Pentecost.[132] At the conclusion of a sermon on tithing, delivered at harvest time just before the feast,[133] Caesarius advised an audience of mainly

---

[129] Caesarius attacked this practice in a number of sermons delivered at parish churches: *serm.* 13. 4; 16. 3; 19. 3. [130] *supra*, p. 198.

[131] Christian, *Local Religion*, 117. On the roots of early Christian opposition to dancing, see C. Andresen, "Altchristliche Kritik am Tanz – ein Ausschnitt aus dem Kampf der Alten Kirche gegen heidnische Sitte," in *Kirchengeschichte als Missionsgeschichte*, I, *Die Alte Kirche*, ed. H. Frohnes and U. W. Knorr (Munich, 1974), 344–76.

[132] Agde (506), can. 21.

[133] "By the favor of Christ, dearest brethren, the days are drawing near in which we are to collect the harvest," *serm.* 33. 1.

landowners "to warn all your neighbors, all your households (*familiae*), and all those who belong to you [i.e., slaves and tenants]…not to dare to bathe in springs, lakes, or rivers during the night before or on the morning of the feast of St. John, for this unfortunate custom carries over from the devotion of pagans" (*serm. 33. 4*). In condemning this practice as pagan, Caesarius likely had in mind the custom of bathing in sacred springs, rivers, and lakes as part of the rites of the summer solstice, which occurred around June 22. Inspired by the close association of healing waters, rain, fertility, and the sun in Celtic religion,[134] these rites were designed to ensure the success of the wheat harvest, which in hot, dry coastal areas like lower Provence was carried out around the end of June.[135] By deferring their ablutions to the evening of June 23 and the morning of June 24, the Christians of Arles enlarged the scope of this practice to symbolize baptism as well, both John's baptism of Jesus and their own Christian baptism, and thereby acknowledged their Christian affiliation. Although they still celebrated the life-giving properties of the sun and rain by bathing in streams and lakes on the feast of John the Baptist – and would continue to do so into modern times[136] – they now did so as Christians, synchronizing the church calendar with the local agricultural calendar. It was likewise as Christians that Augustine's congregation had gone down to the sea on the feast of John the Baptist and "baptized themselves." Criticized by the clergy for their action, they replied that they never would have performed it if they had known it derived from "pagan superstition,"[137] a response which suggests that the impulse for this religious accommodation came from the people themselves rather than the clergy.

We can see in this ritual the salient features of a community Christianity that gradually developed out of the continuities, adaptations, and reinterpretations we have discussed. It was a form of Christianity that was defined as much by local custom as by outside authority; it was a form of Christianity that permitted the continuation of many traditional observances; and above all it was

---

[134] Green, *The Gods of the Celts*, 164–65.

[135] "nunc etiam mense postremo locis maritimis et calidioribus ac siccis tritici messis absciditur," Palladius, *opus agriculturae* VII. 2. 2, ed. R. H. Rodgers (Leipzig, 1975).

[136] F. Benoit, "Le rite de l'eau dans la fête du solstice d'été en Provence et en Afrique," *Revue anthropologique* 45 (1935), 13–30; A. van Gennep, *Manuel de folklore français contemporain*, III, 371–85. [137] Augustine, *serm.* 196. 4.

a form of Christianity that the rural population actually practiced. As a result, it was a form of Christianity that local communities saw as better suited to their interests than the Christianity proposed by Caesarius and practiced by the "good Christians" of his sermons.[138] This was exactly the sort of religious autarky that Caesarius's whole training and way of life left him unable to tolerate. And it inspired a broad range of strategies designed to define the limits of authorized behavior, to enforce religious conformity, to eradicate all traces of deviant and "pagan" belief and behavior, and to disrupt the culture that allowed these to flourish.

STRATEGIES OF CHRISTIANIZATION AND DEPAGANIZATION

In order to transform the community religion of the peasants of Arles into the ideal Christianity he espoused, Caesarius attempted to set in motion two separate processes of religious change: a process of "christianization," by which he hoped to inculcate Christian rituals and beliefs, and a process of "depaganization," by which he hoped to obliterate pagan rituals and beliefs.[139] Although they were closely bound up with one another, and in the larger sense of "christianization" cannot be separated, these processes posed different problems and called for different strategies. The program of christianization Caesarius carried out in the countryside did not differ markedly from the efforts he made in the city to define the habits, values, attitudes, and practices of an ideal Christian life, and to persuade his people to abide by these norms. It was a program of religious instruction, which aimed at the initial conversion of non-Christians and the deeper indoctrination of Christians. As an essentially constructive effort, it depended mainly on persuasion and forms of "indirect compulsion,"[140] such as social pressure and threats of damnation. Depaganization, on the other hand, involved forcing the population not only to abandon the traditional practices they performed "in parallel" to Christianity, but also to desist from those pagan practices they performed in conjunction with it. It required Caesarius to emphasize the exclusivity and superiority of the Christian system, to undermine cultural patterns that favored traditional habits of thought and

---

[138] E.g., *serm.* 16. 1; 23. 2.
[139] For this distinction, see Kahl, "Die ersten Jahrhunderte," 40.   [140] Ibid., 44.

action, and to disrupt the processes of habituation and cultural transmission by which pagan practices were inculcated and passed on from one generation to the next. As an essentially destructive effort, imposed on an unwilling population, depaganization was more likely to involve coercion, although persuasion was also employed.

The focal point for efforts of christianization and depaganization was the rural parish church, with its resident clergy.[141] It was there that new Christians were instructed and baptized,[142] that Mass was celebrated,[143] and that the bishop preached on his regular tours of the diocese.[144] A number of factors, however, limited the effectiveness of rural parishes as centers of evangelization at the beginning of the sixth century. In the first place, parishes were not spread uniformly over the diocese, but were concentrated in its more populous regions.[145] This meant that they were sometimes inaccessible to those living in remote areas. In addition, many Christians in Arles attended religious services at private churches built by their landlords, which were not always under the bishop's effective supervision, and were therefore incapable of implementing his conversion program.[146] Moreover, even where a parish church was available to the population, it was often prevented by a lack of autonomy from serving as an effective center of christianization and depaganization. As we saw in Chapter 2, priests and deacons were permitted to read the scriptures at Mass, but not to explain them in sermons; they could accept donations to the church, but were required to turn control of these over to the bishop; endowments of land to support the parish likewise remained under his control. Without an autonomy of action that allowed clergy to offer, for instance, a "persuasive" commentary on the far from transparent meanings of sacred scripture,[147] or to spend church funds on patronage, it is doubtful that they could have had much success in inculcating Christian beliefs, let alone in obliterating paganism.

---

[141] E. Griffe, "A travers les paroisses rurales de la Gaule au VIe siècle," *Bulletin de littérature ecclésiastique* 76 (1975), 3–26.

[142] For instance, the "ignorant peasant women" who were to be taught by widows and nuns before baptism, according to *stat. eccl. ant.*, can. 100. For baptismal instruction in Spanish parishes, see Braga (572), can. 1, *Concilios Visigóticos*, 81.

[143] E.g., *vita* II. 20.   [144] *serm.* 6. 1; 19. 1; 22. 1; 29. 1; 151. 1.

[145] G. Fournier, "La mise en place du cadre paroissial et l'évolution du peuplement," in *Cristianizzazione ed organizzazione*, I, 495–563: 498–500.

[146] Orléans (541), can. 7.   [147] Augustine, *doctr. christ.* II. ix. 14.

Over the course of his career, Caesarius took a number of actions to remedy these shortcomings. As early as 506, the Council of Agde decreed that while rural dwellers were permitted to hear Mass in private churches on most Sundays and feast days, they were required on Easter, Christmas, and other important feasts to attend the urban cathedral or parish churches, where they could be more directly influenced by the bishop or his representatives.[148] In 524, to provide a larger pool of clergy for the "growing number of churches," the Council of Arles reduced to a year the length of time that laymen were required to live as *conversi* before being ordained as bishops, priests, and deacons.[149] More important than this change in recruitment standards is the evidence that additional churches were being founded within the province, both villa churches and parishes.

Granting increased autonomy to parishes encountered greater resistance, however, especially outside the diocese of Arles, since bishops saw in this reform a usurpation of their exclusive rights to preach and control finances within their own dioceses. Thus it was only later in his career, when he had finally established control over his suffragan bishops, that Caesarius was able to promulgate church legislation requiring bishops to share these rights with their parish clergy. It was to argue for these reforms that Caesarius composed an encyclical letter to his fellow bishops in the late 520s, conventionally referred to as *Sermon* 1.[150] In the letter Caesarius defined the bishop's role in such a way as to convince bishops that greater parish autonomy would not pose a threat to their status, but would rather enhance it. Above all, Caesarius argued that the bishop's responsibility was the spiritual cultivation of his congregation, through preaching and constant vigilance:

Bishops are called overseers because they are placed in a high place, as at the top of a citadel, that is the church. Having been established on the altar, they should be concerned for the city and the countryside of the Lord, that is the whole church, and not only guard the wide spaces of the gates, that is prevent mortal sins, by very vigorous preaching, but also watch the small rear gates, that is the lesser sins that creep in daily, by constantly advising that they be eliminated by fasting, almsgiving, and prayers. Acting as very zealous cultivators of souls, they should carefully

---

[148] Agde (506), can. 21.   [149] Arles (524), can. 2.

[150] Delage provides the best edition of the letter. For a date between 506 and 529, see Delage I, 276, n. 1. A date after 524 is suggested by the reference to can. 2 of the Council of Arles (524), which mandated a year's probation for laymen wishing to be ordained, *serm.* 1. 14.

watch over the vineyard of the Lord from a higher place, like vineyard workers, and protect it from spiritual beasts and birds and any kind of harmful or impure animals. (4)

This metaphor of spiritual cultivation allowed Caesarius to criticize bishops for their excessive concern with the management of property, both their own and the church's (5). He advised them instead to turn these responsibilities over to laymen and junior clerics, as he himself had done (6). The relevance of this advice to the issue of parish autonomy is clear. By turning day-to-day management of church property, including parish property, over to others, bishops would in Caesarius's eyes give themselves more time for their proper concerns. The objections he anticipated make it clear that bishops feared that the loss of direct control over church property would reduce their capacity to give alms, assist the poor, and put on impressive displays of wealth: "But someone might say, 'I devote a lot of attention [to the management of estates] because I want to give more abundant alms to the poor.' I judge no one, but I am afraid that there are some who concern themselves with earthly cultivation in order to put on sumptuous banquets rather than to give alms" (9).[151] It was to forestall such objections that Caesarius argued that of the kinds of alms bishops could give, the spiritual alms of pastoral care were superior to any other (8); his disapproval of luxurious feasts needed no elaboration.

In the second half of the letter, Caesarius concentrated on preaching. He called upon bishops to preach "not only on the most important feasts, but also every Sunday" (10). Because their responsibilities extended over the whole church, city and country-side alike (4), Caesarius argued that not only bishops but also priests and deacons should be permitted and required to preach frequently in parishes (12), a reform long sought by Gallic reformers.[152] To those bishops who objected that they themselves (and by implication their clergy) lacked the necessary eloquence and memory for preaching, Caesarius responded that simple themes and everyday language were all the preacher needed (13). And if this was not reassurance enough, he said, bishops could introduce a custom practiced in the east, by which priests and even deacons read out the sermons of the fathers in church (15), a practice Augustine had also recommended.[153] "For if a deacon is

---

[151] See also *serm.* 1. 7, 17.   [152] *stat. eccl. ant.*, can. 56.
[153] *doctr. christ.* IV. xxix. 62.

worthy of reading what Christ said [in the gospels], he should not be deemed unworthy of reciting what Saints Hilarius, Ambrose, and Augustine, and the rest of the fathers, have preached" (15).

These arguments seem to have convinced Caesarius's suffragan bishops. In 527, at the Council of Carpentras, they gave parishes in the province of Arles the right to dispose of their own revenues for the support of their clergy and the upkeep of their buildings.[154] The only exception involved bishops whose dioceses were in financial straits: they could retain a portion of parish revenues after allowances had been made for supporting clergy and maintaining buildings. By this regulation, parishes in the province of Arles obtained far more control over donations than parishes under Frankish jurisdiction were currently permitted. According to the Council of Orléans (511), all lands, vineyards, and slaves given to parishes were to remain in the bishop's control, as were one third of the gifts of wine, oil, bread, and money brought to the altar at Mass.[155]

In 529, meeting at Vaison, the bishops of the province extended parish autonomy still further. Enacting Caesarius's reform proposals to the letter, they gave priests of the province the authority to preach "not only in the cities, but also in all the parishes;" in the absence of priests, deacons were permitted to recite homilies written by fathers of the church.[156] Such privileges were still rare in the west. Priests in Spain were not granted general permission to preach until the seventh century.[157]

The council also authorized parish priests to create a pool of successors for themselves by bringing up young unmarried lectors in their homes, a practice Caesarius claimed was common in Italy.[158] "Spiritually nourishing these boys like good fathers, they should strive to teach them the Psalms, immerse them in scriptural readings, and educate them in the law of God, so as to furnish themselves with worthy successors and receive eternal rewards from God. When they become adults, if anyone wants to take a wife, because of fragility of the flesh, he should not be denied the right to marry."[159] Lectors were singled out for this special education because, besides being young in most cases, and therefore more easily trained, especially in the difficult work of

---

[154] Carpentras (527), can. 1.   [155] Orléans (511), can. 15.
[156] Vaison (529), can. 2.   [157] Toledo (633), can. 25, *Concilios Visigóticos*, 202.
[158] C. E. Boyd, *Tithes and Parishes in Medieval Italy* (Ithaca, N.Y., 1952), 52.
[159] Vaison (529), can. 1.

memorizing the Psalms, they were also literate, which suggests that they were recruited from the upper strata of the local population.[160] They were thus ideal candidates for the diaconate and priesthood.

The chief beneficiaries of these changes were the clerics in charge of local parishes, normally priests.[161] By virtue of their control over church property, they could begin to exercise on a smaller scale the same style of patronage as bishops. By virtue of their license to preach, they could begin to address their congregations with the same teaching authority as bishops addressed theirs. Moreover, like bishops, they could form around themselves clerical communities made up of junior clergy.[162] These rights did not only raise the status of parish priests; they also permitted them to engage in a more intensive conversion effort. Under the right conditions, parish priests could offer the favors of patronage in return for loyalty to the church. They could use donations made in honor of local saints to foster increased devotion to their cults.[163] Most importantly, they could preach the Christian system of values and practices to their congregations on a regular basis, a form of pastoral care that Caesarius began requiring of priests and deacons as well as bishops.[164]

The right to preach, however, meant little without the proper preparation. Caesarius therefore took steps to encourage priests and deacons to preach effectively. He continued to insist on a minimum degree of education for the clergy. Priests and deacons, for instance, were required to have read the books of the Bible at least four times over,[165] and lectors, as we have seen, were taught the psalms and sacred scriptures. He also made collections of his sermons available to priests and deacons.[166] His preface to one of these collections tells us something of the procedure by which these were copied and distributed at the parish level.[167] "By our paternal piety and pastoral care, we have collected in this little book simple admonitions necessary in parishes, which holy priests

[160] Lectors were traditionally young: the eight-year-old cleric cured of possession in *vita* II. 20 was probably a lector. On their ages and social standing, see H. Leclercq, "Lecteur," *DACL* VIII. 2 (1929), cols. 2247–49.

[161] de la Tour, *Les Paroisses*, 61–62.   [162] Beck, 79.

[163] de la Tour, *Les Paroisses*, 42–49.   [164] *serm.* 2; 183. 1.

[165] *vita* I. 56; Riché, *Education and Culture*, 124–28.

[166] *vita* I. 54–55; *serm.* I. 15; 2.

[167] Represented by the eleventh-century MS Zwifalt. 49, the collection includes 27 sermons by Caesarius: *serm.* 2, 3, 13, 16, 17, 33, 36, 37, 41, 43, 44, 46, 47, 54, 55, 154, 179, 187, 188, 192, 199, 200, 202, 207, 210, 216, 223, Morin I, lxx–lxxiii.

and deacons ought to recite on the greater feasts of the church to the people entrusted to them" (*serm.* 2). Because his scribes in Arles, including the sisters of his monastery (*vita* I. 58), were inexperienced, and because they had had to make multiple copies of the collection, Caesarius asked that his readers pardon any errors they might find in the work and emend the text where necessary. He then requested that they have further copies made, in a better hand and on parchment if they could afford it, and send these on to neighboring parishes. It was through such cooperation that Caesarius expanded his influence not only within his own diocese, but also far outside of it.[168] Although he himself was normally able to visit his own rural parishes only once a year,[169] and those outside his diocese almost never, the spread of his sermons from parish to parish ensured that his reform message would be widely propagated by priests and deacons, with or without the approval of their bishops.

As important as they were to Caesarius's program, rural parishes were not the only centers of christianization in the diocese. Many peasants, as we have seen, attended Mass along with their landlords in oratories erected on the estates they worked. Not all of these were officially classified as parishes.[170] Although ordained by the bishop, their resident clergy remained under the effective control of the landlord; their property remained the landlord's property.[171] Because they were not considered parishes, these churches were not affected by the legislation of 527/29. Whether their priests were authorized to preach or not depended entirely on the landlord's rather than the bishop's decision. Caesarius tried to reach the congregations of these churches not only on the holy days when they were required to attend Mass at the cathedral or rural parishes, but also on the occasions when he made direct visits to local villas, often in the context of his visits to parishes (*vita* I. 50; II. 27).

In order to implement his program of conversion, Caesarius employed a variety of strategies, which ranged along a spectrum from persuasion to coercion, and often included elements of both. Like other Christian missionaries, Caesarius was more inclined to favor predominantly persuasive techniques when he believed

---

[168] Arnold, 355–56.   [169] *serm.* 6. 1; 151. 1.   [170] Agde (506), can. 21.
[171] Lesne, *Histoire de la propriété*, I, 55–58. In Italy, on the other hand, strenuous efforts were made by the bishops of Rome to plce the endowments of proprietary churches under church control, Boyd, *Tithes*, 51.

potential converts shared a common frame of mind and common culture with him, and to favor coercive techniques when he believed they did not, especially in the case of depaganization, where coercion was more easily justified.[172] His strategies therefore varied as much according to individual status as according to the particular behavior he was trying to inculcate or eradicate. The use of varying degrees of force on persons of low status, such as women, children, tenants, and slaves, was more acceptable than it was on persons of higher status, because their powers of free choice were restricted and their powers of rationality doubted. Likewise, peasants were more likely than townspeople to be compelled to abandon their traditional practices, because Caesarius had less respect for their culture and more trouble understanding it. He was thus more inclined to disrupt it and less capable of framing effective arguments against it. Nonetheless, fundamental similarities between urban and rural culture and a staunch confidence in the universality of human rationality[173] predisposed Caesarius to prefer persuasion, or at least those forms of "indirect compulsion" that could be disguised as persuasion.

His persuasive strategy was threefold. First he tried to demolish the cognitive framework that made paganism meaningful, in the hope that people would cease to engage in pagan practices when they began to perceive them as irrelevant, ineffective, impractical, or meaningless. Second, he tried to present Christian beliefs and practices as effective and meaningful alternatives to paganism. Finally, he tried to demonstrate that these Christian alternatives constituted the only legitimate means of access to the understanding and control of the world.

It was of course in his sermons that Caesarius attempted to use this three-part strategy most directly, marshalling arguments, threats, and scriptural admonitions to persuade peasants to abandon their pagan practices. In a sermon on lunar eclipses, for instance, he tried to convince his audience that the practice of sounding horns and ringing bells was unnecessary and ineffective. The moon, he said, was "a sphere set afire by a natural physical cause, which was hidden at fixed times or overcome by the nearby glow of the setting sun" (*serm.* 52. 3). It was wrong to think that

---

[172] For a theoretical overview of this point, see Kahl, "Die ersten Jahrhunderte," 36–38; for a convincing demonstration, see S. MacCormack, "'The Heart Has Its Reasons': Predicaments of Missionary Christianity in Early Colonial Peru," *Hispanic American Historical Review* 65 (1985), 443–66.   [173] *vita* I. 32; *serm.* 52. 3.

"sacrilegious noise-making" could make it propitious. "If this heavenly body is inferior to you, why do you fear to offend it by your silence? If it is superior to you, why do you think it needs your help?" (*serm.* 52. 3). In a sermon condemning the use of pagan names for the days of the week, he explained that the days of the week were named after men and women mistakenly thought to be gods: "Mercury was a wretched man, greedy, cruel, impious, and proud; and Venus was a most shameless prostitute" (*serm.* 193. 4). These individuals were born, he maintained, while the children of Israel were in Egypt, which led to a contradiction with scripture. "If they were born at that time," he said, "then certainly the days named after them were already in existence, and in accordance with what God established, they were named 'first' and 'second' and 'third' and 'fourth' and 'fifth' and 'sixth day'" (*serm.* 193. 4). Following his usual custom, Caesarius then underscored the difference between pagan and Christian practice by referring to the great divide between the demonic and the divine, and presented his audience with a Christian alternative to the pagan practice: "Let us, brothers, who are known to have hope not in lost and impious people, but in the living and true God, judge no day worthy of the name of demons... Let us disdain to speak those most sordid names and never let us say 'Mars's day', 'Mercury's day', or 'Jupiter's day', but rather 'first day', 'second day', or 'third day'; according to what has been written [in Genesis], let us call the days" (*serm.* 193. 4).

Caesarius's argument in this sermon ultimately turned on a contradiction between scripture and traditional custom. Not surprisingly, appeals to the authority of the scriptures were frequently the basis of his persuasive efforts. In a sermon condemning the use of amulets as remedies for sickness, Caesarius relied on two approaches: pointing out the demonic power behind the effectiveness of amulets, an explanation which itself relied on biblical cosmology, and directly quoting the Bible's disapproval:

Let us consider the matter, dearly beloved, with a penetrating insight, and by careful investigation examine our own actions, so that a malevolent spirit does not secretly creep up on us, and does not deceive us by the appearance of goodness, if it cannot do so openly. For he has "a thousand ways of doing harm,"[174] and he abuses all of these to deceive

---

[174] Vergil, *Aen.* VII. 337–38. Caesarius also quotes this verse in *serm.* 152. 2 and 207. 1, probably unaware of its source.

the human race. "For we are not ignorant," says the apostle, "of his cunning" (2 Cor. 2: 11). And Christ himself condemned amulets among the Pharisees when he said, "They make their phylacteries broad, and lengthen their fringes" (Mt. 23: 5). It is better to keep the words of God in your heart than to hang writings around your neck. (*serm*. 50. 2)

Such admonitions were backed up by the authority of the scriptures and the threat of eternal punishment. "Those who make amulets, along with those who ask that they be made and those who agree [to allow this] are all made into pagans. Unless they perform a suitable penance, they cannot avoid punishment" (*serm*. 50. 1).[175] Descriptions of hell alternated with promises of eternal happiness.[176]

Yet, as Caesarius well knew, direct experience often furnished a more powerful motivation for religious change than episcopal rhetoric.[177] And so he endeavored to persuade and influence his audiences by convincing acts of patronage and healing. We have already examined the ways in which Caesarius established himself as the principal patron of his community through numerous acts of charity. By these, he not only provided concrete material benefits to his people; he also placed himself in a position to demand benefits in return, such as cooperation in his effort to instill Christian values and eradicate paganism. For example, by ransoming pagan Frankish prisoners of war after their attack on the city of Arles in 507/8, he may have converted some of those who felt obligated to him for rescuing them.[178] By the same mechanism, Caesarius's patronage toward the natives of Arles might be expected to bind them more closely to the Christianity he espoused. To the extent that pagan officials and institutions were no longer available to perform the same function, depaganization was also served. Under the bishop's supervision, the cathedral and parish churches regularly collected food, clothing, and money,[179] and distributed these to the poor, widows, orphans, and other needy persons.[180] With the decentralization of control over parish property in 527, rural priests began to exercise this form of

---

[175] See also *serm*. 14. 4; 53. 3; 54. 1, 5.   [176] *serm*. 19. 6; 52. 6; 54. 5.

[177] For examples from the analogous problem of modernization in traditional cultures, see F. G. Bailey, "The Peasant View of the Bad Life," in *Peasants and Peasant Societies*, ed. T. Shanin (Harmondsworth, 1971) 298–321: 316–20.   [178] *supra*, pp. 116–17.

[179] *serm*. 30–32, and for parish churches, *serm*. 13. 2; 19. 2, 3.

[180] Perhaps through archdeacons or archpriests, as recommended by *stat. eccl. ant.*, can. 7; Beck, 330–31.

patronage on their own. By 567 in the province of Tours, parish priests and their congregations were being commanded to feed the poor in their own region.[181] And by the end of the century, it is clear that many affluent churches and shrines maintained a list of the poor who were entitled to receive regular benefits from them, a custom that certainly began much earlier.[182] Gregory of Tours vividly depicted the crowds of poor men and women who gathered at these places to receive alms.[183] Each church thus became a center not only for the preaching of Christian virtues such as generosity and love of neighbors, but also for the practical validation of these virtues. Those who depended on these gifts for their survival might therefore be doubly motivated to affiliate themselves more closely with a local church or shrine: by their gratitude and continued need for support, and by the ideals of righteousness they saw enacted there. Loyalties could run deep. When the poor attached to the burial church of St. Martin in Tours saw a murder committed in the atrium, they rushed in to seize the malefactors.[184]

In addition to the institutional forms of patronage that Caesarius and his clergy controlled, they also engaged in individual acts of patronage, with potentially the same results. Caesarius himself frequently gave gifts of food, clothing, and money to captives and the poor (*vita* I. 20, 44; II. 23–24), as his clergy probably also did. He was prepared to help in other ways too, for instance when the peasants responsible for tending a property of the women's monastery asked him to do something about the hunting of wild boars on their property by Gothic counts and soldiers (*vita* I. 48). Such favors called for repayment, and the poor paid as they could, in loyalty, deference, and piety.

Miracles, in turn, could promote christianization and depaganization in three ways. First, like acts of charity, miracles offered a means of demonstrating that Christian leaders could deliver material benefits like good health and successful harvests even more effectively than pagan figures.[185] Also like acts of charity,

---

[181] Tours (567), can. 5.
[182] Lesne, *Histoire de la propriété*, I, 380–89. Remigius mentions the *matricula* of the church of Reims in his will, *test.*, 337, line 17. [183] *virt. Mart.* II. 7, 8, 22, 23, etc.
[184] Gregory of Tours, *hist.* VII. 29.
[185] On the importance of visual proof for conversion, see R. Van Dam, "Hagiography and History: The Life of Gregory Thaumaturgus," *Classical Antiquity* I (1982), 272–308: 274–75; on the role that healing could play, see A. Rousselle, "Du sanctuaire au thaumaturge," 1101–5.

miracles produced tangible *beneficia* that created intangible networks of *clientela* and obligation. Finally, miracles provided visual proof of the bishop's self-proclaimed ability to mediate between the distant power of God and the pressing needs of his people. Not only was this intended to validate the bishop's authority; it was also calculated to verify the Christian model of the universe which the bishop proposed to the peasants, a universe of good and evil powers whose hidden energies, processes, and forces were deemed to be legitimately accessible only through the organized church.

Among the miraculous events attributed to Caesarius by his biographers, several took place in rural parishes. On a tour of his parishes, at a fortified place called Luco, a woman named Eucyria brought forward one of her slave girls, who she claimed was being secretly beaten at night by "a demon the peasants call Diana," an identification which itself reveals the church's success in defining the pagan gods as malevolent demons.[186] When he received the report, Caesarius sent a priest and two deacons, including his biographer Stephanus, to investigate the case. After Eucyria's claims had been verified, the girl was taken to Caesarius, who placed his hand on her head, blessed her, and gave her consecrated oil with which to anoint herself at night. Thus the demonic Diana was immediately driven out. Similar miracles are recorded on other parish visits. At the church of Berre, during the celebration of Mass, Caesarius exorcised a demon from an eight-year-old cleric; the boy later became a subdeacon in the church (*vita* II. 20). At the parish of la Ciotat, in front of the altar in the parish church, he cured the daughter of Novatus of demon possession, who "returned down the street to her home in good health while everyone watched" (*vita* II. 21). To observers and participants in these cases, Caesarius's exorcisms validated the church's contention that the pagan gods were deeply malevolent to mankind, and served to demonstrate that God's power, exercised through Caesarius, was superior to theirs. Miracles of healing in rural places, such as the incident in which Caesarius and Eucherius (probably of Avignon[187]) cured a crippled woman in the Alpilles (*vita* I. 47), made the additional point that the approved remedies offered by clerics were more powerful than the herbs and potions of folk healers. The use of Caesarius's relics by rural folk

---

[186] *vita* II. 18–19. The same demon appears in *vita patrum Iurensium* 144.
[187] Duchesne I, 267, n. 7; see also *CCSL* 148A, 45.

themselves suggests that there was some acceptance of these claims. When peasants in the parish of Succentriones found the bishop's staff, which had been left there by mistake, they hung it from the wall of an abandoned bath house to drive out the demons that had taken up residence there (*vita* II. 22). When a landowner in the Alpilles found the same object at his house on another occasion, he had it made into a cross and erected on a hilltop to counteract hailstorms, common in Provence (*vita* II. 27). It was by such contests waged between Christian and pagan divinities, and Christian and traditional systems of therapy, that Caesarius could hope that the Christian God would emerge not merely as a useful supplement to the pagan gods, but as the only god whose power counted.

But however successful these persuasive methods might have been – and we should not overestimate their success – Caesarius did not rely exclusively on them. He also advocated direct religious repression, as tolerated, advocated, and practiced by bishops of the later fourth and fifth centuries[188] with the authorization of imperial law.[189] Unlike his predecessors, however, Caesarius could not rely on imperial power to back up sanctions against paganism. Nor is there any evidence to suggest that he made use of what little anti-pagan legislation the *Breviary* of Alaric[190] and the *Edict* of Theoderic[191] had taken over from Roman law. Not only would this have undermined his opposition to Arianism, but such laws had never had as much practical effect in the countryside as the repressive powers of landowners and *patresfamilias*.[192] Childebert's *praeceptum* of *c*. 554, which mandated severe floggings for slaves who practiced paganism, simply confirmed what landlords and slave owners had been urged to do all along.[193] To constrain the peasantry, Caesarius therefore turned to the same forms of power Augustine and other bishops had relied upon: the power patrons exercised over their clients and

---

[188] For example, Augustine, *ep.* 91. 8; Sulpicius Severus, *vita Martini* 12–15; Maximus of Turin, *serm.* 91, 106, 107, 108. For Augustine's attitude to religious coercion, see Brown, "St. Augustine's Attitude," and *Augustine of Hippo* (Berkeley and Los Angeles, 1967), 226–43.   [189] *CTh* XVI. 10.

[190] *brev. Al., nov.* 3, although the interest of the compilers in this law was evidently focused on its anti-Jewish provisions, Schäferdiek, *Die Kirche*, 46, n. 132.

[191] *edict. Theod.* 108.

[192] P. Brown, "Religious Coercion in the Later Roman Empire: The Case of North Africa," in his *Religion and Society in the Age of Saint Augustine* (London, 1972), 301–31: 311; Dölger, "Christliche Grundbesitzer."

[193] Childebert, *praeceptum*, ed. A. Boretius, *MGH Capit.*, I, 2–3.

dependants, landlords over their tenants and slaves, and *patres-familias* over their wives, children, and household slaves.[194] Caesarius had often asked members of his audience to communicate to their relatives, friends, clients, and slaves what he preached in his sermons (*vita* 1. 61). He now asked them to reinforce this message with forms of compulsion appropriate to the status of the offender: "Not only should you frequently reproach those who are yours with severity; you should also constantly admonish those who are not with charity" (*serm.* 193. 4).

The coercive tasks he assigned varied from sermon to sermon. In several sermons, landowners were asked to cleanse their property of pagan holy places: "And so, whoever has any trees, altars, or shrines in his fields or in his villa or next to his villa, where wretched people customarily offer prayers, if he does not tear them down or cut them down, he will doubtless be an accessory to what is done there" (*serm.* 54. 5).[195] In addition, landlords were asked to control the behavior of those who worshiped at these sites. "Chastise those whom you know to be [guilty]; warn them very harshly; scold them very severely. And if they are not corrected, beat them if you have the power; if they are not improved by this, cut off their hair too. And if they still persevere, bind them in iron shackles, so that those whom the grace of Christ does not hold, a chain may hold" (*serm.* 53. 2). In another sermon Caesarius asked the heads of households to "reprove, correct, and reproach" those who engaged in unauthorized practices on the Kalends of January, and to "banish these practices from their households" (*serm.* 192. 3). By such tactics, Caesarius clearly advocated more than simple persuasion. Where equals were involved, he recommended social pressure; where dependants were involved, corporal punishment. As he said in condemning those who kept Jupiter's day holy, "Scold those who do such things very severely. If they are unwilling to change, do not permit them to speak with you or to celebrate festivities with you. If they belong to you, however, beat them even with whips, so that they might fear a blow to their bodies who do not think about the salvation of their souls" (*serm.* 13. 5).

These repressive measures were implicitly justified by the deeply held assumption that dependent persons were endowed

---

[194] Augustine, *serm.* 302. 19–21.   [195] See also *serm.* 14. 4; 53. 1.

with a diminished capacity for rational thought and a restricted power of free choice. But Caesarius also justified them explicitly. Those who reverted to paganism after baptism, he said, were choosing the devil over Christ and death over life. "They desert the light and run to darkness; they despise God and embrace the devil; they desert life and pursue death; they repudiate Christ and have recourse to sacrileges" (*serm.* 53. 1). The image of the military deserter, who could under Roman law be punished with death,[196] helped to justify Caesarius's threats of force. In advocating attendance at church during the Rogations Caesarius delivered a warning that applied all the more to the practice of paganism.

No one should desert the spiritual camp. For you know, dearest brothers, that if anyone who serves an earthly king as a soldier leaves the battle line at the moment of combat because he is afraid, not only does he not receive glory and the rewards that have been prepared, but he also risks his life. The man who deserts the church of Christ on these three days must therefore without doubt be judged the same as the man who deserts the army of a terrestrial king...Like a fugitive and a deserter from the celestial camp, he will undergo eternal damnation and a punishment worthy of his deeds. (*serm.* 207. 2)

Essential to this justification for repression was the threat of eternal punishment: "Whoever does not want to observe [this prohibition of pagan activity] will be tortured by eternal fire without any remedy" (*serm.* 53. 3).[197] Unless radical measures were taken in this life, Caesarius could argue, apostates would suffer unceasingly in the next (*serm.* 1. 13; 13. 5; 54. 1, 5).

The repressive measures Caesarius proposed were not only designed to define his opposition to paganism with terrifying clarity; they were also intended to be put into effect. But how were these measures intended to promote depaganization? Certainly, punishments like shunning, beating, and imprisonment could have prevented peasants from publicly practicing paganism when they were in danger of being discovered. But how could these sanctions have kept them from "thinking" like pagans and returning to traditional rituals as soon as possible? The answer would seem to depend on the time frame involved. Over the short term, Caesarius was content to prevent forbidden activities whenever possible, relying on his rhetoric to alter patterns of

---

[196] *CTh* VII. 18. 4, 11, 15.   [197] See also *serm.* 14. 4.

thought. Over the long term, however, he aimed at interrupting the process of transmission by which pagan customs and beliefs were passed down from one generation to the next through storytelling, ritual performances, proverbs, and the like. He was aware that the complex body of beliefs and practices that he called paganism was kept alive by continual repetition and reinforcement within the community and the family (*serm.* 6. 2). Curtailing these beliefs and practices, or suppressing their transmission, for instance by substituting the reading of Christian scriptures for non-Christian activities (*serm.* 6. 1, 2), would certainly have made it more difficult for children to appropriate the full details of the traditional religious system. But it is unclear how successful such measures could be. Much depended on the willingness of the men in Caesarius's congregation to punish their wives, children, tenants, and slaves for religious infractions. In view of the resistance many of these men had already mounted against Caesarius's other prescriptions, we cannot assume that they responded enthusiastically. Moreover, even those landlords and *patresfamilias* who did carry out religious repression for Caesarius could never have entirely prevented peasants from practicing traditional religion or transmitting it to their children. Repressed rituals could be performed in secret and taught as part of a child's normal upbringing, thus remaining completely inaccessible to outside interference.

A more effective method of disrupting the transmission of pagan beliefs and practices was to remove young people from the process entirely, and submit them to an orthodox Christian education. Not only did this method avoid the problem of parental influence; it could also be directly imposed by the church, without lay intermediaries. Caesarius took one obvious step in this direction with his decision at the Council of Vaison to have young unmarried lectors leave their homes, and receive a Christian upbringing in the homes of local priests.[198] In addition to providing the local parish with a reliable pool of recruits, this measure was intended to produce a corps of adult males who had been isolated during their formative years from the sources of traditional peasant culture. Having received a thoroughly Christian education (at least to the extent that local priests could supply this), and learned to prefer the authority of their "spiritual

[198] Vaison (529), can. 1.

fathers" to the authority of their natural fathers, they could function as effective models for Christian behavior, even if they never entered the higher ranks of the clergy. Indeed, they were perhaps more effective if they chose not to, and raised "Christian" families of their own instead.

On what scale this operation was conducted it is difficult to say. Certainly it did not approach either the magnitude or the degree of ruthlessness evident in sixteenth-century New Spain, where the children of native elites were taken by force to live with Christian missionaries, who taught them the "errors of idolatry" and afterwards sent them back to destroy temples and indoctrinate their parents.[199] The children taken to live with parish priests in Gaul were already Christians, as were their parents, and they remained in the priests' control until their ordination or their marriage. Furthermore, they were probably never as numerous as the child interns of the New World, since parishes probably did not support large numbers of lectors under any conditions. But there are noteworthy parallels between the two practices: a concentration on the children of native elites, an emphasis on Christian education, provisions for the eventual marriage of interns, and an insistence on the role of the clergy as "spiritual fathers." The important differences that remain between the two cases help to illuminate the religious situation Caesarius faced as a missionary. The peasants he was trying to christianize did not belong to an alien culture or speak a foreign language, like the Aztec, the Inca, or their subject populations;[200] they were part of his own culture and spoke his own language. It was largely because they did not live in an entirely separate culture that Caesarius was content to advocate the use of force only against dependent persons with limited rights, such as slaves, tenants, women, and children, and not against everyone who practiced "pagan" customs. It was for the same reason that the religion peasants practiced in response to his program of christianization was in fact a form of Christianity not essentially different from the religion townspeople were practicing at the same time. In fact, as religious options grew narrower over the course of the fifth and sixth

---

[199] R. Trexler, "From the Mouths of Babes: Christianization by Children in 16th Century New Spain," in *Religious Organization and Religious Experience*, ed. J. Davis (London, 1982), 115–35.

[200] See now S. MacCormack, *Religion in the Andes: Vision and Imagination in Early Colonial Peru* (Princeton, 1991).

centuries, the question that both urban and rural populations increasingly faced was not whether they would become Christians, but what kinds of Christians they would become. The community religion they designed for themselves constituted their answer to this question.

Chapter 9

THE COMING OF THE FRANKS

Caesarius emerged from the Council of Vaison at the height of his political power, the uneven success of his programs of christianization and depaganization notwithstanding. His suffragans had supported his reform program at the Councils of Arles, Carpentras, and Vaison, joined him in censuring Agroecius at the Council of Carpentras, and together with Liberius and other lay aristocrats, endorsed his definition of grace at the Council of Orange. Theoderic had made these councils possible in the first place by incorporating the rest of Caesarius's metropolitan province into the Ostrogothic kingdom, thus allowing Caesarius to confirm in practice the metropolitan authority he claimed in theory. Popes Symmachus and Hormisdas, moreover, had extended valuable privileges to his monastery for women, and Pope Felix had supported his actions against Agroecius. By the late 520s, however, the political environment that Caesarius had found so favorable to his own ambitions was already beginning to deteriorate. Within six years of the Council of Vaison, largely as a result of events outside of his control, he was to lose much of the support he had come to depend upon from the Ostrogothic administration, his suffragan bishops, and the bishops of Rome.

RAVENNA AND ROME: 526–35

When Theoderic died in 526, he was succeeded by his ten-year-old grandson Athalaric, whose mother Amalasuintha was appointed to serve as regent.[1] Without the powers of a king or the capacity to lead the Gothic army, Amalasuintha found it difficult to maintain Theoderic's delicate balance between aspirations to *Romanitas* and fidelity to Gothic tradition.[2] In diplomatic terms

---

[1] *PLRE* II, 175–76.

[2] "It may be that Theoderic's roles were less clearly demarcated for his barbarian contemporaries than they are for us. What worried them was not what sort of a Germanic leader he was but whether he were not more of a Roman official. It was

this tension was often expressed as a conflict over relations with the imperial government in Constantinople.[3] Amalasuintha's own sympathies were strongly pro-imperial, as were those of other Goths and many Romans. As regent, she consistently acted to carry out Theoderic's dying request for peace with the emperor and good relations with the senate and people.[4] But she had to contend with a powerful party of Goths and Romans who favored distinctly cooler relations with Constantinople. They were well represented in her government. Tuluin was put in charge of the army, and Boethius's accuser Cyprianus served as praetorian prefect of Italy. A third potential rival, willing to ally himself with anyone who could further his own ambitions, was her cousin Theodahad, who had been denied the kingship despite his descent from Theoderic's father.[5] In late 532 this party organized a conspiracy against Amalasuintha on the pretext that Athalaric was not being raised as a Goth.[6] She reacted by sending the three chief conspirators to the frontiers and then having them assassinated.[7] Tuluin, probably one of those killed, was replaced as army commander by Liberius, and Cyprianus was replaced as praetorian prefect of Italy by Cassiodorus.[8] For the moment, pro-imperial forces had regained control.

In addition to these internal dangers, Amalasuintha was beset by external threats, which closely affected southern Gaul as well. The Franks under Chlothar and Childebert had resumed their push to the Mediterranean, and invaded Burgundy in 532.[9] Around the same time, Provence was invaded from the west by Theudebert, who reached the territory of Béziers and Arles, but withdrew shortly afterward.[10] Amalasuintha reacted to this threat by ceding back to the Burgundians the territory between the Durance and the Isère captured in 523.[11] She thereby gave up a buffer zone against the Franks, but also made the northern and western frontier of Provence more defensible.[12] In the meantime, the

Romanitas that discredited his dynasty in the end," J. M. Wallace-Hadrill, *Early Germanic Kingship in England and on the Continent* (Oxford, 1971), 11.

[3] Wolfram, *Goths*, 286–90. For a concise statement of Theoderic's constitutional position which does not rule out the possibility of conflict within Italy over relations with the emperor, see A. H. M. Jones, "The Constitutional Position of Odoacer and Theoderic," *JRS* 52 (1962), 126–30.   [4] Jordanes, *Getica* 304–5.

[5] Wolfram, *Goths*, 327–33.   [6] Procopius, *de bellis* v. 2. 8–17.

[7] Procopius, *de bellis* v. 2. 21–29.   [8] Wolfram, *Goths*, 336–37.

[9] Schmidt, *Ostgermanen*, 165.   [10] Gregory of Tours, *hist.* III. 21–23.

[11] Stein, *Histoire*, II, 332.   [12] Cassiodorus, *var.* XI. I. 13.

Franks pressed on against Burgundy. With the death of King Godomar in 534, Childebert, Chlothar, and Theudebert took Burgundy.[13] The death of Athalaric on October 2, 534 prompted Amalasuintha to declare herself queen. Because she could no longer ignore Theodahad's claim to the throne, she named him co-ruler, eliciting his solemn promise to respect her superior authority.[14] Theodahad not surprisingly broke his promise, and deposed her at the end of 534. Although he was warned by Justinian not to harm her,[15] Theodahad allowed her to be assassinated in the spring of 535 by the relatives of the men she had put to death in the conspiracy of 532.[16] Eager to recover the Ostrogothic kingdom, Justinian used her death as a pretext for war in June 535.[17]

Besides threatening the general peace, security, and stability of Provence, these events brought about a concrete reduction in Caesarius's power. With the return to Burgundian control of the territory between the Durance and the Isère, Caesarius lost metropolitan control over the dioceses he had regained in 523. This change did not take immediate effect: bishops from Apt, Vaison, Saint-Paul, and Orange all attended the Council of Marseille in May 533 as if their sees still belonged to the Gothic kingdom. By June 534, however, when Caesarius issued the second edition of the rule for virgins, none of the bishops who signed came from north of the Durance.[18]

Continuing political conflict in Ravenna also affected Roman politics, and between 526 and 535 Caesarius found himself dealing with a series of "pro-Gothic" bishops of Rome appointed against the wishes of the largely "pro-imperial" Roman clergy and senate. Felix IV (526–30), was appointed pope "by the orders of King Theoderic" just before the king's death.[19] The climate of fear that prevailed in Italy in the wake of Pope John's tragic death may have deterred the Roman clergy from objecting to this irregular event.[20] Four years later, before his death on September 22, Felix appointed his archdeacon Boniface to succeed him.[21] This time the Roman clergy reacted to the assault on its prerogatives by electing Dioscorus as an alternative.[22] Although Dioscorus's death on October 14 left Boniface in sole possession of the see, it took

---

[13] Gregory of Tours, *hist.* III. 11; Marius of Avenches, *chron.* a. 534, *MGH AA*, XI, 235; Schmidt, *Ostgermanen*, 165.   [14] Procopius, *de bellis* v. 4. 4–11.
[15] Procopius, *de bellis* v. 4. 22.   [16] Procopius, *de bellis* v. 4. 26–28.
[17] Jordanes, *Romana* 368.   [18] Morin II, 124.   [19] *LP* I, 106.
[20] Caspar, *Geschichte des Papsttums*, II, 194.   [21] *LP* I, 282, n. 4.
[22] *LP* I, 282, n. 8.

him several months to consolidate his authority over the dissident clergy and establish himself in full authority.[23] These events help to explain his delay in answering Caesarius's request for confirmation of the canons of Orange. Caesarius had requested this confirmation because "some Gallic bishops" still opposed the council's decisions on grace.[24] He had written in the belief that Pope Felix was still alive, that is in the autumn of 530, with every expectation of receiving the same favorable treatment that he had received in the affair of Agroecius. It was Boniface who responded, however, and he did not do so until late January 531. Nonetheless, he provided the confirmation Caesarius sought, to the mutual benefit of both parties. Caesarius won papal support for a controversial position, and Boniface strengthened his own insecure authority by being seen to provide it. But Caesarius's need for papal confirmation of the conciliar decisions of Carpentras and Orange signals his weakness rather than his strength, and suggests that his influence as metropolitan of Provence and vicar of Gaul was not particularly strong. This impression is confirmed by his unsuccessful effort to suppress opposition arising out of the affair of Contumeliosus, bishop of Riez.

Contumeliosus was a powerful bishop. He was the most senior suffragan in Caesarius's province,[25] and an aristocrat whose literary tastes Avitus of Vienne openly admired.[26] He had in the past generally supported Caesarius's councils.[27] In May 533 Caesarius and fifteen of his suffragans assembled in Marseille to consider charges against him of sexual misconduct,[28] and illegal alienation of church property.[29] Presented with the evidence against himself, Contumeliosus admitted his guilt and agreed to undergo penance at the *monasterium Casense* (location unknown) and to pay the church back for the property he had sold.[30] The council was

---

[23] *LP* I, 281.   [24] Caesarius, *ep.* 20, Morin II, 67–70.

[25] His signature appears immediately after Caesarius's at the Councils of Arles (*CCSL* 148A, 45, line 4), Carpentras (*CCSL* 148A, 49, line 4), and Vaison (*CCSL* 148A, 80, line 4). He did not attend the Council of Orange, possibly to avoid the necessity of condemning the theological opinions of his predecessor, Faustus of Riez.

[26] Avitus of Vienne, *ep.* 15.

[27] He signed the letter of Hormisdas, and the canons of Arles, Carpentras, and Vaison.

[28] The sources are, characteristically, imprecise: "multa turpia et inhonesta," *CCSL* 148A, 85; "indignas familiaritates extranearum mulierum," *CCSL* 148A, 94; "in adulterio deprehensi," *CCSL* 148A, 90.

[29] Specifically, he was accused of alienating houses belonging to his diocese without the consent of his fellow bishops, in violation of Agde (506), can. 7.

[30] *CCSL* 148A, 85.

divided, however, on the length of time Contumeliosus should be suspended from office. Some of his colleagues believed he should be suspended from the position only while he performed his penance. Others, including Caesarius, maintained that he should be permanently deposed from office. Precedents could be cited for both positions.[31] It was a sign of the deep loyalty that Contumeliosus commanded among his colleagues and of Caesarius's lack of influence over his suffragans that all efforts to agree on this point failed. The council therefore left unresolved both the duration of Contumeliosus's penance and the question of his continuation in office.

In response to this blow against his authority, Caesarius once again appealed to the bishop of Rome for confirmation of his position. Boniface had died in October 532, and was succeeded after a long vacancy by the priest Mercurius, consecrated in January 533, who took the name John II.[32] In April 534, the pontiff responded with three letters, addressed to the bishops of Gaul, the clergy of Riez, and Caesarius.[33] As requested, he upheld Caesarius's view. He ordered Contumeliosus to be suspended from office, and to submit to Caesarius a signed and dated confession, which suggests that he had already recanted his previous confession to the council.[34] In his place a visitor was to be appointed to run the diocese until a new bishop could be elected. John supported his position with a selection of evidence from papal letters and church councils.[35] To these Caesarius added his own canons, accompanied by a sharply worded letter to his suffragan bishops, in which he argued that the desire to have mercy on Contumeliosus was misguided since no one but God could truly pardon his sins.[36] The angry tone of this letter and the fact that he felt compelled to write it reveals the depth of opposition Caesarius faced among his own suffragans.

What Rome could give, however, it could also take away. Pope John died on May 8, 535, and was succeeded a few days later by the archdeacon Agapitus, whom Symmachus had ordained in 502.[37] With the help of a *defensor* of the Roman church named Emeritus, Contumeliosus appealed his case to Rome. He had chosen the right

---

[31] Arnold, 374–78.

[32] He was the first pope to change his name, probably to avoid connotations of paganism, Caspar, *Geschichte des Papsttums*, II, 199.   [33] *CCSL* 148A, 86–87.

[34] Arnold, 379.   [35] *CCSL* 148A, 88–89.   [36] Ibid., 89–95.

[37] *LP* I, 285 and 286, n. 5; J. Richards, *The Popes and the Papacy in the Early Middle Ages, 476–752* (London, 1979), 127.

moment to do so. Because Agapitus was not a Gothic partisan, he
was less likely to feel bound by the decisions of his immediate
predecessors. The offspring of a noble Roman family,[38] his first act
in office had been to order the documents of anathema issued
against Dioscorus by Boniface destroyed.[39] This is not to say that
Agapitus was not consecrated with the approval of King
Theodahad, for in the wake of the murder of Amalasuintha and
the threat of war with Justinian, a Roman who could find favor in
Constantinople was just the sort of pope he needed to have.[40] But
in addition to his services to the Goths, Agapitus also appears to
have acted independently of the king in the interests of the Roman
church. On July 18, 535, after Emeritus erroneously informed him
that Contumeliosus had received Caesarius's permission to return
to his church,[41] the pope ordered a retrial, which was to be
conducted by a commission appointed in Rome rather than a
Gallic synod.[42] In the meantime, he permitted the bishop to live in
Riez in full possession of his property, although he prohibited him
from celebrating Mass in the diocese or managing church
property. In reversing Pope John's support for Caesarius, Agapitus
acted both to distance himself from his predecessor, and to curb
the power of the metropolitan of Arles.[43] It did not hurt that
Contumeliosus had already declared his ardent support for the
papacy by taking the unusual step in his signature of the canons of
Vaison of further underscoring his support for canon 4: "I
Contumeliosus have consented to every point in such a way that
when the holy pope of Rome has given his offering, let us recite his
name before the altar of the Lord."[44]

In the affair of Contumeliosus we have perhaps the clearest
indication of Caesarius's incapacity to impose his own vision of
church reform and church order upon his suffragan bishops.
Indeed, Contumeliosus may be taken as the most visible representative of a class of cultivated and high-ranking bishops who
rejected Caesarius's calls for radical changes in their pastoral

[38] Caspar, *Geschichte des Papsttums*, II, 200.   [39] *LP* I, 287.
[40] For Agapitus's embassy to Constantinople in 535/36, see *LP* I, 287–88.
[41] *CCSL* 148A, 97, lines 25–27; Arnold, 390, n. 1247.   [42] *CCSL* 148A, 96–97.
[43] Arnold, 389–90.
[44] "Contumeliosus ita consensi in omnibus, ut, cum sanctus papa Urbis suam oblatam
dederit, recitemus ante altarium Domini," *CCSL* 148A, 80. The meaning of *suam
oblatam* here is obscure. Arnold thought it referred to offerings of consecrated bread
(*eulogiae*) that the bishop of Rome sent to other sees, 354, n. 1142. *Eulogiae* in fact could
be gifts of various kinds; see A. Stuiber, "Eulogia," *RAC* VI (1966), col. 925.

practices and way of life, and continued to run their dioceses and live their lives as they saw fit. Besides Contumeliosus, this group included Agroecius of Antibes and those unnamed suffragans who opposed Caesarius's hard-line actions at the Council of Marseille, and resisted his efforts at the councils of 524–29 to promote the kinds of pastoral reform he had initiated in his own diocese. Their independence from Caesarius was demonstrated not only by their continued unwillingness to promulgate his most radical reforms, but also by their reluctance to abide by the reforms to which they did agree. In the past Caesarius had relied on papal intervention to fortify his own faltering authority. His failure to win even that assistance in 535 signals a further decline in his political position.

On the same day he issued his decision on Contumeliosus, Agapitus sent Caesarius another unfavorable decision. In keeping with the decisions of the Roman council of 502, which he had attended as a deacon,[45] Agapitus prohibited Caesarius from alienating church property on behalf of the poor.[46] It is uncertain exactly which church property and which poor he meant. Commentators have generally assumed that the property belonged to the church of Arles, as in the previous requests Caesarius had made to the bishops of Rome.[47] Caspar suggested, however, that the property belonged to the Roman patrimony in the territory of Arles, and that Caesarius was asking the pope for a gift of some of this land.[48] This suggestion is supported by Agapitus's comment that his refusal was not due to parsimony (*tenacitatis studio*). But the actual ownership of the land is less important than the identity of the poor Caesarius intended to support with it. Were they the "poor" virgins of the women's monastery, as in his requests to Popes Symmachus and Hormisdas? We do not know for certain, but such an intention would not be inconsistent with other steps he took at this time to guarantee the security and independence of the women's monastery.

PROTECTING THE WOMEN'S MONASTERY

From the very beginning, Caesarius had placed control over the monastery in the hands of his own family: himself, his sister Caesaria, his niece Caesaria, and his nephew Teridius. He realized,

---

[45] *MGH AA*, XII, 443. [46] Caesarius, *ep.* 15.
[47] Arnold, 388; Malnory, 119; Lesne, *Histoire de la propriété*, I, 294.
[48] Caspar, *Geschichte des Papsttums*, II, 205, n. 8.

however, that a family devoted to celibacy could not retain control over it into future generations. As he reached the end of his life, he therefore began to take further steps to ensure the institution's survival and independence after his death.

The first of these steps was to produce a final version of the monastery's rule (*reg. virg.* 48). In keeping with this intention, Caesarius composed a *recapitulatio* of the rule, which he issued on June 22, 534. To add to its authority he noted in three places that he had written the document in his own hand.[49] Moreover, in addition to signing it himself, he had it signed by seven of his suffragans, as he had also done with Pope Hormisdas's letter of exemption. In large part the *recapitulatio* simply summarized and expanded on regulations that appeared in earlier versions of the rule. It laid particular stress on the maintenance of a strict cloister (*reg. virg.* 50, 53, 54, 59, 73), the rejection of personal property (*reg. virg.* 52), the proper conduct of the common life (*reg. virg.* 51, 57), and the practice of an ascetic lifestyle (*reg. virg.* 55, 56, 60). But this document also introduced two new measures designed to ensure the independence of the monastery from Caesarius's successors. First, it provided a mechanism for the selection of future abbesses. They were no longer to be appointed by the bishop of Arles, as Caesaria the Elder and Caesaria the Younger had been, but were to be chosen by the sisters themselves, on the grounds of merit rather than popularity, noble birth, wealth, or kinship (*reg. virg.* 61). This was precisely the same right the Council of Arles had confirmed for the monks of Lérins in 449/61.[50] Second, it warned the sisters (*reg. virg.* 48, 62) and especially their leaders (*reg. virg.* 64) not to make any changes in the rule. In particular, Caesarius warned abbesses against falling under the control of future bishops of Arles "either because of kinship or for any other reason" and against making changes in the rule that would compromise the autonomy, isolation, or security of the monastery. It was at this juncture that Caesarius reminded the nuns of the privileges granted by Pope Hormisdas *c.* 515 which could be used, as could the *recapitulatio* itself, to defend their lands and their institution from episcopal interference.

Caesarius also produced two other documents around this time. One was a rule for monks based upon his final version of the rule

---

[49] *reg. virg.* 49 (Morin II, 115, lines 14, 27), 64 (Morin II, 119, line 16).
[50] *CCSL* 148, 134; de Vogüé and Courreau, 244, n. 61.

for nuns.[51] Much shorter than the rule for nuns, it may have been written for the men's monastery in Arles. After the bishop's death, the rule was transmitted by Caesarius's nephew Teridius to other monasteries.[52] The other, more important document was the final version of his testament.[53] It served two purposes: to distribute to his heirs and other beneficiaries what little personal property he owned, and more importantly, to confirm the arrangements he had made during his lifetime for his monastery's well-being. Toward this end, he designated two heirs, the monastery for women and his successor in the see of Arles, and appealed to both abbess and bishop to abide by the arrangements he had made for the monastery's protection.[54] Embodied in the form of a will, these appeals acquired added force, since heirs were legally obliged to honor testamentary provisions.

Caesarius made specific bequests to his heirs and other beneficiaries. To his successor in the see of Arles, Caesarius bequeathed his paschal vestments and some articles of personal clothing,[55] along with his chamber servants.[56] To the monastery for women, he bequeathed his slave Agritia, quite possibly given to him by Liberius's wife of the same name.[57] To the abbess Caesaria he bequeathed a cloak.[58] The rest of his personal effects were to be divided up at his death among his clerical and lay attendants,[59] the priest Leo,[60] and his biographer Bishop Cyprianus.[61] Small gifts he had made to his slave Bricianus were confirmed, but not specified, as were gifts made to others during his lifetime.[62]

Of much greater importance than these bequests were the specific provisions Caesarius made for his monastery's independence and financial security. These were directed chiefly at his successor, who might be tempted, as Caesarius feared, to meddle in the monastery's internal affairs or to seize its property or revenues for his own use. Since the fifth century, when monasteries were first established in Gaul, bishops had attempted to exercise

---

[51] de Vogüé, "La Règle."   [52] Morin II, 149.

[53] de Vogüé and Courreau, 362–64. On its authenticity, initially denied by Krusch, see G. Morin, "Le testament de S. Césaire d'Arles et la critique de M. Bruno Krusch," *RBen* 16 (1899), 97–112. For Krusch's later admission of error, see *MGH SRM*, IV, 770–71.

[54] *test.*, 283, line 16–284, line 2. See further, Klingshirn, "Caesarius's Monastery," 460–62.

[55] *test.*, 284, lines 15–16.   [56] *test.*, 289, lines 12–13.

[57] *test.*, 289, lines 10–11. Although individual sisters in the monastery were prohibited by the rule (7) from owning slaves, the monastery as such was not.

[58] *test.*, 289, lines 5–6.   [59] *test.*, 285, lines 1–3.   [60] *test.*, 289, line 7.

[61] *test.*, 289, lines 7–8.   [62] *test.*, 289, lines 8–9, 11–12.

progressively greater control over them: to authorize their initial foundations,[63] regulate their clergy,[64] restrict their rights over their own property,[65] and supervise their abbots and abbesses.[66] Increasingly, bishops began to realize that it was in their interest to treat monasteries as the organizational equivalent of parishes, their rights of control and supervision over which could not be questioned.[67] Monasteries and their founders viewed these developments with alarm, and, by the seventh century, conciliar legislation and charters of immunity began to reflect a growing concern not with preventing abuses by abbots, but with preventing abuses by bishops, particularly the despoliation of monasteries.[68]

Caesarius had already taken steps to protect the monastery from such abuses through the monastic rule and the letter of Hormisdas. In his testament, he confirmed these and added new provisions. To give the monastery maximum control over its relations with the outside world, and as a corollary to its right to elect its own abbess, he insisted that it be permitted to appoint its own steward and its own priest for the burial church of St. Mary.[69] In addition, he directed his successor to allow the steward of the monastery to live in a cell in the atrium of the cathedral church, both to protect his reputation and to allow him to watch over the monastery's interests from the center of ecclesiastical administration, where the greatest power for the monastery and the greatest threat against it might be exercised.[70]

Caesarius was particularly concerned about actions his successors might take to deplete the monastery's resources. First, he feared an attempt to remove from the monastery's control those lands or funds which it owned outright.

And although I shall take for granted your piety, lord bishop, nevertheless, in the fear that you might by chance adopt the dangerous suggestions of others to the detriment of our monastery, I entreat you earnestly by the Father, the Son, and the Holy Spirit, and by the fearful

---

[63] Agde (506), can. 27; Orléans (511), can. 22; Epaone (517), can. 10.

[64] Arles (449/61); Orléans (538), can. 21.

[65] Epaone (517), can. 8; Orléans (538), can. 26; Orléans (541), can. 11.

[66] Orléans (511), can. 7; Orléans (533), can. 21.

[67] Epaone (517), can. 8; Orléans (538), can. 21; Gregory of Tours, *hist.* IX. 40; T. P. McLaughlin, *Le Très Ancien Droit monastique de l'Occident* (Paris, 1935), 137.

[68] Paris (614), can. 10; Chalon (647/53), can. 7; McLaughlin, *Le Très Ancien Droit*, 137, 152–67.   [69] *test.*, 285, lines 10–13.   [70] *test.*, 285, lines 5–10.

day of the Last Judgment, that the ancient enemy might never prevail over you in such a way that you allow your servants to be unjustly saddened or that you permit any of the possessions that we have bestowed upon them to be taken away from them.[71]

To justify the monastery's separate ownership of property and protect it from confiscation by the bishop, Caesarius referred to a number of properties in this category. For instance, to refute the objection that his generosity to the monastery had been unfair to the church, he compared for a single estate the amount of land that he had granted to the monastery with that left in the control of the church. The ratio was 3 : 1 in favor of the church for arable and 10 : 3 in favor of the church for vineyards.[72] At another point in the will he referred to property that had come into the monastery's possession after a sale of lands deemed useless to the church, which was alienated in strict adherence to canons 7 and 45 of the Council of Agde. He implored his successor to allow the monastery to keep what had been legally transferred to it from the church.[73] He also confirmed in general the donations he had made to the monastery.[74]

The second threat Caesarius feared was an attempt to deprive the monastery of the income from properties that belonged to the church of Arles, but were reserved for the support of the nuns of St. John.[75] To prevent this from happening, he listed the properties in this category, carefully distinguishing them from the properties in the first category by the stipulation that they belonged to the church "with every right."[76]

Caesarius's last fear was that his successor might not allow the monastery any share in new gifts presented by pious Christians for the joint benefit of church and monastery. In a way, this was the most important concern of all, because gifts from outside donors constituted the only category of monastic property likely to grow after Caesarius's death. He exhorted his successor to respect donors' wishes. "for this reason, holy bishop, I earnestly entreat you that if almighty God should give any greater gift to this holy

---

[71] *test.*, 285, lines 14–19. Cf. also *test.*, 285, lines 3–4 and 289, lines 4–5.

[72] *test.*, 287, line 11–288, line 1. The estate was the *agellus Ancharianus*, on which the church possessed about 100 *aripenni* of vines, and enough arable land to sow 300 *modii* of grain; the monastery, on the other hand, possessed 30 *aripenni* of vines and land capable of being sown with 100 *modii* of grain. For the calculations, see Klingshirn, *Life, Testament, and Letters*, ad loc.   [73] *test.*, 285, line 19–286, line 5.

[74] *test.*, 289, lines 4–5.   [75] *test.*, 288, lines 7–8.   [76] *test.*, 288, lines 1–8.

mother church and the monastery of holy virgins through the generosity of those who fear him, your holy love not detach one from the other."[77]

In his testament, Caesarius not only reminded his successor of his responsibilities toward the monastery; he also reminded the nuns of their duty to obey the bishop. Indeed, as the letter of Hormisdas had specified and Caesarius had repeated in instituting his monastery as heir, the bishop was permitted to exercise a general oversight over the monastery, and the sisters were expected to respect and obey him.[78] But his primary purpose in making this statement was clearly to underscore the point that obedient nuns were all the more deserving of the bishop's protection and support. "For we trust in God's mercy [that it will deign to inspire] all bishops to weigh out for you with a pure love what has been given by the pious, so that they permit you to lack nothing that is necessary for bodily sustenance."[79]

In general, then, Caesarius used his will to urge his immediate successor and all future successors to watch over his foundation. "I ask you again and again, holy bishop, through divine grace that above all you treat the monastery of holy virgins as having been entrusted to your very great care, and that you very kindly allow the community of these women to be provided for. And if anyone wishes to give you bad advice, dutifully answer that what was done or granted with the advice of the bishop not only should not, but cannot, in any way be reversed."[80] This exhortation was immediately followed by a reminder of the support Popes Symmachus and Hormisdas had extended to the monastery,[81] and of the financial benefits Caesarius had procured for the church of Arles. "[For] through my efforts, the wealth [of the church] has increased a great deal for you: it has almost doubled. In addition, through my humble self, merciful God has for the most part granted immunity from taxation [to the church], not only in the immediate vicinity of the city and within it, but also in the suburban villas."[82] It was by such provisions that Caesarius's testament became part of a valuable dossier of documents for the monastery's future use, which already included the letter of Hormisdas and the Rule, and would soon include the *vita Caesarii* as well.[83]

[77] *test.*, 288, lines 9–14.   [78] *test.*, 286, lines 6–10.   [79] *test.*, 286, lines 10–13.
[80] *test.*, 286, line 14–287, line 3.   [81] *test.*, 287, lines 3–4.
[82] *test.*, 287, lines 6–10.   [83] Klingshirn, "Caesarius's Monastery," 475.

THE FRANKISH TAKEOVER

In the summer of 535 war broke out between the empire and the Ostrogothic kingdom. Taking the offensive, Justinian sent Mundus to attack Gothic territory in Dalmatia,[84] and Belisarius against Sicily.[85] The unwarlike Theodahad vacillated between abandoning Italy to the Romans and defending his kingdom at any cost. At the end of November 536, when Belisarius had conquered Naples and threatened Rome, the city's Gothic nobility deposed Theodahad and replaced him with Vitigis, an army commander.[86] At the end of 536 or beginning of 537, in order to protect the kingdom's northern and western frontiers, and free up badly needed troops, Vitigis concluded negotiations with the Franks begun under Theodahad. Under the terms of the agreement, the Goths were to relinquish their holdings in Gaul and Alamannia, and pay an indemnity of 2,000 pounds of gold in return for Frankish support in their war against Justinian.[87] Provence was turned over to Childebert (*vita* I. 34; II. 45), and Alamannia to Theudebert.[88]

It was thus in late 536 or early 537 that the Franks took possession of Arles. The authors of the *vita* sought to absolve Caesarius of blame for this outcome. "There appeared in Arles, with tranquillity and peace and by God's consent, the kingdom of the most glorious Childebert, a most Catholic kingdom in Christ's name. The bishop did not betray the city, as the Arians charged, but rather prayed constantly for all" (*vita* II. 45). By "Arians" here, Messianus and Stephanus meant the Goths and their supporters, who stood to lose the most by a Gothic withdrawal to Italy. Their accusations of betrayal come as no surprise. Not only had Caesarius been accused of such machinations before, but in some respects he might have seemed to gain from Frankish control: his city would be ruled by a Catholic rather than an Arian king, and the dioceses across the Durance that he lost in 533/34 would once more fall under his metropolitan control. But Caesarius faced danger in this outcome at the same time. Abandonment by the Goths meant losing the independence he had

---

[84] Procopius, *de bellis* v. 5. 2.   [85] Procopius, *de bellis* v. 5. 6.

[86] Jordanes, *Getica* 309; Procopius, *de bellis* v. 11. 1–9.

[87] Procopius, *de bellis* v. 13. 14; Buchner, *Die Provence*, 4; E. Zöllner, *Geschichte der Franken bis zur Mitte des 6. Jahrhunderts* (Munich, 1970), 88–89.

[88] Agathias, *hist.* 1. 6. 6.

been able to exercise in southern Gaul, where the Arian identity of the Goths, and the distance between Arles and Ravenna, had left him relatively free from interference in church matters. Annexation by the Franks, on the other hand, meant enduring the kinds of meddling in church affairs that the Catholic identity of the Frankish nobility warranted, and their proximity encouraged. It is thus not at all clear that he thought that annexation by the Franks lay in his best interests, despite their orthodox Christology[89] and the chance to regain metropolitan control over his lost dioceses. Indeed, as it happened, while the Frankish takeover brought few changes to the civil administration of Arles and Provence, it markedly altered the balance of ecclesiastical power in the region.

When Childebert took over Provence, he left in place the existing Roman and Ostrogothic system of civil administration, and simply replaced its personnel. Franks took the place of Goths, and Gallo-Roman aristocrats the place of Italo-Roman aristocrats.[90] The Ostrogothic *praefectus praetorio Galliarum* became the Frankish *praefectus* (or *rector*) *Provinciae*,[91] a post the Gallo-Roman patrician Parthenius may have been the first to hold.[92] Frankish counts replaced Gothic counts, and Frankish soldiers Gothic soldiers. The local council probably continued to function as before.[93] Thus in 542, at the end of his life, Caesarius could commend the women's monastery not only to the bishops and clergy, but also to "the office of the prefect, the counts, and the citizens" (*vita* II. 47).

What changed the most for Caesarius after 536 was not the structure of civil and military power, but the balance of ecclesiastical power. Before 536 he had operated in Gothic Provence as the ecclesiastical equivalent of a praetorian prefect, with the full cooperation of the Goths and the bishops of Rome. As the sole metropolitan in this province, his only serious rivals had been senior suffragans like Agroecius and Contumeliosus. After 536, however, Provence was incorporated into the administrative structure of Childebert's kingdom and the larger Gallic church. While Caesarius retained control over his traditional province, he had become only one among several metropolitan bishops of Childebert's kingdom and the fifteen or so metropolitan bishops of the whole Frankish church. He was thus far more likely to see

---

[89] *pace* Malnory, 162.   [90] Buchner, *Die Provence*, 15–29.   [91] Ibid., 16.
[92] *vita* I. 49; Buchner, *Die Provence*, 91; *PLRE* II, 834.
[93] Buchner, *Die Provence*, 19–21.

his claims to power challenged by powerful colleagues. Moreover, Merovingian kings were more likely to intervene in church matters that directly concerned their interests. We can see the beginnings of this new order in the church councils of 538 and 541.

The first general council held in Childebert's kingdom after the annexation of Provence took place in May 538 at Orléans. Neither Caesarius nor any of his suffragans attended or sent representatives to it.[94] Their absence may simply suggest an uncertainty over the civil status of Provence. Possibly they awaited Justinian's ratification of the agreement between the Goths and the Franks before committing themselves to a Frankish council.[95] But it is also possible that a more fundamental disagreement was involved. Caesarius claimed after all to be the papal vicar of Gaul. That he had never tried to enforce this claim outside of Provence was due to political divisions outside of his control, not to limited ambition on his part. When Arles and Provence were turned over to the Franks, these political divisions were removed, and Caesarius could at last promote himself as the papal vicar for the whole of Frankish Gaul, or at least Childebert's share of it.[96] If he chose to press this claim, he might have objected to attending or allowing his suffragans to attend a general council that he himself did not call. That Caesarius could present himself as a rival source of authority in these times is clear from a story told in the *vita* of Albinus, bishop of Angers from *c.* 530 to *c.* 550. Having been forced by a synod of his fellow bishops to reverse his excommunication of a man guilty of incest, a penalty fully in accord with the Council of Orléans (538),[97] Albinus went to Arles to consult Caesarius, and ultimately prevailed by his authority.[98] Respect for Caesarius's authority is further demonstrated by the council's approval (can. 6) of several provisions from his councils of 506 and 524: the setting of minimum ages for deacons and

---

[94] C. de Clercq, *La Législation religieuse Franque de Clovis à Charlemagne* (Louvain and Paris, 1936), 20.

[95] Procopius, *de bellis* VII. 33. 3; Malnory, 162–63; Buchner, *Die Provence*, 15.

[96] Pope Vigilius may have reflected this new understanding of Caesarius's position when he charged him with supervising the penitence of a man guilty of incest, about whom King Theudebert had written for advice, Caesarius, *ep.* 17. Unfortunately, we do not know the identity or location of this penitent. If he belonged to Caesarius's province, as some of Theudebert's subjects undoubtedly did (Buchner, *Die Provence*, 8), the pope would have been writing to Caesarius in his capacity as metropolitan; if he did not belong to Caesarius's province, however, the pope would have been writing to Caesarius as vicar. [97] can. 11.

[98] Venantius Fortunatus, *vita Albini* xviii. 49–53.

priests,[99] the enforcement of a one-year period of preparation for laymen to be ordained as clerics,[100] and the barring from ordination of men married twice, the husbands of women married twice, and penitents.[101]

It was only with the Council of Orléans in 541 that Provençal bishops began to attend Frankish councils.[102] Sixteen of the twenty-three bishops from the province of Arles attended in person, and two sent representatives.[103] Prominent among those who attended was Maximus of Aix, who managed to reassert his metropolitan status by signing with the other metropolitan bishops and identifying himself as "the bishop of Narbonensis II."[104] This short-lived success[105] was made possible by the fact that Caesarius neither attended the council nor sent a representative to it. His absence has usually been attributed to the frailties of old age.[106] This might explain his absence from the council, but it does not explain his failure to send a representative, at least if he remained faithful to the principles he had recited to Ruricius of Limoges thirty-five years earlier (*ep.* 3). The explanation would rather appear to be political.[107] Caesarius simply did not see his claims to primacy taken seriously by his fellow bishops in the new order of the Frankish church, an interpretation that the council's favorable treatment of Maximus simply confirmed.[108] The choice of Orléans as the venue for general councils – a tradition that went back to Clovis – underscores the fact that the church's center of gravity had shifted away from Provence and into the Frankish heartland,[109] where Caesarius had little influence. His world was no longer Roman, but Merovingian. It is one symbol of this change that Orléans (541) was the last Gallic council to be dated by a consular formula: *Basilio console*.[110] Henceforth bishops used a regnal formula: *anno XXXVIII regni domni Childeberthi*.[111] The reason was not so much that bishops (or their kings) had come to prefer this formula, as that 541 was the last year in which a citizen

---

[99] Agde (506), can. 16, 17; Arles (524), can. 1.   [100] Arles (524), can. 2.
[101] Agde (506), can. 43; Arles (524), can. 3.   [102] de Clercq, *La Législation*, 27–28.
[103] For the list, see Pontal, *Synoden*, 87, n. 62.   [104] *CCSL* 148A, 142, line 11.
[105] By the Council of Orléans (549), the bishop of Aix could be found signing with the other suffragans, *CCSL* 148A, 159, line 302. See also Macon (585), *CCSL* 148A, 249, line 373.   [106] Pontal, *Synoden*, 87; Malnory, 164.   [107] Arnold, 394–95.
[108] Loening, *Geschichte des deutschen Kirchenrechts*, II, 75–84.
[109] Wallace-Hadrill, *The Frankish Church*, 99.   [110] *CCSL* 148A, 142, line 3.
[111] Orléans (549), *CCSL* 148A, 157, line 250. This formula first appeared at Orléans (533), *CCSL* 148A, 102.

consul was appointed. After Basilius, only emperors held this ancient office, rendering the formula unacceptable to other sovereigns.[112]

THE DEATH OF CAESARIUS

Caesarius died on August 27, 542 at the age of 72 (*vita* II. 46).[113] In recounting his last days and death, his biographers followed a standard hagiographical pattern.[114] They began with the topos of his last illness and his premonitions of death (*vita* II. 46), which were reportedly preceded two years earlier by a vision of the celestial glories to come (*vita* II. 36). They then recalled his last words, which were addressed not to his own clergy but to the women of his monastery on the thirtieth anniversary of its foundation (*vita* II. 48). Their narrative of his death the following day (*vita* II. 48) was followed by a typical account of the grief of the people as a whole and the cures worked by his relics (*vita* II. 39–44, 49). Finally they described his burial in the church of St. Mary alongside his sister Caesaria the Elder and her fellow nuns (*vita* II. 50).[115]

The function of this stylized account was not so much to relate the facts of Caesarius's demise as to lay the foundation for his future cult. Descriptions of his growing intimacy with God, his peaceful death, the lamentations of the entire community, the frenzied grasping for his relics, and the miracles they worked – all confirmed his portrait in the *vita* as a venerable and powerful holy man. The information that he was buried in a privileged holy place at the women's monastery,[116] which also retained relics of his clothing and vestments,[117] provided a focal point for his cult.

---

[112] A. Cameron and D. Schauer, "The Last Consul: Basilius and his Diptych," *JRS* 72 (1982), 126–45.

[113] For the date, see Klingshirn, "Church Politics and Chronology," 81–84.

[114] For an account of this pattern, see P. Boglioni, "La scène de la mort dans les premières hagiographies latines," in *Le Sentiment de la mort au moyen âge*, ed. C. Sutto (Montréal, 1979), 185–210, and G. Schieberreiter, *Der Bischof in merowingischer Zeit* (Vienna, 1983), 240–53.

[115] F. Benoit, "La tombe de saint Césaire d'Arles et sa restauration en 883," *Bulletin monumental* 94 (1935), 137–43.

[116] This place was in fact triply privileged since it was located within the walls of the city, in the floor of a consecrated church, and in the midst of the graves of holy women. See M. Fixot, "Les inhumations privilegiées en Provence," in *L'Inhumation privilégiée du IVᵉ au VIIIᵉ siècle en occident*, ed. Y. Duval and J.-Ch. Picard (Paris, 1986), 117–28: 118.   [117] Benoit, "Les reliques."

This cult operated principally for the benefit of the women's monastery. Indeed, having himself buried in the basilica of St. Mary rather than at the tomb of St. Genesius, where the bishops of Arles were traditionally buried, represented Caesarius's last act of protection for the monastery.[118] The fact that the basilica served as the burial place for a congregation of cloistered nuns need not have restricted access to Caesarius's grave. The basilica was clearly thought of as exterior to the cloister, whatever its location,[119] and the nuns themselves, who worshiped in an oratory located within the monastic enclosure,[120] were strictly prohibited by the rule from entering it.[121] Normal observance of the rule would thus have permitted the basilica to be left open to outsiders.

The usefulness of such veneration to the monastery seems clear. Not only could a cult of St. Caesarius encourage gift-giving to the monastery that guarded his relics. It could also help to ensure the monastery's independence and survival. Popular validation of the founder's sanctity could stimulate respect for his final wishes. Most importantly, a monastery's patron saint could be expected to retaliate if he sensed a threat to its well-being. When a group of Franks robbed the monastery of Latte, despite warnings that the place was protected by the relics of St. Martin, their boat was reported to have capsized in the river, killing them instantly.[122] It was through fear of their power that saints protected fragile foundations.

ARLES AFTER CAESARIUS

The full effects of Merovingian control over Arles and its church only began to appear after Caesarius's death. These effects included royal interference in the episcopal succession, involvement in the appointment of papal vicars, interest in the monastery of St. John, and eventually the city's demise as a political and ecclesiastical capital. A brief survey of the history of Arles from Caesarius's death in 542 to Charles Martel's conquest of Provence in 739 will demonstrate these effects. At the same time, because the history of the church in Merovingian Arles reflects the history of the larger Merovingian church, this narrative will provide the background

[118] Klingshirn, "Caesarius's Monastery," 471–72.
[119] de Vogüé and Courreau, 108.
[120] *reg. virg.* 36, 38, 69; de Vogüé and Courreau, 108, n. 2.
[121] *reg. virg.* 2, 50, 59. These passages speak simply of a *basilica*, which I would identify with the funerary *basilica* referred to in *reg. virg.* 70.
[122] Gregory of Tours, *hist.* IV. 48.

for our discussion in Chapter 10 of the later implementation of Caesarius's reform program.

Although Caesarius's death provided Childebert with an opportunity to install one of his own supporters in the see, he appears instead to have ratified the choice of the local clergy, a priest by the name of Auxanius, whose election Pope Vigilius praised as entirely regular.[123] Auxanius's lack of strong royal support, however, appears clear from the fact that he was forced to wait for over two years before his request for vicarial status was approved, a decision that was now effectively made by the king and the emperor on the recommendation of the pope.[124] When he was finally named papal vicar in May 545, his jurisdiction extended only as far as his own ecclesiastical province and Childebert's kingdom, a further sign of the limits of papal power and the increasing dependence of local bishops on secular rulers.[125] As vicar, Auxanius was directed to convene synods of the bishops under his jurisdiction and to supervise their movements abroad.[126] In 546, however, he died without having had an opportunity to exercise any of these powers.

Childebert took a direct role in the choice of Auxanius's successor. He selected Aurelianus, the twenty-three-year-old relative (probably son[127]) of the patrician Sacerdos, whom he had named metropolitan bishop of Lyon in 541 in return for his political support.[128] It was a sign of the king's favor (and Justinian's approval) that Aurelianus was almost immediately granted vicarial status by Pope Vigilius.[129] When Childebert convened the Council of Orléans in 549, Aurelianus ranked second in the signature list, just behind his father. The close connection between Aurelianus and the king is further demonstrated by their cooperation in the foundation of monasteries for men and women in Arles.[130] The building of churches and monasteries was an activity in which Childebert and his wife Ultrogotha were particularly interested:

---

[123] *ep. Arel.* 39. On the king's role in the appointment and approval of bishops, see D. Claude, "Die Bestellung der Bischöfe im merowingischen Reiche," *ZRG KA* 49 (1963), 1–75: 31–38.

[124] *ep. Arel.* 39. The delay may also have been due in part to the bubonic plague that afflicted the territory of Arles in 543, Gregory of Tours, *glor. mart.* 50; *hist.* IV. 5; *vita patrum* 6. 6. For a summary of its extent and its effects, see J.-N. Biraben and J. Le Goff, "La peste dans le Haut Moyen Age," *Annales ESC* 24 (1969), 1484–1510.

[125] *ep. Arel.* 40.   [126] *ep. Arel.* 40.

[127] Heinzelmann, *Bischofsherrschaft*, 136–37.   [128] Ibid., 146–52.

[129] *ep. Arel.* 43, 44 (August 23, 546).

[130] "iubente rege Childeberto," *regula ad monachos*, proemium, *PL* 68: 385.

these displays of patronage furnished opportunities for forging good relations with the Gallo-Roman cities under their control.[131] Located inside the city walls, probably on the site of the medieval church of Sainte-Croix,[132] the men's monastery in Arles was dedicated on November 17, 547.[133] Its first abbot was Florentinus, possibly a relative of Aurelianus,[134] who was installed on October 12, 547 and served until his death in April 553.[135] At the dedication of the monastery a number of relics were installed, including those of several local Gallic saints: Genesius, Hilarius (probably of Poitiers[136]), Martin of Tours, and Caesarius.[137] Childebert saw to it that the monastery was richly endowed,[138] and persuaded Pope Vigilius to grant it certain privileges of autonomy, including the right to manage its own property and the right to choose its own abbot.[139] The date of the foundation of the women's monastery is unknown, but it is plausibly assigned to the same year. The institution was located within the city walls, but exactly where is unknown.[140] Childebert probably cooperated with Aurelianus in founding and endowing this monastery too, which was dedicated to Mary.[141] In addition to founding these monasteries, Aurelianus wrote rules for both of them, largely modeled on Caesarius's rules for monks and nuns.[142]

It is not likely that Aurelianus's monasteries directly threatened the survival of the existing men's and women's monasteries in Arles, since his foundations were separately (and richly) funded by the royal family. But they did challenge the undivided prestige the older monasteries had enjoyed as the city's original (and only) monastic foundations. In addition, by adopting Caesarius's mon-

---

[131] Among other institutions, Childebert and his wife founded a *xenodochium* in Lyon and the church of St. Vincentius (later Saint-Germain-des-Prés) in Paris, where the king was buried; for details, see Prinz, *Frühes Mönchtum*, 153–57.

[132] Février, "Arles," 82–83.

[133] H. Atsma, "Die christlichen Inschriften Galliens als Quelle für Klöster und Klosterbewohner bis zum Ende des 6. Jahrhunderts," *Francia* 4 (1976), 1–57: 25. R. Collins has rightly argued against the view that Childebert temporarily lost control over the territory of Arles to Theudebert sometime between 546 and 548, "Theodebert I, 'Rex Magnus Francorum,'" in *Ideal and Reality in Frankish and Anglo-Saxon Society*, ed. P. Wormald with D. Bullough and R. Collins (Oxford, 1983), 7–33: 18–19.

[134] Heinzelmann, *Bischofsherrschaft*, 151, n. 356.   [135] *ILCV* 1644.

[136] Atsma, "Die christlichen Inschriften," 30.

[137] Aurelianus, *regula ad monachos*, PL 68: 396.   [138] *regula ad monachos* 54.

[139] Gregory the Great, *ep.* IX. 216.

[140] Aurelianus, *regula ad virgines*, PL 68: 399; Johannes, *ep. ad virgines monasterii Sanctae Mariae*, PL 72: 859. See also Février, "Arles," 83.

[141] Prinz, *Frühes Mönchtum*, 154–55; for the endowment, see Aurelianus, *regula ad virgines* 39.   [142] Texts available in *PL* 68: 385–404.

astic rules and incorporating his relics, these new foundations claimed for themselves an association with the prestige of St. Caesarius and threatened to displace the memory of his original connections with the city's first monasteries for men and women. Furthermore, with their large endowments and royal patronage, Aurelianus's monasteries were poised to attract wealthier recruits and supporters than Caesarius's monasteries, whose donations would further enrich the new monasteries rather than the old. The uncertain date of the *vita* of Caesarius makes it impossible to determine whether Caesaria the Younger originally commissioned the *vita* to counteract the attractions of Aurelianus's monastery for women. But even if she did not, this would soon have been recognized as a use for which the document was well suited.

Aurelianus died on June 16, 551,[143] and was buried in the family tomb in the church of Saint-Nizier in Lyon, where Sacerdos was to be buried a few months later. He was succeeded by Sapaudus, son of the patrician Placidus, who served as governor of Provence in the late 550s.[144] The fact that almost six years passed before he was finally granted the papal vicariate and *pallium* in February 557 should not be attributed to any lack of support from the king, but rather to the fact that Pope Vigilius spent the last eight years of his life at Justinian's court embroiled in the controversy over the Three Chapters. It was only with the consecration of Pope Pelagius in April 556, itself a contentious affair, that Sapaudus was granted the status he sought.[145] Even without official status as papal vicar, however, Sapaudus enjoyed royal and papal favor. In 551 King Childebert placed him in charge of a general council he convened in Paris.[146] Moreover, as soon as Pelagius was elected bishop of Rome and before he had even reached the city, Sapaudus could be found serving as his intermediary with the bishops of Gaul, the king, and royal officials.[147] After the death of his patron in 558, Bishop Sapaudus continued to hold a position of political prominence in the Gallic church, first under Childebert's brother Chlothar from 558 to 561 and then under Chlothar's son Guntram.

---

[143] For his epitaph, see *CE* 2100.

[144] *ep. Arel.* 49 (December 14, 556), 53 (April 13, 557). [145] *ep. Arel.* 50.

[146] This council is usually dated to 552. But if Sacerdos died in September 551 rather than September 552, as Heinzelmann has argued (*Bischofsherrschaft*, 130, n. 211), then the Council of Paris must have taken place in the summer of 551, since Gregory of Tours (*hist.* IV. 36) says that Sacerdos died shortly after the council that deposed Saffrac of Paris.   [147] *ep. Arel.* 47–49.

In 558/59 Pope Pelagius wrote to him to defend his support for the fifth ecumenical council and to call for an end to idolatry and the irregular promotion of laymen to the episcopate.[148] In 573 Sapaudus was the first bishop to sign the letter the Council of Paris sent to King Sigibert to reproach him for violating the rights of jurisdiction of the bishop of Chartres.[149] In 583/85 he signed the acts of the Council of Valence ahead of his fellow metropolitans Priscus of Lyon and Evantius of Vienne.[150] Finally, although he did not attend the Council of Macon in 585, the representative he sent signed ahead of other representatives.[151]

The reputation of Caesarius's monastery for women continued to spread under Sapaudus, who took steps at the Council of Arles in 554 to confirm episcopal responsibility for monasteries, and to ensure in particular that abbesses observed their rules.[152] Although this is a direct reflection of Caesarius's own advice in the *regula virginum*, and suggests that his wishes for the monastery's autonomy continued to be respected after his death, it also signals Sapaudus's attempt to solidify his control over the city's most prestigious institution. It is one measure of the monastery's continued reputation for success that Queen Radegund decided to adopt its rule for the monastery she founded in Poitiers, after having received a copy of it from Caesaria the Younger between 552 and 557.[153] Caesaria the Younger died shortly after this in *c.* 560. She was succeeded by Liliola, who presided as abbess until 574.[154] The monastery continued to attract royal interest during her term in office. Radegund visited the institution in *c.* 570 to win support at a time of difficulty for her own foundation.[155] It may have been at this time that she obtained copies of important documents in the monastery's dossier, such as Caesarius's *testamentum*, which she had certainly read, and his *vita*, which her

---

[148] *MGH Ep.*, III, 442–45. For the date, see P. M. Gasso and C. M. Batlle, *Pelagii I papae epistolae quae supersunt* (Montserrat, 1956), *ep.* 19.

[149] *CCSL* 148A, 216, line 36.   [150] *CCSL* 148A, 235, line 31.

[151] *CCSL* 148A, 249, line 369.

[152] Arles (554), can. 2, 3, 5. See Orléans (511), can. 19.

[153] This dating is based on Caesaria's statement in her letter to Richild and Radegund that she was also sending along a copy of the rule of Caesarius: "Ego feci quod praecepistis: transmisi exemplar de regula, quam nobis beatae et sanctae recordationis domnus papa Caesarius fecit," de Vogüé and Courreau, 486 (= *MGH Ep.*, III, 451). On the contradictory account offered by Gregory of Tours, *hist.* IX.40, see de Vogüé and Courreau, 444–48.   [154] de Vogüé and Courreau, 30, 440–41.

[155] Gregory of Tours, *hist.* IX. 40; R. Aigrain, "Le voyage de Sainte Radegonde à Arles," *Bulletin philologique et historique* (1926–27), 119–27; de Vogüé and Courreau, 448–50.

biographer Baudonivia liberally quoted.[156] With its provisions for strict cloister, Caesarius's monastery could also serve the king as a place of permanent exile for political opponents. In *c.* 567, Guntram sent Theudechild, wife of the recently deceased King Charibert, to live out the rest of her life in "a monastery in Arles."[157] If this was Caesarius's monastery for women – and the connection between Liliola and Guntram through Bishop Syagrius of Autun suggests that it was[158] – Liliola would then have been the abbess who prevented Theudechild from escaping and kept her imprisoned in the cloister. Under different circumstances the abbey's strict provisions for cloister could also make it a welcome refuge. In 561 Liliola welcomed into the monastery the five-year-old Rusticula, whom Syagrius of Autun and King Guntram helped to escape an unwanted engagement.[159] When Liliola died in 574, it was the eighteen-year-old Rusticula who succeeded her.[160] The monastery's reputation as a place of refuge persisted under Rusticula, who was falsely accused in 613 of having hidden the young Childebert II there to prevent his capture by Chlothar II.[161] Forced to leave the cloister for a hearing before the king, she was exonerated and permitted to return to Arles, where she remained until her death in *c.* 632.[162]

It was during Sapaudus's tenure in Arles that the seeds of the city's demise as a political capital (and hence an ecclesiastical center) were sown. When Childebert died without heirs in 558, his kingdom fell into the hands of Clovis's last surviving son Chlothar I.[163] At his death in 561, the unified Frankish kingdom he ruled – the remainder had come under his control in 555 at the death of Theudebert's son Theudebald – was divided among his four sons, just as Clovis's kingdom had been in 511.[164] Provence was divided between two brothers. Guntram, whose main possessions lay in Burgundy, took possession of most of the region, including Arles.

[156] Klingshirn, "Caesarius's Monastery," 474–80.
[157] Gregory of Tours, *hist.* IV. 26.
[158] *vita Rusticulae* 3; Gregory of Tours, *vita patrum* 8. 10.   [159] *vita Rusticulae* 3.
[160] *vita Rusticulae* 7.
[161] Fredegar, *chronica* IV. 42; *vita Rusticulae* 9; P. Riché, "Note d'hagiographie mérovingienne: La vita S. Rusticulae," *Analecta Bollandiana* 72 (1954), 369–77: 373–75.
[162] *vita Rusticulae* 10–17.
[163] Gregory of Tours, *hist.* IV. 20; James, *Franks*, 169; E. Ewig, "Die fränkischen Teilungen und Teilreiche (511–613)," in his *Spätantikes und fränkisches Gallien*, I, 114–71: 133–35.
[164] Gregory of Tours, *hist.* IV. 22; Buchner, *Die Provence*, 10; Ewig, "Die fränkischen Teilungen," 135–38.

Sigibert received Marseille and parts of the territories of Aix and Avignon, which formed a corridor between his possessions in the Auvergne and the sea. To rule his possessions in Provence, Sigibert established his own governor in Marseille, which thereby became a separate regional capital.[165] In time, he sought to occupy the entire region. Although he took Arles in *c.* 568, Guntram regained it, reportedly because of a trick played on Sigibert's army by Bishop Sapaudus.[166] At Guntram's death in 592, however, Sigibert's heir Childebert II gained possession of the whole of Provence.[167] For strategic and political reasons he chose to keep the governor's residence at Marseille.[168] Arles remained important as a port,[169] but except at times when the region was divided, Marseille served as its capital.[170] Although these changes did not affect the metropolitan status of the bishop of Arles, they did weaken his claim to a larger role in the Merovingian church as papal vicar, since Pope Symmachus had originally bestowed the vicariate on Caesarius in large part because of the city's status as a provincial capital. The loss of this justification clearly contributed to the diminished prestige of Sapaudus's successors.

When Sapaudus died in 586, he was succeeded by Licerius, the referendary of King Guntram, who held the see for only two years.[171] At Licerius's death in 588, acting on the recommendation of Bishop Syagrius of Autun, Guntram appointed as his successor Virgilius, the abbot of the monastery of St. Symphorian in Autun.[172] Two years later, on September 3, 590, Gregory the Great succeeded Pelagius as bishop of Rome. It was not, however, until August 12, 595, that Gregory honored a joint request from Virgilius and King Childebert for the *pallium* and papal vicariate. The delay may indicate that Virgilius lacked support from a king who had not appointed him, or that the pope was in no particular hurry to fill a position that had lost most of its political significance anyway.[173] When the honor was finally conferred, in addition to its traditional responsibilities, Gregory directed Virgilius to work with the king and his fellow bishops for the reform of the Gallic church.[174] Specifically, he urged his vicar to eliminate simony and the promotion of bishops directly from the laity. In later

---

[165] Buchner, *Die Provence*, 22; Gregory of Tours, *hist.* IV. 43. For the commercial importance of Marseille at this time, see Loseby, "Marseille."
[166] Gregory of Tours, *hist.* IV. 30.   [167] Buchner, *Die Provence*, 11.
[168] Ibid., 23.   [169] Ibid., 45.   [170] Ibid., 13.
[171] Gregory of Tours, *hist.* VIII. 39.   [172] Gregory of Tours, *hist.* IX. 23.
[173] Gregory the Great, *ep.* V. 58.   [174] *ep.* V. 59, 60.

correspondence to Gaul, he also condemned, along with simony, the use of ties of kinship or patronage to achieve the episcopacy.[175] He demanded, moreover, that idolatry be suppressed,[176] that clerics cease cohabitation with women,[177] and that a nun's right to resist forcible marriage be enforced.[178] These complaints had been previously raised by Gallic bishops themselves, including Caesarius. But it was increasingly unlikely that the bishops of Gaul could promote the sorts of reform Gregory demanded without the cooperation of their rulers. Gregory accordingly addressed additional appeals for reform directly to the Merovingian royalty. When Childebert II died in March 596, Gregory appealed to the king's mother Brunhild,[179] and to his heirs and sons Theuderic II and Theudebert II,[180] for whom she served as regent. While such appeals did not bypass the papal vicar entirely, they did indicate his relative lack of power. Virgilius's weak position was confirmed and further undermined in September 597 when Gregory acceded to Brunhild's wish that Syagrius of Autun, one of her strongest allies,[181] be awarded a *pallium* as well, although he was only a suffragan bishop in the province of Lyon.[182] Two years later Gregory directed that Syagrius lead the reform synod he urged Brunhild to convene.[183] This was a role traditionally reserved for the papal vicar, and Gregory's conferral of it on Syagrius strongly suggests not so much Virgilius's lack of ardor for reform as his inability to promote it effectively.[184]

It was not, however, Brunhild or her grandchildren who answered the pope's call for a reform synod, but Chlothar II, king of Neustria, who gained control over the whole Frankish kingdom by deposing Brunhild in 613. The following year he convened two national councils in Paris, one for bishops and the other for bishops and lay aristocrats together.[185] Widely considered the greatest of the Merovingian councils,[186] the Council of Paris assembled twelve of the fourteen metropolitans in the Frankish realm and sixty-seven other bishops.[187] The council was led by

[175] *ep.* VIII. 4.   [176] *ep.* VIII. 4.   [177] *ep.* IX. 218.   [178] *ep.* IX. 224.
[179] *ep.* VIII. 4; IX. 213; XI. 49.   [180] *ep.* IX. 215; XI. 47; XI. 50.
[181] J. L. Nelson, "Queens as Jezebels: The Careers of Brunhild and Balthild in Merovingian History," in *Medieval Women*, ed. D. Baker (Oxford, 1978), 31–77: 52–57, esp. 55.   [182] *ep.* VIII. 4.   [183] *ep.* IX. 213, 222.
[184] Indeed, Virgilius's career as an abbot, tolerance for the forced baptism of Jews (Gregory, *ep.* I. 45), and later reputation for sanctity (*vita Virgilii, Acta Sanctorum*, March, vol. 1, [Paris and Rome, 1865], 397–402) all testify to a particular zeal for the church.   [185] de Clercq, *La Législation*, 57–62.
[186] Wallace-Hadrill, *Frankish Church*, 104–5.   [187] Pontal, *Synoden*, 183–84.

Aridius of Lyon and not by Virgilius's successor Florianus of Arles, who signed second. Although he had been awarded the *pallium* by Pope Boniface IV in 613 at the request of Brunhild's grandson Theuderic II, Florianus did not receive the vicariate that traditionally accompanied it, a clear indication that the ecclesiastical pre-eminence of Arles had come to an end.[188] At their synod, among other reforms, the bishops condemned the payment of gifts or money for episcopal office and demanded elections by the clergy and people.[189] Eight days later, the king issued an edict to the council of bishops and laymen.[190] He affirmed several of the bishops' canons, including prohibitions against a bishop's consecration of his own successor[191] and forcible marriage to a woman vowed to religious life.[192] Most importantly, however, he declined to forbid simony or rule out the royal appointment of bishops,[193] and revised a number of other canons in favor of royal interests as well.[194] His actions made it clear that even a reform-minded king was not prepared to give the church the kind of autonomy its leaders sought for themselves.

The Council of Paris was the last Merovingian council known to have been attended by a bishop of Arles. No bishop from the province of Arles attended the Council of Clichy in 626. Florianus's successor Theodosius (*fl.* 630/50)[195] refused to attend the Council of Chalon-sur-Saône in 647/53, after learning upon his arrival that he would be charged with leading an "unseemly way of life and violating the canons."[196] For his refusal to answer charges against him, Theodosius was suspended from office until the next council; his subsequent fate is unknown. Only three of his immediate successors can be confirmed: Johannes (*fl.* 660/68), Felix (*fl.* 679), and Wolbertus (*fl.* 683).[197] After Wolbertus a secure list of the bishops of Arles does not resume until 794 when Bishop Elifantus held the see.[198] This interruption might not signal a break in the episcopate itself – Paris B.N. lat. 2812, a sacramentary

---

[188] For the award of the *pallium*, see *MGH Ep.*, III, 454. On the new ecclesiastical pre-eminence of Lyon, see H. Mordek, *Kirchenrecht und Reform im Frankenreich* (Berlin and New York, 1975), 70–79. [189] Paris (614), can. 2.
[190] *Edict of Paris*, ed. A. Boretius, *MGH Capit.*, I, 20–23. [191] *Edict* 2 = can. 3.
[192] *Edict* 18 = can. 15. [193] *Edict* 1. [194] *Edict* 3, 4, 6, 7.
[195] *vita Rusticulae* 25.
[196] *epistula synodi ad Theodorium Arelatensem episcopum*, *CCSL* 148A, 310.
[197] Duchesne I, 260–61.
[198] Duchesne I, 261. Elifantus is attested by can. 8 of the Council of Frankfurt (794), *MGH Conc.*, II, 1. 167, which tried once again to settle the longstanding dispute between the bishops of Arles and Vienne over metropolitan control.

of the church of Arles dated to *c.* 900, lists eleven bishops between Wolbertus and Elifantus[199] – but rather a gap in the flow of evidence, especially the signature lists of church councils and other ecclesiastical documents, that would verify and date these names.

The causes of this interruption in the episcopal *fasti* of Arles were largely political. Like other regions of Gaul, Provence began to fall out to effective Merovingian control after 639 when Chlothar's son Dagobert died and left his kingdom to his minor sons Sigibert III and Clovis II. Over the next century power increasingly lay in the hands of local dukes, who often ruled independently of both the Merovingians and their mayors of the palace.[200] Closely connected to these rulers by ties of kinship, patronage, and common interest, bishops showed little enthusiasm for ecclesiastical responsibilities. Those who met at the last three Merovingian councils whose canons survive – Bordeaux (662/75), Autun (663/80), and Saint-Jean-de-Losne (673/75) – had to urge their colleagues to say Mass in their own cathedrals on Easter, Christmas, and Pentecost,[201] to preach to their congregations on Sundays and feast days,[202] to live in a spiritual fashion,[203] and not to carry weapons[204] or spend their time hunting.[205] None of these canons was entirely new, but their cumulative effect points to a deeply troubled church.[206] The fact that no councils are attested in Gaul between the diocesan synod of Auxerre in 692/96 and the German council in 743 signals further disorganization in the Frankish church.[207] Reform traditions were kept alive during this period not primarily in episcopal sees, but in monasteries such as Corbie, where the collection of canons known as the Vetus Gallica received its final redaction in the second quarter of the eighth century.[208]

With the consolidation of political power in the 730s by Charles

---

[199] Duchesne I, 250.

[200] A. R. Lewis, "The Dukes in the *Regnum Francorum*, A.D. 550–751," *Speculum* 51 (1976), 381–410: 399–408; P. Geary, *Before France and Germany: The Creation and Transformation of the Merovingian World* (New York and Oxford, 1988), 204–8.

[201] Saint-Jean-de-Losne (673/75), can. 8. At the Council of Agde, bishops had urged Christians to take communion on at least these three days.

[202] Saint-Jean-de-Losne (673/75), can. 18.

[203] Bordeaux (662/75), can. 4; Saint-Jean-de-Losne (673/75), can. 10.

[204] Bordeaux (662/75), can. 1; Saint-Jean-de-Losne (673/75), can. 2.

[205] Saint-Jean-de-Losne (673/75), can. 15.

[206] Wallace-Hadrill, *Frankish Church*, 106–7.

[207] For the date of the Council of Auxerre, see *CCSL* 148A, 323; for the date of the German council, see *infra*, p. 275, n. 14.   [208] Mordek, *Kirchenrecht und Reform*, 86.

Martel, ruler of Austrasia, the political prerequisites for a well-ordered church began to be put into place. After his victory over the Muslims at Poitiers in 732, Charles began to make war on the rulers of other Frankish subkingdoms. He turned to Provence in 736 after securing Burgundy (733)[209] and Aquitaine (735).[210] According to the Continuator of Fredegar, "he subjected to his rule the chief men and officials of that province and placed his judges over the whole region as far as Marseille and Arles."[211] To defend his territory, Maurontus, duke of Provence, appealed to Yūsuf, Muslim governor of Narbonne, who sent armies to occupy the cities of Avignon and Arles and ravage their countryside.[212] Charles fought these for several years and in 739 finally regained Provence.[213] When he died in 741, the region passed to his son Pippin III, the first Carolingian king.[214]

CONCLUSIONS

As this chapter has demonstrated, Caesarius's efforts at pastoral reform and christianization owed as much to favorable political conditions as to his own interests and capacities. Within his own diocese, like any bishop, he had needed only the cooperation of the senior clergy and local aristocracy to carry out his reforms. To promote these outside his diocese, however, he required the cooperation of his fellow bishops, the bishops of Rome, and the king and his local officers. When the Merovingians annexed Provence in 536/37, all these forms of outside cooperation had to be renegotiated. Caesarius died, however, before he could institutionalize most of his reforms in the larger Frankish church. Although some of his restrictions on the ordination of clergy, such as minimum age limits and a year of preparation for laymen, were taken up by the Councils of Orléans in 538 and 549,[215] no subsequent Merovingian council mentioned these, either because they were regularly observed, or, more likely, because there was no longer any interest in maintaining them. Prohibitions against simony were frequently repeated by later Merovingian coun-

---

[209] Fredegar, *contin.* 14. [210] Ibid., 15. [211] Ibid., 18, trans. Wallace-Hadrill.
[212] *chron. moissiacense*, ed. G. H. Pertz, *MGH Script.*, I, 291–92; P. Geary, *Aristocracy in Provence: The Rhône Basin at the Dawn of the Carolingian Age* (Philadelphia, 1985), 127–28. [213] Fredegar, *contin.* 20–21. [214] Ibid., 23.
[215] Orléans (538), can. 6; Orléans (549), can. 9.

cils,[216] but as we have seen, in the case of episcopal appointments at least, these could have no effect without the cooperation of the king. Most importantly, no Merovingian council repeated the canons of Carpentras (527) and Vaison (529) that had allowed greater autonomy to the rural clergy, and so promoted the christianization of the peasantry.

Reasons for Caesarius's pronounced lack of influence in the later Merovingian period are not difficult to discover. Even in his own lifetime, Caesarius advocated ideals of pastoral reform that few of his colleagues shared. Profound changes in the episcopate of the seventh and early eighth centuries made these ideals even less appealing. Far more than their aristocratic counterparts of the sixth century, bishops of the later Merovingian period came to define their prestige by their vast personal wealth, their exclusive control over wealthy sees, their close connections to kings and powerful magnates, and their lavish endowment of family monasteries and shrines.[217] Such men were even more unlikely than Caesarius's colleagues to embrace a program of church reform that required them to relinquish their personal property, live in ascetic communities with their lower clergy, share their prerogatives of church governance with priests and deacons, and travel throughout the countryside to preach to rural populations. It is thus all the more noteworthy that after some two centuries of dormancy, Caesarius's ideas were taken up again by reformers in the later eighth and early ninth centuries. This development constituted a decisive further step in the making of a Christian society, and merits our attention as a fitting epilogue to Caesarius's career.

[216] Orléans (549), can. 10; Tours (567), can. 28; Paris (614), can. 2; Chalon (647/53), can. 16.

[217] Prinz, *Frühes Mönchtum*, 489–501; idem, "Die bischöfliche Stadtherrschaft," 1–26; Geary, *Before France and Germany*, 171–78, 210–14.

Chapter 10

THE LEGACY OF CAESARIUS

In a famous letter of 742 to Pope Zacharias, Boniface called attention to what he perceived as an alarming disarray in the Frankish church:

The Franks, according to their elders, have not held a council for more than eighty years, nor have they had an archbishop or established or restored anywhere the canon law of the Church. For the most part the episcopal sees in cities are in the hands of greedy laymen or are exploited by adulterous and vicious clergymen and publicans for secular uses ... And certain bishops are to be found among them who, although they deny that they are fornicators or adulterers, are drunkards and shiftless men, given to hunting and to fighting in the army like soldiers and by their own hands shedding blood, whether of heathens or Christians.[1]

Boniface informed the pope that it was for these reasons that Carloman had decided to convene a council to re-establish ecclesiastical discipline. At the same time, to strengthen his own efforts to convert the Alamanni, Bavarians, and Franks, Boniface called upon Zacharias to prohibit "pagan" practices that had long been tolerated in Rome, including the observance of the Kalends of January and the wearing of amulets.[2] He confirmed his appeal by a passage he mistakenly thought Augustine had written; it was in fact written by Caesarius: "He who believes in these evils, that is, fortunetellers, diviners, and soothsayers, or phylacteries and other auguries of any kind, even if he fasts, prays, constantly attends church, gives abundant alms, and mortifies his body with every affliction, will gain nothing unless he abandons these sacrileges" (*serm.* 54. 5).

However one-sided and unreliable Boniface's assessment of the

---

[1] Boniface, *ep.* 50, MGH Ep., III, 299–300, trans. E. Emerton, *The Letters of Saint Boniface*, Records of Civilization, Sources and Studies 31 (New York, 1940), 79–80.
[2] Boniface, *ep.* 50, MGH Ep., III, 301.

Frankish church may be, his letter nicely illustrates the link between Caesarius and the Carolingian reforms: its call for church reform and conversion directly recalls Caesarius's own program of reform and christianization while at the same time prefiguring the Carolingian reforms and missionary enterprises to follow. Boniface's direct, albeit unconscious, quotation of Caesarius not only confirms this link, but also reveals the anonymity of much of Caesarius's influence on the Frankish church. Whatever authority Caesarius's writings were thought to possess did not depend primarily on his personal reputation for sanctity or learning, but rather on the simplified and codified patristic teaching his work embodied. To reformers who depended as much on written documents as the Carolingians,[3] what mattered most of all was the immediate practical relevance of the documents Caesarius had produced, especially sermons and conciliar canons. It is the aim of this chapter to survey the impact of these writings on the Frankish church in the later eighth and early ninth centuries. For it was not until this time that the program of reform they implicitly contained was finally embraced on the scale Caesarius originally envisioned, with essentially the same vision of a total Christian society in mind, and probably with the same complicated and limited record of success. An exhaustive survey of this theme is not necessary. Instead, we shall concentrate on those features of the Carolingian reforms that reflect Caesarius's own program, and help to illuminate its coherence and, under the right circumstances, its practical applicability.

Although few Merovingian manuscripts of Caesarius's writings remain, the later survival of these writings demonstrates that they were continuously copied throughout the period before Boniface.[4] Indeed, it is clear that Merovingian churchmen continued to make use of Caesarius's writings after his death. The monastic rules of Aurelianus of Arles (546–51),[5] Ferreolus of Uzès (d. 581),[6] Donatus

---

[3] R. McKitterick, *The Frankish Church and the Carolingian Reforms, 789–895* (London, 1977). The following pages demonstrate my extensive debt to this superb study.

[4] Morin dates one MS of Caesarius's sermons to the seventh century (M[1]), six to the seventh/eighth century (W[2], H[5], H[25], H[36], H[39], H[49]), and 236 to the eighth and later centuries, Morin I, xxv–cxv = *CCSL* 103, xxiv–cxxii. See also R. Grégoire, "Les homéliaires mérovingiens du VIIe–VIIIe siècle," *Studi medievali*, ser. 3, 13 (1972), 901–17. In addition, one MS of the rule for nuns dates to the beginning of the ninth century and three to the tenth and later centuries; one MS of the rule for monks dates to the eighth century and the other to the ninth, Morin II, 99–101, 149.

[5] C. de Clercq, *La Législation*, 79–83.   [6] Ibid., 83–85.

of Besançon (627–58),[7] and the anonymous sixth-century *regula Tarnantensis*[8] all depend on Caesarius's rule for women. Likewise, the authentic sermon fragments of Eligius of Noyon[9] (641–60) as well as the *liber scintillarum* of Defensor of Ligugé[10] (*c.* 700) contain many direct quotations from Caesarius's sermons.[11] In addition, the canons of Agde, Arles, Carpentras, and Vaison continued to be included in Merovingian conciliar collections, as well as in systematic compilations like the Vetus Gallica.[12] It was not until the middle of the eighth century, however, that Caesarius's ideas and writings began to be employed in a systematic program of christianization and reform.

The first hints of such a program appear in three church councils of 743/44, influenced by Boniface and held under the auspices of Charles Martel's sons, Carloman in Austrasia and Pippin III in Neustria.[13] These were the first councils held in the Frankish church since the seventh century, and the few bishops who took part in them devoted themselves to the most pressing matters at hand. Behind their efforts to restore the "decrees of the canons and the rights of the church"[14] can be seen elements of the same program proposed centuries earlier by Caesarius, Pomerius, Augustine, and other reformers: the imposition of an ascetic style of life on the clergy, including a condemnation of hunting parties, military expeditions, and sexual liaisons;[15] the regulation of lay

---

[7] Ibid., 85–88; A. de Vogüé, "La règle de Donat pour l'abbesse Gauthstrude," *Benedictina* 25 (1978), 219–313.

[8] F. Villegos, "La *regula monasterii Tarnantensis*. Texte, sources et datation," *RBen* 84 (1974), 7–65.

[9] Ed. B. Krusch, *MGH SRM*, IV, 751–61. The anti-pagan sermon attributed to Eligius in *vita Eligii* II. 16 would seem to have been inserted by the Carolingian editor of the work, Markus, "From Caesarius to Boniface." For the career of Eligius and other seventh-century missionaries, see P. Fouracre, "The Work of Audoenus of Rouen and Eligius of Noyon in Extending Episcopal Influence from the Town to the Country in Seventh-Century Neustria," in *The Church in Town and Countryside*, ed. D. Baker (Oxford, 1979), 77–91.   [10] Ed. H. M. Rochais, *CCSL* 117 (1957), 1–234.

[11] For the general influence of Caesarius's sermons on this genre, see H. Millemann, "Caesarius von Arles und die frühmittelalterliche Missionspredigt," *Zeitschrift für Missionswissenschaft und Religionswissenschaft* 23 (1933), 12–27.

[12] *Les Canons des conciles mérovingiens (VIe–VIIe siècles)*, ed. J. Gaudemet and B. Basdevant, I, *SC* 353 (Paris, 1989), 13–19.

[13] Texts of these councils can be found in *MGH Conc.*, II. 1, 1–7, 33–36.

[14] German council (743), can. 1. The date is disputed; see W. Hartmann, *Die Synoden der Karolingerzeit im Frankenreich und in Italien* (Paderborn, 1989), 51, n. 14.

[15] German council (743), can. 2, 6; Les Estinnes (744), can. 1; Soissons (744), can. 3. For the dating of the Council of Les Estinnes to 744 rather than 743, see A. Dierkens, "Superstitions, christianisme et paganisme à la fin de l'époque mérovingienne," in *Magie, sorcellerie, parapsychologie*, ed. H. Hasquin (Brussels, 1984), 9–26: 15–16.

behavior, for instance in cases of adultery and perjury;[16] and the definition and condemnation of paganism, whether practiced by prospective converts or baptized Christians.[17] Caesarius's preoccupation with defining and condemning paganism can be seen in other contemporary documents as well. The *indiculus superstitionum et paganiarum*, composed in connection with the councils of 743/44, lists thirty forbidden practices, some of which closely resemble those condemned by Caesarius.[18] Extensive direct quotations from Caesarius's sermons against paganism are also evident in other documents that may be dated to the middle of the eighth century: the *dicta* or *scarapsus* attributed to Pirmin[19] and the anonymous sermons "Necessarium est"[20] and "Gratias agimus."[21] For Boniface and his fellow reformers, as for Caesarius, defining what it meant to be a pagan helped to define what it meant to be a Christian. And it was defining what it meant to be a Christian that lay at the heart of their programs of church reform.

As his own correspondence shows, however, Boniface's reform program soon encountered widespread opposition from Frankish bishops and lay aristocrats whose own positions of privilege and power it threatened to undermine.[22] With Carloman's decision to become a monk and his departure for Italy in 747, Boniface lost a valuable supporter. Increasingly thereafter his activities were confined to his bishopric at Mainz, his abbey at Fulda, and his missionary work in Hesse-Thuringia and ultimately Frisia, where he was murdered in 754.[23] At his death, the initiative for church

---

[16] Les Estinnes (744), can. 3; Soissons (744), can. 4.

[17] German council (743), can. 5; Les Estinnes (744), can. 4.

[18] *indiculus superstitionum et paganiarum* 10, 12, 13, 14, 21, ed. Dierkens, "Superstitions, christianisme et paganisme."

[19] Ed. G. Jecker, *Die Heimat des hl. Pirmin des Apostels der Alamannen* (Münster-in-Westphalia, 1927), 34–73. For arguments against this attribution, see J.-P. Bouhot, "Alcuin et le 'De catechizandis rudibus' de saint Augustin," *Recherches augustiniennes* 15 (1980), 176–240: 180–84. The treatise's dependence on Caesarius is discussed in Millemann, "Caesarius von Arles," 21, and Jecker, *Die Heimat*, 89–158.

[20] Ed. W. Scherer, "Eine lateinische Musterpredigt aus der Zeit Karls des Grossen," *Zeitschrift für deutsches Altertum* 12 (1865), 436–46.

[21] Partial edition in W. Levison, *England and the Continent in the Eighth Century* (Oxford, 1946), 302–314; reprinted in *PLS* 4: 967–69.

[22] Boniface, *ep.* 60, 63, 65, 77, 78, 87. See further, T. Schieffer, *Winfrid-Bonifatius und die christliche Grundlegung Europas* (Freiburg, 1954), 225–28, and E. Ewig, "Milo et eiusmodi similes," in his *Spätantikes und fränkisches Gallien*, II, 189–219.

[23] E. Ewig, "The Revival of the Frankish Kingdom," in *Handbook of Church History*, ed. H. Jedin and J. Dolan, III, *The Church in the Age of Feudalism*, trans. A. Biggs (New York, 1969), 7–16: 15–16.

reform was taken up by Chrodegang, bishop of Metz (742–66).
Under his leadership and with the support of Pippin III, a new
series of councils was held from 755 to 760/2. Much concerned
with church organization and episcopal authority, these councils
clearly reflected Chrodegang's own preoccupations as a reformer.[24] His links with the reform tradition of Augustine,
Pomerius, and Caesarius are most evident in his rule for the
cathedral clergy of Metz.[25] Composed around 754, the *regula
canonicorum* organized the clergy into a quasi-monastic community
in which clerics ate, slept, prayed, and worked together in a
common dwelling, just as Augustine's and Caesarius's clergy had
done. As Chrodegang's prologue states, the intentions behind this
reform were essentially pastoral.[26] Having noticed in general the
growing "negligence" of bishops and clergy, he conceived of the
need to lead his own clergy back to the path of righteous living.
By remaining united in mind and heart, devoting themselves to
the divine office and holy scriptures, obeying the bishop, and
leading lives of virtue, the clergy of Metz could become the kinds
of "good servants" that Christ would reward on Judgment Day.[27]
In practical terms this meant that Chrodegang's clergy were in
many ways to live like monks, and Chrodegang accordingly
borrowed liberally from the *Rule of Benedict*.[28] He did not,
however, require his cathedral clergy to make the most radical
monastic sacrifice of all – the renunciation of property – the very
point on which Pomerius had insisted with such force in the *de vita
contemplativa*. Although Chrodegang believed with Pomerius that
clerics should renounce their property, he acknowledged that few
could be persuaded to do this.[29] He therefore recommended that
clerics give their property to the church while still enjoying the
usufruct for the remainder of their lives. He further recommended
that those who maintained an income of their own not accept a
stipend from the church, which would deprive the poor of what
they needed. In directly quoting Pomerius on this point,[30]

---

[24] E. Ewig, "Saint Chrodegang et la réforme de l'église franque," in his *Spätantikes und
fränkisches Gallien*, II, 232–59.
[25] Ed. J.-B. Pelt, *Etudes sur la cathédrale de Metz*, I, *La Liturgie* (Metz, 1937), 7–28.
[26] G. Hocquard, "La Règle de Saint Chrodegang," in *Saint Chrodegang* (Metz, 1967),
55–89: 80–88.   [27] *regula canonicorum*, prol.
[28] E. Morhain, "Origine et histoire de la 'regula canonicorum' de saint Chrodegang," in
Miscellanea Pio Paschini, Lateranum, n.s. 14 (Rome, 1948), I, 173–85: 176–77.
[29] "nostris temporibus persuaderi non potest," *regula canonicorum* 31.
[30] *vita contempl.* II. 12.

Chrodegang demonstrated his own debt to a tradition that had already begun to exercise a strong influence on Carolingian views of clerical life.[31] Influenced by Augustine and Pomerius, his rule influenced other reformers in turn, as calls for reform of the clergy increased.[32]

Pippin's reputation as a reformer rests not only on the church councils he convened and ratified,[33] but also on the legislation he promulgated on his own.[34] His most far-reaching contribution to this effort was his command that "every individual, whether he wishes to or not, should pay tithes."[35] This made the payment of tithes a requirement of civil as well as ecclesiastical law,[36] and supplied the foundation for later legislation that made tithes available to local parishes for the needs of their clergy, their buildings, and their poor.[37] Support of this kind was crucial for the reform movement for, as we shall see, local parishes lay at the heart of Carolingian efforts to christianize the population.

It was on these first tentative and disparate elements of church reform and christianization that Charlemagne and his advisors built the far more comprehensive and systematic program they hoped would produce a totally Christian society. "For we read in the Book of Kings how Josiah was eager to recall the kingdom given him by God to the worship of the true God by going around, correcting, and admonishing."[38] This ideal was not only much like the one Caesarius had envisioned; it also seemed attainable by many of the same methods. And so it was that the Carolingian reformers turned to Caesarius and other church fathers, notably Augustine and Gregory the Great, for the practical instruments of christianization and reform. Caesarius's influence on church reform in the age of Charlemagne can be detected in comprehensive royal legislation, such as the *admonitio generalis* of 789 and the later capitularies that supplemented it, as well as in the

[31] J. Devisse, "L'influence de Julien Pomère sur les clercs carolingiens," *Revue d'histoire de l'église de France* 56 (1970), 285–95.
[32] Morhain, "Origine et histoire," 179–82.
[33] Ver (755), prol. *MGH Capit.*, I, 33.
[34] *capitulare* of 754/55, *MGH Capit.*, I, 31–32.
[35] *Pippini ad Lullum epistola, MGH Capit.*, I, 42 = *MGH Ep.*, III, 408.
[36] G. Constable, *Monastic Tithes* (Cambridge, 1964), 28–30.
[37] de la Tour, *Les Paroisses*, 148–53. On the very complicated subject of tithes, see Lesne, *Histoire de la proprieté*, II, part 1, 98–111; Boyd, *Tithes*, 26–46; and Constable, *Monastic Tithes*, 1–56.
[38] *admonitio generalis*, pref., *MGH Capit.*, I, 54. For commentary, see McKitterick, *The Frankish Church*, 2–3.

local enactments of bishops, including their deliberations at the reform councils of 813 and the statutes, or *capitula*, they issued to their diocesan clergy.[39] We shall discuss the royal legislation first.

Like Caesarius, Charlemagne worked to transform churches, especially parish churches, into centers of christianization, where congregations could express their concord and harmony at the ritual of the Mass,[40] and could learn proper Christian behavior from the preaching, teaching, and good example of the local clergy.[41] In the tradition of Caesarius, Charles directed parishioners to learn prayers by heart, at a minimum the Lord's Prayer and the Creed.[42] He also placed a similar emphasis on proper behavior in church, commanding congregations to refrain from "secular business" and "vain speech" in church, to pay attention for the duration of the service, and not to leave until the final blessing.[43] In addition, to ensure that the norms of Christian behavior were widely propagated, Charles authorized and required parish priests to preach,[44] a prerogative still reserved for bishops alone,[45] despite Caesarius's earlier enactment of the same reform. Finally, to further promote Christian instruction, and to provide a source of recruits for the local clergy, he encouraged bishops to create local schools where boys of every class might learn to read, a proposal that directly recalls Caesarius's establishment of parish schools.[46]

Further evidence of Caesarius's impact on the Carolingian reforms can be seen in the councils of 813 and the statutes of individual bishops, which worked out many of the details of Charlemagne's general program at the local level. Held in Reims, Mainz, Chalon, Tours, and Arles (which had regained some of its earlier secular and ecclesiastical administrative importance[47]), the councils were intended to promote church reform throughout the

---

[39] McKitterick, *The Frankish Church*, 45–79. [40] *admonitio generalis* 62.

[41] *admonitio generalis* 61.

[42] *capitulare missorum item speciale* 30, MGH *Capit.*, I, 103; *capitulare missorum* 2, MGH *Capit.*, I, 147. [43] *admonitio generalis* 71.

[44] "The first requirement of all is that bishops and priests thoroughly learn the Catholic faith through their reading and preach it to the whole people," *admonitio generalis* 61.

[45] McKitterick, *The Frankish Church*, 87. Alcuin reports in a letter of 798 that some bishops still prohibited their priests and deacons from preaching, *ep.* 136, MGH *Ep.*, IV, 209.

[46] *admonitio generalis* 72; *epistola de litteris colendis*, MGH *Capit.*, I, 78–79. See P. Riché, *Ecoles et enseignement dans le Haut Moyen Age*, 2nd edn. (Paris, 1989), 69–73, 192–93.

[47] From at least 794 the city was again recognized as a metropolitan see, Frankfurt (794), can. 8, MGH *Conc.*, II. 1, 167, and coinage was struck there under Charlemagne, P. Grierson, "Money and Coinage under Charlemagne," in *Karl der Große. Lebenswerk und Nachleben*, ed. W. Braunfels, I (Düsseldorf, 1965), 501–36: 523.

Frankish realm.[48] Individual bishops further elaborated these reforms for their own dioceses in the form of *capitula* issued to their clergy. Although Caesarius, unlike Augustine[49] and Gregory the Great,[50] was not referred to by name in any of these documents, his influence is unmistakable, most obviously in legislation on preaching. For example, in authorizing priests to preach in rural parishes, "for the edification of all the churches and for the benefit of the whole people," the Council of Arles quoted directly from the second canon of the Council of Vaison (529).[51] The councils of 813 also followed Caesarius in advising bishops and other preachers to read and deliver the "sermons and homilies of the holy Fathers," and to do so in language the congregation could easily understand, whether "rustic Latin" or German.[52] Preaching in the vernacular was in fact the ninth-century equivalent of the *sermo rusticus* for which Caesarius was famous:[53] both aimed at a syntax, diction, and pronunciation that everyone could understand. To communicate the correct message, priests were also required to learn the *quicumque vult*, also known as the *fides Athanasii*,[54] a compendium of Christian doctrine that has been plausibly linked to Caesarius.[55]

In addition to reforms directly related to preaching, the councils of 813 and episcopal statutes also tried to strengthen parishes as centers of christianization along the lines suggested by royal legislation and Caesarius's earlier work. Parish priests were once more prohibited from secular pursuits such as hunting,[56] carrying arms,[57] drinking in taverns,[58] and unseemly joking, singing, or

---

[48] McKitterick, *The Frankish Church*, 12, 217. Texts of the councils can be found in *MGH Conc.*, II. 1, 245–306.   [49] Mainz (813), can. 3, 15.

[50] Mainz (813), pref., can. 1, 16; Chalon (813), can. 1; Tours (813), can. 3.

[51] Arles (813), can. 10.

[52] Reims (813), can. 15; Tours (813), can. 17. For the interpretation of *rustica Romana lingua* as a form of Latin rather than Old French, see M. Van Uytfanghe, "The Consciousness of a Linguistic Dichotomy (Latin–Romance) in Carolingian Gaul: The Contradictions of the Sources and of their Interpretation," in *Latin and the Romance Languages*, ed. Wright, 114–29: 120, and R. McKitterick, "Latin and Romance: An Historian's Perspective," in ibid., 130–45: 137–38.

[53] For pseudo-Eligius's use of this phrase in *serm.* 6 and 11, *PL* 87: 612 and 630, see McKitterick, *The Frankish Church*, 85, n. 4.

[54] Theodulf, *capitula* II. 1. 2, ed. P. Brommer, *MGH Capit. Episc.*, I, 149; *quae a presbyteris discenda sint* 1, *MGH Capit.*, I, 235. See McKitterick, *The Frankish Church*, 75–76.

[55] G. Morin, "L'origine du symbole d'Athanase: témoignage inédit de s. Césaire d'Arles," *RBen* 44 (1932), 207–19. The text is found in Morin's edition of Caesarius as *serm.* 3.   [56] Tours (813), can. 8; Chalon (813), can. 9.

[57] *capitulare episcoporum* 7, ed. E. Baluze, *Capitularia Regum Francorum* I (Paris, 1780), col. 359.

storytelling.[59] The role of the parish as a center of Christian charity
was strengthened by canons directing that local tithes should be
distributed to the local poor,[60] and that clergy should live in
common and open their houses to the needs of the poor.[61] Its role
as a center of education was promoted by Theodulf's ruling that
local priests set up schools "on villas and in villages."[62]

Caesarius's example also stood behind episcopal legislation
about the behavior of the laity. This is directly reflected in themes
appropriated from his most popular sermons: condemnations of
drunkenness,[63] "pagan" healing practices,[64] the singing of
"shameful and lewd songs" in the vicinity of churches,[65] and the
"vain conversations, idle and useless words, and dangerous
thoughts" engaged in during Mass.[66] Caesarius's advice is likewise
reflected in the setting of minimum standards of Christian piety,
such as the memorization of the Lord's Prayer and Creed,[67] the
teaching of children by their parents and godparents,[68] and the
sending of sons to monasteries or local priests for education.[69]

The growing popularity of Caesarius's sermons in the later
eighth and early ninth centuries was both a cause and a
consequence of the reform movement we have described. By his
insistence on church reform, and specifically on the responsibility
of bishops and priests to preach to their congregations, Caesarius
had helped to create a demand for sermons that would embody the
reform ideas he promoted. To respond to this demand, Carolingian compilers continued to copy Caesarius's sermons[70] and
collect them into homiliaries.[71] In one such collection, the late
eighth-century homiliary attributed to Burchard of Würzburg,
thirty-three of forty-five sermons were written by Caesarius.[72]

---

[58] Reims (813), can. 26; Chalon (813), can. 44; Tours (813), can. 21; Theodulf, *capitula*
I. 13; *capitulare episcoporum* 14, 19; *capitula in dioecesana quadam synodo tractata* 7, *MGH
Capit.*, I, 237.   [59] Tours (813), can. 7, 8; Chalon (813), can. 9.

[60] Tours (813), can. 16.   [61] *statuta synodalia ecclesiae Remensis* 17, *PL* 135: 408.

[62] "Per villas et vicos," Theodulf, *capitula* I. 20.

[63] Mainz (813), can. 46; Tours (813), can. 48.   [64] Tours (813), can. 42.

[65] Mains (813), can. 48.   [66] Tours (813), can. 38; Theodulf, *capitula* I. 10.

[67] Reims (813), can. 2; Mainz (813), can. 45; Theodulf, *capitula* I. 22; *capitulare episcoporum*
5.   [68] Arles (813), can. 19.   [69] Mainz (813), can. 45.

[70] Of the 243 manuscripts of Caesarius's sermons cited by Morin, fourteen can be dated
to the eighth century, six to the end of the eighth or beginning of the ninth century,
and twenty-three to the ninth century, Morin I, xxv–cxv.

[71] McKitterick, *The Frankish Church*, 90–92.

[72] G. Morin, "L'homéliaire de Burchard de Würzburg," *RBen* 13 (1896), 97–111. For the
date, see T. L. Amos, "The Origin and Nature of the Carolingian Sermon" (Ph.D.
diss., Michigan State University, 1983), 113.

But it was just as frequent that Caesarius's sermons were adapted or used as sources for original sermons, much as he himself had used the works of Augustine. Hrabanus Maurus, for example, drew on Caesarius, as well as other patristic authors, for the seventy sermons that made up his first homiliary (814/26), but he also included material of his own devising.[73] A similar pattern of composition holds for other sermon writers of the late eighth and early ninth centuries.[74]

Carolingian preachers chiefly esteemed Caesarius's sermons for their definition of the proper Christian life. An anonymous fragmentary sermon of the late eighth or early ninth century offers a typical example.[75] Apparently delivered around Easter Sunday, the sermon opens with an exhortation to keep holy the Lord's day. There follow rules for fasting during Pentecost and the admonition to act charitably toward friends, relatives, widows, orphans, pilgrims, the sick, and guests. More rules follow for fasting and limiting sexual relations during Lent. Next, avarice is condemned, followed by a long passage on the need to pay tithes and help the poor. After this the sermon condemns drunkenness, concubinage, incest, and divorce. Next, the faithful are warned to carry out the duties of their social rank. Husbands should love their wives, and wives their husbands. Children should obey their parents, and slaves their masters. Masters should do no violence against their slaves. Everyone, the preacher repeats, should refrain from working on the Lord's day, including male and female slaves and farm animals. Parents and godparents should teach their children and godchildren to recite the Creed and the Lord's Prayer and to believe in the Trinity and the Resurrection of the Dead. Explaining that these prayers and beliefs constitute the only protection Christians need in times of trouble, the preacher next turns to the prohibition of unauthorized observances. His list comes straight from Caesarius. When parishioners go to church, the sermon

[73] Hrabanus Maurus, *homeliae*, PL 110: 10–134. His most obvious borrowings from Caesarius can be seen in *hom.* 1, 2, 16, 21, 40, 43, and 44, which contain passages from Caesarius, *serm.* 187, 188, 204, 210, 227, 54, and 16, respectively. See R. Cruel, *Geschichte der deutschen Predigt im Mittelalter* (Detmold, 1879), 59–66.

[74] For Caesarius's influence on the fifteen sermons of pseudo-Boniface (PL 89: 843–79), see Millemann, "Caesarius von Arles," 23–24 and Bouhot, "Alcuin," 184–91. For his influence on the sixteen sermons of pseudo-Eligius (PL 87: 593–654), see Millemann, "Caesarius von Arles," 18–19. For a list of edited Carolingian sermons composed before 825, see Amos, "The Origin," 201–4.

[75] G. Morin, "Textes inédits relatifs au symbole et à la vie chrétienne," *RBen* 22 (1905), 515–19.

warns, they should avoid "lewd or shameful songs." When there is sickness in their houses, they should not seek the help of folk healers or soothsayers (*caragii*, *divini*, or *praedicatores*), but rather the prayers of parish priests. When a storm threatens, heads of households ought to pray for the safety of their wives and children and for rain for their crops and animals. If they promise to pay their tithes and help the poor, the preacher assures them, God will certainly hear their prayers. Moreover, he says, it is not witches who are the source of evil, but the devil, who "deceives men in a thousand ways" (Caesarius's favorite classical quotation[76]). The sermon closes with condemnations of women who curse their own children, kill them, or practice abortion or contraception. It finally breaks off with the admonition to go to (private) confession and do penance.

This sermon makes it clear that Caesarius's writings were still making an impact on the way preachers thought and spoke long after his death. But it is important to be clear about the nature of that impact. The borrowing of themes and phrases from Caesarius did not take place in a vacuum; it had a contemporary purpose. Carolingian sermons were, after all, delivered to Carolingian audiences, and the preachers who composed them did so with those audiences in mind.[77] When they borrowed from Caesarius, it was in the belief that his sermons made a relevant contribution to the edification of their listeners. This is even true of Carolingian sermons against "superstition," despite the recently expressed view that "the ecclesiastical literature of superstition...does not reflect reality, but rather transmits it and passes it down."[78] Motivated by the same pastoral intentions as their Gallo-Roman predecessors, Carolingian preachers would not have quoted from Caesarius's anti-pagan sermons unless they believed that their congregations were engaged in similar practices. Although some of their descriptions of "pagan" or "superstitious" acts were drawn from sixth-century models, these texts still supply valuable evidence for ninth-century attitudes and behaviors. The actual procedures condemned as pagan matter less than the fact of their condemnation. Moreover, it was not only the literature of superstition that was traditional, but also superstitious practices

[76] Vergil, *Aen.* VII. 337–38; Caesarius, *serm.* 50. 2; 152. 2; 207. 1.
[77] T. L. Amos, "Preaching and the Sermon in the Carolingian World," in *De Ore Domini: Preacher and Word in the Middle Ages*, ed. T. L. Amos, E. A. Green, and B. M. Kienzle (Kalamazoo, Mich., 1989), 41–60.   [78] Harmening, *Superstitio*, 72.

themselves, for which there is abundant evidence outside of sermons.[79] A contemporary focus is also indicated by the widespread condemnation in Carolingian sermons of practices unattested in their Gallo-Roman models, for instance, witchcraft. Treating Carolingian sermons in this way not only restores their value as evidence for actual practice; it also allows us to identify the particular nature and limitations of Caesarius's influence.

What Carolingian preachers took from Caesarius was not only a catalogue of virtues and vices, and authorized and unauthorized practices, but more importantly the image of Christian life that these embodied. This was essentially a life of ascetic spirituality, a life of selfless charity, and a life within the official church. It was not, as we have seen, a life that many of the laity or even the clergy had hitherto been interested in leading. And from this follows the central paradox of Caesarius's influence on the Carolingian church. The more evidence we find of his influence on themes of preaching and church reform, the more unsuccessful the Carolingian church appears in suppressing the social and religious practices of local congregations and imposing the official Christianity of the king and his bishops.

The details of this scenario are familiar. One anonymous sermon warns the congregation against keeping concubines, kissing the dead farewell, practicing divination, shopping or hunting on Sundays, celebrating feast days too boisterously, singing, kissing, talking, eating, or drinking in church, swearing by the sun and the moon, and spreading malicious stories about their neighbors.[80] Another condemns the consultation of the *sortes sanctorum*,[81] the use of contraceptives or abortifacients,[82] the recital of incantations over the sick as a supplement to the Lord's Prayer and Creed,[83] and noisemaking at lunar eclipses or hailstorms.[84] References to churches and Christian prayers in these documents make it clear that they were not intended for true pagans or new converts but for the populations of settled Christian areas. The

---

[79] "…il me paraît difficile de perdre de vue que ces textes ne constituent qu'une parte de notre documentation sur ces sujets: il faut leur ajouter l'hagiographie, la littérature des *mirabilia*, la littérature en langue vulgaire, les *exempla*, c'est-à-dire une immense documentation, peut-être moins répétitive, ayant une meilleure prise sur les pratiques réellement observées, et qui permet une découverte plus complète et une mise en perspective historique du folklore médiéval," J.-C. Schmitt, review of *Superstitio* by D. Harmening in *Archives de sciences sociales des religions* 53 (1982), 298.

[80] Morin, "Textes inédits," 519-23.   [81] *sermo de sacrilegia* iii. 7.

[82] Ibid., vi. 18.   [83] Ibid., iv. 14-15.   [84] Ibid., v. 16.

reform councils of 813 and early episcopal statutes convey much the same impression, all the more convincingly since they were certainly not intended for mission areas. Among other problems, they legislated against the storing of grain in churches[85] and the use of magical formulas and phylacteries to cure illness.[86] By the close of the ninth century not much had changed. The lists of questions that Regino of Prüm drew up in 906 for bishops to ask on their annual parish visits portray a developed community religion whose earliest formation can be traced back to the fifth and sixth centuries.[87] Again, the details are familiar. Among other offenses, such as drinking in taverns,[88] carrying arms,[89] and hunting,[90] priests were suspected of commemorating the deaths of parishioners with shameful jokes, indecent songs, and toasts to the angels or the deceased.[91] Peasants neglected to attend Mass some Sundays,[92] and worked instead,[93] particularly swineherds and other herdsmen whose work carried them far from churches.[94] When they did attend, they talked, ignored the service, and left before it was over;[95] sometimes they sang shameful and humorous songs around churches.[96] Moreover, instead of attending funeral services in churches, people held services outside at night, where they would eat, drink, and sing diabolic songs.[97] They also observed the Kalends of January,[98] consulted diviners,[99] protected animals with incantations and charms,[100] and collected medicinal herbs by demonic rites.[101] Women were suspected of pagan activities in their spinning and weaving[102] and of witchcraft to induce love or hatred.[103] These were aspects of local behavior and especially local religion that might not have come to our attention without the insistence of Caesarius and his Carolingian heirs on a set of religious standards that specifically excluded such practices. Indeed, it is by virtue of such standards that we can speak not only of the ideals but also of the limits of reform and christianization in the Carolingian church.[104]

Despite its systematic scope, its official sanction by the govern-

---

[85] Theodulf, *capitula* 1. 8.   [86] Tours (813), can. 42.
[87] Regino of Prüm, *de synodalibus causis*, ed. F. G. A. Wasserschleben (Leipzig, 1840). His list of ninety-six questions for the clergy is found in the preface to Book I, 19–26, and his list of eighty-nine questions for the laity is found in Book II, chapter 5, 208–216.
[88] Book I, quest. 26 (= I, 26).   [89] I, 24.   [90] I, 25.   [91] I, 40.
[92] II, 63.   [93] II, 57; I, 71.   [94] II, 64.   [95] II, 88; I, 72.   [96] II, 87.
[97] II, 55; I, 73.   [98] II, 51.   [99] II, 42.   [100] II, 44.   [101] II, 52.
[102] II, 53.   [103] II, 45.
[104] J. L. Nelson, "On the Limits of the Carolingian Renaissance," in *Renaissance and Renewal in Christian History*, ed. D. Baker (Oxford, 1977), 51–69.

ment and the church, and the considerable intellectual resources dedicated to its success, the Carolingian reform movement encountered many of the same limits that Caesarius had earlier faced. As we have seen, what ordinary Christians continued to prefer, peasants and townspeople alike, was a religion that did not always observe clerical regulations, a religion both traditional and Christian, and above all a religion people chose for themselves rather than a religion imposed by outsiders, from whatever motives. To those who were allowed as little autonomy in their lives as these men and women, the family, community, and religious traditions they preserved for themselves appeared exceedingly precious. It was just such traditions that stood at the center of the way they lived their lives, and the religion they developed for themselves depended on a loyalty to those traditions. From this point of view, it was not christianization itself that failed to achieve its ideals, but only a particular form of christianization – abrupt, centralized, and unresponsive to local conditions. What succeeded in its place was a gradual and exceedingly diverse process of religious change that depended above all on the choices made by countless individuals in countless communities, a process that necessarily produced a wide variety of Christian practices and beliefs over time. But even if this was not exactly the form of christianization that Caesarius and subsequent reformers had worked to achieve, it still depended in the last analysis on the elements of reform they had so painstakingly assembled: the organization of parishes, support for the poor, education of the clergy, and universal preaching. The degree of their success is illustrated by the central role that the local parish had come to play in rural life by the later middle ages. "The parish had clear boundaries and watchfully imposed them on the human reality. Thanks to its organization, it was present and active in all events of both the individual and the collective existence: spiritually (in the broad sense the period gave to the term, including charity and teaching) as well as materially, worldly. It associated its members in its management. It infused cohesion and strength into the group, especially by imposing common duties and obligations."[105] It was in such a fashion that civil communities had become Christian communities and the Christian religion a community religion.

---

[105] L. Genicot, *Rural Communities in the Medieval West* (Baltimore, 1990), 90.

SELECT BIBLIOGRAPHY

ANCIENT SOURCES

Ancient sources cited more than once are listed here. Sources referred to only once are cited in full in the notes where they appear. Place and date of publication are not given for works published in *CCSL*, *CSEL*, *MGH*, *PL*, or *SC*. Classical texts not listed are available in the Loeb Classical Library. Editions of inscriptions not edited in *CE*, *CIL*, or *ILCV* are listed by editor's name in the bibliography of secondary works.

admonitio generalis. Ed. A. Boretius. *MGH Capit.*, I, 52–62.

Agathias, *historiae*. Ed. R. Keydell. *Corpus Fontium Historiae Byzantinae* 2. Berlin, 1967.

Ammianus Marcellinus. Ed. W. Seyfarth. 2 vols. Leipzig, 1978.

Augustine, *confessiones*. Ed. L. Verheijen. *CCSL* 27.

Augustine, *de bono coniugali*. Ed. H. Zycha. *CSEL* 41, 185–231.

Augustine, *de catechizandis rudibus*. Ed. I. B. Bauer. *CCSL* 46, 115–78.

Augustine, *de civitate dei*. Ed. B. Dombart and B. Kalb. 2 vols. Leipzig, 1928–29.

Augustine, *de doctrina christiana*. Ed. J. Martin. *CCSL* 32.

Augustine, *epistulae*. *CSEL* 34, 44, 57, 58, 88.

Augustine, *praeceptum*. Ed. L. Verheijen. *La Règle de Saint Augustine*. II. Paris, 1967, 417–37.

Augustine, *sermones ad populum*. *PL* 38–39.

Aurelianus, *regula ad monachos*. *PL* 68: 385–398.

Aurelianus, *regula ad virgines*. *PL* 68: 399–408.

Ausonius, *Mosella*. Ed. R. P. H. Green. *The Works of Ausonius*. Oxford, 1991, 115–30.

Ausonius, *ordo nobilium urbium*. Ed. R. P. H. Green. *The Works of Ausonius*. Oxford, 1991, 169–75.

Avitus of Vienne, *epistulae ad diversos*. Ed. R. Peiper. *MGH AA*, VI. 2, 35–103.

Avitus of Vienne, *homiliae*. Ed. R. Peiper. *MGH AA*, VI. 2, 103–57.

Boniface, *epistolae*. Ed. E. Dümmler. *MGH Ep.*, III, 231–431.

breviarium Alarici. Ed. G. Haenel. *Lex Romana Visigothorum*. Repr. Aalen, 1962.

Caesarius, *epistulae*. Ed. Morin II, 3–32, 65–70, 125–27, 134–44. Eng. trans. W. E. Klingshirn. *The Life, Testament, and Letters of Caesarius of Arles*. Translated Texts for Historians. Liverpool, forthcoming. (The numbering system in this translation, which differs slightly from Morin's system, has been adopted here as well. See the concordance, pp. xviii–xix above.)

Select bibliography

Caesarius, *regula monachorum*. Ed. Morin II, 149–55. Also ed. and trans. J. Courreau and A. de Vogüé. *Césaire d'Arles. Œuvres monastiques*. II. *Œuvres pour les moines*. SC, forthcoming.

Caesarius, *regula virginum*. Ed. Morin II, 99–124. Also ed. and trans. de Vogüé and Correau, 35–273. Eng. trans. M. C. McCarthy. *The Rule for Nuns of St. Caesarius of Arles*. The Catholic University of America Studies in Mediaeval History, n.s. 16. Washington, D.C., 1960.

Caesarius, *sermones*. Ed. Morin I, 1–2, repr. *CCSL* 103–104. *Sermons* 1–80 also ed. and trans. Delage. Editions of recently discovered sermons by R. Etaix, R. Grégoire, A. Höfer, J. Lemarié, and A. M. G. Vichi listed in bibliography of secondary works. Eng. trans. M. M. Mueller. *Caesarius of Arles. Sermons*. 3 vols. Fathers of the Church 31, 47, 66. Washington, D.C., 1956–73.

Caesarius, *testamentum*. Ed. Morin II, 281–89. Also ed. and trans. de Vogüé and Courreau, 360–97. Eng. trans. W. E. Klingshirn. *The Life, Testament, and Letters of Caesarius of Arles*. Translated Texts for Historians. Liverpool, forthcoming.

capitulare episcoporum. Ed. E. Baluze. *Capitularia Regum Francorum*. I. Paris, 1780, cols. 357–60.

capitulare missorum generale. Ed. A. Boretius. *MGH Capit.*, I, 91–99.

Cassian, *conlationes*. Ed. M. Petschenig. *CSEL* 13.

Cassian, *de institutis coenobiorum*. Ed. M. Petschenig. *CSEL* 17.

Cassiodorus, *variae*. Ed. T. Mommsen. *MGH AA*, XII, 1–385.

Chrodegang of Metz, *regula canonicorum*. Ed. J.-B. Pelt. *Etudes sur la cathédrale de Metz*. I. *La Liturgie*. Metz, 1937, 7–28.

codex Justinianus. Ed. P. Krueger. *Corupus Iuris Civilis*. II. Berlin, 1929.

codex Theodosianus. Ed. T. Mommsen and P. M. Meyer. *Theodosiani Libri XVI*. 2nd edn. Berlin, 1954.

Concilia aevi Karolini. Ed. A. Werminghoff. *MGH Conc.*, II, 1–2.

Concilia Africae, A. 345–A. 525. Ed. C. Munier. *CCSL* 149.

Concilia Galliae, A. 314–A. 506. Ed. C. Munier. *CCSL* 148.

Concilia Galliae, A. 511–A. 695. Ed. C. de Clercq. *CCSL* 148A.

Concilios Visigóticos e Hispano-Romanos. Ed. J. Vives. Barcelona and Madrid, 1963.

Constantius of Lyons, *vita Germani*. Ed. R. Borius. *SC* 112.

constitutiones Sirmondianae. Ed. T. Mommsen and P. M. Meyer. *Theodosiani Libri XVI*. 2nd edn. Berlin, 1954, 907–21.

Cyprianus of Toulon *et al.*, *vita Caesarii*. Ed. Morin II, 293–349. Eng. trans. W. E. Klingshirn. *The Life, Testament, and Letters of Caesarius of Arles*. Translated Texts for Historians. Liverpool, forthcoming.

edictum Theodorici. Ed. S. Riccobono. *FIRA* II, 683–710.

Ennodius, *epistulae*. Ed. G. Hartel. *CSEL* 6, 1–260.

Ennodius, *vita Antonii*. Ed. F. Vogel. *MGH AA*, VII, 185–190.

Ennodius, *vita Epiphani*. Ed. F. Vogel. *MGH AA*, VII, 84–109.

epistulae Arelatenses. Ed. W. Gundlach. *MGH Ep.*, III, 1–83.

Eucherius, *de laude eremi*. Ed. S. Pricoco. *Eucherii. De Laude Eremi*. Catania, 1965.

288

Eusebius Gallicanus, *homiliae*. Ed. F. Glorie. 3 vols. *CCSL* 101, 101A, 101B.

expositio totius mundi et gentium. Ed. J. Rougé. *SC* 124.

Faustus of Riez, *epistulae*. Ed. A. Engelbrecht. *CSEL* 21, 159–219.

Fredegar, *chronica*. Ed. J. M. Wallace-Hadrill. *The Fourth Book of the Chronicle of Fredegar with its continuations*. London, 1960, 1–79.

Fredegar, *continuationes*. Ed. J. M. Wallace-Hadrill. *The Fourth Book of the Chronicle of Fredegar with its continuations*. London, 1960, 80–121.

Gennadius, *de viris illustribus*. Ed. E. C. Richardson. Texte und Untersuchungen 14. 1. Leipzig, 1896.

Ps.-Gennadius, *de viris illustribus*. Ed. E. C. Richardson. Texte und Untersuchungen 14. 1. Leipzig, 1896.

Gregory of Tours, *de passione et virtutibus sancti Iuliani martyris*. Ed. B. Krusch. *MGH SRM*, I. 2, 112–134.

Gregory of Tours, *de virtutibus sancti Martini*. Ed. B. Krusch. *MGH SRM*, I. 2, 134–211.

Gregory of Tours, *historiae*. Ed. B. Krusch and W. Levison. 2nd edn. *MGH SRM*, I. 1.

Gregory of Tours, *in gloria confessorum*. Ed. B. Krusch. *MGH SRM*, I. 2, 294–370.

Gregory of Tours, *in gloria martyrum*. Ed. B. Krusch. *MGH SRM*, I. 2, 34–111.

Gregory of Tours, *vita patrum*. Ed. B. Krusch. *MGH SRM*, I. 2, 211–294.

Gregory the Great, *dialogi*. Ed. A. de Vogüé. *SC* 251, 260, 265.

Gregory the Great, *epistulae*. Ed. P. Ewald and L. M. Hartmann. *MGH Ep.*, I–II.

Hilarius, *vita Honorati*. Ed. S. Cavallin. *Vitae Sanctorum Honorati et Hilarii*. Lund, 1952, 48–78.

Isidore, *de viris illustribus*. Ed. C. Codoñer Merino. *El "De Viris Illustribus" de Isidoro de Sevilla*. Salamanca, 1964.

Isidore, *historia Gothorum*. Ed. T. Mommsen. *MGH AA*, XI, 267–295.

Jonas, *vita Johanni*. Ed. B. Krusch. *MGH SRM*, III, 502–17.

Jordanes, *Getica*. Ed. T. Mommsen. *MGH AA*, V. 1, 53–138.

Jordanes, *Romana*. Ed. T. Mommsen. *MGH AA*, V. 1, 1–52.

Justinian, *edicta*. Ed. R. Schoell and W. Kroll. *Corpus Iuris Civilis*. III. Berlin, 1928, 759–93.

lex coloniae Genetivae Iuliae Ursonensis. Ed. S. Riccobono. *FIRA* I, 177–98.

liber pontificalis. Ed. L. Duchesne. *Le liber pontificalis*. 2nd edn. 3 vols. Paris, 1955–57.

Martin of Braga, *de correctione rusticorum*. Ed. C. W. Barlow. *Martini Episcopi Bracarensis Opera Omnia*. Papers and Monographs of the American Academy in Rome 12. New Haven, 1950, 183–203. Corrections in A. M. Kurfess, "Textkritische Bemerkungen zu sancti Martini Bracarensis sermo de correctione rusticorum," *Aevum* 29 (1955), 181–86.

Maximus of Turin, *sermones*. Ed. A. Mutzenbecher. *CCSL* 23.

notitia dignitatum in partibus Occidentis. Ed. O. Seeck. *Notitia Dignitatum*. repr. Frankfurt am Main, 1962.

passio sancti Genesii Arelatensis. Ed. S. Cavallin. "Saint Genès le notaire." *Eranos* 43 (1945), 150–75.

Select bibliography

Peter Chrysologus, *sermones*. Ed. A. Olivar. *CCSL* 24, 24A, 24B.

Julianus Pomerius, *de vita contemplativa*. *PL* 59: 411–520.

Porcarius, *monita*. Ed. D. A. Wilmart. "Les *Monita* de l'abbé Porcaire." *RBen* 26 (1909), 475–80.

Possidius, *vita Augustini*. Ed. H. T. Weiskotten. *Sancti Augustini Vita Scripta a Possidio Episcopo*. Princeton, 1919.

Procopius, *de bellis*. Ed. J. Haury and G. Wirth. 2 vols. Leipzig, 1962–63.

Regino of Prüm, *de synodalibus causis*. Ed. F. G. A. Wasserschleben. Leipzig, 1840.

regula Benedicti (*RB*). Ed. A. de Vogüé and J. Neufville. *SC* 181–86.

regula Macarii (*RMac*). Ed. A. de Vogüé. *SC* 297, 372–88.

regula magistri (*RM*). Ed. A. de Vogüé. *SC* 105–7.

regula orientalis (*ROr*). Ed. A. de Vogüé. *SC* 298, 462–94.

regula sanctorum patrum (*RIVP*). Ed. A. de Vogüé, *SC* 297, 180–204.

regula "tertia" patrum (*3RP*). Ed. A. de Vogüé. *SC* 298, 532–42.

Remigius, *testamentum*. Ed. B. Krusch. *MGH SRM*, III, 336–39.

Ruricius, *epistulae*. Ed. A. Engelbrecht. *CSEL* 21, 349–442.

Salvian, *ad ecclesiam*. Ed. C. Halm. *MGH AA*, I. 1, 120–68.

Salvian, *de gubernatione dei*. Ed. C. Halm. *MGH AA*, I. 1, 1–108.

Salvian, *epistulae*. Ed. C. Halm. *MGH AA*, I. 108–19.

de septem ordinibus ecclesiae. Ed. W. Kalff. "Ps.-Hieronymi, *De septem ordinibus ecclesiae*." Diss. University of Würzburg, 1935.

sermo de sacrilegia. Ed. C. P. Caspari. *PLS* 4: 969–73.

sermo seu narratio de miraculo s. Genesii. *PL* 50: 1273–76.

Sidonius Apollinaris, *epistulae*. Ed. C. Luetjohann. *MGH AA*, VIII, 1–172.

sortes Sangallenses. Ed. A. Dold. "Die Orakelsprüche im St. Galler Palimpsest-codex 908 (die sogenannten 'Sortes Sangallenses')." *Österreichische Akademie der Wissenschaften*, Philosophisch-historische Klasse, Sitzungsberichte 225, Band 4, Abhandlung (1948). Commentary in "Die Orakelsprüche im St. Galler Palimpsestcodex 908 (die sogenannten 'Sortes Sangallenses'): Erläuterungen," ed. R. Meister, *Österreichische Akademie der Wissenschaften*, Philosophisch-historische Klasse, Sitzungsberichte 225, Band 5, Abhandlung (1951).

statuta ecclesiae antiqua. Ed. C. Munier. *Les Statuta Ecclesiae Antiqua*. Paris, 1960.

statuta patrum (*2RP*). Ed. A. de Vogüé. *SC* 297, 274–82.

Sulpicius Severus, *chronica*. Ed. C. Halm. *CSEL* 1, 1–105.

Sulpicius Severus, *vita Martini*. Ed. C. Halm. *CSEL* 1, 107–37.

Symmachus, *epistulae*. Ed. O. Seeck. *MGH AA*, VI. 1, 1–278.

Theodulf, *capitula*. Ed. P. Brommer. *MGH Capit. Episc.*, I, 103–84.

Valentinian, *novellae*. Ed. T. Mommsen and P. M. Meyer. *Theodosiani Libri XVI*. 2nd edn. II. Berlin, 1954, 69–154.

Venantius Fortunatus, *carmina*. Ed. F. Leo. *MGH AA*, IV. 1, 1–270.

Venantius Fortunatus, *vita Albini*. Ed. B. Krusch. *MGH AA*, IV. 2, 27–33.

Venantius Fortunatus, *vita Germani*. Ed. B. Krusch. *MGH AA*, IV. 2, 11–27.

vita Apollinaris. Ed. B. Krusch. *MGH SRM*, III, 194–203.

vita Hilarii. Ed. S. Cavallin. *Vitae Sanctorum Honorati et Hilarii.* Lund, 1952, 80–109.

vita Leobini. Ed. B. Krusch. *MGH AA,* IV. 2, 73–82.

vita Lupi. Ed. B. Krusch. *MGH SRM,* VII. 1, 284–302.

vita patrum Iurensium. Ed. F. Martine. *SC* 142.

vita Rusticulae. Ed. B. Krusch. *MGH SRM,* IV, 337–51.

vitas patrum Emeretensium. Ed. J. N. Garvin. *The Vitas Sanctorum Patrum Emeretensium.* The Catholic University of America Studies in Medieval and Renaissance Latin Language and Literature 19. Washington, D.C., 1946.

SECONDARY WORKS

This list includes all works cited in the notes (with the exception of most encyclopedia articles, book reviews, and translations), as well as selected studies consulted but not cited.

Abel, A.-M. "La pauvreté dans la pensée et la pastorale de saint Césaire d'Arles." In *Etudes sur l'histoire de la pauvreté (Moyen âge-XVIᵉ siècle),* ed. M. Mollat. I. Paris, 1974, 111–21.

Adkin, N. "A Problem in the Early Church: Noise During Sermon and Lesson." *Mnemosyne* 38 (1985), 161–63.

"Some Notes on the Dream of St. Jerome." *Philologus* 128 (1984), 119–26.

Aigrain, R. "Le voyage de Sainte Radegonde à Arles." *Bulletin philologique et historique* (1926–27), 119–27.

Alliez, L. *Histoire du monastère de Lérins.* 2 vols. Paris, 1862.

Amos, T. L. "The Origin and Nature of the Carolingian Sermon." Ph.D. diss., Michigan State University, 1983.

"Preaching and the Sermon in the Carolingian World." In *De Ore Domini: Preacher and Word in the Middle Ages,* ed. T. L. Amos, E. A. Green, and B. M. Kienzle. Kalamazoo, Mich., 1989, 41–60.

Amy, R. "Les cryptoportiques d'Arles." In *Les Cryptoportiques dans l'architecture romaine.* Collection de l'école française de Rome 14. Rome, 1973, 275–91.

Andresen, C. "Altchristliche Kritik am Tanz – ein Ausschnitt aus dem Kampf der Alten Kirche gegen heidnische Sitte." In *Kirchengeschichte als Missionsgeschichte,* ed. H. Frohnes *et al.* I. *Die Alte Kirche,* ed. H. Frohnes and U. W. Knorr. Munich, 1974, 344–76.

Angenendt, A. "Die Liturgie und die Organisation des kirchlichen Lebens auf dem Lande." In *Cristianizzazione ed organizzazione,* I, 169–226.

Anné, L. *Les Rites des fiançailles et la donation pour cause de mariage sous le Bas-Empire.* Louvain, 1941.

Antin, P. "Autour du songe de S. Jérôme." In *Recueil sur Saint Jérôme.* Collection Latomus 95. Brussels, 1968, 71–100.

Arbesmann, R. "The 'cervuli' and 'anniculae' in Caesarius of Arles." *Traditio* 35 (1979), 89–119.

Arcelin, P. "Arles protohistorique." In *Du nouveau sur l'Arles antique,* ed. C. Sintès, 17–23.

Select bibliography

"Les fouilles du Jardin d'Hiver." In *Du nouveau sur l'Arles antique*, ed. C. Sintès, 24–31.

Arnold, C. F., *Caesarius von Arelate und die gallische Kirche seiner Zeit*. Leipzig, 1894, repr. Leipzig, 1972.

Atsma, H. "Die christlichen Inschriften Galliens als Quelle für Klöster und Klosterbewohner bis zum Ende des 6. Jahrhunderts." *Francia* 4 (1976), 1–57.

Audin, P. "Césaire d'Arles et le maintien de pratiques païennes dans la Provence du VIᵉ siècle." In *La Patrie Gauloise d'Agrippa au VIᵉᵐᵉ siècle*. Lyons, 1983, 327–38.

Auerbach, E. *Literary Language and its Public in Late Latin Antiquity and in the Middle Ages*. Trans. R. Manheim. London, 1965.

Aune, D. E. "Magic in Early Christianity." *ANRW* II. 23. 2 (1980), 1507–57.

Bailey, F. G. "The Peasant View of the Bad Life." In *Peasants and Peasant Societies*, ed. T. Shanin, 298–321.

Baratier, E. *et al. Atlas historique. Provence, Comtat, Orange, Nice, Monaco*. Paris, 1969.

Bardy, G. "L'attitude politique de saint Césaire d'Arles." *Revue d'histoire de l'église de France* 33 (1947), 241–56.

"Les origines des écoles monastiques en Occident." *Sacris Eruditi* 5 (1953), 86–104.

Barnish, S. J. B. "Transformation and Survival in the Western Senatorial Aristocracy, *c*. A.D. 400–700." *Papers of the British School at Rome* 56 (1983), 120–55.

Baronius, C. *Annales Ecclesiastici*. 12 vols. Rome, 1588–1607.

Barruol, G. *Les Peuples préromains du Sud-Est de la Gaule. Revue archéologique de Narbonnaise*, Suppl. 1. Paris, 1969.

"La résistance des substrats préromains en Gaule méridionale." In *Assimilation et résistance à la culture gréco-romaine dans le monde ancien*, ed. D. M. Pippidi. Bucharest and Paris, 1976, 389–405.

Barry, M. I. *St. Augustine, the Orator: A Study of the Rhetorical Qualities of St. Augustine's Sermones ad Populum*. The Catholic University of America Patristic Studies 6. Washington, D.C., 1924.

Beaujard, B. "Chalon-sur-Saône." In *Topographie chrétienne des cités de la Gaule*, ed. N. Gauthier and J.-Ch. Picard. IV. *Province ecclésiastique de Lyon*. Paris, 1986, 65–74.

Beck, H. G. J. *The Pastoral Care of Souls in South-East France During the Sixth Century*. Rome, 1950.

Bedard, W. M. *The Symbolism of the Baptismal Font in Early Christian Thought*. The Catholic University of America Studies in Sacred Theology, 2nd ser., 45. Washington, D.C., 1951.

Bell, C. and H. Newby. *Community Studies: An Introduction to the Sociology of the Local Community*. New York, 1972.

Benoit, F. "L'archéologie sous-marine en Provence." *Rivista di studi liguri* 18 (1952), 237–307.

"Les chapelles triconques paléochrétiennes de la Trinité de Lérins et de la Gayole." *Rivista di archeologia cristiana* 25 (1949), 129–54.

Les Cimetières suburbains d'Arles dans l'Antiquité chrétienne et au Moyen Age. Studi di antichità cristiana 11. Rome, 1935.

"Le développement de la colonie d'Arles et la centuriation de la Crau." *CRAI* (1964), 156–69.

"L'économie du littoral de la Narbonnaise à l'époque antique : le commerce du sel et les pêcheries." *Rivista di studi liguri* 25 (1959), 87–110.

"Essai de quadrillage d'un plan d'Arles." *CRAI* (1941), 92–100.

"Fouilles aux Aliscamps." *Provence historique* 2 (1952), 115–32.

"Informations archéologiques : XII⁰ circonscription." *Gallia* 8 (1950), 116–32.

"Informations archéologiques : Circonscription d'Aix-en-Provence (région sud)." *Gallia* 18 (1960), 287–327.

"Informations archéologiques : Circonscription d'Aix-en-Provence (région sud)." *Gallia* 20 (1962), 687–716.

"Informations archéologiques : Circonscription d'Aix-en-Provence (région sud)." *Gallia* 22 (1964), 573–610.

"Le premier baptistère d'Arles et l'abbaye Saint-Césaire." *Cahiers archéologiques* 5 (1951), 31–59.

Recherches sur l'hellénisation du Midi de la Gaule. Paris, 1965.

"Les reliques de saint Césaire, archevêque d'Arles." *Cahiers archéologiques* 1 (1946), 51–62.

"Le rite de l'eau dans la fête du solstice d'été en Provence et en Afrique." *Revue anthropologique* 45 (1935), 13–30.

"La romanisation de la Narbonnaise à la fin de l'époque républicaine." *Rivista di studi liguri* 32 (1966), 287–303.

"Le sanctuaire d'Auguste et les cryptoportiques d'Arles." *Revue archéologique* 39, part 1 (1952), 31–67.

Sarcophages paléochrétiens d'Arles et de Marseille. Gallia, Suppl. 5. Paris, 1954.

"La tombe de saint Césaire d'Arles et sa restauration en 883." *Bulletin monumental* 94 (1935), 137–43.

"Topographie monastique d'Arles au VIᵉ siècle." In *Etudes mérovingiennes*, Actes des Journées de Poitiers, 1er–3 mai 1952. Paris, 1953, 13–17.

"L'usine de meunerie hydraulique de Barbegal (Arles)." *Revue archéologique* 15, part 1 (1940), 19–80.

ed. *Forma Orbis Romani : Carte archéologique de la Gaule romaine.* V. Paris, 1936.

Béranger, J. "Le refus du pouvoir." *Museum Helveticum* 5 (1948), 178–96.

Bieler, L. "Zur Mosella des Ausonius: 'cliens' in der Bedeutung 'colonus.'" *Rheinisches Museum* 86 (1937), 285–87.

Biraben, J.-N. and J. Le Goff. "La peste dans le Haut Moyen Age." *Annales ESC* 24 (1969), 1484–1510.

Blumenkranz, B. "'Iudaeorum convivia' à propos du concile de Vannes (465), c. 12." In *Etudes d'histoire du droit canonique dédiées à Gabriel le Bras.* II. Paris, 1965, 1055–58.

"Die Juden als Zeugen der Kirche." *Theologische Zeitschrift* 5 (1949), 396–98.

Juifs et chrétiens dans le monde occidental. Paris, 1960.

Boese, R. *Superstitiones Arelatenses e Caesario collectae.* Marburg, 1909.

Boglioni, P. "La scène de la mort dans les premières hagiographies latines." In *Le Sentiment de la mort au moyen âge*, ed. C. Sutto. Montréal, 1979, 185–210.

Bonini, I. "Lo stile nei sermoni di Cesario di Arles." *Aevum* 36 (1962), 240–57.

Bossy, J. "Postscript." In *Disputes and Settlements: Law and Human Relations in the West*, ed. J. Bossy. Cambridge, 1983, 287–93.

Boswell, J. *The Kindness of Strangers: The Abandonment of Children in Western Europe from Late Antiquity to the Renaissance.* New York, 1988.

Bouhot, J.-P. "Alcuin et le 'De catechizandis rudibus' de saint Augustin." *Recherches Augustiniennes* 15 (1980), 176–240.

Boulouis, A. "Références pour la conversion du monde païen aux VIIe et VIIIe siècles: Augustin d'Hippone, Césaire d'Arles, Grégoire le Grand." *REAug* 33 (1987), 90–112.

Bourdieu, P. *Outline of a Theory of Practice.* Trans. R. Nice. Cambridge, 1977.

Boyd, C. E. *Tithes and Parishes in Medieval Italy.* Ithaca, N. Y., 1952.

Braudel, F. *Civilization and Capitalism, 15th–18th Century.* I. *The Structures of Everyday Life.* Trans. S. Reynolds. New York, 1981.

Braun, J. *Die liturgische Gewandung im Occident und Orient.* Freiburg im Breisgau, 1907.

Brown, P. "Art and Society." In *Age of Spirituality: A Symposium*, ed. F. Weitzmann. New York, 1980, 17–37.

Augustine of Hippo. Berkeley and Los Angeles, 1967.

The Body and Society: Men, Women, and Sexual Renunciation in Early Christianity. New York, 1988.

The Cult of the Saints: Its Rise and Function in Latin Christianity. Chicago, 1981.

"Dalla 'plebs romana' alla 'plebs dei': aspetti della cristianizzazione di Roma." In *Governanti e intellettuali: popolo di Roma e popolo di Dio (I–VI secolo)*, ed. P. Brown, L. Cracco Ruggini, and M. Mazza Passatopresente 2. Turin, 1982, 123–45.

The Making of Late Antiquity. Cambridge, Mass., 1978.

Religion and Society in the Age of Saint Augustine. London, 1972.

"Religious Coercion in the Later Roman Empire: The Case of North Africa." In his *Religion and Society in the Age of Saint Augustine*, 301–31.

"St. Augustine's Attitude to Religious Coercion." In his *Religion and Society in the Age of Saint Augustine*, 260–78.

Society and the Holy in Late Antiquity. Berkeley and Los Angeles, 1982.

Brown, T. *Gentlemen and Officers: Imperial Administration and Aristocratic Power in Byzantine Italy* A.D. *554–800.* Rome, 1984.

Brühl, C. *Palatium und Civitas.* I. *Gallien.* Cologne, 1975.

Brun, J.-P. "L'habitat de hauteur de Saint-Estève (Evenos, Var)." *Revue archéologique de Narbonnaise* 17 (1984), 1–28.

"L'oléiculture antique en Provence d'après les recherches archéologiques récentes." *Echos du monde classique/Classical News* 28 (1984), 249–62.

Bruun, P. *The Constantinian Coinage of Arelate.* Helsinki, 1953.

Buchner, R. *Die Provence in Merowingischer Zeit.* Stuttgart, 1933.

Burnand, Y. *Domitii Aquenses. Une famille de chevaliers romains de la région d'Aix-*

en-Provence. Mausolée et domaine. Revue archéologique de Narbonnaise, Suppl. 5. Paris, 1975.

Cameron, A. and D. Schauer. "The Last Consul: Basilius and his Diptych." *JRS* 72 (1982), 126–45.

Cappuyns, D. M. "L'origine des 'Capitula' d'Orange 529." *Recherches de théologie ancienne et médiévale* 6 (1934), 121–42.

Carrias, M. "Vie monastique et règle à Lérins au temps d'Honorat." *Revue d'histoire de l'église de France* 74 (1988), 191–211.

Carruthers, M. J. *The Book of Memory: A Study of Memory in Medieval Culture.* Cambridge Studies in Medieval Literature 10. Cambridge, 1990.

Carson, R. A. G. *Coins of the Roman Empire.* London and New York, 1990.

Caspar, E. *Geschichte des Papsttums.* 2 vols. Tübingen, 1930–33.

Cavallin, S. *Literarhistorische und textkritische Studien zur Vita S. Caesarii Arelatensis.* Lund, 1934.

"Eine neue Handschrift der Vita S. Caesarii Arelatensis." *Kungl. Humanistiska Vetenskapssamfundet i Lund, Årsberättelse = Bulletin de la Société Royale des Lettres de Lund* (1935–36), 9–19.

Cavallo, G. "Libro e pubblico alla fine del mondo antico." In *Libri, editori e pubblico nel mondo antico*, ed. G. Cavallo. Rome and Bari, 1975, 81–132.

Cayré, F. *La Contemplation augustinienne.* Paris, 1927.

Chadwick, O. "Euladius of Arles." *JTS* 46 (1945), 200–5.

Chaillan, M. and C. Jullian. "Inscriptions de Fabregoules." *REA* 13 (1911), 466.

Chalon, M. and M. Gayraud. "Notes de géographie antique, II." *Revue archéologique de Narbonnaise* 15 (1982), 399–406.

Chastagnol, A. "Le repli sur Arles des services administratifs gaulois en l'an 407 de notre ère." *Revue historique* 249 (1973), 23–40.

Chaume, M. "Le mode de constitution et de délimitation des paroisses rurales aux temps mérovingiens et carolingiens." *Revue Mabillon* 27 (1937), 61–73.

Chevallier, R. "Gallia Narbonensis. Bilan de 25 ans du recherches historiques et archéologiques." *ANRW* II. 3 (1975), 686–828.

Provincia. Paris, 1982.

Christian, W. A. *Local Religion in Sixteenth-Century Spain.* Princeton, 1981.

Christophe, P. *Cassien et Césaire, prédicateurs de la morale monastique.* Gembloux, Belgium, 1969.

Chuvin, P. *A Chronicle of the Last Pagans.* Trans. B. A. Archer. Cambridge, Mass., 1990.

Claude, D. "Die Bestellung der Bischöfe im merowingischen Reiche." *ZRG KA* 49 (1963), 1–75.

Clavel, M. *Béziers et son territoire dans l'antiquité.* Paris, 1970.

Clerc, M. "Inscriptions romaines de Garéoult (Var)." *REA* 16 (1914), 79–80.

de Clercq, C. *La Législation religieuse Franque de Clovis à Charlemagne.* Louvain and Paris, 1936.

Clerici, E. "Il sermo humilis di Cesario d'Arles." *Rendiconti dell'Istituto Lombardo. Classe di lettere, scienze morali e storiche* 105 (1971), 339–64.

Collins, R. *Early Medieval Spain: Unity in Diversity, 400–1000.* New York, 1983.

"Theodebert I, 'Rex Magnus Francorum.'" In *Ideal and Reality in Frankish and*

Select bibliography

Anglo-Saxon Society, ed. Patrick Wormald with D. Bullough and R. Collins. Oxford, 1983, 7–33.

Congès, G. "L'Esplanade." In *Du nouveau sur l'Arles antique*, ed. C. Sintès, 33–37.

"L'histoire d'Arles romaine precisée par les fouilles archéologiques." *Archéologia*, no. 142 (May 1980), 10–23.

"Un dépotoir de la fin de l'Antiquité dans la grotte de la Fourbine, Saint-Martin-de-Crau (B.-du-Rh.)." *Revue archéologique de Narbonnaise* 16 (1983), 347–64.

Constable, G. *Monastic Tithes*. Cambridge, 1964.

Constans, L.-A. *Arles antique*. Bibliothèque des écoles françaises d'Athènes et de Rome 119. Paris, 1921.

Cottineau, L. H. and G. Poras, eds. *Répertoire topo-bibliographique des abbayes et prieurés*. 3 vols. Macon, 1935–70.

Courcelle, P. "Nouveaux aspects de la culture lérinienne." *Revue des études latines* 46 (1968), 379–409.

Courreau, J. "Saint Césaire d'Arles et les Juifs." *Bulletin de littérature ecclésiastique* 71 (1970), 92–112.

Cracco Ruggini, L. *Economia e società nell'* "*Italia Annonaria.*" Milan, 1961.

Cristianizzazione ed organizzazione ecclesiastica delle campagne nell'alto medioevo: espansione e resistenze. Settimane di Studio 28. 2 vols. Spoleto, 1982.

Cruel, R. *Geschichte der deutschen Predigt im Mittelalter*. Detmold, 1879.

Dalloni, M. "Grotte votive de l'époque gallo-romaine à Gignac (Bouches-du-Rhône)." In *Cinquième Congrès international d'archéologie*. Alger, 1933, 153–57.

Daly, W. M. "Caesarius of Arles. A Precursor of Medieval Christendom." *Traditio* 26 (1970), 1–28.

Davis, J. "Introduction." In *Religious Organization and Religious Experience*, ed. J. Davis. Association of Social Anthropologists, Monograph 21. London, 1982, 1–8.

Defarrari, R. J. "St. Augustine's Method of Composing and Delivering Sermons." Parts 1, 2. *American Journal of Philology* 43 (1922), 97–123, 193–219.

Delage, M.-J., ed. *Césaire d'Arles. Sermons au Peuple*. 3 vols. SC 175, 243, 330. Paris, 1971–86.

"Le séjour de Césaire d'Arles en Italie." In *Studia Patristica* 23, ed. E. A. Livingstone. Louvain, 1989, 103–10.

Delatte, A. *Herbarius: Recherches sur le cérémonial usité chez les anciens pour la cueillette des simples et des plantes magiques*. 3rd edn. Brussels, 1961.

Demougeot, E. "Remarques sur les débuts du culte impérial en Narbonnaise." *Provence historique* 18 (1968), 39–65.

Devisse, J. "L'influence de Julien Pomère sur les clercs carolingiens." *Revue d'histoire de l'église de France* 56 (1970), 285–95.

Dierkens, A. "Superstitions, christianisme et paganisme à la fin de l'époque mérovingienne." In *Magie, sorcellerie, parapsychologie*, ed. H. Hasquin. Brussels, 1984, 9–26.

Dill, S. *Roman Society in Gaul in the Merovingian Age*. London, 1926.

Dobrowolski, K. "Peasant Traditional Culture." In *Peasants and Peasant Societies*, ed. T. Shanin, 277–98.

Dölger, F. J. "Christliche Grundbesitzer und heidnische Landarbeiter." *Antike und Christentum* 6 (1950), 297–320.

Douglas, M., ed. *Constructive Drinking: Perspectives on Drink from Anthropology*. Cambridge, 1987.

Dozier, E. P. "Rio Grande Pueblos." In *Perspectives in American Indian Culture Change*, ed. E. H. Spicer. Chicago, 1961, 94–186.

Drinkwater, J. F. *Roman Gaul*. Ithaca, N.Y., 1983.

Duchesne, L. *Fastes épiscopaux de l'ancienne Gaule*. 2nd edn. 3 vols. Paris, 1907–15.

Duprat, E. "Histoire des légendes saintes de Provence." Parts 1, 2. *Mémoires de l'Institut historique de Provence* 17 (1940), 118–98; 18 (1941), 87–125.

Duval, P.-M. *Les Dieux de la Gaule*. 2nd edn. Paris, 1976.

Engelbrecht, A. *Patristische Analecten*. Vienna, 1892.

Ernout, A. "Du latin aux langues romanes." *Revue de philologie* 43 (1969), 7–14.

Espérandieu, E. *Recueil général des bas-reliefs de la Gaule romaine*. 14 vols. Paris, 1907–55.

Etaix, R. "Deux nouveaux sermons de saint Césaire d'Arles." *REAug* 11 (1965), 9–13.

"Les épreuves du juste. Nouveau sermon de Saint Césaire d'Arles." *REAug* 24 (1978), 272–77.

"Nouveau sermon pascal de Saint Césaire d'Arles." *RBen* 75 (1965), 201–11.

"Sermon pour la fête des apôtres Jacques et Jean attributable à Saint Césaire." *RBen* 67 (1957), 3–9.

"Trois notes sur saint Césaire d'Arles." In *Corona Gratiarum*. I. Brugge, 1975, 211–27.

Euzennat, M. "Informations archéologiques: Circonscription de Provence-Côte d'Azur-Corse (région sud)." *Gallia* 25 (1967), 397–435.

"Informations archéologiques: Circonscription de Provence-Côte d'Azur-Corse (région sud)." *Gallia* 27 (1969), 419–63.

Ewig, E. "Beobachtungen zu den Klosterprivilegien des 7. und frühen 8. Jahrhunderts." In his *Spätantikes und fränkisches Gallien*, II, 411–26.

"Le culte de saint Martin à l'époque franque." In his *Spätantikes und fränkisches Gallien*, II, 355–70.

"Die fränkischen Teilungen und Teilreiche (511–613)." In his *Spätantikes und fränkisches Gallien*, I, 114–71.

"Die Kathedralpatrozinien im römischen und im fränkischen Gallien." In his *Spätantikes und Fränkisches Gallien*, II, 260–317.

"Milo et eiusmodi similes." In his *Spätantikes und fränkisches Gallien*, II, 189–219.

"The Revival of the Frankish Kingdom." In *Handbook of Church History*, ed. H. Jedin and J. Dolan. II. *The Church in the Age of Feudalism*. Trans. A. Biggs. New York, 1969, 7–16.

"Saint Chrodegang et la réforme de l'église franque." In his *Spätantikes und fränkisches Gallien*, II, 232–59.

Select bibliography

Spätantikes und Fränkisches Gallien, Gesammelte Schriften (1952–1973). Ed. H. Atsma. 2 vols. Beihefte der Francia 3. Munich, 1976–79.

Eyben, E. "Family Planning in Antiquity." *Ancient Society* 11–12 (1980–81), 5–82.

Eydoux, H.-P. "La meunerie hydraulique de Barbegal." *Congrès archéologique de France* 134 (1979), 165–71.

Ferreiro, A. "*Frequenter legere*: The Propagation of Literacy, Education, and Divine Wisdom in Caesarius of Arles." *Journal of Ecclesiastical History* 43 (1992), 5–15.

Février, P.-A. "A propos du *vicus* en Gaule méridionale." *Le vicus gallo-romain. Caesarodunum* 11 (1976), 309–21.

"Arles." In *Topographie chrétienne des cités de la Gaule*, ed. N. Gauthier and J.-Ch. Picard. III. *Provinces ecclésiastiques de Vienne et d'Arles*. Paris, 1986, 73–84.

"Arles au IVe et Ve siècles: ville impériale et capitale régionale." *XXV Corso di cultura sull'arte Ravennate e Bizantina*. Ravenna, 1978, 127–58.

Le Développement urbain en Provence de l'époque romaine à la fin du XIVe siècle. Paris, 1964.

"The Origin and Growth of the Cities of Southern Gaul to the Third Century, A.D.: An Assessment of the Most Recent Archaeological Discoveries." *JRS* 63 (1973), 1–28.

"Problèmes de l'habitat du midi méditerranéen à la fin de l'antiquité et dans le haut moyen âge." *Jahrbuch des römisch-germanischen Zentralmuseums Mainz* (1978), 208–47.

"La sculpture funéraire à Arles au IVe et début du Ve siècle." *XXV Corso di cultura sull'arte Ravennate e Bizantina*. Ravenna, 1978, 159–81.

"Toulon." In *Topographie chrétienne des cités de la Gaule*, ed. N. Gauthier and J.-Ch. Picard. II. *Provinces ecclésiastiques d'Aix et d'Embrun*. Paris, 1986, 61–63.

"Vetera et nova: le poids du passé, les germes de l'avenir, IIIe–VIe siècle." In *Histoire de la France urbaine*, ed. G. Duby. I. *La Ville antique*. Paris, 1980, 393–493.

Février, P.-A. and F. Leyge, eds. *Premiers temps chrétiens en Gaule méridionale : antiquité tardive et haut moyen âge, IIIème–VIIIème siècles*. Lyon, 1986.

Fiches, J.-L. "L'éspace rural antique dans le sud-est de la France: ambitions et réalités archéologiques." *Annales ESC* 42 (1987), 219–38.

Fixot, M. "Les inhumations privilégiées en Provence." In *L'Inhumation privilégiée du IVe au VIIIe siècle en occident*, ed. Y. Duval and J.-Ch. Picard. Paris, 1986, 117–28.

Flint, V. I. J. *The Rise of Magic in Early Medieval Europe*. Princeton, 1991.

Fouracre, P. "The Work of Audoenus of Rouen and Eligius of Noyon in Extending Episcopal Influence from the Town to the Country in Seventh-Century Neustria." In *The Church in Town and Countryside*, ed. D. Baker. Studies in Church History 16. Oxford, 1979, 77–91.

Fournier, G. "La mise en place du cadre paroissial et l'évolution du peuplement." In *Cristianizzazione ed organizzazione*, I, 495–563.

Select bibliography

Frank, K. S. "*Vita apostolica*. Ansätze zur apostolischen Lebensform in der alten Kirche." *Zeitschrift für Kirchengeschichte* 82 (1971), 145–66.

Frézouls, E. "La vie rurale au Bas-Empire d'après l'œuvre de Palladius." *Ktema* 5 (1980), 193–210.

Fritz, G. "Orange." *DTC* XI. 1 (1931), cols. 1087–1103.

Gabba, E. "Literature." In *Sources for Ancient History*, ed. M. Crawford. Cambridge, 1983, 1–79.

Gagnière, S. and J. Granier. "L'occupation des grottes du IIIe au Ve siècle et les invasions germaniques dans la basse vallée du Rhône." *Provence historique* 13 (1963), 225–39.

Ganszyniec, R. "Les Sortes Sanctorum." In *Congrès du Christianisme. Jubilé Alfred Loisy*. III. *Annales d'histoire du Christianisme* 3 (1928), 41–51.

Garnsey, P. *Famine and Food Supply in the Graeco-Roman World: Responses to Risk and Crisis*. Cambridge, 1988.

Garnsey, P. and G. Woolf. "Patronage of the Rural Poor in the Roman World." In *Patronage in Ancient Society*, ed. A. Wallace-Hadrill. London, 1989, 153–70.

Gaudemet, J. "Concile d'Epaone." *DHGE* XV (1963), cols. 524–45.

L'Eglise dans l'empire romain. Paris, 1958.

Gaudemet, J. and B. Basdevant, eds. *Les canons des conciles mérovingiens (VIe–VIIe siècles)*. 2 vols. *SC* 353–54. Paris, 1989.

Gauthier, M. "Informations archéologiques: Circonscription de Provence-Alpes-Côte d'Azur." *Gallia* 44 (1986), 375–483.

Geary, P. *Aristocracy in Provence: The Rhône Basin at the Dawn of the Carolingian Age*. Philadelphia, 1985.

Before France and Germany: The Creation and Transformation of the Merovingian World. New York and Oxford, 1988.

Geertz, C. "Religion as a Cultural System" In his *The Interpretation of Cultures*. London, 1975, 87–125.

Gellert, B. F. "Caesarius von Arelate." Part 1. "Das Leben des Caesarius." *Programm des städtischen Realgymnasiums zu Leipzig*. Progr. Nr. 553. Leipzig, 1892, 3–48. Part 2. "Seine Schriften." *Jahresbericht des städtischen Realgymnasiums in Leipzig*. Progr. Nr. 554. Leipzig, 1893, 3–30.

Genicot, L. *Rural Communities in the Medieval West*. Baltimore, 1990.

van Gennep, A. *Manuel de folklore français contemporain*. 4 vols. (Vol. 2 lacking). Paris, 1937–58.

Gerberding, R. A. *The Rise of the Carolingians and the Liber Historiae Francorum*. Oxford, 1987.

Ghysens, G. and P.-P. Verbraken. *La Carrière scientifique de Dom Germain Morin (1861–1946)*. Instrumenta Patristica 15. Steenbrugge, 1986.

Gill, S. D. *Native American Religions*. Belmont, Calif., 1982.

Glorie, Fr. "La culture lérinienne." *Sacris Erudiri* 19 (1969–70), 71–76.

Goelzer, H. and A. Mey. *Le Latin de Saint Avit*. Paris, 1909.

Goffart, W. *Barbarians and Romans: The Techniques of Accommodation*. Princeton, 1980.

Goody, J. *The Development of the Family and Marriage in Europe*. Cambridge, 1983.

The Interface Between the Written and the Oral. Cambridge, 1987.

Goudineau, C. *Les Fouilles de la Maison au Dauphin. Recherches sur la romanisation de Vaison-la-Romaine. Gallia*, Suppl. 37. Paris, 1979.

"Les villes de la paix romaine." In *Histoire de la France urbaine*, ed. G. Duby. I. *La Ville antique*. Paris, 1980, 234–390.

Grabar, A. *Christian Iconography. A Study of its Origins*. Princeton, 1968.

Green, M. *The Gods of the Celts*. Gloucester, 1986.

Green, R. P. H. *The Works of Ausonius*. Oxford, 1991.

Grégoire, R. "Les homéliaires mérovingiens du VIIe–VIIIe siècle." *Studi medievali*, ser. 3, 13 (1972), 901–17.

"Homiliare Floriacense. Homilia 15." *PLS* 4, cols. 1903–10.

Grenier, A. "Aspects de la religion romaine en Provence." *CRAI* (1954), 328–35.

Manuel d'archéologie gallo-romaine. 4 vols. Paris, 1931–60.

Grierson, P. "Money and Coinage under Charlemagne." In *Karl der Große. Lebenswerk und Nachleben*, ed. W. Braunfels. I. Düsseldorf, 1965, 501–36.

Griffe, E. "A travers les paroisses rurales de la Gaule au VIe siècle." *Bulletin de littérature ecclésiastique* 76 (1975), 3–26.

La Gaule chrétienne à l'époque romaine. 2nd edn. 3 vols. Paris, 1964–66.

"L'idéal pastoral selon Saint Césaire d'Arles." *Bulletin de littérature ecclésiastique* 81 (1980), 50–54.

Grodzynski, D. "Superstitio." *REA* 76 (1974), 36–60.

Gros, P. "Un programme Augustéen: le centre monumental de la colonie d'Arles." *Jahrbuch des deutschen archäologischen Instituts* 102 (1987), 339–63.

Guild, R. *et al.* "Saint-Sauveur d'Aix-en-Provence: La cathédrale et le baptistère." *Congrès archéologique de France* 143 (Paris, 1988), 17–64.

Guiraud, H. "Une intaille magique au Musée d'Arles (Bouches-du-Rhône)." *Revue archéologique de Narbonnaise* 7 (1974), 207–11.

Gurevich, A. *Medieval Popular Culture: Problems of Belief and Perception*. Trans. J. M. Bak and P. A. Hollingsworth. Cambridge, 1988.

Guyon, J. "L'évolution des sites urbains en Provence (Antiquité et Haut Moyen Age). L'exemple de Marseille, Aix, Arles, et Riez à la lumière des recherches et fouilles récentes." *Ktema* 7 (1982), 129–40.

Hallier, G. "Le cirque romain: Etude historique et monumentale." In *Du nouveau sur l'Arles antique*, ed. C. Sintès, 56–62.

Harmand, L. *Le Patronat sur les collectivités publiques des origines au bas-empire*. Paris, 1957.

Harmening, D. *Superstitio. Überlieferungs- und theoriegeschichtliche Untersuchungen zur kirchlich-theologischen Aberglaubensliteratur des Mittelalters*. Berlin, 1979.

Harris, W. V. *Ancient Literacy*. Cambridge, Mass., 1989.

War and Imperialism in Republican Rome. Oxford, 1979.

Hartmann, W. *Die Synoden der Karolingerzeit im Frankenreich und in Italien*. Paderborn, 1989.

Hefele, C. J. and H. Leclercq. *Histoire des conciles*. 11 vols. Paris, 1907–52.

Select bibliography

Heinzelmann, M. *Bischofsherrschaft in Gallien*. Beihefte der Francia 5. Munich, 1976.

"Gallische Prosopographie, 260–527." *Francia* 10 (1982), 531–718.

Hochstetler, D. "The Meaning of Monastic Cloister for Women according to Caesarius of Arles." In *Religion, Culture, and Society in the Early Middle Ages*, ed. T. F. X. Noble and J. J. Contreni. Kalamazoo, Mich., 1987, 27–40.

Hocquard, G. "La Règle de Saint Chrodegang." In *Saint Chrodegang*. Communications présentées au colloque tenu à Metz à l'occasion du douzième centenaire de sa mort. Metz, 1967, 55–89.

Hoeflich, M. H. "The Concept of Utilitas Populi in Early Ecclesiastical Law and Government." *ZRG KA* 67 (1981), 36–74.

Höfer, A. "Zwei unbekannte Sermones des Caesarius von Arles." *RBen* 74 (1964), 44–53.

Hopkins, K. "Contraception in the Roman Empire." *Comparative Studies in Society and History* 8 (1965), 124–51.

Horton, R. "African Conversion." *Africa* 41 (1971), 85–108.

"On the Rationality of Conversion." Parts 1, 2. *Africa* 45 (1975), 219–35, 373–99.

Hubert, J. *L'Art pré-roman*. Paris, 1938.

"La topographie religieuse d'Arles au VIᵉ siècle." *Cahiers archéologiques* 2 (1947), 17–27.

Jacob, J.-P. *et al.* "Provence-Alpes-Côte d'Azur." *Gallia Informations* (1987–88), part 2, 185–343.

"Provence-Alpes-Côte d'Azur." *Gallia Informations* (1990), 81–315.

James, E. "'Beati pacifici': Bishops and the Law in Sixth-Century Gaul." In *Disputes and Settlements: Law and Human Relations in the West*, ed. John Bossy. Cambridge, 1983, 25–46.

The Franks. Oxford, 1988.

The Origins of France: From Clovis to the Capetians, 500–1000. London, 1982.

Jecker, G., ed. *Die Heimat des hl. Pirmin des Apostels der Alamannen*. Beiträge zur Geschichte des alten Mönchtums und des Benediktinerordens 13. Münster-in-Westphalia, 1927.

Jones, A. H. M. "The Constitutional Position of Odoacer and Theoderic." *JRS* 52 (1962), 126–30.

The Later Roman Empire, 284–602. 3 vols. Oxford, 1964, repr. Baltimore, 1986.

Jones, A. H. M., P. Grierson, and J. A. Crook. "The Authenticity of the 'Testamentum S. Remigii.'" *Revue belge de philologie et d'histoire* 35 (1957), 356–73.

Jullian, C. *Histoire de la Gaule*. 8 vols. Paris, 1909–26.

"Inscriptions de la vallée de l'Huveaune." Parts 1–6. *Bulletin épigraphique* 5 (1885), 7–16, 71–83, 117–30, 165–84, 240–57, 279–301.

"Inscriptions de la vallée de l'Huveaune. Appendice." *Bulletin épigraphique* 6 (1886), 167–82.

"Notes gallo-romaines." *REA* 2 (1900), 233–36.

Juster, J. *Les Juifs dans l'empire romain*. 2 vols. Paris, 1914.

Kahl, H.-D. "Die ersten Jahrhunderte des missionsgeschichtlichen Mittelalters.

Bausteine für eine Phänomenologie bis ca. 1050." In *Kirchengeschichte als Missionsgeschichte*, ed. H. Frohnes *et al.* II. Part 1. *Die Kirche des früheren Mittelalters.* ed. K. Schäferdiek. Munich, 1978, 11–76.

Katz, S. *The Jews in the Visigothic and Frankish Kingdoms of Spain and Gaul.* Cambridge, Mass., 1937.

Kessler, H. L. "Pictorial Narrative and Church Mission in Sixth-Century Gaul." In *Pictorial Narrative in Antiquity and the Middle Ages*, ed. H. L. Kessler and M. S. Simpson. Studies in the History of Art 16 (1985), 75–91.

Klauser, T. *Der Ursprung der bischöflichen Insignien und Ehrenrechte.* Bonn, 1948.

Klingshirn, W. E. "Caesarius's Monastery for Women in Arles and the Composition and Function of the 'Vita Caesarii.'" *RBen* 100 (1990), 441–81.

"Charity and Power: Caesarius of Arles and the Ransoming of Captives in Sub-Roman Gaul." *JRS* 75 (1985), 183–203.

"Church Politics and Chronology: Dating the Episcopacy of Caesarius of Arles." *REAug* 38 (1992), 80–88.

The Life, Testament, and Letters of Caesarius of Arles. Translated Texts for Historians, Liverpool, forthcoming.

Konda, G. *Le Discernement et la malice des pratiques superstitieuses d'après les sermons de s. Césaire d'Arles.* Rome, 1970.

König, D. *Amt und Askese: Priesteramt und Mönchtum bei den lateinischen Kirchenvätern in vorbenediktinischer Zeit.* Regulae Benedicti Studia, Suppl. 12. St. Ottilien, Germany, 1985.

König, I. *Die Meilensteine der Gallia Narbonensis.* Itinera Romana 3. Bern, 1970.

Krautheimer, R. *Early Christian and Byzantine Architecture.* 3rd rev. edn. Harmondsworth, 1981.

Three Christian Capitals: Topography and Politics. Berkeley and Los Angeles, 1983.

Kroeber, A. L. *Anthropology.* New York, 1948.

Labande, L. H. "Etude historique et archéologique sur Saint-Trophime d'Arles du IVe au XIIIe siècle." Parts 1, 2. *Bulletin monumental* (1903), 459–97 and (1904), 3–42.

Ladner, G. *The Idea of Reform.* Cambridge, Mass., 1959.

Lambrechts, P. "Le commerce des 'Syriens' en Gaule du Haut-Empire à l'époque mérovingienne." *L'Antiquité classique* 6 (1937), 35–61.

Langgärtner, G. *Die Gallienpolitik der Päpste im 5. und 6. Jahrhundert. Eine Studie über den apostolischen Vikariat von Arles.* Theophaneia 16. Bonn, 1964.

Lauwers, M. "'Religion populaire', culture folklorique, mentalités: notes pour une anthropologie culturelle du moyen âge." *Revue d'histoire ecclésiastique* 82 (1987), 221–58.

Lavagne, H. "Les dieux de la Gaule Narbonnaise: 'romanité' et romanisation." *Journal des savants* (1979), 155–97.

Le Blant, E., ed. *Inscriptions chrétiennes de la Gaule antérieures au VIIIe siècle.* 2 vols. Paris, 1856–65.

Le Blant, E., ed. *Nouveau recueil des inscriptions chrétiennes de la Gaule antérieures au VIIIe siècle.* Paris, 1892.

Select bibliography

Le Bras, G. *L'Eglise et le village*. Paris, 1976.

Le Glay, M. "La Gaule romanisée." In *Histoire de la France rurale*, ed. G. Duby and A. Wallon. I. *La Formation des campagnes françaises*. Paris, 1975, 191–285.

Le Goff, J. *Time, Work and Culture in the Middle Ages*. Trans. A. Goldhammer. Chicago, 1980.

Lemarié, J. "Trois sermons fragmentaires inédits de saint Césaire d'Arles conservés à 'l'Arxiu capitular' de Vich." *RBen* 88 (1978), 92–110.

Lesne, E. *Histoire de la proprieté ecclésiastique en France*. 6 vols. Lille, 1910–43.

Lévi, I. "Saint Césaire et les Juifs d'Arles." *Revue des études juives* 30 (1895), 295–98.

Lévi-Strauss, C. "The Sorcerer and His Magic." In his *Structural Anthropology*, trans. C. Jacobson and B. Grundfest Schoepf. Garden City, N.Y., 1967, 161–180.

Levillain, L. "La crise des années 507–508 et les rivalités d'influence en Gaule de 508 à 514." In *Mélanges offerts à Nicholas Iorga*. Paris, 1933, 537–67.

Levison, W. "Zur Geschichte des Frankenkönigs Chlodowech." *Bonner Jahrbücher* 103 (1898), 42–86.

Lewis, A. R. "The Dukes in the *Regnum Francorum*. A.D. 550–751." *Speculum* 51 (1976), 381–410.

Lienhard, J. T. "Patristic Sermons on Eusebius of Vercelli and their Relation to his Monasticism." *RBen* 87 (1977), 164–72.

Lizzi, R. "Ambrose's Contemporaries and the Christianization of Northern Italy." *JRS* 80 (1990), 156–73.

Lloyd, G. E. R. *Science, Folklore, and Ideology*. Cambridge, 1983.

Loening, E. *Geschichte des deutschen Kirchenrechts*. 2 vols. Strasburg, 1878.

Longnon, A. *Géographie de la Gaule au VIe siècle*. Paris, 1878.

Loseby, S. T. "Marseille: A Late Antique Success Story?" *JRS* 82 (1992), 165–85.

Lotter, F. "Methodisches zur Gewinnung historischer Erkenntnisse aus hagiographischen Quellen." *Historische Zeitschrift* 229 (1979), 298–356.

Loyen, A. *Sidoine Apollinaire et l'esprit précieux en Gaule aux derniers jours de l'empire*. Paris, 1943.

MacCormack, S. *Art and Ceremony in Late Antiquity*. Berkeley and Los Angeles, 1981.

"Change and Continuity in Late Antiquity: The Ceremony of Adventus." *Historia* 21 (1972), 721–52.

"'The Heart Has Its Reasons': Predicaments of Missionary Christianity in Early Colonial Peru." *Hispanic American Historical Review* 65 (1985), 443–66.

Religion in the Andes: Vision and Imagination in Early Colonial Peru. Princeton, 1991.

McKenna, S. *Paganism and Pagan Survivals in Spain up to the Fall of the Visigothic Kingdom*. The Catholic University of America Studies in Medieval History 1. Washington, D.C., 1938.

McKitterick, R. *The Carolingians and the Written Word*. Cambridge, 1989.

"Conclusion." In *The Uses of Literacy in Early Mediaeval Europe*, ed. R. McKitterick. Cambridge, 1990, 319–33.

The Frankish Church and the Carolingian Reforms, 789–895. London, 1977.

"Latin and Romance: An Historian's Perspective." In *Latin and the Romance Languages in the Early Middle Ages,* ed. R. Wright, 130–45.

McLaughlin, T. P. *Le Très Ancien Droit monastique de l'Occident.* Paris, 1935.

MacMullen, R. "Late Roman Slavery." *Historia* 36 (1987), 359–82.

"Peasants during the Principate." *ANRW* II. 1 (1974), 253–61.

Malnory, A. *Saint Césaire, évêque d'Arles.* Bibliothèque de l'école des hautes études 103. Paris, 1894, repr. Geneva, 1978.

Manselli, R. "Resistenze dei culti antichi nella practica religiosa dei laici nelle campagne." In *Cristianizzazione ed organizzazione ecclesiastica,* I, 57–108.

Marignan, A. *Etudes sur la civilisation française.* 2 vols. Paris, 1899.

Markus, R. "The Cult of Icons in Sixth-Century Gaul." *JTS* n.s. 29 (1978), 151–57.

The End of Ancient Christianity. Cambridge, 1990.

"From Caesarius to Boniface: Christianity and Paganism in Gaul." In *Le Septième Siècle: changements et continuités. The Seventh Century: Change and Continuity,* ed. J. Fontaine and J. N. Hillgarth. London, 1992, 154–72.

"The Legacy of Pelagius: Orthodoxy, Heresy, and Conciliation." In *The Making of Orthodoxy: Essays in Honour of Henry Chadwick,* ed. R. Williams. Cambridge, 1989, 214–34.

Marrou, H.-I. "Les deux palliums de Saint Césaire d'Arles." In his *Christiana Tempora.* Rome, 1978, 251–52.

"Le dossier épigraphique de l'évêque Rusticus de Narbonne." *Rivista di archeologia cristiana* 46 (1970), 331–49.

M. Marshall, ed. *Beliefs, Behaviors, and Alcoholic Beverages: A Cross-Cultural Survey.* Ann Arbor, Mich., 1979.

Mathisen, R. W. "The Ecclesiastical Aristocracy of Fifth-Century Gaul: A Regional Analysis of Family Structure." Ph.D. diss., University of Wisconsin-Madison, 1979.

Ecclesiastical Factionalism and Religious Controversy in Fifth-Century Gaul. Washington, D.C., 1989.

"Episcopal Hierarchy and Tenure in Office in Late Roman Gaul: A Method for Establishing Dates of Ordination." *Francia* 17 (1990), 125–38.

"PLRE II: Suggested Addenda and Corrigenda." *Historia* 31 (1982), 364–86.

Matthews, J. *Western Aristocracies and Imperial Court, A.D. 364–425.* Oxford, 1975.

Meslin, M. *La Fête des kalendes de Janvier dans l'empire romain.* Collection Latomus 115. Brussels, 1970.

"Persistances païennes en Galice, vers la fin du VIᵉ siècle." In *Hommages à Marcel Renard.* II. Collection Latomus 102. Brussels, 1969, 512–24.

Meyer, E. A. "Literacy, Literate Practice, and the Law in the Roman Empire, A.D. 100–600." Ph.D. diss., Yale University, 1989.

Meyer, P. M. *Der römische Konkubinat nach den Rechtsquellen und den Inschriften.* Leipzig, 1895, repr. Aalen, 1966.

Millemann, H. "Caesarius von Arles und die frühmittelalterliche Missionspredigt." *Zeitschrift für Missionswissenschaft und Religionswissenschaft* 23 (1933), 12–27.

Miller, T. *The Birth of the Hospital in the Byzantine Empire.* Baltimore, 1985.

Mohrmann, C. *Die altchristliche Sondersprache in den Sermones des hl. Augustin.* Nijmegen, 1932.

"Encore une fois: Paganus." *Vigiliae Christianae* 6 (1952), 109–21.

Mordek, H. *Kirchenrecht und Reform im Frankenreich.* Berlin and New York, 1975.

Morhain, E. "Origine et histoire de la 'regula canonicorum' de saint Chrodegang." In *Miscellanea Pio Paschini.* I. *Lateranum* n.s. 14 (1948), 173–85.

Morin, G. "Comment j'ai fait mon édition des œuvres de saint Césaire d'Arles." *Nouvelle Revue de Hongrie* 58 (1938), 225–32.

"L'homéliaire de Burchard de Würzburg." *RBen* 13 (1896), 97–111.

"Mes principes et ma méthode pour la future édition de saint Césaire." *RBen* 10 (1893), 62–78.

"L'origine du symbole d'Athanase: témoignage inédit de s. Césaire d'Arles." *RBen* 44 (1932), 207–19.

"Le prêtre Arlésien Teridius." *Recherches de science religieuse* 28 (1938), 257–63.

"Quelques raretés philologiques dans les écrits de Césaire d'Arles." *Bulletin du Cange* 11 (1936), 5–14.

"Le testament de S. Césaire d'Arles et la critique de M. Bruno Krusch." *RBen* 16 (1899), 97–112.

"Textes inédits relatifs au symbole et à la vie chrétienne." *RBen* 22 (1905), 515–19.

Munier, C. *Les Statuta Ecclesiae Antiqua.* Paris, 1960.

Nardi, E. *Procurato aborto nel mondo grecoromano.* Milan, 1971.

Nehlsen, H. "Codex Euricianus." *Reallexikon der germanischen Altertumskunde.* 2nd edn. V. Berlin and New York, 1984, 42–47.

"Lex Visigothorum." *Handwörterbuch zur deutschen Rechtsgeschichte.* II. Berlin, 1978, cols. 1966–79.

Nelson, J. L. "On the Limits of the Carolingian Renaissance." In *Renaissance and Renewal in Christian History,* ed. D. Baker. Studies in Church History 14. Oxford, 1977, 51–69.

"Queens as Jezebels: The Careers of Brunhild and Balthild in Merovingian History." In *Medieval Women,* ed. D. Baker. Studies in Church History, Subsidia 1. Oxford, 1978, 31–77.

Nilsson, M. P. *Greek Folk Religion.* Philadelphia, 1940.

"Studien zur Vorgeschichte des Weihnachtfestes." *Archiv für Religionswissenschaft* 19 (1916–19), 50–150.

Nock, A. D. *Conversion: The Old and the New in Religion from Alexander the Great to Augustine of Hippo.* Oxford, 1933.

Noonan, J. T. *Contraception. A History of its Treatment by Catholic Theologians and Canonists.* Cambridge, Mass., 1965.

Norberg, D. *Manuel pratique de latin médiéval.* Paris, 1968.

O'Donnell, J. "Liberius the Patrician." *Traditio* 37 (1981), 31–72.

Select bibliography

Olsen, G. W. "Reform after the Pattern of the Primitive Church in the Thought of Salvian of Marseille." *Catholic Historical Review* 68 (1982), 1–12.

d'Ors, A. "La territorialidad del Derecho de los Visigodos." In *Estudios Visigoticos*. I. Rome and Madrid, 1956, 91–150.

Palanque, J.-R. "La date du transfert de la Préfecture des Gaules de Trèves à Arles." *REA* 36 (1934), 359–65.

"Du nouveau sur la date du transfert de la préfecture des Gaules de Trèves à Arles." *Provence historique* 23 (1973), 29–38.

Parkes, J. *The Conflict of the Church and the Synagogue*. New York, 1961.

Patlagean, E. *Pauvreté économique et pauvreté sociale à Byzance, 4e–7e siècles*. Paris, 1977.

"Sur la limitation de la fécondité dans la haute époque byzantine." *Annales ESC* 24 (1969), 1353–69.

Payer, P. J. "Early Medieval Regulations Concerning Marital Sexual Relations." *Journal of Medieval History* 6 (1980), 353–76.

Peel, J. D. Y. "Conversion and Tradition in Two African Societies: Ijebu and Buganda." *Past and Present* 77 (1977), 108–41.

Pellegrino, M. "General Introduction." In *The Works of Saint Augustine*, ed. J. E. Rotelle. Part 3. *Sermons*. I. Brooklyn, N.Y., 1990, 13–137.

Pfeilschifter, G. *Der Ostgotenkönig Theoderich der Grosse und die katholische Kirche*. Münster-in-Westphalia, 1896.

Phillips, C. R. "The Sociology of Religious Knowledge in the Roman Empire to A.D. 284." *ANRW* II. 16. 3 (1986), 2677–2773.

Pietri, C. *Roma christiana*. 2 vols. Rome, 1976.

"Le sénat, le peuple chrétien et les partis du cirque à Rome sous le pape Symmaque (498–514)." *Mélanges d'archéologie et d'histoire de l'Ecole Française de Rome* 78 (1966), 123–39.

Pietri, L. *La Ville de Tours du IVe siècle au VIe siècle: naissance d'une cité chrétienne*. Collection de l'Ecole Française de Rome 69. Rome, 1983.

Pitt-Rivers, J., ed. *Mediterranean Countrymen*. Paris, 1963.

de Plinval, G. "L'activité doctrinale dans l'église gallo-romaine." In *Histoire de l'église*, ed. A. Fliche and V. Martin. IV. *De la mort de Théodose à l'avènement de Grégoire le Grand*. Paris, 1948, 397–419.

Plumpe, J. C. *Mater Ecclesia*. The Catholic University of America Studies in Christian Antiquity 5. Washington, D.C., 1943.

"Pomeriana." *Vigiliae Christianae* 1 (1947), 227–39.

Pontal, O. *Die Synoden im Merowingerreich*. Paderborn, 1986.

Price, S. R. F. *Rituals and Power: The Roman Imperial Cult in Asia Minor*. Cambridge, 1984.

Pricoco, S. *L'isola dei santi. Il cenobio di Lerino e le origini del monachesimo gallico*. Rome, 1978.

Prinz, F. "Die bischöfliche Stadtherrschaft im Frankenreich vom 5. bis zum 7. Jahrhundert." In *Bischofs- und Kathedralstädte des Mittelalters und der frühen Neuzeit*, ed. F. Petri. Cologne and Vienna, 1976, 1–26.

Frühes Mönchtum im Frankenreich. Munich and Vienna, 1965.

Select bibliography

Quacquarelli, A. *Lavoro e ascesi nel monachesimo prebenedettino del IV e V secolo.* Bari, 1982.

Rapisarda, C. A. "Lo stile umile nei sermoni di S. Cesario d'Arles. Giustificazioni teoriche e posizioni polemiche." *Orpheus* 17 (1970), 115–59.

Rawson, E. "Roman Concubinage and Other *de facto* Marriages." *Transactions of the American Philological Association* 104 (1974), 279–305.

Redfield, R. *Peasant Society and Culture.* Chicago, 1956.

Reynolds, R. E. "The Pseudo-Hieronymian 'De septem ordinibus ecclesiae': Notes on its Origins, Abridgments and Use in Early Medieval Canonical Collections." *RBen* 80 (1970), 238–52.

Rice, E. *St. Jerome in the Renaissance.* Baltimore, 1985.

Richards, J. *The Popes and the Papacy in the Early Middle Ages, 476–752.* London, 1979.

Riché, P. *Ecoles et enseignement dans le Haut Moyen Age.* 2nd edn. Paris, 1989.
Education and Culture in the Barbarian West, Sixth Through Eighth Centuries. Trans. J. J. Contreni. Columbia, S.C., 1976.
"Note d'hagiographie mérovingienne: La vita S. Rusticulae." *Analecta Bollandiana* 72 (1954), 369–77.

Rivet, A. L. F. *Gallia Narbonensis: Southern Gaul in Roman Times.* London, 1988.

Rolland, H. *Fouilles de Glanum. Gallia*, Suppl. 1. Paris, 1946.
Fouilles de Glanum, 1947–1956. Gallia, Suppl. 11. Paris, 1958.
Fouilles de Saint-Blaise (Bouches du Rhône). Gallia, Suppl. 3. Paris, 1951.
Fouilles de Saint-Blaise (1951–1956). Gallia, Suppl. 7. Paris, 1956.
"Inscriptions antiques de Glanum." *Gallia* 3 (1944), 167–223.

Rostaing, Ch. *Essai sur la toponymie de la Provence.* Paris, 1950.

Rouche, M. *L'Aquitaine des Wisigoths aux Arabes, 418–781.* Paris, 1979.

Rouquette, J.-M. "Les découvertes du Crédit Agricole." In *Du nouveau sur l'Arles antique*, ed. C. Sintès, 70–77.
"Mosaïque du génie de l'année." In *Du nouveau sur l'Arles antique*, ed. C. Sintès, 89–93.
Provence romane. I. *La Provence rhodanienne.* La Pierre-qui-Vire, 1974.
"Trois nouveaux sarcophages." *CRAI* (1974), 257–63.

Rousseau, P. *Ascetics, Authority and the Church in the Age of Jerome and Cassian.* Oxford, 1978.

Rousselle, A. "Du sanctuaire au thaumaturge: La guérison en Gaule au IVe siècle." *Annales ESC* 31 (1976), 1085–1107.

Saint-Saëns, A. "Césaire d'Arles et les Juifs." Mémoire de Maîtrise, University of Strasburg, 1979.

Salin, E. *La Civilisation mérovingienne.* 4 vols. Paris, 1949–59.

Salvatore, A. "Uso delle similitudini e pedagogia pastorale nei Sermones di Cesario di Arles." *Rivista di cultura classica e medioevale* 9 (1967), 177–225.

Salviat, F. "Informations archéologiques: Circonscription de Provence." *Gallia* 30 (1972), 511–41.
"Informations archéologiques: Circonscription de Provence." *Gallia* 32 (1974), 501–28.

"Informations archéologiques: Circonscription de Provence." *Gallia* 35 (1977), 511–37.

Samson, R. "Rural Slavery, Inscriptions, Archaeology and Marx: A Response to Ramsey MacMullen's 'Late Roman Slavery.'" *Historia* 38 (1989), 99–110.

Scavi di Ostia. 10 vols. Rome, 1953–79.

Schäferdiek, K. *Die Kirche in den Reichen der Westgoten und Suewen bis zur Errichtung der westgotischen katholischen Staatskirche.* Berlin, 1967.

"Remigius von Reims: Kirchenmann einer Umbruchszeit." *Zeitschrift für Kirchengeschichte* 94 (1983), 256–78.

"Das sogenannte zweite Konzil von Arles und die älteste Kanonessammlung der arelatenser Kirche." *ZRG KA* 71 (1985), 1–19.

Scheibelreiter, G. *Der Bischof in merowingischer Zeit.* Veröffentlichungen des Instituts für Österreichische Geschichtsforschung 27. Vienna, 1983.

"Der frühfränkische Episkopat: Bild und Wirklichkeit." *Frühmittelalterliche Studien* 17 (1983), 131–47.

Schieffer, T. *Winfrid-Bonifatius und die christliche Grundlegung Europas.* Freiburg, 1954.

Schmidt, L. *Die Ostgermanen.* 2nd edn. Munich, 1941.

Schmitt, J.-C. "'Religion populaire' et culture folklorique." *Annales ESC* 31 (1976), 941–53.

Seeck, O. *Regesten der Kaiser und Päpste für die Jahre 311 bis 476 n. Chr.* Stuttgart, 1919.

Shanin, T., ed. *Peasants and Peasant Societies.* Harmondsworth, 1971.

Shaw, B. and R. P. Saller. "Close-Kin Marriage in Roman Society?" *Man* n.s. 19 (1984), 432–44.

Shils, E. "Center and Periphery." In his *Center and Periphery: Essays in Macrosociology.* Chicago and London, 1975, 3–16.

Sintès, C. "Le cirque romain: Les fouilles récentes." In *Du nouveau sur l'Arles antique*, ed. C. Sintès, 63–65.

"L'évolution topographique de l'Arles du Haut-Empire à la lumière des fouilles récentes." *Journal of Roman Archaeology* 5 (1992), 130–47.

"Les fouilles de l'Hôpital Van-Gogh." In *Du nouveau sur l'Arles antique*, ed. C. Sintès, 44–48.

"Les fouilles de la Verrerie de Trinquetaille." In *Du nouveau sur l'Arles antique*, ed. C. Sintès, 80–88.

"L'habitat du haut-empire au Jardin d'Hiver." In *Du nouveau sur l'Arles antique*, ed. C. Sintès, 41.

"La nécropole protohistorique de l'Hôpital Van-Gogh." In *Du nouveau sur l'Arles antique*, ed. C. Sintès, 100–104.

"Les nécropoles." In *Du nouveau sur l'Arles antique*, ed. C. Sintès, 95–99.

"Le site aux IVe et Ve siècles: une tentative de reconstitution." In *Carnets de fouilles d'une presqu'île. Revue d'Arles* 2. Arles, 1990, 59–62.

ed. *Du nouveau sur l'Arles antique. Revue d'Arles* 1. Arles, 1987.

Smith, I. M. "The Lérins Survey." Durham University Excavation Committee and Committee for Excavation and Fieldwork, University of Newcastle upon Tyne. *Archaeological Reports for 1983* (1984), 61–66.

Select bibliography

Smith, J. M. H. "Oral and Written: Saints, Miracles, and Relics in Brittany, c. 850–1250." *Speculum* 65 (1990), 309–43.

Smith, J. Z. *Imagining Religion: From Babylon to Jonestown.* Chicago, 1982.

Solignac, A. "Les fragments du De natura animae de Pomère." *Bulletin de littérature ecclésiastique* 75 (1974), 41–60.

"Julien Pomère." *DS* VIII (1974), cols. 1594–1600.

Stancliffe, C. E. "From Town to Country: The Christianisation of the Touraine." In *The Church in Town and Countryside*, ed. D. Baker. Studies in Church History 16. Oxford, 1979, 43–51.

Stein, E. *Histoire du Bas-Empire.* Ed. J.-R. Palanque. 2 vols. Paris, 1949–59.

Stevens, C. E. "Agriculture and Rural Life in the Later Roman Empire." In *The Cambridge Economic History of Europe*, ed. M. M. Postan. 2nd edn. I. Cambridge, 1966, 92–124.

Sidonius Apollinaris and his Age. Oxford, 1933.

Sticca, G. "La biografia di Cesario vescovo di Arles, 470–549." Tesi di Laurea, University of Turin, 1954.

Stroheker, K. F. *Der senatorische Adel im spätantiken Gallien.* Tübingen, 1948.

Suelzer, M. J., ed. *Julianus Pomerius. The Contemplative Life.* Westminster, Md., 1947.

Tchernia, A. "Italian Wine in Gaul at the End of the Republic." In *Trade in the Ancient Economy*, ed. P. Garnsey *et al.* London, 1983, 87–104.

Terraneo, G. "Saggio bibliografico su Cesario vescovo di Arles." *La scuola cattolica* 91 (1963), Suppl. bibliogr. 272*–94*.

Theis, L. "Saints sans famille? Quelques remarques sur la famille dans le monde franc à travers les sources hagiographiques." *Revue historique* 255 (1976), 3–20.

Thirion, J. "Saint-Trophime d'Arles." *Congrès archéologique de France* 134 (1976), 360–479.

Tibiletti, C. "La teologia della grazia in Giuliano Pomerio." *Augustinianum* 25 (1985), 489–506.

Tjäder, J.-O., ed. *Die nichtliterarischen lateinischen Papyri Italiens aus der Zeit 445–700.* 2 vols. I: Lund, 1955. II: Stockholm, 1982.

de la Tour, I. *Les Paroisses rurales du 4ᵉ au 11ᵉ siècle.* Paris, 1900, repr. Paris, 1979.

Toutain, J. *Les Cultes païens dans l'empire romain.* 3 vols. Paris, 1907–20.

Treggiari, S. "Concubinae." *Papers of the British School at Rome* 49 (1981), 59–81.

Trexler, R. "From the Mouths of Babes: Christianization by Children in 16th Century New Spain." In *Religious Organization and Religious Experience*, ed. J. Davis. Association of Social Anthropologists, Monograph 21. London, 1982, 115–35.

Turcan, R. *Les Religions de l'Asie dans la vallée du Rhône.* Leiden, 1972.

Ueding, L. *Geschichte der Klostergründungen der frühen Merowingerzeit.* Historische Studien 261. Berlin, 1935.

Vacandard, E. "L'idolatrie en Gaule au VIᵉ et au VIIᵉ siècle." *Revue des questions historiques* 65 (1899), 424–54.

Vaccari, A. "Volgarismi notevoli nel latino de S. Cesario di Arles (†543)." *Archivum Latinitatis Medii Aevi* 17 (1943), 135–48.

Select bibliography

Valentin, M.-D., ed. *Hilaire d'Arles. Vie de Saint Honorat. SC* 235. Paris, 1977.

Van Buchem, L. A. *L'Homélie pseudo-eusébienne de Pentecôte.* Nijmegen, 1967.

Van Dam, R. "Hagiography and History: The Life of Gregory Thaumaturgus." *Classical Antiquity* 1 (1982), 272–308.

"Images of Saint Martin in Late Roman and Early Merovingian Gaul." *Viator* 19 (1988), 1–27.

Leadership and Community in Late Antique Gaul. Berkeley and Los Angeles, 1985.

Van Engen, J. "The Christian Middle Ages as an Historiographical Problem." *American Historical Review* 91 (1986), 519–52.

Van Uytfanghe, M. "The Consciousness of a Linguistic Dichotomy (Latin–Romance) in Carolingian Gaul: The Contradictions of the Sources and of their Interpretation." In *Latin and the Romance Languages in the Early Middle Ages,* ed. R. Wright, 114–29.

"Histoire du latin, protohistoire des langues romanes et histoire de la communication." *Francia* 11 (1983), 579–613.

Varagnac, A. *Civilisation traditionelle et genres de vie.* Paris, 1948.

Verbraken, P.-P. *Etudes critiques sur les sermons authentiques de Saint Augustin.* Instrumenta Patristica 12. Steenbrugge, 1976.

Verdon, M. "Virgins and Widows: European Kinship and Early Christianity." *Man* n.s. 23 (1988), 488–505.

Vichi, A. M. G. "Un'omelia della perduta 'Collectio Tripartita Longipontana' ritrovata in un codice vallicelliano." *Accademie e Biblioteche d'Italia* 21 (1953), 335–42.

Villegos, F. "La *regula monasterii Tarnantensis.* Texte, sources et datation." *RBen* 84 (1974), 7–65.

Villevieille, U. *Histoire de saint Césaire, évêque d'Arles.* Aix-en-Provence, 1884.

de Vogüé, A. "Marie chez les vierges du sixième siècle: Césaire d'Arles et Grégoire le Grand." *Benedictina* 33 (1986), 79–91.

"La Règle de Césaire d'Arles pour les moines: un résumé de sa Règle pour les moniales." *Revue d'histoire de la spiritualité* 47 (1971), 369–406.

"La Règle de Donat pour l'abbesse Gauthstrude." *Benedictina* 25 (1978), 219–313.

ed. *Règles des saints pères.* 2 vols. SC 297–98. Paris, 1982.

de Vogüé, A. and J. Courreau, eds. *Césaire d'Arles. Œuvres monastiques. I. Œuvres pour les moniales.* SC 345. Paris, 1988.

Völker, W. "Studien zur päpstlichen Vikariatspolitik im 5. Jahrhundert." *Zeitschrift für Kirchengeschichte* 46 (1928), 355–80.

Walker, S. "La campagne lyonnaise du 1er siècle av. J. C. jusqu'au 5ème siècle ap. J. C." In *Récentes recherches en archéologie gallo-romaine et paléo-chrétienne sur Lyon et sa région.* BAR International Series 108. Oxford, 1981, 279–325.

Wallace-Hadrill, J. M. *Early Germanic Kingship in England and on the Continent.* Oxford, 1971.

The Frankish Church. Oxford, 1983.

Ward-Perkins, B. *From Classical Antiquity to the Middle Ages: Urban Public Building in Northern and Central Italy, AD 300–850.* Oxford, 1984.

von Wartburg, W. "Les noms des jours de la semaine dans les langues romanes."
    In his *Von Sprache und Mensch*. Bern, 1956, 45–60.
Wemple, S. F. *Women in Frankish Society. Marriage and the Cloister, 500–900*.
    Philadelphia, 1981.
Whatmough, J. "Κελτικά, Being Prolegomena to a Study of the Dialects of
    Ancient Gaul." *Harvard Studies in Classical Philology* 55 (1944), 68–76.
Wightman, E. M. *Gallia Belgica*. Berkeley and Los Angeles, 1985.
"Peasants and Potentates." *American Journal of Ancient History* 3 (1978),
    97–128.
Roman Trier and the Treveri. London, 1970.
"Rural Settlement in Roman Gaul." *ANRW* II.4 (1975), 584–657.
Williamson, L. "Infanticide: An Anthropological Analysis." In *Infanticide and the
    Value of Life*, ed. M. Kohl. Buffalo, N.Y., 1978.
Wolfram, H. *History of the Goths*. Trans. T. J. Dunlap. Berkeley and Los Angeles,
    1988.
Wood, I. N. "The Audience of Architecture in Post-Roman Gaul." In *The
    Anglo-Saxon Church*, ed. L. A. S. Butler and R. K. Morris. The Council for
    British Archaeology, Research Report 60. London, 1986, 74–79.
"Avitus of Vienne: Religion and Culture in the Auvergne and the Rhône
    Valley, 470–530." D. Phil. thesis, Oxford University, 1980.
"Early Merovingian Devotion in Town and Country." In *The Church in
    Town and Countryside*, ed. D. Baker. Studies in Church History 16. Oxford,
    1979, 61–76.
"The Ecclesiastical Politics of Merovingian Clermont." In *Ideal and Reality in
    Frankish and Anglo-Saxon Society*, ed. P. Wormald. Oxford, 1983, 34–57.
"Gregory of Tours and Clovis." *Revue Belge de philologie et d'histoire* 63 (1985),
    249–72.
"Pagans and Holy Men, 600–800." In *Irland und die Christenheit: Bibelstudien
    und Mission*, ed. Próinséas Ní Chatháin and M. Richter. Stuttgart, 1987,
    347–61.
"A Prelude to Columbanus: The Monastic Achievement in the Burgundian
    Territories." In *Columbanus and Merovingian Monasticism*, ed. H. B. Clarke
    and M. Brennan. BAR International Series 113. Oxford, 1981, 3–32.
Woodruff, H. "The Iconography and Date of the Mosaics of La Daurade." *Art
    Bulletin* 13 (1931), 80–104.
Worsley, P. *The Trumpet Shall Sound*. 2nd edn. New York, 1968.
Wright, R. *Late Latin and Early Romance*. Liverpool, 1982.
    ed. *Latin and the Romance Languages in the Early Middle Ages*. London and New
    York, 1991.
Zöllner, E. *Geschichte der Franken bis zur Mitte des 6. Jahrhunderts*. Munich, 1970.
Zumkeller, A. *Augustine's Ideal of the Religious Life*. Trans. E. Colledge. New
    York, 1986.
Zurek, A. "L'etica coniugale in Cesario di Arles: Rapporti con Agostino e nuovi
    orientamenti." *Augustinianum* 25 (1985), 565–78.

INDEX

Cambridge Studies in Medieval Life and Thought
Fourth series

★ Also published as a paperback

GENERAL THEOLOGICAL SEMINARY
NEW YORK

DATE DUE

Printed
in USA